The New China-Russia Alignment

Recent Titles in
The Changing Face of War

The New China-Russia Alignment

Critical Challenges to U.S. Security

Richard Weitz

The Changing Face of War
James Jay Carafano, Series Editor

 PRAEGER®

An Imprint of ABC-CLIO, LLC
Santa Barbara, California • Denver, Colorado

Library of Congress Cataloging-in-Publication Data

Names: Weitz, Richard, author.
Title: The new China-Russia alignment : critical challenges to U.S.
   security / Richard Weitz.
Other titles: Critical challenges to U.S. security
Description: Santa Barbara : Praeger, An Imprint of ABC-CLIO, LLC, [2022] |
   Series: The changing face of war | Includes bibliographical references and index.
Identifiers: LCCN 2022006719 (print) | LCCN 2022006720 (ebook) | ISBN
   9781440847363 (hardcover) | ISBN 9781440847370 (ebook)
Subjects: LCSH: United States—Relations—China. | United States—Relations—
   Russia (Federation) | China—Relations—United States. | China—Relations—
   Russia (Federation) | Russia (Federation)—Relations—United States. | Russia
   (Federation)—Relations—China. | United States—Foreign relations—
   21st century. | National security—United States.
Classification: LCC E183.8.C6 W45 2022 (print) | LCC E183.8.C6 (ebook) | DDC
   327.73051—dc23/eng/20220210
LC record available at https://lccn.loc.gov/2022006719
LC ebook record available at https://lccn.loc.gov/2022006720

ISBN: 978-1-4408-4736-3 (print)
      978-1-4408-4737-0 (ebook)

26 25 24 23 22   1 2 3 4 5

This book is also available as an eBook.

Praeger
An Imprint of ABC-CLIO, LLC

ABC-CLIO, LLC
147 Castilian Drive
Santa Barbara, California 93117
www.abc-clio.com

This book is printed on acid-free paper ∞

Manufactured in the United States of America

Contents

Contents

Preface

This volume examines the unprecedented alignment between the Russian Federation and the People's Republic of China (PRC) that has developed in recent years. It analyzes the main drivers of the Sino-Russian relationship—its sources, nuances, and manifestations in detail—and assesses its consequences, especially for the United States. Over the past three decades, Moscow and Beijing have moved increasingly close in critical security, economic, and regional areas. They have pursued harmonious regional policies toward the Korean Peninsula, Central Asia, and the Middle East while better institutionalizing and integrating their security ties. China has become Russia's leading national trade partner, gateway to other Asian markets, and an important energy importer. The leaders of both countries have engaged in numerous high-level exchanges, made many mutually supportive statements, and manifested other dimensions of their developing strategic partnership. Both regimes view their improved ties as a tremendous success that they must sustain. Their nonconfrontational relationship benefits both countries. Russian leaders can focus on advancing their interests in the former Soviet republics, Europe, and the Middle East, while Beijing can pursue primacy in the Indo-Pacific region. Shared opposition to the United States and its values partly explains their tightening ties. As a result, Moscow and Beijing have adopted coordinated as well as separate policies to counter U.S. power and influence.

The Sino-Russian relationship has moved considerably closer than many expected in recent years. Scholars have traditionally downplayed the potential for an enduring and comprehensive Russia-China alignment against the United States. Many analysts have argued that Sino-Russian cooperation is constrained by the two countries' interest in sustaining favorable ties with the United States and the relatively benign nature of U.S. hegemony, which provides many benefits to Russia and the PRC. It was thought that Moscow's and Beijing's centuries-long history of conflict and distrust as well as Russia's and China's strong capacity to defend against external military threats presented additional barriers. Until recently, the concept of "triangular diplomacy" has been out of fashion in Washington. Whereas Russian and Chinese writers have regularly employed a triangular framework in their discourse on great power politics, most U.S. foreign policies have typically addressed each country separately rather than considering their combined weight. For many years after the end of the Cold War, U.S. national security decision makers rarely considered how U.S. dealings with Moscow or Beijing would affect the Sino-Russian alignment, let alone what tactics Washington could use to shape the relationship. In contrast, Russian and Chinese policies have striven to exploit U.S. tensions with the other state. Prudence warrants more consideration of the effects an enduring Sino-Russian alignment could have on the United States. Not only do strong Russian-Chinese ties look likely to persist for years, and they could plausibly broaden and deepen this alignment in the future, but Russia and China have also already experienced an impressive geopolitical resurgence since the Cold War. U.S. policy makers need to acknowledge and understand how U.S. decisions and other factors impact Sino-Russian ties. At a minimum, U.S. policy makers should make a greater effort to assess how Russian-Chinese collaboration presents a more challenging environment for U.S. foreign policy. Even better, U.S. leaders could try to redirect the relationship in ways that benefit U.S. interests. Toward that end, this manuscript examines several complementary case studies encompassing geographic and functional issues that are critically important for all three countries. These cases reveal various pathways, events, and drivers that have most impacted the dynamics shaping the Russia-China relationship.

The first part of this book reviews the changing nature of Sino-Russian ties since the Cold War, focusing on their governments' strengthening connections and increasingly anti-American worldviews. The Russian and PRC political systems have become more similar under their current national leaderships. Since the end of the Cold War, both governments have become more authoritarian under preeminent leaders who dominate national policies. Neither country tries to export its authoritarian ideology as ardently as their Cold War–era predecessors, who adhered to (and fought over) Marxist-Leninist principles. Yet, both governments have become less tolerant of domestic and international opposition. Since becoming Russia's president in 2000, Vladimir Putin has suppressed the limited political and economic pluralism that arose during the presidency of his weaker predecessor, Boris Yeltsin. The PRC had been moving in a more politically liberal direction in the late 1990s, with previously rigorous controls slightly loosened, while the ruling Chinese Communist

Party (CCP) maintained the requirement for a more collective leadership and the obligatory rotation of political elites. After Xi Jinping became the country's paramount leader, however, the PRC became even more authoritarian. In 2018, the CCP National Party Congress abolished the two-term limit (i.e., two periods of five years) on presidential terms, while Xi has assumed a cult of personality, and Chinese censorship, drawing on technological advances, has become more severe. Xi is scheduled to remain China's unelected president until 2022, while Putin's presidency extends until 2024, but both presidents seem able to extend their limits indefinitely. Along with other members of governing elites in both Moscow and Beijing, the presidents display resolute ideological opposition to Western values. They view U.S. professions of promoting democracy and human rights as a conceptual guise to subvert their regimes and those of their allies while advancing U.S. commercial and strategic interests. They vehemently insist that the United States and other foreign governments should respect traditional interpretations of state sovereignty, territorial integrity, and national autonomy—which includes nonintervention in their internal affairs. At the same time, both regimes violate these principles in their foreign policies while employing nationalism and anti-Americanism to rally domestic support behind their policies. They emphatically oppose U.S. interference in their perceived regional spheres of influence, especially Washington's siding with their neighbors in their disputes with Beijing and Moscow.

The second section of this book details several major geographic regions of trilateral interaction. In the Arctic, Beijing has scaled back its previously expansive status and resource claims, which aroused unease in Moscow, to facilitate Sino-Russian collaboration on joint energy extraction and other commercial projects. In East Asia, the two countries have aligned their policies regarding the Korean Peninsula, to include launching joint peace plans; neither country wants near-term regime change in Pyongyang even as they promote peace and nonproliferation. In contrast, Russian-Chinese coordination has remained minimal regarding Japan and South Asia. Though China has gingerly increased its economic and political influence in the adjacent region of Central Asia, PRC officials have taken care not to overtly challenge Russian security interests in the region's group of former Soviet republics, which still purchase primarily Russian weapons. For decades, South Asia had been a region central to Sino-Soviet rivalry. Following independence from the United Kingdom, India became a de facto Soviet ally, buying enormous quantities of weapons from the Soviet Union and aligning with Moscow against Beijing. Meanwhile, Pakistan became the PRC's closest foreign ally, receiving privileged access to Chinese defense and even nuclear technology. Since the Cold War, however, New Delhi has improved relations with Washington, while Islamabad has largely reconciled with Moscow. The Middle East, Africa, and South America present a more mixed picture. Moscow and Beijing have no open disagreements in the region, but they tend to prioritize different countries, employ different policy tools, and do not closely coordinate their policies.

The third part of this text surveys several critical functional areas of Sino-Russian interaction that transcend geographic regions. Moscow and Beijing have become each other's most important security partners. Their governments have adopted several arms control and confidence-building measures, broadened contacts between their national security establishments, and institutionalized their defense and regional security dialogues, military exchanges, and strategic consultations within both bilateral and multilateral frameworks. Their common security objectives encompass averting bilateral conflicts, maintaining border security, sustaining arms transfers, and influencing third parties such as the United States. Following several years of stagnation, Russia has resumed large-scale arms sales to China. These transfers were prominent in the 1990s and included complete warships and warplanes before sharply declining in the mid-2000s due to concerns about Chinese violations of Russian intellectual property agreements and Beijing's demands that Russia offer more advanced weapons than the surplus Soviet-era systems sold in the 1990s. The past few years have seen a rapid renewal of these sales, as Russia has delivered some of its most advanced fighter planes and air defense missiles. The scale, scope, and sophistication of Russian-Chinese military exercises have also grown remarkably in the past decade. There are now several major drills each year that occur in multiple domains to include ground, sea, air, and aerospace forces. Importantly, neither Moscow nor Beijing views the other as a near-term military threat. In September 2001, the two countries signed the Sino-Russian Treaty of Good-Neighborliness and Friendly Cooperation, with provisions for nonaggression and mutual security consultations. Sino-Russian economic and energy ties have also increased though not as extensively as their security ties. In the diplomatic realm, though Russian and Chinese opposition to U.S. defense alliances and military policies in Europe and the Indo-Pacific region are long-standing, both governments have more assertively challenged these alliances in recent years. Moscow has strived to impede further North Atlantic Treaty Organization's (NATO) enlargement and more vigorously contested the alliance's ties with the former Soviet republics. Whereas PRC leaders previously prioritized cooperating with foreign partners to achieve economic growth, they now aim to become the dominant Asian power without war by pushing U.S. military forces away from China's borders. Moreover, following many years of false hopes and frustrated deals, the two countries have consummated their long-anticipated energy partnership. Russia's large but undeveloped Asian hydrocarbon deposits, combined with China's increasingly voracious demand for imported energy, make them natural energy partners. For years, inadequate transportation infrastructure, diverging pricing perceptions, and novel energy technologies kept Chinese purchases of Russian energy at relatively low levels. However, recent oil and gas deals as well as newly built energy pipelines have secured Russia's position as one of the PRC's largest foreign energy suppliers, probably for decades. The two countries are considering extending cooperation in the cyber and outer space realms, such as by launching joint projects to pool their scientific and technical resources to affirm their sovereignty claims in these domains.

The final section of this volume considers possible future scenarios for Russian-Chinese relations, assesses the impact of these developments on U.S. foreign policy, and offers some recommendations for U.S. policy makers to drive future events in favorable directions. Importantly, the degree of Russian-Chinese cooperation has varied substantially—by location, issue, and time. In some cases, they cooperate closely against U.S. interests; in other instances, Moscow and Beijing pursue policies marked by mutual indifference and even rivalry. The manifestations of the Sino-Russian alignment are global but most evident in only a few geographic regions, such as Central Asia. In terms of functional issues, their security and diplomatic cooperation is greater than their still minimal social and humanitarian collaboration. Bilateral economic exchanges between the two countries also remain modest compared to those found between most friendly countries, let alone allies. Russian and Chinese approaches to a range of significant subjects remain frequently uncoordinated.

The "Return of Great Power Competition" is the term used in many U.S. national security documents to describe the deterioration of U.S. political-military relations with Russia and China. Yet, the three legs that comprise the Russia-China-U.S. strategic triangle display clear differences. The Sino-Russian relationship is much more stable and stronger than the ties either state has with the United States. Whereas Russian-U.S. exchanges remain dominated by Cold War–era issues such as arms control and regional security, the Sino-U.S. and even Russian-Chinese dialogue extends to encompass many more nonmilitary issues. While relations between Moscow and Beijing have never been better, Russian-U.S. ties have never been worse, at least since the Cold War. However, the third leg of the triangle, the Sino-American connection, is still in flux. Beijing and Washington have a mixed relationship in which they cooperate in some areas and compete in many others, though the divergences have grown considerably in recent years. Current Sino-American differences range from unfair trading and investment practices to cyber confrontations to human and civil rights. In any case, all three countries enjoy substantial strategic autonomy, which they freely exercise through unilateral actions, due to their great power.

One could imagine scenarios that could lead the Sino-Russian relationship to regress to its traditional state of tensions and troubles. Demographic developments, leadership changes, and other transformations could eventually undermine their current alignment. Russian concerns about China could grow if the PRC continues to ascend to superpower status, displacing Russia as the main global rival to the United States. Alternatively, Russian plans to create an European Union (EU)-like arrangement among the former Soviet republics could provoke Beijing's resistance since such a development could impede China's economic access to Central Asia. Beijing's growing economic interests in the Arctic and Central Asia, combined with the improving power projection capabilities of the People's Liberation Army (PLA), could induce the PRC to cease deferring to Moscow's lead in these regions. If the PLA establishes bases in the former Soviet republics surrounding Russia, or the Chinese economic and military presence in these states displaces Russian companies or arms sales, many Russians will become alarmed. But these and other potential divisive developments are unlikely to occur soon if, as seems probable, Russian and PRC diplomats continue to manage adroitly possible pitfalls in their bilateral relationship. In some cases, critical time periods may arise that create windows of opportunity or vulnerability for U.S. influence. Like all authoritarian systems, the selection of leaders in either country is opaque and prone to factional infighting. At some point, new leaders will arise in Russia and China who could, as in the past, be more wary of cooperating with the other country and be more open to cooperating with the United States. But forecasting when and how this may occur is probably impossible.

The growing Sino-Russian collaboration has already challenged important U.S. security, economic, and ideological interests. These challenges could intensify if Moscow and Beijing align even more strongly behind anti-American positions. For instance, Russia may sell more advanced weaponry to the PLA as well as begin buying substantial military technologies from Chinese manufacturers. Since their strategic partnership is not binding, constraining, or exclusive, their low-cost, multidimensional alignment is resilient against many potential U.S. countermeasures. The United States should apply more resources to evaluating Sino-Russian defense ties, understanding the evolving dynamic in order to prepare for its future evolution, and ensuring that U.S. defense dialogues with allies and friends address this issue. Washington should do more to discourage technology transfers and other exchanges that can strengthen Sino-Russian military cooperation. Enhancing U.S. alliances and security partnerships with other countries is also imperative since these networks provide the United States with unique strategic advantages regarding Russia and China. Furthermore, the United States can profitably apply some of the tools it has developed to counter Russian sub-conventional aggression to constraining PRC assertiveness in this domain as well. At some point, arms control issues could give Washington a tool to divide Beijing from Moscow, since some Russian officials would likely share U.S. concerns about China's rising military power and stubborn strategic opacity. But overall, there are no easy policy solutions by which Washington can break apart the Russian-Chinese partnerships. Some developments and U.S. policies might eventually drive Moscow and Beijing apart, but the United States and its allies should prudently plan for this Sino-Russian alignment to persist for decades.

The author would like to thank the Smith Richardson Foundation for providing funding for this project. He would also like to thank his colleagues and interns for the numerous insights they have offered over the years regarding the issues addressed in this book.

Introduction

Trilateral Great Power Politics in Theory and History

President Joe Biden has called the challenge presented by the Russian Federation and the People's Republic of China a "fundamental debate about the future and direction of our world."[1] Like its predecessor, the Biden administration perceives Russia and China as the most substantial great power strategic competitors of the United States. The "Interim National Security Strategic Guidance," released in early March 2021, states that the PRC "has rapidly become more assertive. It is the only competitor potentially capable of combining its economic, diplomatic, military, and technological power to mount a sustained challenge to a stable and open international system." The Guidance further affirms that "Russia remains determined to enhance its global influence and play a disruptive role on the world stage." In short, "[b]oth Beijing and Moscow have invested heavily in efforts meant to check U.S. strengths and prevent us from defending our interests and allies around the world."[2] These interests include maintaining favorable regional balances of power, defending allies against military aggression, bolstering partners against coercion, reinvigorating and modernizing U.S. alliances and partnerships, developing new capabilities for emerging technologies, and augmenting the competitiveness of the U.S. defense economy and supply chains.

Until recently, U.S. national security planners had shown little public concern regarding Sino-Russian cooperation. They may have presumed that the partnership was inherently limited due to the well-known differences between the countries, downplayed the military potential of both countries' armed forces given U.S. military strengths and the superior U.S. global network of allies and partners, or feared that expressing open unease about their collaboration would encourage it or at least make Moscow and Beijing believe that they gained leverage in Washington from cooperating with each other.

The closest link U.S. officials used to make would be criticizing both Russia and China for violating international norms or when justifying some recent U.S. defense and foreign policy initiatives, such as to strengthen U.S. cyber defenses or fortify international security institutions upholding Western liberal values. The idea that Moscow and Beijing will not form a comprehensive anti-U.S. alignment—one that encompasses multiple geographic regions and functional areas and attracts other partners—has been one of the most widely accepted propositions in contemporary international relations thought and practice. According to many scholars, economic interdependence, mutual distrust, nuclear deterrence, and the U.S. contribution to maintaining the global commons mean that Moscow and Beijing will accept, if with resentment and sometimes under protest, U.S. military and political supremacy in managing global affairs.[3] Analysts have perceived Moscow and Beijing as sharing important interests in maintaining good ties with the United States, recalled the lengthy legacy of Russian-Chinese conflict and distrust, and depicted U.S. primacy as benign and beneficial for all countries due to the U.S. role in preserving peace and stability in the "global commons"—the maritime, air, outer, and cyberspace domains.[4] Additionally, the advent of nuclear weapons makes an all-out war between Russia, China, and the United States both unthinkable and unnecessary since countries that possess robust nuclear deterrents are largely invulnerable against external threats.[5] This interpretation holds that Russian and Chinese leaders will avoid actions that could jeopardize their national security or economic health—something best achieved in a peaceful world without major military conflicts or other impediments to commerce. In September 2018, U.S. secretary of defense James Mattis said that "I see little in the long term that aligns Russia and China."[6]

While the conventional wisdom may prove correct, accepting untested assumptions regarding such an important issue is dangerous. Influential analytical and political figures have challenged this consensus. International relations theorists have long predicted that balances of power tend to form naturally, both at the regional and at the global levels. Great powers strive to prevent the enduring primacy of one of their members out of fear that it would exploit its preeminent status to their detriment.[7] History has regularly witnessed such balancing coalitions. In Europe, Britain would often serve as an offshore balancer against a potential hegemon on the continent, which at various times has included Spain, France, Germany, and Russia. Power transitions are primed for problems no matter which actors are involved. The rise and fall of great powers due to major changes in resource distributions among countries have produced power vacuums and hegemonic transitions, sometimes with violent consequences. Ascending powers typically try to apply their growing economic and military capacity to alter international institutions and norms to their advantage as well as pursue territorial, commercial, and other concrete gains. By the same token, existing hegemonic powers strive to maintain the prevailing world order of norms, institutions, rules, and practices that benefit them.[8] When confronted by rising powers, the established state can respond in several ways, from graceful retrenchment, as occurred during the transition from British to U.S. leadership, to preemptive war, as several powers responded to the growing power of Germany.

Today, Russia and China are the most prominent great power balancers against the United States; they sometimes enjoy backing from other dissatisfied countries, such as Iran and North Korea. Prominent analysts have faulted U.S. policies for driving Russia and China together in alignment against the United States. For example, University of Chicago professor John Mearsheimer has argued that the last few years have seen a great power politics renewal in which the United States again faces, as during the Cold War, near peer rivals for preeminence. He has also criticized U.S. policy for confronting both states simultaneously, thereby driving them together, rather than trying to maneuver between them.[9] When Donald Trump ran for president, he and his advisers criticized previous U.S. administrations for not doing more to avert a stronger Sino-Russian alignment against the United States. Global developments in recent years have further challenged conventional wisdom. The Russian and Chinese governments have over time more consistently supported one another in these challenges against U.S. leadership. Whereas Washington might have largely ignored Moscow's and Beijing's opposition to U.S. policies in the 1990s, this approach has become less tenable. The U.S. position in the triangular relationship between Russia and China has deteriorated since the Cold War ended. As Sino-Russian ties have improved, U.S. relations with both countries have worsened. Through their diplomatic and security cooperation, Russia and China have threatened more U.S. national interests. If these trends continue, the United States could confront a potentially greater challenge than Washington encountered during the Cold War due to the complex asymmetries involved in countering two nuclear-armed states that possess a diverse, complementary, and historically unique range of assets.

RUSSIA'S RESURGENCE

Under its current government, the Russian Federation is a dissatisfied, revisionist power seeking to comprehensively replace the existing U.S.-led world order with one more favorable to Russian interests. Russia is one of the most important global security actors besides the United States. In addition to having a permanent seat on the United Nations Security Council (UNSC) and remaining a leading exporter of oil and natural gas, the Russian armed forces possess sufficient offensive nuclear forces to destroy the United States or any other country. Putin has overseen an upsurge in Russian defense spending and foreign military interventionism. The Syrian war has also confirmed the improved effectiveness of Russia's conventional military capacity following its decay in the post-Soviet era. Additionally, the Russian national security establishment has adroitly applied political-military "hybrid" tools in the gray zone between peace and war, such as internet-enhanced media and cyber instruments. Russia also regularly uses arms and energy exports as foundational instruments to develop more comprehensive ties. Since the Soviet era, Russian diplomacy has become more flexible in pursuing short-term pragmatic partnerships, prioritizing foreign engagements, and exploiting U.S. diplomatic setbacks.[10] Moscow has been striving to establish buffers against Western influence by promoting international disorder through ambiguous actions that impede Western governments from reaching a consensus on an effective response against Moscow.

During the 1990s, the newly created Russian Federation underwent several traumatic transformations. The breakup of the Soviet Union in 1991 consummated the dissolution of the previously integrated Soviet political, economic, and military structures that sustained Moscow's status as the capital of a global superpower. As Russia's first president, Yeltsin identified his main tasks as dismantling the Communist Party's legally enshrined political monopoly, reining in the Russian security services, ending the inherent economic inefficiencies of the country's command economy, and ending Russia's alienation from the West. At home, Yeltsin not only empowered a group of young free-thinking economists who introduced radical and rapid free market reforms that destroyed the vestiges of the Soviet command economy but also enriched a select group of nouveau riche oligarchs and harmed the well-being of many Russians.[11] Yeltsin's rule was marked by protracted struggles among the factions within his administration, between the president and a parliament filled with influential opposition legislators, and between the central federal government in Moscow and several semiautonomous regional entities that at times appeared out of Moscow's control. On the international stage, Yeltsin more frequently aligned Russia with the United States and the other Western democracies while curtailing the direct use of Russian military power beyond the former Soviet space. Though the Russian military retained a presence in some other Soviet republics, and Moscow exploited divisions within and between these states, Moscow's influence in many of the former Soviet republics atrophied even as innumerable Russian national security managers perceived threats in the strengthening security ties of some of these newly independent states with Western countries.

Since Yeltsin's surprising resignation as president at the end of 1999, the Russian Federation has experienced a remarkable geopolitical resurgence. The previously chaotic politics of the Yeltsin years were replaced by a tightly controlled political process under Putin. The president and his closest allies have regained control over the country's political parties, judicial branch, media, corporations, and other key national actors. Due to higher world oil prices and other favorable developments, the Russian economy stabilized as did Moscow's international influence. However, the extent and duration of Russia's great power revival remain uncertain since the economy suffers from serious problems, including underinvestment in critical infrastructure and next-generation technological sectors, dismal demographic and health figures, and limited progress in diversifying the economy away from hydrocarbon exports. President Putin's foreign policy has also alienated Western states, while the country's post-Putin political transition remains unresolved. The Russian-U.S. relationship is more confrontational now than at any time since the Cold War. Moscow perceives major threats in North Atlantic Treaty Organization's (NATO) enlargement, Western democracy promotion, and other U.S. policies. The Russian government has strived to minimize U.S. influence in neighboring countries where Moscow claims a special sphere of influence. Beyond the former Soviet space, the Russian government has also contested U.S. influence in Europe, Asia, and the Middle East. Suspicions linger that Russian leaders have adopted a firmer nationalist posture to compensate for Russia's domestic shortcomings. Hostility to the West benefits the Moscow elite politically but harms the nation. Russian national security officials regularly presume malign motives behind almost any U.S. policy affecting their country. For instance, influential Russians frequently claim that Washington wants to force regime change in Russia and elsewhere under the guise of advancing liberalization and democracy. In response, Russian officials have severely curtailed U.S. government and Western-backed nongovernmental organizations' (NGO) involvement in their internal affairs. Besides overstating the desire and capacity of the U.S. government to threaten their regime, these curtailments weaken the socioeconomic foundation needed for better long-term Russian-U.S. ties. The chances of a direct military conflict are low given Russian conventional inferiority to NATO, but the adverse consequences of a war due to misunderstanding or miscalculation would be catastrophically high.[12] The Obama administration addressed these challenges by enhancing Western defense and deterrence capabilities while trying to cooperate with Moscow on areas of mutual interest. The Trump and Biden administrations generally continued and augmented these policies by further strengthening U.S. military capabilities in Europe, reinvesting in intelligence and other enabling capabilities, pushing for higher European defense spending, supporting Europe's energy independence, and fortifying U.S. allies against Russian non-kinetic challenges. Presidents Putin and Trump continued to praise each other in public, but governmental relations below the presidential level remain overwhelmingly confrontational. President Biden initially tried to work out a modus vivendi with Putin so that the United States could concentrate on managing China's rise, but the Russian invasion of Ukraine that began in February 2022 brought Russian-U.S. relations to their worst state since the end of the Cold War.

CHINA'S RISE

China's unprecedented growth in economic, diplomatic, and military power has propelled the PRC to the forefront of global players for the first time in centuries. During the past three decades, the country has grown more rapidly than any other large economy while maintaining domestic stability and increasing its international clout. Following its decisive turn toward economic reforms and openness to the outside world in the 1980s, the PRC overtook many other countries and has become the world's second-largest economy after the United States. China is now the largest energy consumer and importer and depends on reliable access to foreign markets and resources. From the mid-1980s until a few years ago, the PRC transformed from a revolutionary state whose government advocated global revolution into a "status quo" power that sought gradual integration into the existing international system instead of trying to overthrow it. Former paramount leader Deng Xiaoping adeptly described this foreign policy as "Observe calmly; secure our position; cope with affairs calmly; hide our capacities and bide our time; be good at maintaining a low profile; and never claim leadership."[13] Through pacific speeches and announcing generous economic aid, trade, and investment deals, PRC leaders strived to portray China as a benevolent rising power pursuing a peaceful development path that does not threaten other countries. PRC foreign policy has continued this pro-globalism line and "win-win" rhetoric of mutual benefits. In his speech at the 2019 Munich Security Conference, Yang Jiechi, Director of the Office of the Central Commission for Foreign Affairs, said, "Guided by a vision of global governance featuring consultation, cooperation and benefit for all, China has actively engaged in the reform of the global governance system. . . . We believe that the purpose of the reform is not to overturn the current system or start something new, but to improve the existing framework to reflect new realities and increase the representation and voice of emerging markets and developing countries."[14]

Even so, the demise of the mutual Soviet threat ended the de facto security alliance that had existed between China and the West during the late 1970s and 1980s. At the same time, the international outrage over the military crackdown at Tiananmen Square induced Western governments to impose an arms embargo on China. These developments led to a substantial reorientation in PRC strategic concerns. Previously, the focus had been on defending against a Soviet attack along China's northern and western borders, whereas since the early 1990s, the PRC national security establishment has worried more about maritime and aerospace clashes with the United States and its Pacific allies.

The Chinese government has used its improving economy to acquire more powerful warships, warplanes, and unconventional space and cyber capabilities. For example, the People's Liberation Army (PLA) Navy has been acquiring a "bluewater" naval force with modern oceangoing vessels, including aircraft carriers as well as a fleet of modern military aircraft.[15] Defense reforms have enhanced inter-service cooperation under new joint commands. There have also been substantial investments in asymmetric warfare capabilities for cyber and space warfare and a small but growing nuclear deterrent. Furthermore, Chinese diplomats have been active in building a China-centric network of bilateral and multilateral institutions. Xi's "Chinese Dream" envisages a resurgence of scientific, technological, cultural, and military power intended for both civilian and military purposes, within the framework of a national spirit of "rejuvenation." The Chinese military-civilian fusion strategy, as outlined in the 2016 "Opinions on the Integration of Economic and National Defense Building," aims to expand collaboration between the country's military and civilian sectors, especially in the realm of technology and know-how.[16]

The fundamental question facing the world is whether the international system can manage China's rise without large-scale loss of life and strife. Power transition theory posits that the PRC has the same general goal as other rising powers—to apply its growing economic, military, and other capabilities to remake the international order more in line with Beijing's preferences. Even though China's rise benefited from the U.S.-made global order, Beijing is now trying to replace that order with institutions and norms that PRC leaders believe would better advance its economic and security interests under current conditions. Historically, rising powers tend to free ride off the global hegemon and only challenge it when they conclude that they have accumulated sufficient strength to overthrow the international system. China is a rising power whose recent actions suggest that it is following this opportunistic path through carefully calibrated actions to strengthen its position in Asia, with the goal of establishing a Sino-centric order in the region, while benefiting from the U.S.-sustained world order in the interim. Like earlier rising great powers, the PRC might use its growing economic and military power to uphold common interests, but such a benign power transition is rare and certainly cannot be presumed. These power transitions often lead to major wars between the rising and the already dominant powers, a development sometimes referred to in Sino-American discourse as "The Thucydides Trap," which Chinese and U.S. policy makers are striving to avoid.[17] Beijing aims to dominate the Indo-Pacific region without war. Chinese leaders have demanded more influence within the world's key international institutions while making excessive claims to sovereignty over neighboring territories. The United States and other countries are torn between wanting to benefit from China's economic rise and fearing its political-military implications. Like Russia, however, China faces major obstacles to its great power ambitions. Its economic model relies on high rates of growth driven by large state-directed corporations supported by massive public subsidies, loans from state-owned banks, and access to global markets now focused inward due to the COVID-19 pandemic. The lack of a free media, an independent judiciary, and popular elections all encourage official corruption and abuses of power. The government continues to deny Chinese citizens basic civil and political rights, making integration with the mainland unattractive to countless people in Hong Kong and Taiwan. Rising prosperity could lead more PRC citizens to demand political rights to correspond with their new economic power, which would challenge the political monopoly of the ruling Chinese Communist Party (CCP).

A DEVELOPING ALIGNMENT

Soviet president Mikhail Gorbachev's landmark visit to Beijing in 1989 signified the dissipation of Cold War–era animosity between Moscow and Beijing. Since then, Russian-Chinese relations have been on an upward trajectory. Following the 1991 demise of the Soviet Union, Russia again became an important source of defense products and technology for China as well as an important economic and diplomatic partner. The PRC's growing need for raw materials and energy due to its expanding economic activity has aligned with Russian export priorities and need for foreign investment. Putin has accurately described the relationship as both "comprehensive"—involving diverse political, economic, and military ties—and "strategic" in that Beijing and Moscow consider their partnership fundamentally important.[18] In 2017, President Xi argued that, in an era of global complexity and uncertainty, good Sino-Russian relations promote revitalization of both nations as well as international peace and stability.[19] Developments between Russia and China since the Cold War are at odds with earlier periods of world history. Moscow and Beijing have often been rivals, not partners. Their relationship has most often been characterized by bloody wars, imperial conquests, and mutual denunciations. Sino-Russian ties have been particularly uneasy for the past few centuries. Although China was the strongest power in the 17th and 18th centuries, during the 19th century, Tsarist Russia surpassed China in terms of economic and military power. The growing power imbalance between a rising Russia and a weakening China enabled the Russian empire to annex territories claimed by China. These "unequal treaties" resembled how the divided Chinese were also suffering humiliating treatment at the hands of the Europeans, Japanese, and eventually Americans. Later in the 20th century, the Soviet Union and Maoist China were initially close allies due to their shared Marxist-Leninist outlook. Following a decade of close partnership after World War II, however, diverging ideological interpretations and personality issues turned into fierce rivals over leadership of the world communist movement. Their 1969 border skirmishes raised the risk of escalating into a nuclear war as PRC leaders raised the issue of revising the unequal treaties and Soviet leaders considered a preventive war before China could develop a secure nuclear deterrent. Sino-Soviet relations remained tense during the 1970s, with proxy wars in Angola, Mozambique, and Vietnam. In the 1980s, China aligned with the United States as a less threatening global power than the Soviet Union. The PRC and the United States collaborated to expel the Soviet occupation forces from Afghanistan, which in turn helped precipitate the collapse of Soviet power worldwide. Seeking to break the Chinese-U.S. alignment against Moscow, Gorbachev made major concessions to overcome the "three obstacles" that PRC leaders had identified to improved relations by curtailing the Soviet military presence in Afghanistan, Cambodia, and the Sino-Soviet border region. This process culminated in Gorbachev's 1989 state visit to Beijing, where Soviet and PRC leaders pledged to overcome their decades-long split and launch a new era of cooperation.

Since the Cold War, Russian policy makers have been striving to improve relations with the PRC. The disintegration of the Soviet Union essentially negated the threat from Russia in China's eyes and vastly reduced the element of their great-power rivalry. Though Yeltsin ended Moscow's Cold War rivalry with the West and the Sino-U.S. alignment atrophied due to the absence of the mutual Soviet threat, Sino-Russian relations stalled for a few years as both governments became preoccupied with domestic challenges. Russian leaders confronted the simultaneous need to transition their new country from single-party rule to a multiparty state, convert a command economy to one respecting market principles, and manage the loss of a Soviet multinational empire and the Russian military withdrawal from most of its foreign bases. PRC leaders had to sustain their CCP-dominant political system and global influence in the face of mass protests and years of political ostracism by Western governments following the armed repression of peaceful protesters in 1989. Russian and Chinese leaders convened regular high-level meetings, but it took some time before Sino-Russian cooperation began to resolve tensions such as their boundary dispute and develop mutual economic and diplomatic interests. Though Yeltsin faced major domestic opposition to transferring some disputed territory to Beijing, Putin managed to concentrate sufficient power to override this resistance. In July 2008, the Russian and Chinese governments demarcated the last pieces of their 4,300-km frontier, one of the world's longest land borders. They then demilitarized this area through arms reduction and confidence-building measures. Some Russian authors have developed a new conceptual framework to characterize the Russia-China relationship, that of the "Greater Eurasian Partnership." The term embeds growing Sino-Russian ties within a broader group of non-Western countries, and their multilateral frameworks, on the Asian mainland that Russian experts believe will fortify Russia's influence in East Asia and revitalize the Russian Far East's connections with the rest of Russia.[20] Russian leaders hope to harness China's rise to advance the two countries' shared interests. Russian officials would welcome greater Chinese investment to help modernize the Russian economy. The current Kremlin leadership is unenthusiastic about political reform as a means of imparting greater dynamism to the Russian economy. They appreciate how the PRC has been able to combine an authoritarian political system with a vigorous economy. Throughout his years in power, but especially in the last decade, Putin has made developing strong relations with the PRC a foreign policy priority. Russians describe their alignment with China as both comprehensive and enduring. In January 2017, Foreign Minister Sergey Lavrov observed, "Our relations with China ... are rich, trusting, friendly and effective like never before with regard to bilateral cooperation in all areas and our cooperation and coordination of steps in the international arena. I do not think that prospects for the development of relations with any country in the world should call into question Russian-Chinese strategic partnership and multilateral cooperation."[21] At his December 2017 news conference, Putin observed "that there is a nationwide consensus in Russia concerning the development of relations with China. . . . Russia and China will remain strategic partners for the long-term historical perspective."[22] In an October 2019 presentation to the Valdai International Discussion Club, Putin said that the Sino-Russian connection had become "an allied relationship in the full sense of a multifaceted strategic partnership."[23]

Though numerous factors account for better Sino-Russian relations, one of the drivers has been the two governments' similar foreign-policy outlook and shared opposition to many U.S. policies. In October 2021, presidential spokesperson Dmitry Peskov acknowledged, "There is quite a common ground between Moscow and Beijing in terms of what we dislike in Washington's politics."[24] Russia and China are now the most influential revisionist powers seeking to alter the U.S.-designed economic and security structures established after World War II, which they perceive as failing to adequately recognize their status or ensure their security and other national interests. Neither Russia nor China is content with the existing U.S.-led global order rooted in liberal internationalist principles, norms, and institutions. They dismiss U.S. claims to stewardship in upholding benign principles of international behavior as hypocritically deceptive professions to obscure how Washington pursues U.S. interests under the guise of defending universal values. They further denounce U.S.-led military alliances as anachronistic legacies of the Cold War and reflections of an outdated "bloc" mentality of containing Moscow and Beijing. Maintaining traditional interpretations of international law upholding national sovereignty, dispersing power away from the United States, and preserving their UNSC veto have been important tools for constraining U.S. foreign policy and buttressing their claims to great power status. Both governments have tried to weaken U.S. alliances by driving wedges between U.S. partners and pulling them toward its orbit. Moreover, Russian and Chinese representatives vehemently insist that they do not view each other as military threats and avoid publicly expressing concern about the other's military activities, the potential for future Sino-Russian rivalry, or other issues that might challenge their official line of an enduring Sino-Russian strategic partnership.

Moscow and Beijing both want a more powerful United Nations and UNSC, where Russian and PRC delegates can veto U.S.-backed resolutions that authorize sanctions or military force against Russia, China, or any governments friendly to them. Since the Cold War, Russia has cast more UNSC vetoes than any of the other four permanent Council members. In his 2015 speech before the UN General Assembly (UNGA), Putin said, "The United Nations is unique in terms of legitimacy, representation and universality."[25] The 2016 "Foreign Policy Concept of the Russian Federation" also highlighted Moscow's view that the United Nations had a "central and coordinating role" in regulating international relations.[26] In contrast, the PRC's involvement in the United Nations was initially circumscribed. Although "China" is technically one of the charter members of the United Nations, the PRC only assumed China's UN seat from the government of Taiwan in 1971. At first, Beijing sought to avoid directly confronting other countries and regularly abstained on resolutions that China opposed rather than veto them. The PRC also became a leading contributor to UN peacekeeping missions, supplying a substantial number of medical, engineering, and transportation assets to these UN "blue helmet" missions. Besides highlighting China's commitment to world peace, participating in UN missions allowed the PLA to gain valuable foreign military experience. In recent years, however, PRC representatives have become more assertive in defending Beijing's interests through UN speeches as well as casting vetoes. In a 2015 interview with the *Wall Street Journal*, Xi described the United Nations as the "most representative and authoritative international organization" and insisted on "the central role" of the United Nations and the UNSC in maintaining peace and security.[27] Beijing has aligned its own UN stances closer to those of Moscow in recent years. Their solidarity within the UNSC can include casting joint affirmative votes, issuing parallel vetoes, or arranging for one country (typically China) to abstain on resolutions that the other will unilaterally veto in any case.[28] Russian foreign minister Lavrov has attacked Western governments' use of the term "a rules-based order" as an attempt to denigrate the United Nations and international law in order to "uphold their exclusive position on these issues and do not want to negotiate."[29] The Russian and Chinese delegations to the UNSC have frequently collaborated to dilute resolutions seeking to impose sanctions on governments they consider friendly, including vetoing resolutions they have opposed in tandem several times since 2011.[30] Russia has vetoed more than a half dozen resolutions condemning the Moscow-backed government of Syria in the past five years. Beijing has joined Moscow on some of those vetoes while abstaining on others. Their 2016 Joint Declaration on Promotion and Principles of International Law calls for acceptance of the primacy of the UNSC in ensuring peace and security and for the resolution of disputes through predominately diplomatic and peaceful means.[31] Beyond voting on, or vetoing, UN actions, the United Nations provides Russian and Chinese representatives with a stage to express mutual diplomatic solidarity, share aversion to Western policies, and prominently enjoy equal status with the United States. Cooperating within the United Nations makes it harder for Western governments to isolate or ignore them. They also see the United Nations, which enjoys great international legitimacy, as a key tool to support their vision of a new system of global governance. Whereas the Trump administration withdrew the United States from various international bodies such as the UN Human Rights Council, Russia and especially China doubled down on their professed commitment to multilateralism and international organizations and strove to fill a perceived multilateral leadership vacuum. Moscow and Beijing have regularly pushed to have their candidates assume leadership positions in the United Nations and other major international institutions, insisting that their relative global importance warrants their having a share of senior positions. Western governments and NGOs have resisted these demands due to concerns about the commitment of Moscow and Beijing to defend UN values like human rights and rule of law. Russia and China also similarly employ the UNGA, despite its having only nonbinding votes, as another platform along with the UNSC to advance their positions on international issues. In particular, they have both used the opening fall session of the UNGA, attended by world leaders, to affirm similar principles on world-order issues. Nonetheless, despite their shared preferences for a powerful United Nations, their financial contributions to UN operations typically lag behind those of the United States.

Russian and Chinese leaders engage in numerous other high-level exchanges, make innumerable mutually supportive statements, and manifest other displays of Sino-Russian cooperation in what both governments regularly describe as their best relations in history. In March 2017, Putin said Sino-Russian ties have reached an "unprecedentedly high level" and served as "a model of interaction between great powers in the modern world."[32] On June 8, 2017, PRC president Xi Jinping emphasized the importance of the Sino-Russian strategic partnership as "vital to the revitalization of both nations, as well as to world peace and stability."[33] Russian leaders perceive the PRC's growing economic, diplomatic, and military weight in the world as an unavoidable development that in any case offers Moscow important benefits.

Whatever their private feelings, PRC leaders make sure to show public respect for Russia and Putin's achievements, with the Chinese media emphasizing Xi's knowledge of, and admiration for, Russian history and culture. (Russian leaders reciprocate through fulsome praise of China's achievements.) PRC leaders are solicitous of Moscow's hurt pride and make sure to show deference to the former superpower in public, praising Russian culture, Putin's skilled leadership, and anything else that resonates well in Moscow. Chinese officials have described their goal as striving to build a new type of great power relationship with Russia based "on non-conflict, non-confrontation, mutual respect and common development through win-win cooperation."[34] Since Xi had his first meeting with Putin in Moscow in 2013 as the PRC's president, the two leaders have made countless similar anti-American speeches. Yet, Putin regularly denies that Sino-Russian collaboration has been driven by common hostility toward the United States. Rather, the Russian president claimed that "Russia and China are not directing their policy against anyone," and instead, "we are just consistently implementing our plans for expanding cooperation." Putin asserted that such plans were based on the goals laid out in their 2001 bilateral friendship treaty.[35] This "Treaty of Good-Neighborliness and Friendly Cooperation between the People's Republic of China and the Russian Federation," signed by Chinese president Jiang Zemin and Putin in 2001, has established a flexible legal instrument for bilateral collaboration. Its five core principles include "mutual respect of state sovereignty and territorial integrity, mutual non-aggression, mutual non-interference in each other's internal affairs, equality and mutual benefit and peaceful co-existence." Article 2 has a mutual non-aggression clause in which Russia and China agree to never employ or threaten the use of military force against each other. The article also extends their earlier nuclear missile nontargeting pledge to include mutual adoption of a "no first use" nuclear weapons posture toward each other. Articles 3–5 affirm that each party will not challenge the others' political-economic orientation or territorial integrity, which in Moscow's case includes reaffirming recognition of Beijing's sovereignty over Taiwan. In Article 7, the parties commit to supporting arms reduction and confidence-building measures along their joint border. Article 8 contains a standard nonaggression clause: "The contracting parties shall not enter into any alliance or be a party to any bloc nor shall they embark on any such action, including the conclusion of such treaty with a third country which compromises the sovereignty, security and territorial integrity of the other contracting party." Article 9 provides for holding immediate mutual consultations "when a situation arises in which one of the contracting parties deems that peace is being threatened and undermined or its security interests are involved or when it is confronted with the threat of aggression." Article 10 calls for regular meetings "at all levels" to allow both sides to exchange views and "co-ordinate their stand on bilateral ties and on important and urgent international issues of common concern." Article 13 states that they will work to strengthen "the central role of the United Nations as the most authoritative and most universal world organization composed of sovereign states in handling international affairs, particularly in the realm of peace and development." Article 20 states that both governments "shall actively cooperate in cracking down on terrorists, splittists [commonly referred to as 'separatists' in later declarations] and extremists, and in taking strong measures against criminal activities of organized crimes, illegal trafficking of drugs, psychotropic substances and weapons." The treaty's initial duration is 20 years, but the accord automatically renews every 5 years unless a party notifies the other, one year prior to expiration, of its intent to terminate the treaty.[36] Unlike the earlier bilateral Cold War defense treaty signed between China and the Soviet Union in 1950, the 2001 treaty lacks a mutual defense clause in which both parties commit to providing military assistance, in case the other is attacked by a third party. In fact, the document resembles more of a declaration of mutual goodwill than a treaty of alliance. Much of the text affirms policies of noninterference and nonaggression toward the other country or pledges to consult on issues of mutual security concern.

In their joint statements, Russian and Chinese officials present a shared vision for global affairs, profess their commitment to enhancing bilateral security cooperation and mutual support, express solidarity against transnational terrorism and other mutual menaces, affirm mutual trust and understanding, and advocate nonaggression, antiterrorism, and international law. They also castigate the United States, sometimes by name but normally by allusion, by calling on all countries to abide by international rules, avoid expanding exclusive alliances and political-military blocs and eschew actions that enhance their own security at the expense of other states. Russian and PRC officials uphold traditional interpretations of national sovereignty, which severely limit the right of external actors to challenge a country's domestic policies. They both resent what they perceive as Washington's proclivity to interfere in their internal affairs as well as in their geographic regions. Russian and PRC strategists both think in terms of buffer states and spheres of influence. For Moscow, the U.S. presence in the former Soviet republics is a major irritant, whereas for Beijing, U.S. intervention in China's Indo-Pacific territorial conflicts and support for Taiwan's autonomy from the mainland represent major sore spots. Russian and Chinese officials openly call on their U.S. counterparts to stay out of these issues, which they view as vital interests for Moscow and Beijing but of only peripheral concern for Washington. Moscow views Ukraine as a barrier between Russia and NATO, while China views North Korea as a buffer from the U.S. military forces stationed in South Korea and Japan. Moreover, a recurring feature of Sino-Russian statements has been the call for a "multipolar" world in which Russia and China would occupy key positions, and no one great power—such as the United States—would predominate. In their historical narratives, both see themselves as victims of Western policies.[37] The Russian and Chinese governments make these joint statements because they often resonate louder than unilateral pronouncements. In the words of their March 2007 summit declaration, "The shared position on major international political issues of principle and the common or similar positions on important international and regional issues between China and Russia enable them to take part in international cooperation more effectively and meet new challenges and threats."[38]

A combination of aversion and opportunity fuels Sino-Russian revisionism. The governments of Russia and China are dissatisfied with various elements of the U.S.-led "global order." They each believe that it unduly constrains their power and prestige. Both greater powers are surrounded by weaker and divided countries—presenting an inviting security vacuum that the United States has only partly tried to or been able to fill. They also have specific territorial grievances and ambitions. Many Russians believe that, for various historical and cultural reasons, eastern Ukraine and other former Soviet territories should fall under Moscow's rule. In Asia, the Chinese widely believe that the contested islands in the East and South China Seas belong to China due to considerations of history and geography. Over the years, Russian and PRC writers have developed a shared narrative of U.S. hostility. They perceive Washington as pursuing "absolute" rather than "equal" security, thereby disregarding Russian-Chinese interests surrounding missile defense among other issues, misapplying sanctions selectively to promote U.S. commercial rather than multinational interests, and overlooking misbehavior by regimes and nonstate actors friendly to the United States. According to this Sino-Russian narrative, Washington took advantage of the weakness of its main geopolitical rivals after the Cold War to construct an exclusionary world order that privileged U.S. interests and values at the expense of Russia, China, and other countries. In Putin's words, Western leaders "chose the road of globalization and security for their own beloved selves, for the select few, and not for all. But far from everyone was ready to agree with this."[39] Confronted by obstacles, the United States intended to contain Russian and Chinese power and subvert regimes aligned with Beijing and Moscow through the use of propaganda, terrorism, and other unconventional means under the guise of promoting democracy, humanitarian intervention, and mass-based "social revolutions."[40] Putin apparently blamed the Obama administration for instigating the mass street protests that arose in Russia after he declared his intent to return to the presidency in September 2011, as well as the 2013–2014 demonstrations that catalyzed regime change in Ukraine. Like Russian leaders, Xi has criticized U.S. unilateralism and the U.S.-led world order, stating that "[t]he global governance system is built and shared by the world, not monopolized by a single country." He also joined Putin in averring that "[n]o country can maintain absolute security with its own effort, and no country can achieve stability out of other countries' instability." Just like his Russian counterpart, Xi called for an end to a "Cold War mentality in all its manifestation."[41] Russian and Chinese leaders perceive the United States as constantly manipulating global rules and principles for its benefit. According to the Sino-Russian narrative, when the rules favor Washington, the United States upholds them. When the rules impede the realization of U.S. interests, U.S. decision makers disregard even long-standing practices to create new rules more to their liking. They cite examples such as the U.S. withdrawals from the Anti-Ballistic Missile Treaty and Paris Climate Accords. They also object to the frequent U.S. military interventions in foreign countries, especially those without UNSC approval such as the U.S.-led wars in Kosovo and Iraq or the U.S. military activities in Syria without the approval of the pro-Russian Assad government in Damascus. They worry that Washington might intervene militarily to defend Taiwan against Beijing or assist separatists in Chechnya, Xinjiang, or other regions of Russian or Chinese concern. Throughout the COVID-19 crisis, Russian and Chinese officials have defended each other's responses to the pandemic—in unilateral, bilateral, and multilateral settings. In May 2020, Russian deputy foreign minister Sergei Ryabkov said, "There is no reason to blame China for doing something untimely, wrong or inadequate during the entire period of the fight against COVID-19," and criticized U.S. political leaders who "literally on a daily basis multiply the list of complaints addressed to China and try to impose anti-Chinese discourse in the entire international community."[42] Benefiting from the declining dominance of Western global news outlets, Russia and China have rapidly built influential state-owned broadcast networks, supplemented by additional state-controlled media and other influential outlets. During the pandemic, Russian and PRC broadcast and social media outlets have reinforced one another's messaging that has been critical of the Western response to the crisis.[43] When U.S. and European Union (EU) institutions criticized their propaganda campaigns, Ryabkov denounced the "accusations hurled at Russia and China for spreading 'disinformation' about COVID-19 [a]s nothing but the West demonstrating its anti-Russian and anti-Chinese prejudice" as well as reflecting a Western attempt to exploit the pandemic and compensate for its loss of global influence by scoring points against its geopolitical rivals.[44] Still, one continuing difference between Russia and China is that only Moscow has been annexing new territories, supporting armed proxies in neighboring countries, and regularly making implicit and explicit nuclear threats against other states. PRC leaders have generally been more subdued in their language, warning that others' actions will threaten regional stability but eschewing threats of force.

In essence, since the Soviet Union's disintegration in the early 1990s, Moscow and Beijing have achieved a benign geopolitical equipoise in which neither state immediately threatens the other and both regimes have incentives to cooperate in important areas. Whereas in the past one country tended to have clear power superiority over the other, now a multilevel balance has arisen. China's superior economic performance has allowed the PRC to catch up with Russia's previous lead, but Russia has more energy assets than China, whereas Russia sells oil and gas to many countries, the PRC has become highly dependent on imported energy. Although Russia and China are both military great powers, their relative strength differs. Russia's strength lies in its nuclear forces as well as its land and air power, whereas China's main power projection instrument has rapidly become its navy. Russia retains more advanced military weapons, but China is located at a distance from the core of Russian military power, which remains oriented toward the European theater. Both governments have carefully avoided taking provocative public actions against the other. Many earlier suspicions between Russian and Chinese nationals have dissipated as it has become clear that the PRC leadership has no intention of soon challenging their historically disputed Sino-Russian border and that, while large numbers of Chinese citizens work and travel in eastern Russia, few become permanent residents there. The constant anti-Americanism in the Russian and Chinese media has also diverted popular concerns away from each other and toward the United States. Furthermore, Russian and Chinese security concerns emanate from different areas with the exceptions of Central Asia and North Korea. Most Russian analysts, typically based in Moscow, perceive their main security challenges to the west and south as well as in Washington. They discount the emergence of a genuine military threat to Russia from China for at least the next decade. With their blessing, the Russian defense industry has sold the Chinese military billions of dollars' worth of weapons, though these systems have typically been optimal for fighting a maritime war in the Pacific rather than a land war in the Russian Far East. In light of the powerful U.S. military forces in the Pacific and potentially threatening developments in Taiwan, Japan, India, and North Korea, PRC policy makers eagerly bought these weapons. Russian policy makers believe that stronger ties with Beijing will help realize their long-term ambition of rebalancing economic ties away from the West, diversifying its exports beyond hydrocarbons, all while increasingly integrating Russia into the dynamic economy. While Western sanctions did not alone cause Moscow's turn eastward, they have probably reinforced it. Like others, Russian officials see China's rising power as unstoppable, at least by Moscow. Russian analysts think that even if the PRC surpasses the United States as the world's leading global power, Beijing would never be able to attain the kind of primacy that allowed the United States to construct a Washington-centered world order, whose norms and institutions allow Washington to sanction and constrain both Russia and China. Moscow has set aside its concerns over Beijing's Arctic ambitions; the two sides increasingly collaborate on natural resource exploitation and infrastructure development in northern

Russia and on developing the maritime Northern Sea Route connecting Asia to Europe via polar regions newly opened due to melting ice. The PRC offers investment funds and commercial shipping demand for northern transport routes that shave one-third of the time and expense of sending goods from China to Europe via the Suez Canal, while Russia brings land and long experience in the region. Moscow and Beijing have managed to agree to disagree even on issues where they differ—this compartmentalization helps sustain in other areas. Moscow has attempted but failed to reach out to other Asian players to pursue a more geographically diverse, less Sinocentric, Asia policy.

Still, the relationship is fluid, even in the short term. Several recent developments have abruptly altered the negotiating balance between Moscow and Beijing. A turning point in Sino-Russian relations occurred in 2014, when Moscow confronted the West over Ukraine's foreign-policy orientation, annexed Crimea, and supported rebel movements in eastern Ukraine. The 2014 Ukraine crisis placed China in a more advantageous relationship with Russia due to the Western sanctions and the resulting greater desire of Moscow to obtain PRC investment, technologies, and markets. Russia's economic problems, exacerbated by the depreciation of both its currency and world hydrocarbon prices, helped shrink Russia's gross domestic product to one-tenth of the Chinese economy. Having severely degraded relations with the West, Russian leaders believed that they had no choice but to pursue stronger ties with China. In effect, Moscow's "turn to Asia" strategy has become a "bet on China" policy, with President Putin leading the charge. Russia set aside the reservations that had limited its cooperation with China in areas such as energy, regional infrastructure development, security in Central and South Asia, and the sale of advanced weaponry. Furthermore, the Ukraine crisis advanced Beijing strategically by diverting U.S. rebalancing efforts in Asia, thereby enhancing China's leverage vis-à-vis both Russia and the United States. For example, Moscow became more open to transferring some of its sophisticated weaponry to the PLA. Yet, Russian leaders soon realized that China's economic and diplomatic support for Russia in its confrontation with the United States would remain circumscribed due to China's economic slowdown, desire to keep doors open to the West, and unrelenting Chinese hard bargaining.[45] To Moscow's annoyance, President Trump was unable to realize his stated goal of improving relations with Russia, though Moscow has arguably benefited from Trump's anti-Chinese measures and Beijing's interest in securing Russian support for its Eurasian integration initiatives such as the Belt and Road Initiative (BRI). With China's economy recovering more rapidly than Russia from the COVID-19 pandemic, however, Russian dependence on its Chinese ties may even increase.

I
Part

Regional
Alignments

1 Chapter **Korea**

For decades, Russia, China, and the United States, in coordination with Japan and the Republic of Korea (ROK, also known as "South Korea"), have endeavored to prevent the Democratic People's Republic of Korea (DPRK, commonly referred to as "North Korea") from possessing nuclear weapons. However, neither diplomacy nor sanctions nor military countermeasures have yet curbed North Korea's nuclear or missile ambitions. For years, the DPRK has developed nuclear weapons and long-range missiles in violation of UN resolutions and its international commitments. Pyongyang pursues nuclear weapons for leverage, power, prestige, and money. The DPRK employs nuclear weapons to extract concessions and blackmail Moscow and Beijing as well as Washington. Past diplomatic deals involving North Korea, such as the 1994 Agreed Framework that froze the DPRK's nuclear activities and the 2005 Six Party accord that established an agreed path toward denuclearizing the Korean Peninsula, have failed to halt the DPRK programs for any significant period. UN resolutions and sanctions have not proven more successful. The Pyongyang regime has reportedly circumvented even the tighter sanctions enacted in recent years through creative cyber theft of bitcoins and other innovative criminality, which provides the regime's core members and supporters resources to sustain their rule.[1] The DPRK seeks security assurances, sanctions relief, and diplomatic recognition from the United States. North Korea's definition of peace requires total regime security—something the ROK and the United States can pledge but not guarantee. In January 2021, Kim Jong-un insisted that the regime was now a permanent nuclear weapons state and that Washington must deal with it as such.[2] The United States and its allies have continuously refused to accept a mutual deterrence relationship with an aggressive, congenitally anti-American, and frighteningly unpredictable DPRK regime.

North Korea is one of the few places on the globe where Russia and China jointly border a third country in a tripoint. During the Cold War, Beijing and Moscow aligned with Pyongyang against Washington and its regional allies. More recently, Russian and Chinese leaders have shared some U.S. concerns regarding Korea. For example, they want to avert war on the Peninsula or a DPRK nuclear arsenal. Russian and Chinese officials have opposed the DPRK's testing of nuclear weapons or of long-range ballistic missiles because these actions have led to U.S. defense enhancements in East Asia, such as the deployment of more advanced missile defenses in the ROK and Japan. Russian and Chinese analysts do not think that North Korea would deliberately attack their countries, the United States, or other states. More generally, North Korea's belligerence harms Sino-Russian strategic interests, complicates their regional economic ambitions, and arouses Sino-Russian angst about the DPRK dragging them into conflict.

Nevertheless, Moscow and Beijing have prioritized preservation of the DPRK regime over competing objectives. Though Russia, China, and the United States oppose North Korea's nuclear weapons program, that issue has not consistently been Moscow's and Beijing's highest priority among the issues related to the Korean Peninsula. The Russian and Chinese governments have often been more concerned that the two Korean states might reunify and within the framework of a U.S.-led political-military alliance system— precisely what happened with the reunification of Germany at the end of the Cold War. To address this concern, they have striven to avert instability in the DPRK, especially trying to avoid the collapse of the Kim regime, or a strengthening U.S. military presence in South Korea or Japan. Moscow and Beijing still consider the regional chaos that could follow the precipitous collapse of the DPRK a more severe menace than the potential adverse impact of Pyongyang's nuclear and missile development programs, which they see as primarily motivated by defense and deterrence concerns. For this reason, they have regularly opposed U.S.-led efforts to impose strong sanctions on the DPRK—and at times, Moscow and Beijing have combined forces at the UN Security Council (UNSC) to defend North Korea from potentially destabilizing coercive measures promoted by the United States and its allies. Russian and Chinese officials calculate that pressing too forcefully to coerce North Korea's behavior could backfire and lead Pyongyang to engage in still riskier behavior. They regularly call on the United States to eschew military threats, promote diplomatic solutions, and make concessions to reduce tensions on the Korean Peninsula. Moscow and Beijing favor incremental disarmament with reciprocal reductions in international sanctions—a "step-by-step" approach—and have not backed U.S. demands for the complete, verifiable, and irreversible DPRK denuclearization. In 2017, the two governments called for a halt to major ROK-U.S. military drills along with a suspension of DPRK missile and nuclear tests.[3]

More recently, Russia and China encouraged the Trump administration's reconciliation with North Korea while urging Pyongyang to refrain from further nuclear and missile testing. Russian and Chinese leaders were generally pleased by the lessening of tensions on the Peninsula that occurred in 2018 and 2019. These manifestations have included a cessation of DPRK nuclear and missile testing, curtailment of major ROK-U.S. military exercises, and renewal of intra-Korean economic and diplomatic engagement to include some family reunifications, inter-Korean sports and cultural exchanges, and modest confidence- and security-building measures. Nonetheless, plans for major joint Korean economic cooperation or an inter-Korean peace regime remained largely unrealized. Moscow and Beijing are now pressing for a removal of sanctions on North Korea and a further reduction of U.S. military activities in South Korea in exchange for more DPRK disarmament measures. However, they still fear that their strategic interests could suffer with reunification. As a result, trilateral collaboration regarding North Korea has waxed and waned over the years. Looking ahead, U.S. diplomacy must persuade Russian and Chinese leaders that they no longer need the DPRK to act as a strategic buffer against the United States. Furthermore, Washington must convince Moscow and Beijing that Russia and China would attain more net strategic and economic gains from the return of a unified Korean state under Seoul's democratic and benign leadership than from a continuation of the dangerously unstable division of the Peninsula. Long-term regime change and reunification, which are the optimal enduring solutions to the Korean crisis, will invariably require extensive Russian, Chinese, and U.S. (as well as South Korean and Japanese) cooperation to achieve.

RUSSIAN GOALS AND POLICIES

The DPRK's military activities present Russia with a thorny dilemma. Various considerations give Moscow an ineluctable strategic interest in all Korean questions. The Russian Federation shares a land border with North Korea, with Russia's main Pacific port of Vladivostok situated nearby. Accordingly, the Russian government does not want North Korea to have nuclear weapons, test missiles, or take other provocations that could spur U.S. missile defenses or other U.S. military activities in the Indo-Pacific region. At the same time, Moscow wants to avert U.S. unilateral action against North Korea and reduce the U.S. military presence in the region. Russian officials also fear the potential geopolitical repercussions of regime collapse in Pyongyang, which could generate a regional economic crisis, large refugee flows, and armed conflicts in its proximity. Furthermore, the prospect of an alliance between the United States and the reunified Korea alarms the Kremlin.

To promote these goals, Russian policies insist on Moscow's having a prominent role in negotiations regarding North Korea and related issues. The Russian Federation has always officially rejected the DPRK's claims to nuclear weapons status, urged restraint on its missile launches, and declined to sell weapons to North Korea or directly assist the DPRK's military programs. Yet, President Putin has reversed the previous Russian policy of distancing Moscow from the DPRK while aligning closer to the ROK. For the past two decades, Russian officials have typically devalued threatening North Korean military advancements, argued that the DPRK seeks advanced weapons primarily for defensive purposes, urged more U.S. concessions in negotiations with North Korea, called for reduced U.S. military activities in Northeast Asia, and pro-tected the DPRK from Western coercion while pressing Pyongyang to volun-tarily restrain from provocative activities. Moscow has, unsuccessfully, tried to coax the DPRK into accepting limits on its nuclear and missile testing in exchange for international economic assistance and security assurances. Fur-thermore, Moscow has regularly employed public diplomacy and UN vetoes to constrain the ROK-U.S. response to DPRK provocations.

Russia had accepted some multilateral sanctions on North Korea to gen-erate leverage on Pyongyang, discourage additional DPRK actions that Mos-cow opposes, and obviate tougher Western responses that could threaten the country's stability. Russian diplomats regularly resist more severe sanctions on the grounds that all parties must minimize tensions. As one of the five permanent members of the UNSC, Russia can veto resolutions that would impose harsher multilateral sanctions on the DPRK or authorize the use of force against North Korea. Jealous of its veto power, Moscow has therefore considered any sanctions adopted by U.S. authorities outside the UNSC, espe-cially those levied against Russian entities, as unacceptable. When the United States imposed unilateral sanctions on North Korea following the assassina-tion of Kim Jong-un's half-brother, which Kim allegedly ordered, Russia con-demned the measures as "illegitimate" since they lacked the UNSC's approval.[4] Besides preventing actions Russia opposes, exercising its veto power makes it harder for the United States and its allies to ignore Russian interests regarding the Korean Peninsula.

In a parallel track, Moscow pursues expanded economic ties with both Koreas. Securing greater South Korean trade and investment helps stimulate Russia's growth and modernization as well as reduce Russia's economic depen-dence on China. Increasing connectivity with both Koreas deepens Russian integration into the prosperous East Asian region, which enhances the Russian national economy, in general, and the Russian Far East, in particular. Toward this end, Russian entrepreneurs have sought to construct trans-Korean rail-roads, pipelines, and other conduits linking eastern Russia with the Koreas. Specific projects have aimed to expand Russia's role as a transit country for trade between Europe and East Asia while increasing Russian energy and economic exports to Asian countries. For instance, Russian energy conglomerate Gazprom seeks pipelines that pass through the Koreas in order to shift Russian energy sales toward Asia. Moreover, Russian businesses would like to develop North Korea's minerals and other natural resources. Like earlier Soviet economic assistance to North Korea and other clients, Russian economic activity with the DPRK has the added benefit from Moscow's perspective of helping to fortify the DPRK government against regime change. Despite Moscow's aspirations, the adverse security situation in Northeast Asia has impeded both intra-Korean economic collaboration and Russian ambitions for regional connectivity. Officially declared bilateral trade between Russia and North Korea has remained severely limited. Investors are concerned about potential disruptions of pipelines and other conduits by the North and other risks. Despite major efforts, Russia has also proved unable to secure substantial South Korean high-technology investment.

CHINA'S GOALS AND POLICIES

PRC policy makers favor denuclearization since North Korea's nuclear program provides a rationale for U.S. military deployments and a possible pretext for U.S. military intervention in the North. It also prompts U.S. regional allies such as Japan and South Korea to strengthen their defensive capabilities, which Beijing also perceives as inimical to China's security. Beijing therefore favors a dual-track approach that involves "phased and synchronized" steps by the DPRK and other states toward denuclearization and peace on the Korean Peninsula. Chinese leaders fear that abrupt regime change in Pyongyang could harm their country's economic and security interests by leading to a unified Korean state that would distance itself from Beijing and align with Washington and other Western partners. PRC policy makers also strive to avoid antagonizing the DPRK leadership to the extent that North Korea would retaliate against Chinese interests. Although Beijing wants Pyongyang to end its nuclear program, the Chinese perception is that denuclearization should be an end goal of negotiations rather than a precondition for talks.[5] Furthermore, some PRC writers sympathize with Pyongyang's motivations. They see the DPRK responding to plausible U.S. threats by seeking nuclear weapons to deter them as synonymous with the way China reacted to earlier U.S. nuclear intimidation.[6] Conversely, PRC officials have long seen direct DPRK-U.S. engagement, in support of a wider multinational process, as a critical prerequisite for achieving a more enduring resolution of the Korean nuclear crisis.

In this context, PRC representatives have consistently downplayed concerns about North Korea's missile and nuclear activities while sounding the alarm about U.S., ROK, and Japanese defensive countermeasures. As U.S. and allied officials try to build pressure on Pyongyang, PRC policies strive to construct escape paths for the DPRK. They perennially urge Washington and its partners to offer more negotiations and compromises rather than employ punitive measures that they argue could deepen Pyongyang's alienation and intransigence. For example, PRC representatives have urged Washington and its partners to make more concessions to the North—including normalizing diplomatic relations, offering Pyongyang security guarantees, and providing more economic assistance—to secure its denuclearization. PRC diplomats propose that the international community offer Pyongyang more economic inducements, such as a reduction in sanctions pressure and the resumption of limited economic aid, as incentives for negotiations. In November 2021, PRC Foreign Ministry spokesperson Wang Wenbin told the media that "China believes the crux of the Peninsula issue lies in the fact that the denuclearization measures the DPRK has taken have not won due attention, and the country's legitimate concerns have not received due response. The US should face the crux of the problem squarely, propose attractive plans for dialogue and take real actions instead of simply shouting slogans."[7] Conversely, they argue that sanctions and measures designed to increase the isolation of North Korea may induce the DPRK to make erratic and destructive decisions. At a UNSC meeting in April 2017, Foreign Minister Wang Yi urged the parties to set aside questions of "who is right, who is wrong" and instead reach "for low-hanging fruits, defuse any flashpoint endangering peace on the Peninsula, and create conditions for stability in the region."[8]

Despite the international sanctions, the PRC remains the DPRK's main economic partner, providing critical imports, investment, trade, and internet connectivity to the larger world. Rather than exploiting North Korea's economic dependence on China to pressure the DPRK to change its policies, PRC officials have primarily sought to promote economic reform to stabilize the DPRK regime, reduce aid demands on China, and refocus North Koreans' attention toward domestic economic well-being. Beijing also seeks access to the DPRK's labor, natural resources, and trade. PRC decision makers fear that excessively pressuring North Korea would reduce Beijing's influence in Pyongyang or lead DPRK authorities to cut back economic ties with China. Meanwhile, the economic benefits that China gains through its relationship with the DPRK have given influential Chinese figures yet another stake in averting additional economic sanctions. PRC representatives have unsurprisingly vocally opposed the application of U.S. sanctions to PRC companies that engage in certain business with North Korea. Beijing further strives to avert U.S. military actions against the DPRK, including the deployment of missile defenses in South Korea, major U.S.-ROK military exercises, and, worst of all, U.S.-led offensive operations against North Korea. When the United States and South Korea deployed the Terminal High Altitude Area Defense (THAAD) missile defense system despite Chinese objections, Beijing engaged in one of its most assertive influence operations in recent history. The pressure campaign included critical PRC leadership speeches, alarming media commentary, and coercive economic measures such as trade and tourism boycotts. Ultimately, the Chinese government overreached. Beijing's heavy-handed pressure made it harder for the ROK government to back down without losing credibility and suffering embarrassment.

Despite their strategic and economic interests in sustaining positive ties with North Korea, Chinese officials have occasionally employed sharper rhetoric and tactics in response to Pyongyang's nuclear and missile provocations. Bilateral relations reached their nadir soon after DPRK chairman Kim Jong-un gained power in late 2011. For his first few years in power, Kim snubbed China; PRC officials in turn evinced more willingness than ever before to pressure North Korea despite potential economic and security costs. In July 2014, President Xi broke with precedent in deciding to visit Seoul before Pyongyang. Further, the PRC Ministry of Commerce limited petroleum exports to North Korea, banned exports of natural gas, and ceased importing North Korean textiles. On occasions, PRC officials have reluctantly cooperated in imposing collective UN sanctions on the North in the hopes of heading off more severe unilateral U.S. measures. Even when supporting sanctions, however, PRC officials have insisted that such coercive measures can only represent an intermediate step toward the ultimate objective of "bring[ing] the Korean peninsula nuclear issue back to the negotiation table and to seek a final solution through negotiation, until the denuclearization of the Korean peninsula and the long-term peace and stability of the Korean peninsula become reality."[9] An immediate goal has been to avert pressures for escalation between the two sides. On March 8, 2017, Foreign Minister Wang characterized the "two sides [as] like two accelerating trains coming towards each other with neither side willing to give way," such that China's "priority now is to flash the red light and apply brakes on both trains."[10]

RUSSIAN-CHINESE INTERACTIONS

Moscow and Beijing have often pursued parallel or congruent policies toward the Korean Peninsula. Neither wants Washington to pursue a change in the DPRK regime, rapid Korean unification, or military actions against North Korea. Both countries strive to avoid a sudden change of government in Pyongyang, regardless of how difficult it may be to deal with Kim Jong-un, and have sought to play the role of mediator between Pyongyang and Washington. Russian and Chinese analysts argue that North Korea seeks nuclear weapons mainly for deterrence and defense, especially against the United States, rather than as offensive instruments. Russia and China have been more concerned about the regional chaos that would result from the DPRK's abrupt collapse than the adverse impact of Pyongyang's nuclear and missile development programs. For this reason, and to avert measures that could impede their economic projects involving North Korea, they have both opposed strong sanctions on North Korea and, more recently, called for reducing those already levied. The Sino-Russian stance at times seems to presume that Pyongyang will probably continue its prickly policies regardless of Moscow's and Beijing's actions, so they are disinclined to engage in potentially costly confrontations with North Korea that would likely yield few positive results.

Although neither Moscow nor Beijing perceives the DPRK as a direct military threat to their own countries, they have long sought to end North Korea's testing of long-range ballistic missiles and nuclear weapons because these actions encourage other nations, particularly the United States and its allies, to take military measures that could be employed beyond the North Korean context, potentially against Russia and China. Indeed, the United States, Japan, and South Korea have strengthened their ballistic missile defenses and other military capabilities in Northeast Asia to counter the DPRK's nuclear and missile programs. Both Moscow and Beijing also expressed alarm about the initially aggressive rhetoric of the Trump administration regarding North Korea. In his first address to the UN General Assembly in September 2017, Trump admonished the DPRK about the potential consequences of its nuclear provocations, warning that the United States was prepared "to totally destroy North Korea" in self-defense against the regime's "suicide mission."[11] Russian and Chinese security experts argue that military measures and threats counterproductively encourage Pyongyang's intransigence and pursuit of nuclear weapons technology. Indeed, they blame past U.S. pressure on North Korea for making the DPRK leadership pursue nuclear weapons in the first place. Further, some Russian and Chinese officials believe that Washington's goal is to achieve eventual regime change in Pyongyang despite the high risks to Moscow, Beijing, and others. In the interim, they suspect that the United States is exploiting the DPRK threat to justify the U.S. "rebalancing" of its military power to Asia. Until recently, Russian officials objected less vocally than Chinese officials to ROK-U.S. military exercises and other South Korean-American defense cooperation, except in the case of their long-standing concern about U.S. missile defense projects in Asia. In their joint peace plan for the Korean Peninsula, however, Moscow and Beijing have called for a freeze on major ROK-U.S. military drills in return for a suspension of DPRK missile and nuclear tests.[12] (For reasons unrelated to this appeal, North Korea and the United States adopted this dual-freeze path in 2018.)

Russian and Chinese policy makers have employed similar strategies and tactics to achieve their overlapping goals pertaining to the Korean Peninsula. Following particularly egregious DPRK acts, they have employed sharp rhetoric against Pyongyang and have accepted modest international sanctions in order to avert more severe ones, keep the UNSC as the centerpiece of the global response to the Korean crisis, and preclude a U.S.-led coalition that could exclude Russia and China. In place of denunciations, sanctions, and military measures, Moscow and Beijing have generally been trying to induce North Korea to change its behavior voluntarily, through international assistance and security assurances, in an effort to create a climate that facilitates evolutionary, but limited, internal and external reforms and gradual improvements in the DPRK's external behavior. Similar to their position regarding Iran, Russian and Chinese policy makers argue that an incentive-based strategy and renewed multilateral talks offer the optimal means for persuading Pyongyang to denuclearize. Moscow and Beijing together focus on achieving a gradual resolution of the Korean crisis through "step-by-step" negotiations and mutual concessions in pursuit of long-term progress. In recent years, they have jointly backed a three-phased peace process that incorporated cessation of military activities, initiation of bilateral summits, and resumption of multilateral talks. Although they primarily engage in parallel bilateral diplomacy with Pyongyang, as well as regular deputy ministerial level meetings on Korean issues, they do occasionally meet in a trilateral format with a DPRK representative. For example, in October 2018, Russian deputy foreign minister Igor Morgulov, PRC vice foreign minister Kong Xuanyou, and DPRK vice foreign minister Choe Son Hui met together in Moscow.

In the UNSC, the Russians and the Chinese delegations have employed their veto power to block proposed resolutions that would impose severe sanctions on the DPRK or authorize the use of force against the regime. For example, both Russian and Chinese diplomats blocked U.S. efforts in the UNSC in 2018 to impose an embargo on DPRK imports of refined oil products.[13] In 2021, Moscow and Beijing blocked Western efforts in the UNSC to censure the North's missile tests.[14] They have also proposed in recent years to relax UN sanctions on North Korea, citing several reasons to justify their position:

> First, it is aimed to strengthen the trajectory of a political settlement to the Korean Peninsula issue and create an enabling atmosphere to facilitate the early start of dialogue. Second, given that the DPRK has taken multiple denuclearization measures in recent years, its legitimate and reasonable concerns deserve attention and response. Third, the negative impact of international sanctions and COVID-19 on the DPRK's economy and people's livelihood is a cause for concern, so the Security Council should facilitate external support and assistance to the country. Fourth, the Security Council should activate provisions on modifying sanctions in DPRK-related resolutions at an appropriate point to make adjustments to some sanctions concerning

the economy and livelihood, which is in line with the spirit of the resolutions. Fifth, to improve inter-Korean relations and promote reconciliation and cooperation is the overriding trend, which the international community and relevant parties should all support by creating necessary conditions.[15]

In essence, Moscow and Beijing want to reward North Korea for simply eschewing bad behavior like nuclear and missile testing rather than for pursuing good behavior, such as ending its nuclear program.

Furthermore, Russian leaders desire that their Chinese counterparts perceive Moscow as a reliable partner in regional security issues such as that involving North Korea. Joint Sino-Russian statements concerning Korean affairs also help Moscow maintain a high-profile role in the Koreas. Additionally, their senior diplomats engage in regular consultations on Northeast Asian security questions. Moscow and Beijing regularly ask to restart the Six-Party Talks or pursue some other multinational negotiating format. Though this format has been in disuse during the past decade, the framework does guarantee Russia and China (along with both Koreas, Japan, and the United States) seats at the table on discussions concerning North Korea's nuclear program. Though favoring an eventual multilateral peace framework, Russia and China have encouraged direct DPRK-U.S. and intra-Korean discussions as a precursor to a broader dialogue. Moreover, in order to enhance their leverage as well as their defenses, Russia and China have strengthened their military power and engaged in joint exercises near North Korea. These preparations could facilitate their ability to render military and technical support to Pyongyang in possible Korean War scenarios.

Atypically, Beijing has employed more coercive measures toward the Koreas than Moscow has ever utilized. When tensions were high with the current North Korean leadership, Beijing curtailed bilateral economic trade and other exchanges as a form of pressure. Toward South Korea, PRC officials have engaged in harsh criticism of ROK leadership, disseminated threatening media commentary, and implemented strong economic measures, including trade and tourism boycotts, to discourage Seoul from deploying U.S. missile defenses on its territory. Though Russian officials have been willing to criticize the policies of both Koreas, they have limited their intimidating measures against either. One reason for this difference may be that Beijing has more economic tools than Moscow for applying pressure in the case of North Korea. This amplifies Beijing's leverage both with Pyongyang and with other governments that strive to induce the PRC to pressure North Korea. In contrast, Russian-DPRK commercial ties remain minimal despite Moscow's efforts to build a better economic partnership. As a consequence, Russia's primary tools of influence in Asia consist of diplomatic remonstrations, threats of military action, and weapons and energy sales. Whereas China sought to prevent South Korea's deployment of THAAD by leveraging Seoul's economic relations with Beijing, the Russian government has had to resort to threatening vague military retaliation for the ROK-U.S. deployment decision. Even so, Russian and Chinese economic considerations regarding the DPRK are generally harmonious. Russian entrepreneurs and policy makers have visions of developing north-south trans-Korean connectors, such as an energy pipeline and rail links, to integrate Russia more deeply into the prosperous Indo-Pacific region and to resurrect the Russian Far East from its economic lethargy. Although the actualization of Russia's vision of a trans-Korean energy pipeline would slightly weaken China's economic dominance in North Korea, the PRC recognizes that a better integrated North Korean economy would bring benefits to China too. Discussions about trilateral economic transportation and other economic projects on the Peninsula have also occurred, though actual progress on the ground has proved elusive due to unresolved Korean security issues.

Another potential emerging difference between Moscow and Beijing is their partial divergence relating to nuclear weapons proliferation. Though the Russian government formally opposes the acquisition of nuclear weapons by additional countries, some Russian strategists maintain that limited regional nuclear proliferation in Northeast Asia could benefit Russia. They reason that, if South Koreans and Japanese sought nuclear weapons, these countries would both alienate the United States and better balance China's rising power. Furthermore, though Moscow no longer has a bilateral security treaty with Pyongyang, the PRC and North Korea have allowed the Sino-DPRK Treaty of Friendship, Cooperation and Mutual Assistance, initially signed in 1961, to renew automatically in 1981, 2001, and, most recently, in 2021. The treaty's mutual defense clause gives Beijing flexibility to claim legal justification to engage in military activities on the Korean Peninsula.[16] In practice, though, the People's Liberation Army (PLA) would probably consider intervening on Pyongyang's behalf only if the United States and South Korea attacked the DPRK first. If North Korea initiated a conflict, China would not necessarily render military assistance to the North, as it did in 1950.

In addition to Sino-Russian differences in influence and capabilities regarding the Koreas, Russian leaders at times have seemed more open than their Chinese counterparts to future Korean reunification if it would advance Moscow's long-term economic and security interests. For example, some Russians might welcome a reunified Korea that could more effectively balance Chinese influence in northeast Asia and be more independent from the United States. President Putin said in a Korean Broadcasting System interview in late 2013, "We definitely support the aspiration of Koreans for national unification because it would advance regional security and prosperity . . . [but] it should be exclusively peaceful and take into account the interests of the North, as well as of the South."[17] However, the erosion of Russian-U.S. relations in recent years has aligned Russian policy regarding the Koreas closer to that of China. Russians have become more reticent to risk ROK-led Korean unification that could permit U.S. forces to deploy on the entire Korean Peninsula.

IMPLICATIONS AND RECOMMENDATIONS

U.S. cooperation with Russia and China regarding North Korea has therefore waxed and waned over the years. During the Cold War, Moscow and Beijing aligned with Pyongyang against the United States and the ROK. A few years ago, there was a more harmonious trilateral alignment against North Korean assertiveness. Russia and China joined the United States in pressing Pyongyang to suspend its nuclear and long-range missile tests. In recent years, however, Moscow and Beijing have decreased their support for U.S. coercive policies toward the DPRK. North Korea's value to Russia and China has grown due to Moscow's and Beijing's deteriorating relations with the United States. Not only does the DPRK serve as a buffer separating Russian and Chinese territory from the U.S. forces in South Korea but the tensions between Washington and Pyongyang also distract the Pentagon from concentrating against Russia and China. The DPRK-U.S. differences also generate leverage for Moscow and Beijing with Washington on Korean issues.

Moscow and Beijing presently diverge from Washington in their assessment of the severity of the DPRK threat and the tactics they favor to address it. Russia and China typically have been less willing to accept the risks of regime change in Pyongyang and therefore resist imposing severe sanctions against North Korea. They believe that pushing too hard for concessions could reduce their ability to shape DPRK behavior without realizing concrete results. Conversely, they favor rewarding Pyongyang in advance of any positive steps simply to create a more favorable environment for DPRK moderation. The United States has rejected this approach and instead called on Russia and especially China to apply greater pressure on the DPRK to make more progress on denuclearization. In November 2021, Pentagon spokesperson John Kirby said that China has important levels of influence in Pyongyang, including a lengthy border and "significant economic influence," and needed "to put some bite" into their enforcement of UN sanctions. According to Kirby, "They haven't used the influence they have to try to steer Pyongyang to a better, more sustainable path" toward "denuclearization of the peninsula, which one has to assume is also in China's interest as well."[18] The differences between Russia, China, and the United States have been evident in recent UNSC deliberations. In 2021, the U.S. delegation opposed a draft resolution Russia and China submitted to the UNSC in 2021 that would have removed some sanctions on North Korea. In 2022, Moscow and Beijing blocked a U.S.-sponsored draft to levy new UN sanctions on the DPRK for its escalating missile testing.

Furthermore, the United States is significantly more open to Korean reunification than Beijing or even Moscow. If a single Korean state reemerged, Washington would try to retain a greater U.S. military presence in the reunified Korea than either Russia or China would want. Though a new DPRK regime would be welcomed in the United States as a means of solving the North Korean security and human rights problems, many in Russia and China would see such a scenario as more dangerous than a nuclear-armed DPRK. They both anticipate that state failure in North Korea could generate a regional economic crisis, large refugee flows, and military conflict on their doorstep as DPRK warlords and foreign troops battle for control of Korean territory. They also fear Washington's potential geopolitical gains from a powerful reunified Korean ally.

Given these views, Russia and China have objected whenever the United States and its allies have imposed sanctions on North Korea without UNSC's approval. Russian and Chinese officials maintain that the overzealous use of sanctions could provoke unpredictable and destructive outbursts by Pyongyang. They call on Washington to demonstrate greater negotiating flexibility and tend to favor dialogue with North Korea without major preconditions. At the same time, Moscow and Beijing both call on the international community to provide North Korea with international assistance and security assurances to promote a fertile environment for DPRK internal reforms and improved international behavior. They argue that dialogues and negotiations leading to the denuclearization of the Peninsula would best advance regional peace and stability. Unsurprisingly, many proposals in that vein would also yield important strategic benefits for Moscow and Beijing, such as a suspension of large ROK-U.S. military drills and the removal of U.S. missile defenses from South Korean territory. However, Russia and China do accept some multilateral sanctions as a way to censure DPRK actions that they oppose and to generate leverage to induce North Korean concessions. Such sanctions are also accepted to avert tougher U.S. measures, including U.S. national sanctions or military measures. Nevertheless, in the past, the Russian and Chinese governments have not fully applied the sanctions they have formally adopted. Numerous media reports relate that Russian and Chinese entities are inadequately applying the sanctions, suggesting either weak national enforcement or deliberate circumvention.[19]

The Trump administration pursued a wide range of policies to restructure DPRK-U.S. ties, ranging from military threats to intensified sanctions and unprecedented leadership diplomacy. The first year of the administration, 2017, saw the risks of war rise higher than at any time in decades. The administration's policies further presumed that, given the right combination of incentives and disincentives, Russia and China would apply greater economic and diplomatic leverage over Pyongyang to force the DPRK to end its missile and nuclear programs. Besides pressing Moscow and Beijing to apply stronger economic sanctions against the DPRK, including limiting trade and investment on a wide range of items, the Trump administration made greater use of U.S. national sanctions as well as extraterritorial sanctions on Russian and Chinese entities that violate these unilateral measures. The Trump administration renounced the "strategic patience" policy of the Obama administration of waiting for verifiable changes in DPRK policies after its initial policy review concluded that the approach possessed unacceptable risks. Instead, the Trump administration eventually pursued a "grand bargain" approach in which the DPRK would end its nuclear and ballistic missile programs in return for the other parties providing substantial economic assistance, diplomatic initiatives, and security assurances to North Korea. The most unprecedented feature of Trump's policy toward North Korea was his willingness to break decades of taboo against having a U.S. president meet with a DPRK leader in the absence of a denuclearization agreement and engage in personal diplomacy with Kim Jong-un without elaborate preconditions. The administration's diplomacy strategy initially focused on reassuring South Korea and Japan while concurrently inducing Russia and especially China to increase pressure on Pyongyang to end its nuclear and missile tests. These efforts in 2018 led to the first meeting between a U.S. president and a DPRK chairman and to other direct engagements between senior North Korean and U.S. diplomats. The Singapore summit in June of that year produced a joint statement that repeated the language of earlier commitments to improve relations and denuclearize the Peninsula, though the document lacked a sequence of concrete verifiable steps toward this objective or a timeline for compliance. The most tangible effect of the Singapore Summit was the suspension of major ROK-U.S. military exercises and a continuation of the freeze on DPRK nuclear detonations. Additional presidential meetings occurred in Hanoi on February 28, 2019, and at the truce village of Panmunjom in the Korean Demilitarized Zone on June 30, 2019. Like Singapore, these were high-profile meetings that focused attention on the issue but failed to resolve fundamental differences over sequencing regarding sanctions relief and disarmament. Washington and Pyongyang diverged over the definition of denuclearization and how to synchronize steps toward achieving denuclearization, creating a new bilateral relationship, and establishing a peace regime. The Trump administration insisted on up-front DPRK concessions that would achieve irreversible progress on complete nuclear disarmament, with comprehensive and intrusive international inspections of DPRK nuclear assets. In contrast, the North demanded near-term sanctions relief and depicted denuclearization as a result, rather than the cause, of improved relations between Washington and Pyongyang. By 2019, things had regressed to deadlock, stalemate, and mutual patience.

The Biden administration's DPRK policy review, while reaffirming opposition to North Korea's nuclear and missile programs, adopted a "calibrated, practical approach" rather than pursuing Obama's strategic patience approach or Trump's quest for grand bargains.[20] Administration officials have offered to talk with DPRK representatives without preconditions. U.S. officials have also continued dialogue with Russia, China, South Korea, and other interested governments on the DPRK question. Still, the Biden administration has kept the sanctions adopted by the Obama and Trump administrations despite Russian and Chinese pressure to relax them. Thus far, the North Korean government, while eschewing testing of long-range missiles or nuclear weapons, has continued to test shorter-range missiles and refused to engage in direct dialogue with the United States. Despite their different tactics, the Obama, Trump, and Biden administrations have all insisted on DPRK denuclearization because a nuclear-armed DPRK would threaten U.S. allies, destabilize the region, undermine the international treaties, and encourage other states, including U.S. allies as well as adversaries, to seek weapons of mass destruction (WMD).

To be effective, sanctions on North Korea require Moscow's and Beijing's strong support. Yet, Russia's and China's willingness to implement and execute sanctions is suspect because they fear the consequences of regime collapse more than the prospect of a nuclear-armed North Korea, and they do not want to restrict their economic activities in the North. Through poor enforcement and liberal humanitarian exemptions, Russian and Chinese officials have not fully applied the sanctions that their governments formally supported.[21] Moscow and Beijing might demand restrictions on U.S. military activities in Asia or other conditions in exchange for more comprehensively pressuring the DPRK. U.S. diplomacy needs to persuade Russian and Chinese leaders that they no longer need the DPRK as a strategic buffer against the United States and that they would achieve greater net strategic and economic gains with a unified Korean state under Seoul's democratic and benign leadership than with the current dangerously unstable division of the Peninsula. Washington should also insist that Japan and South Korea are fully consulted regarding the Korean peace process. Inadequate consideration of Tokyo's and Seoul's security concerns, above all regarding medium-range missiles, could strengthen the arguments of those in both countries who favor acquiring their own nuclear weapons. U.S. officials must also strive to remain as supportive as possible of Seoul's approach to building a peace regime on the Peninsula while discouraging excessive exuberance in the Blue House. In the diplomatic realm, U.S. leaders need to raise the DPRK issue repeatedly with their Russian and Chinese counterparts to elevate the matter's priority in their decision making. Washington must insist that cooperation concerning North Korea, especially its nuclear weapons program, is critical for U.S. relations with Russia and China.

2
Chapter

Japan

Japanese foreign policy is invariably embedded in the Russia-China-U.S. triangle. Tokyo seeks a peace treaty with Russia and return of Japanese islands seized by Moscow but without jeopardizing critical U.S. defense guarantees). Japan's leaders and public alike have expressed alarm at China's growing foreign-policy assertiveness. Sino-Japanese animosity primarily originates in historical tensions and a territorial dispute over some islands situated between the two countries (known as the Diaoyu Islands in Chinese and the Senkaku Islands in Japanese). Chinese ties with North Korea and Japan's alliance with the United States also divide the two states. The Obama administration initially accepted Japanese efforts to strengthen ties with Russia but became unenthusiastic about their engagement after Moscow seized Crimea from Ukraine. The Trump administration was initially more tolerant about Tokyo's Russian outreach, but the Russian government relied on an unproductive coercive approach, demanding that Japan weaken its defense ties with the United States in exchange for improved relations with Moscow. Following the February 2022 Russian attack on Ukraine, Japan suspended these unproductive talks with Russia and fully supported international sanctions against Moscow. Japanese leaders have been strengthening their national defense efforts and security ties with the United States due to fears that Beijing might follow Moscow's example and try to seize Taiwan by force.

RUSSIAN GOALS AND POLICIES

The Russian-Japanese sovereignty dispute over four islands north of Japan, which the Japanese term their Northern Territories and the Russians call the Southern Kurils, presents a major impediment to improved relations. The

1875 Treaty of St. Petersburg ceded all the Kuril Islands to Japan and assigned the Sakhalin Island to Russia. At the end of World War II, the Soviet government abruptly abrogated the Japan-Soviet Neutrality Pact. The Red Army then rapidly occupied the entire Kuril Island chain in the final days of the war even after the Japanese government had agreed to surrender—including the four islands (Kunashir, known in Japanese as Kunashiri; Iturup [Etorofu]; Shikotan; and Habomai) never historically considered Russian territory near the Japanese island of Hokkaido. Subsequently, the Soviet authorities expelled most of the original inhabitants from the islands and settled Soviet citizens in their place. Though the Joint Declaration between Japan and the Soviet Union of 1956 ended the state of war between the two countries and restored commercial and diplomatic ties between them, the unresolved sovereignty dispute has prevented their signing a formal peace treaty, leaving the Russia-Japan dispute as the only legally unsettled conflict from World War II.[1] The Japanese public has substantial sympathy for these individuals, who have been displaced from their ancestral homes, making any Tokyo government averse to accepting a compromise that would renounce Japan's formal sovereignty over any of the islands. Whenever prominent Japanese have endorsed potential compromises, they have experienced sharp criticism at home. Russian and Japanese historians can cite competing evidence to support their legal claims. The Russian government justifies its possession of the islands by citing several World War II agreements. The Japanese government's position is that, while Tokyo did cede control of the Sakhalin and Kuril Islands to the USSR under the 1951 San Francisco Peace Treaty, which the Soviet government never signed, the treaty's provisions did not apply to the four islands of the Northern Territories because Tokyo has never recognized them as part of the Kuril chain. However, historical or legal reasoning is largely irrelevant since the question has become entangled in competing national interests, opposing economic and military interests, national prestige, and diverging national opinion. Japanese officials have demonstrated flexibility concerning how and when Moscow could return the islands to Tokyo's control and pledged to respect the rights of Russian citizens on the islands. Yet, as a reflection of Japanese public opinion, the government officials have always insisted that Moscow acknowledge Tokyo's sovereignty over all of them. Polls show widespread Russian public opposition to making further territorial concessions.[2] President Putin flatly remarked in 2016 that "[w]e do not trade territories."[3] Soviet propaganda glorified the islands' seizure as symbolic of Moscow's proud victory in the great war of liberation against fascism in the 1940s. Russians still favorably recall how the occupation resulted from the successful Soviet military campaign at the end of World War II, which marked Moscow's recovery in Asia from its disastrous defeat in its 1904–1905 war with Japan. Russian politicians regularly burnish their nationalist credentials by stressing their opposition to returning any island. Accordingly, Russians are equally adamant that Japan recognize Russian sovereignty over the islands as a prerequisite for negotiations, offering Tokyo merely administrative rights over the disputed territory rather than sovereignty. Further, economic considerations discourage Moscow from accepting a loss of the islands, which are surrounded by rich fishing grounds, possible offshore oil and gas reserves, and other valuable natural resources.[4] Additionally, the Russian government has invested millions of dollars to develop the islands' civilian infrastructure as well as to construct military facilities there. The islands' strategic value for Russian naval operations and Japan's homeland defense (the closest point lies 15 kilometers away from Japan's northern island of Hokkaido) presents another obstacle to a territorial settlement. A Japanese-U.S. military presence on the islands, such as the deployment of antiship or antiair missiles or ballistic missile defense (BMD) systems, could threaten Russia's Pacific Fleet, especially the nuclear missile–launching submarines conducting patrols in the Sea of Okhotsk.[5] Russian negotiators want assurances that Tokyo would not permit U.S. military deployments, though the islands fall under the Japanese-U.S. mutual defense treaty. Since any compromise settlement would engender sharp criticism from nationalist politicians, Russian and Japanese leaders typically have found it easier to stand firm on principle regardless of their opportunity costs—notably, the postponement of a formal peace treaty and thwarted commercial deals. Various proposals to divide control of the islands or establish a creative shared sovereignty arrangement have never gained decisive support in both governments simultaneously. Both sides have plausibly believed that time was on their side and that they could firmly hold to their positions and wait for the other to blink first.

When Abe Shinzo became prime minister again in December 2012, he deliberately aimed to expand economic ties with Russia to establish a more benign tone for Russo-Japanese relations and induce Moscow into making territorial concessions to Japan that would lead to an eventual peace treaty. Abe's desire to improve ties with Russia was understandable. Japan has troubled relations with China and both Koreas. Having confrontations with all four neighbors simultaneously constrains Tokyo's leverage and diplomatic opportunities in Asia. Moscow's hope was that Abe would finally lead a strong Japanese government capable of making substantial concessions on their territorial dispute. For the first time in decades, Russia and Japan both had strong leaders with solid nationalist credentials who could have negotiated a territorial compromise and then sell it domestically. Before Abe, Tokyo had a series of weak leaders who lacked the political support to negotiate a compromise deal with Russia and then secure its domestic approval in the Diet and among the Japanese public. Abe had the nationalist credentials and domestic political strength to sell at home the kind of compromise settlement that Moscow has repeatedly offered—that Japan and Russia each agree to accept control over

fewer than all four islands in return for a peace treaty, stronger economic relations, enhanced diplomatic ties, and liberal visiting rights to all the islands.[6]

Furthermore, both countries could benefit from improved ties. The Japanese seek expanded access to Russia's abundant natural resources, especially
its oil and natural gas. Having greater access to Russian hydrocarbons would
reduce Japan's dependence on tanker transits through the South China Sea,
where Beijing's assertive sovereignty claims potentially put this shipping at
risk and help compensate for setbacks in Japan's nuclear energy development
owing to the 2011 Fukushima nuclear plant disaster. For Moscow, Japan can
serve the roles of investor, balancer, and gateway. Russians would like to secure
more Japanese investment, high technology, and access to Japanese consumer
markets to modernize their industries and to develop the Russian Far East.
Russians also hope that Japan can serve as a gateway to help them access other
East Asian markets and thereby add substance to Moscow's weakening pivot to
the Pacific and Asia. Russia and Japan could both benefit from Japanese investment and access to Russia's considerable hydrocarbon deposits in the Arctic
as well as the Northern Sea Route, consisting of direct maritime shipping
lanes Moscow is developing through the Arctic Ocean between Europe and
Asia. The two countries are complementary economic partners, but levels of
Russian-Japanese commerce have remained relatively modest. Only a small
share of Japanese exports and investment flows to Russia, while Japanese
investment in Russia remains low compared with its levels in other countries.[7]

The pace of Japanese-Russian diplomacy accelerated after Abe returned
as prime minister; Abe and Putin frequently met at bilateral and multilateral
events. However, Moscow and Tokyo have never reached a comprehensive
bilateral settlement on the islands or a peace agreement. In April 2013, Abe
became the first Japanese prime minister to conduct an official state visit to
Russia since Junichiro Koizumi's trip a decade earlier. In a joint statement,
he and Putin instructed their foreign ministries to accelerate their search for
"mutually acceptable options" for settling their territorial dispute and signing a peace accord. In November 2013, Russia and Japan held their first "2 + 2"
joint meeting of foreign and defense ministers. On February 6, 2014, Abe was
one of the few Western leaders to attend the Opening Ceremony of the Sochi
Olympics, boycotted by many Western leaders due to the Russian government's
newly adopted antigay legislation and other objectionable domestic policies.
Japan also avoided confronting Russia in Syria.[8] Though Japan did yield to
U.S. pressure to impose sanctions on Russia over Ukraine, Abe strived to keep
them modest, almost symbolic, to balance an affirmation of Western solidarity while maintaining dialogue with Moscow. Russian officials questioned the
autonomy of Japanese foreign policy, but bilateral talks continued. In December 2016, Putin made his first state visit to Japan since 2005, but the trip yielded
no major improvement in relations. Tokyo tried both economic pressure and
inducements, to no avail. Japanese attempts to restrict investment, technology

transfer, and other economic relations with Russia in order to pressure Moscow to make concessions on the island dispute failed. Conversely, the Japanese government decision in the mid-2010s to expand Russian-Japanese economic projects also proved insufficient to mollify Moscow's hardline stance on territorial concessions. The growth in Russian-Japanese trade and investment during the 2010s reduced the opportunity costs for Russia from not negotiating a territorial settlement. Moscow had less incentive to compromise since bilateral economic ties were developing despite the sovereignty dispute and lack of a formal peace treaty. Indeed, Russian leaders threatened that, should Japan fail to meet Russian economic needs, Russia would turn to other Asian partners.[9] Meanwhile, the military units in the Russian Far East have engaged in larger and more frequent exercises, deployed additional military capabilities, and conducted more air patrols near Japan, sometimes in joint strategic aviation patrols with China. Under Prime Minister Kishida Fumio, the Japanese government adopted a strong stance against the Russian attack on Ukraine that began in February 2022. Japan joined other members of the Group of Seven (G-7) industrial states in imposing severe sanctions on Russia, even at the cost of suspending the peace and sovereignty talks with Moscow.

CHINESE GOALS AND POLICIES

Japan's relationship with China, burdened by history and intermittent geopolitical disputes, is complex, made even more so by the meteoric rise of the People's Republic of China (PRC) in recent years. The two countries have a troubled shared history of geopolitical competition and national confrontation. During Japan's invasion of mainland China from 1931 to 1945, Japanese soldiers committed many atrocities; controversies also arise when Japanese officials visit the Yasukuni Shrine, a memorial dedicated to the memory of Japan's fallen war soldiers, and in the context of Japan's portrayal of World War II in its history textbooks, which the Chinese see as negating Japanese apologies for past actions by showing insincerity. PRC officials exploit Japan's wartime aggression to inflame anti-Japanese sentiment in other countries, especially the Koreas. Conversely, the Abe government pointed to China's growing strength and assertiveness to campaign for the repeal of Article 9 of Japan's pacificist constitution, which prohibits some military activities, in order to increase defense spending and enhance Japan's contribution to collective self-defense in partnership with the United States. Japan's security concerns include the PRC's expanding and opaque defense budget as well as Beijing's territorial claims. Many Japanese believe that the PRC is trying to control the Western Pacific, while Chinese analysts complain about Japan's growing military capabilities, expanding security role in the Indo-Pacific region, efforts to revise the pacifist clauses in the Japanese constitution, growing security cooperation with the United States, and Japan's military and industrial potential, including the country's latent nuclear weapons capacity.[10] Coinciding with Japan's decades of economic stagnation, China has enjoyed rapid industrial growth and has surpassed Japan as the world's second-largest economy. It is true that Sino-Japanese economic connections have become much more extensive than those between Japan and Russia. The PRC is a major destination for Japanese direct investment and exports, while Japan imports an enormous volume of Chinese goods. During the 1990s, Japanese aid, investment, and technology transfer helped drive Chinese growth. Yet, the two countries compete for energy imports, and their businesses compete for markets now that Chinese companies have equaled the sophistication of Western corporations. Tokyo has been especially wary of Beijing's Belt and Road Initiative (BRI) and other Chinese efforts to bind countries to the PRC economy, as they represent a direct challenge to Japan's program to build economic ties with these countries through its "Free and Open Indo-Pacific Strategy."[11] Furthermore, Beijing's militarization of the South China Sea poses a direct threat to Japanese economic and energy security since more than half of Japan's oil and gas imports pass through that body of water.[12]

The greatest source of current Sino-Japanese tensions is the East China Sea, centered on an island chain that the Japanese, who administer them, call the Senkaku Islands and the Chinese, who claim them as well, name the Diaoyu Islands. The islands are situated amid rich energy reserves and fishing grounds that fall within both countries' overlapping 200-nautical-mile exclusive economic zones (EEZ).[13] In 2005, anti-Japanese protests in China escalated from a boycott of Japanese goods into mass demonstrations against Japan. In 2014, the United States accepted the Japanese assertion that the islands fall under the U.S.-Japan Security Treaty, meaning the United States would assist Japan to defend them from external attack. In December 2018, PRC sent a research expedition to Okinotori Island, which Tokyo claims as its southernmost territory. The Chinese navy and air force now routinely patrol in the East China Sea region and denounce similar activity conducted by the United States as a "provocative" threat to China's "rights and interests."[14] The bilateral negotiations that began in 2004 to resolve their conflicting sovereignty and territorial claims over the East China Sea have neither ended the dispute nor established an agreed mechanism for joint exploitation of the energy reserves, which lie within the two countries' overlapping maritime economic zones. After Russia attacked Ukraine in February 2022, Japanese anxieties that China would also employ force to seize disputed territories increased still further.

RUSSIAN-CHINESE INTERACTIONS

Though Russia, China, and Japan all support the denuclearization of the Korean Peninsula, Moscow and Beijing have criticized Tokyo for conditioning any nuclear settlement on resolution of the Democratic People's Republic of Korea's (DPRK) past abductions of Japanese citizens. During his September 2002 summit with then Japanese prime minister Junichiro Koizumi, Kim Jong-il admitted that Pyongyang had kidnapped more than a dozen Japanese nationals between 1977 and 1983 to serve as language instructors for DPRK intelligence agents. The acknowledgment backfired after an outraged Japanese government and public opinion demanded more information about the issue than the secretive DPRK leadership proved willing to provide. Many Japanese remain unconvinced that most of the abductees died in North Korea, while DPRK representatives have continued to demand compensation for Japan's colonial occupation and removal of Tokyo's sanctions on DPRK commercial activities.

Russia and China have remained detached from each other's territorial disputes, including the Diaoyu/Senkaku Islands, the South China Sea, and the Kurils. Neither Moscow nor Beijing has a strong interest in seeing either side resolve their respective disagreements with Japan and has therefore not made any notable effort toward that end. A Russian-Japanese reconciliation would diversify Moscow's portfolio of partnerships to reduce dependence on China. Japanese leaders have made clear that they sought closer ties with Moscow to pull Russia away from China and allow Tokyo to better balance against Beijing.[15] Some Russians may have aimed to use better ties with Tokyo to gain leverage with China. Still, the continuation of both disputes gives each party more leverage over Tokyo since Japanese officials, and their U.S. allies, cannot concentrate their response on the other and concurrently worry about driving Russia and China closer to each other. Russia indirectly aides China's aspirations regarding the Diaoyu/Senkaku Islands by selling its advanced weapons technologies, though this is not a primary purpose of these sales. This practice makes their partnership less brittle, but the flexibility does limit the depth of their collaboration on some issues. They have essentially decided to agree to disagree, though some recent developments suggest that they may coordinate their policies more extensively toward Japan. In June 2016, Russian and Chinese naval vessels both sailed into contested East China Sea waters. Starting in 2019, the Russian and Chinese air forces have conducted joint aviation patrols over waters claimed by Japan and South Korea. Russia's aggressive independent air patrols against Japan aim to punish Tokyo for joining other Western countries in imposing sanctions on Russia over Ukraine, provide Russia with information about Japanese defense capabilities as well as the U.S. forces based on Japan, and pressure Tokyo to make concessions on their territorial dispute. But they may also aim to curry favor in China at Japan's expense by distracting Tokyo from concentrating its military resources against Beijing—or they may intend to send a subtle warning to China about contesting Moscow's hold over the Russian Far East.

Yet, some differences exist between Russia and China regarding Japan. Moscow finds the status quo acceptable since Russia possesses the disputed islands of the Southern Kurils, whereas Beijing's outlook is fundamentally revisionist, aiming to take control of islands currently administered by Tokyo. In this regard, Japan stands as a revisionist actor toward Russia, wanting to recover its Northern Territories, but as a status quo state regarding China, seeking to ward off Beijing's claims to the East China Sea. Russian officials have been less concerned than their Chinese colleagues about Abe's military reform program. Whereas Chinese media and officials issued warnings pertaining to renewed Japanese militarism and wars of aggression, the Russian Foreign Ministry said that Moscow did "not want to reach hasty conclusions" concerning the issue and wanted to see its practical effects on Japanese defense policy.[16] The militaries of Russia and China conduct frequent incursions against Japan for different reasons. While Russia attempts to monitor and harass the U.S. military forces based in Japan, Beijing aims to press its territorial claims through displays of its growing power projection capabilities. Whereas Russia's military assertiveness represents a return to Cold War norms, China's growing military power and presence is a new and more disturbing development for the Japanese. Additionally, concerns about the PRC partly shape Moscow's policies toward Japan. One reason Russian and Japanese officials wanted to strengthen bilateral ties was to expand their diplomatic options and gain leverage with third parties, such as China and the Koreas.[17] Tokyo would like to decrease Russian dependence on the PRC as well as Russian military assistance to the People's Liberation Army (PLA) since these Russian arms transfers are bolstering the PLA's ability to project power against Japan and its allies.[18] A Russian-Japanese reconciliation could have induced Beijing to moderate its policies toward Japan. From the converse perspective, Russian officials strived to weaken Japanese-U.S. defense ties and hoped that Tokyo might help ease Western sanctions by acting as a bridge between Moscow and other Western governments.[19] Although not publicly stressed, Russians likely desired to attract more Japan investment to reduce their dependence on China's economy and develop the Russian Far East. That region's lagging economic development and population outflows present Moscow with a long-term challenge given its proximity to the PRC, with its large population and booming economy. Bringing more Japanese investment to eastern Russia would simultaneously help promote the region's development and avert the Russian Far East falling under Beijing's de facto control. Before one of his trips to Japan, Putin observed, "A considerable part of Russia's territory is located in Asia but we are aware—and so is Japan—that the population density is very low there but the resources are enormous . . . the same time we would like to hope that our relations would be gradually diversified, primarily, as I have said, in the sphere of high technologies."[20] Despite falling behind China in terms of size of aggregate gross domestic product (GDP), Japan still has enormous economic potential, including advanced technology that could help Russia raise the lagging socio-economic conditions in the Russian Far East. Yet, neither Moscow nor Tokyo has realized this goal. In recent years, Russia's ties with China have strengthened, while Japan has moved closer in the military domain to the United States in response to China's growing regional assertiveness. In 2014, Russia's aggression against Ukraine led the United States to press a reluctant Tokyo to impose economic and diplomatic sanctions on Russia related to Moscow's annexation of the Crimea.[21] The Russian government termed Tokyo's imposition of sanctions "unfriendly and short-sighted" since Japan was allegedly sacrificing its own interests to please Washington.[22] In 2022, the Japanese government took the lead in organizing Asian opposition to Moscow's attack on Ukraine, partly due to anxieties that China would follow Russia's example and try to resolve Beijing's territorial disputes in Asia with force.

IMPLICATIONS AND RECOMMENDATIONS

U.S. strategists consider Japan the anchor of U.S. strategy in the Indo-Pacific region because of its strategic location, vast economic influence, sophisticated self-defense capabilities, and willingness to host the largest U.S. military presence (more than 50,000 troops) in the region. The two countries have frequently restructured the guidelines of the alliance in accordance with global, regional, bilateral, and unilateral requirements. The United States benefits tremendously from its military bases in Japan, enhancing its power projection and rapid response capabilities in the Pacific. Japan's defense budget has been increasing, as has the capability of the country's air, sea, and ground forces to operate with the U.S. military. Despite doubts over U.S. extended security guarantees, and Japan's possession of the technological capabilities to develop nuclear weapons, mainstream Japanese and U.S. policy makers maintain the country's tradition of nuclear abstention. The alliance between the United States and Japan faces difficulties, but these two countries share common values and security challenges, including proliferation of weapons of mass destruction, terrorism, and threats from North Korea, Russia, and China. The United States offers critical support to Tokyo in the face of these threats. Although the United States has excluded the Northern Territories from the 1960 Japan-U.S. security treaty since they are not administered by Japan (and occupied by foreign troops), Washington has affirmed that the Diaoyu/Senkaku Islands are protected under Article 5 of the mutual U.S.-Japan security treaty.[23] The United States deploys thousands of troops in Japan and engages in large exercises not only in Japanese territory but also in adjacent maritime zones and air space.

The Japanese armed forces have enhanced their capacities to repel and reverse any Chinese military seizure of contested islands. But the Chinese, like the Russians, employ nonmilitary hybrid tactics, such as sending paramilitary forces or even unarmed people to the region. Although threatening, these kinds of activities do not constitute "an armed attack against Japan," so the previous 1997 Japan-U.S. defense cooperation guidelines do not provide definitive direction regarding how the U.S. and Japanese militaries should respond. To address what the Japanese described as these "gray area" challenges, Tokyo has been shifting to a more proactive security policy, which includes the formation of a National Security Council and the reinterpretation of Article 9 of the national constitution to allow the Japanese Self-Defense Forces to support a wider range of international missions, including collective defense in alliance with the United States. Tokyo has also relaxed its traditional arms export restrictions and now only stipulates the prohibition of selling weapons to countries that violate international treaties Japan is a party to, countries that have violated UN Security Council resolutions, and countries involved in international conflict, as determined by the Security Council. The United States should support these initiatives as well as intensify the new Japanese-U.S. focus on the potential for reinforcing Sino-Russian aggression. Since trilateral security arrangements help balance both Russia and China, the United States should actively promote ROK-Japan reconciliation.

3

Chapter

South Asia

India is an attractive partner for Russia, China, and the United States owing to its large economy, expanding military power, and quest for a larger international role. During the Cold War, Moscow was New Delhi's prime economic and security partner, but in recent years, the People's Republic of China (PRC) has become India's most significant economic associate, while the United States is becoming India's most important defense partner. For decades, Russian officials have tried to form a trilateral bloc between Moscow, Beijing, and New Delhi, but these efforts have repeatedly foundered due to persistent Sino-Indian tensions and the countries' diverging priorities. While all three governments want a multipolar order in which they exert greater influence, they differ in their preferred visions. Whereas Russian leaders want to overhaul the existing Western-dominated world order with an entirely new one, their PRC counterparts have tried to reform rather than uproot the current system. In contrast, India's new post–Cold War generation of foreign policy makers want their country to become a more significant actor within the existing international system, including by attaining permanent membership in the UN Security Council (UNSC). While trilateral cooperation among Russia, China, and India is possible, bilateral engagement has been the three countries' preferred mode of engagement. This complex web of agreements and disagreements has prevented these countries from consistently aligning against the United States. Washington has readily taken advantage of these divergences. With Russia no longer able or willing to serve its Cold War role as regional balancer against China and primary great power patron of India, New Delhi has been open to U.S. efforts to deepen military and other ties with the United States.

RUSSIAN GOALS AND POLICIES

The foreign policies of Moscow and New Delhi, like those of Moscow and Beijing, have rarely been in conflict. In 2000, Russia and India signed a strategic partnership agreement in which each pledged to develop economic, security, and other ties and to convene regular senior-level meetings. However, their earlier extensive multidimensional ties of the Cold War have since degraded into more intermittent, narrow, and shallow collaboration centered on energy, security, and diplomacy. Regarding the latter, both countries' regular attendance at major bilateral and multilateral meetings, such as at the Brazil-Russia-India-China-South Africa (BRICS) group, the Shanghai Cooperation Organization (SCO), and the UNSC, has kept Russian-Indian diplomatic ties robust. Furthermore, New Delhi has refrained from fully supporting the West's sanctions against Moscow for the Soviet military occupation of Afghanistan in the 1980s, its occupation of Georgian territory since 2008, or its annexation of Crimea in March 2014 and subsequent interference in eastern Ukraine and other countries. The two countries jointly oppose radical Islamic terrorism, political separatism, and regional instability in Eurasia.

The collapse of the Soviet Union severely reduced bilateral trade, resulting in a sharp fall in Russian purchases of Indian manufactured goods, declining Indian purchases of Russian raw materials, tightening terms for Russian financing of Indian enterprises, and the virtual disappearance of Russian direct investments in India. Russian-Indian trade has yet to recover. Russians still sell mostly weapons, nuclear reactors, and raw materials to India while importing agricultural products, textiles, packaged medicaments, and some equipment.[1] In comparison, India's commerce with other countries, especially China, has progressed at a considerably more rapid pace. In particular, Russian businesses infrequently engage with India's rapidly developing private sector, whose ties are focused on Chinese and Western firms.[2] Realization of the proposed International North-South Transport Corridor (INSTC) connecting India, Iran, Azerbaijan, and Russia, which could spur renewed Indian-Russian commerce, has been stalled.[3]

Russian-Indian energy ties remain comprehensive, embracing hydrocarbons and nuclear power, while Russian and Indian companies have invested billions of dollars in each other's oil and gas sector. Specialists have considered multiple conduits for delivering Russian oil and gas to India via pipelines, but the high costs and major geopolitical challenges of building pipelines through a war-torn Afghanistan, a sanctioned Iran, or an antagonistic Pakistan have impeded their execution so far. India suffers from a perennial energy shortage and hopes that nuclear power will provide a larger share of the country's energy requirements. Despite this expansive need, Russia is the only country to have delivered working nuclear reactors to India; other foreign companies have been wary of India's extremely demanding nuclear accident liability law, in which nuclear suppliers rather than local plant operators are held primarily accountable for nuclear accidents. Russian nuclear providers typically offer more generous terms to Indian buyers than their foreign competitors since Russian public companies enjoy extensive state financial backing. Furthermore, Russian nuclear firms pledge to transfer substantial technology to India, deliver uninterrupted uranium fuel supplies to any Russian reactors India purchases, and conduct joint research and development (R&D) on leading nuclear technologies in return for sales. However, the Indian government has recently cut its planned nuclear power plant construction, challenging Russian plans for this sector.

Russia and India maintain substantial security-related interactions despite the burgeoning Sino-Russian and Indian-U.S. military ties. Not only do Russia and India hold frequent consultations on mutual national security challenges but India has also acquired more weaponry from Russian/Soviet suppliers than from any other country. Moreover, the Russian and Indian armed forces conduct regular military exercises, including, since 2003, the "Indo-Russian Activity" (INDRA) naval maneuvers in varying locations in the Indian and Pacific Oceans. Their fleets have rehearsed maritime law enforcement, sharing intelligence, surface warfare, antiair/anti-sub defense, and countering piracy, terrorism, and narcotics trafficking.[4] The two militaries also hold less frequent joint air force drills. In 2017, Russia and India upgraded their military ties by holding exercises involving personnel from all three military branches for the first time.[5] The goal of all these exercises is to promote mutual interoperability and strengthen other defense ties. Importing weapons from Russia has been especially important to New Delhi since the Indian defense industry has lacked a strong domestic arms industry. During the Cold War, India bought almost all of its major military systems from the Soviet Union. Since 2000, the Russian-Indian Governmental Commission on Military Technical Cooperation, which involves yearly dialogue between defense ministries, has overseen bilateral military industrial collaboration, including arms sales, under 10-year framework agreements. Although Russia's share of the Indian defense market has fallen in the past decade—with Israel, European countries, and especially the United States enjoying greater defense sales—the aggregate value of Russia's defense exports to India has remained large since India has become the leading importer of foreign military technologies, of which Russia still accounts for more than half, measured by value.[6] The large number of weapons Moscow has sold to New Delhi over the years has provided Russian defense companies with many opportunities to sell spare parts, service existing systems, and upgrade some weapons. Indian military platforms consist overwhelmingly of planes, tanks, and warships of Soviet or Russian origin, so they depend heavily on Russian firms for upkeep and upgrading. Based on already planned deliveries and orders, Russia will likely sustain its dominant position as India's arms supplier for at least several more years.[7] Until recently, Russian arms suppliers had a distinct competitive advantage over Western weapons suppliers in India's market due to their lower prices and willingness to transfer more sophisticated defense technologies to India. The Indian government requires any large foreign arms transfer to come with the extensive transfer of technology, large offsets, purchases of source components and subsystems from local companies, eventual production of some imported weapons under license, and shared maintenance and repair work. To meet New Delhi's demands, Moscow has demonstrated flexibility and reconfigured the bilateral relationship from that of buyer-to-seller—through which Russia delivers "turnkey" (ready-to-use) weapons—into a partnership founded on binational research, development, and production of weapons systems for both countries' armed forces as well as for other possible buyers. Besides the convenience of continuing to employ Russian and Soviet defense technologies, some Indians may hope that continued collaboration in this area may preserve New Delhi's influence in Russia despite the growing Sino-Russian military cooperation.

Even the Russian-Indian defense relationship, however, has experienced challenges. The Indian government has always sought to diversify its foreign weapons suppliers despite the higher costs and complexity involved in maintaining a variety of platforms. As a result, the Indian military began buying large quantities of Soviet weapons in the 1960s but always complemented these purchases with European (and later Israeli) systems. India has also regularly equipped the platforms it buys from Russia (such as warplanes and warships) with non-Russian systems and components, either domestically made or purchased from other countries. Furthermore, India has long complained about quality problems with some Russian weapons, lengthy delays in acquiring them, and massive cost overruns on major contracts, such as for a former Russian aircraft carrier India added to its fleet. These problems with past Russian sales, growing competition from the United States and other suppliers, and modest improvements in India's indigenous defense industry have led New Delhi to purchase fewer Russian weapons in recent years. Moscow's developing security partnership with Pakistan, promoted by China, could also present a challenge to Russian-Indian collaboration since Moscow has begun selling weapons to Pakistan (such as four Mi-35M combat helicopters), training Pakistani officers, engaging with the Islamabad-backed Taliban, and conducting joint Russian-Pakistani military exercises.[8] Nevertheless, India will remain a leading global arms buyer for many years owing to its unmet defense needs, growing economy, and weak indigenous defense industry.

Russian-Indian ties may decline further in the future. Russia is less able to provide the kind of economic and security assistance that India needs to address its main development and security priorities. Russia's share of India's total arms imports has fallen steadily over the past decade as New Delhi has bought more Western weapons. Indians have been concerned that Moscow is moving too close to China, a relationship that Beijing might exploit to New Delhi's disadvantage, as well as Pakistan, while Russians are wary of growing Indian-U.S. security ties. Nonetheless, Russians and Indians seem comfortable with their current relationship, in which they have good bilateral ties but not an alliance or exclusive partnership. Since Russian leaders also value their strategic autonomy, they understand Indians' quest for foreign-policy flexibility. Although India's rise has made the country less reliant on Moscow, most Russian analysts have welcomed New Delhi's ascent as contributing toward a more multipolar world order, especially in Asia.

CHINESE GOALS AND POLICIES

Sino-Indian relations reflect a mixture of collaboration and conflict. During the Cold War, New Delhi was de facto aligned with Moscow against Beijing. Relations between India and the PRC from 1962 until 1976 were practically frozen. Although the two governments never formally severed relations, diplomatic and economic ties were severely degraded. Both sides accused the other of supporting insurgent movements in each other's territories while competing for influence with Moscow, a competition New Delhi won due to the Sino-Soviet split. In August 1971, India and the Soviet Union signed a Treaty of Peace, Friendship, and Cooperation. Emboldened by Moscow's support, New Delhi exploited the widespread popular protests in East Pakistan (now Bangladesh) that year and eventually used its military to separate that region from West Pakistan (modern-day Pakistan), leading to the establishment of Bangladesh despite Beijing's opposition. In 1976, India and China upgraded relations and exchanged ambassadors. Beijing viewed Moscow's invasion of Afghanistan in December 1979 as an attempt to encircle China, leading Beijing to improve its relations with India to counterbalance the Soviet Union. However, New Delhi demanded greater border concessions than Beijing was willing to provide. India also stood by Moscow despite Chinese and Western pressure over Afghanistan. The intermittent border talks throughout the 1980s yielded little, as Indians protested Chinese military deployments near India while Beijing refused to recognize New Delhi's sovereignty over Arunachal Pradesh. In 1988, Prime Minister Rajiv Gandhi, encouraged by Moscow to reduce Sino-Indian tensions, became the first Indian head of government to visit the PRC since Nehru's 1954 visit to Beijing. The outcome was to set aside the boundaries issue while reciprocal visits continued, and commercial and cultural ties expanded. The 1993 signing of the Agreement on the Maintenance of Peace and Tranquility along the Line of Actual Control in the India-China Border Areas was followed by many additional rounds of border talks, joint statements affirming shared economic and security interests, reciprocal visits by Chinese and

Indian leaders, and some confidence-building measures such as mutual force reductions, small-scale joint military exercises, and regular defense dialogues. Despite these efforts at reconciliation and their growing trade ties, China and India remain divided by many major sources of tension. Neither country is entirely satisfied with the current situation along the so-called Line of Actual Control, which divides the areas governed by Beijing and New Delhi along the Tibetan Plateau and the Himalayan mountain chains. The disputed territories include the Aksai Chin, controlled by China, and Arunachal Pradesh, in eastern India but claimed by Beijing as an extension of southern Tibet. Indian officials would prefer to use the boundary drawn in 1914 by the British, known as the McMahon Line, as the current delineation between India's northeastern territory and Chinese-occupied Tibet, but Beijing wants a new demarcation of the border. Some PRC actions appear to contest India's influence in Bhutan and Nepal. Beijing and New Delhi also compete for influence in Bangladesh, Myanmar, and Sri Lanka. India has invested in Iran's strategically located Chabahar Port, mainly for economic reasons but partly to develop a transportation route that will circumvent China and Pakistan.[9] Indian support for the Dalai Lama, whom many Tibetans consider their political as well as spiritual leader, represents another source of bilateral conflict.

New Delhi has also warily watched Beijing expand its economic and military footprint around India's neighborhood. Beijing has long cultivated close ties with its "all-weather" ally Pakistan, India's main South Asian rival. Chinese officials have traditionally considered Pakistan a counterweight to India in South Asia, an important foundation for enhancing Beijing's influence in Central Asia, and a significant economic partner, both directly and as a transit country. Beijing's extensive diplomatic, military, and economic cooperation with Pakistan continues to be a major point of contention with New Delhi. India's national security community has viewed Pakistan as an existential threat, while Chinese leaders have seen Pakistan as a valued partner. The PRC and Pakistan have been militarily aligned almost since both states were founded in the late 1940s. Though they have since developed deep economic ties, their shared strategic interests remain the primary binding force in their relationship. PRC officials consider Pakistan a counterweight to India in South Asia, an important base for projecting Beijing's influence in the Muslim world, and a significant economic partner, both directly and as a transit country. PRC policy has been to fortify Pakistan, India's main South Asian rival, with economic and military help, thus preoccupying New Delhi with Islamabad's activities and allowing Beijing to focus on other relationships. The PRC provided Pakistan with vital assistance to develop its civilian and military nuclear programs, including technologies that Islamabad used to create ballistic missiles that target India. In justifying its May 1998 nuclear weapons test, the Indian government cited the threat from China rather than Pakistan.

Interestingly, Indian policy makers have regularly seen China as a much greater threat than PRC policy makers have perceived an Indian military threat to China. Whereas Indian strategists are often fixated on the direct military balance between India and the PRC, Chinese security experts have focused on the balance of power between China and other countries. They seem to discount the prospects of a Sino-Indian war or believe that, if they build forces sufficient to match Japan and the United States, they will have the capacity to deter and defeat India. From New Delhi's perspective, Beijing's strategic and economic relations with Bangladesh, Pakistan, Sri Lanka, the Maldives, and Burma/Myanmar—which include the construction of ports and other potentially militarily useful infrastructure—seemingly aim at surrounding India with PRC clients. Some analysts have referred to this approach as a maritime "String of Pearls" strategy or a "a necklace of refueling and resupply arrangements" in which Beijing, though eschewing the acquisition of official military bases, gains access to military naval and intelligence facilities in South Asian and Southeast Asian countries. These facilities would support a People's Liberation Army (PLA) Navy presence, including submarines as well as surface ships, along the conduit through which tankers carry oil and gas from the Middle East to China through the Malacca Strait and other potential chokepoints. These transit zones are vulnerable to not only pirates but also Indian, U.S., or other foreign maritime interdiction.[10] The PLA Navy base in Djibouti on the Horn of Africa and growing PRC presence in other ports add to this chain defending China's critical sea lines of communication. Beijing and New Delhi also maneuver globally to contain the others' rise. Indians see China as a potential obstacle to their country's great power aspirations despite India's newly accelerated economic growth, stronger ties with Western countries, and other achievements. PRC strategists are aware that India has cultivated ties with China's potential rivals in the Pacific Ocean, including Japan, Vietnam, Singapore, and, above all, the United States. The Indian navy has begun participating in regular joint exercises with these countries in East Asian waters, establishing security ties that make Chinese analysts uneasy. Furthermore, Beijing's opposition presents a major obstacle to India's acquisition of a permanent seat on the UNSC as well as membership in the Nuclear Supplier Group (NSG). Even China and India's growing economic ties are not without tension. India runs a large trade deficit with China, which buys mostly raw materials from India and sends back higher value-added manufactured products.[11] PRC and Indian firms also compete for international hydrocarbon supplies and other markets. India has also resisted Beijing's Belt and Road Initiative (BRI) since, besides worrying about the leverage China will gain through its loans and other economic ties, the proposed PRC-Pakistan Economic Corridor would run through Pakistan-occupied, India-contested Kashmir and develop Pakistan's Gwadar Port, which China might convert into a naval base.[12]

RUSSIAN-CHINESE INTERACTIONS

The Soviet Union also played an important role in Sino-Indian relations, especially after the 1962 Sino-Indian War. Just as Beijing allied with Pakistan to counter India, so too Moscow saw India as an ally against the PRC as Soviet-Chinese relations deteriorated. India started purchasing Soviet weapons in 1959 to address immediate threats from Pakistan and China. The Soviets offered easy terms (long-term payments of nonconvertible rupees), so India did not need to use its valuable hard currency reserves.[13] Despite being allied to Beijing, Moscow adopted a neutral stance during the 1959 China-India border dispute and the 1962 war, furthering the Sino-Soviet split. The massive Soviet economic assistance Indians received, exceeding Moscow's provisions to China, deepened Beijing's irritation. The 1971 Russian-Indian 20-year Treaty of Peace, Friendship, and Cooperation had a security clause that each party would remain neutral if the other were to go to war, which resulted in Moscow's backing New Delhi's war against Pakistan and its occupation of Bangladesh. The treaty acted as a deterrent to an increasingly assertive China, but this dynamic changed after the Soviet Union's collapse. Moscow sought warmer ties with Beijing. The new 1993 Treaty of Peace, Friendship, and Cooperation removed language implying a Chinese threat. For decades, Moscow has strived to reconcile Sino-Indian differences over Kashmir and other issues, without noticeable success. In particular, under Yevgeni Primakov, foreign minister from January 1996 until September 1998, and then prime minister until May 1999, Moscow strived to build a "strategic triangle" that would align both China and India with Russia in support of a multipolar world, powerful state sovereignty, noninterference in their internal affairs, and countering separatism in Chechnya, Kashmir, and Taiwan. Nonetheless, not even Primakov's deft hand could persuade Beijing and New Delhi to abandon their historic rivalries or support Moscow explicitly against Washington. More recently, Russia's split with the West over Ukraine and the exceptional growth of the Chinese and Indian economies have renewed Russian interest in trilateral collaboration. Yet, while Beijing has accepted India's elevation to full membership in the SCO, renewed Sino-Indian border tensions and Indian opposition to China's BRI have constrained trilateral cooperation even when embedded in a broader multilateral framework. While the Russian, Indian, and Chinese foreign ministers have met formally every year since 2001, this troika has also produced little beyond joint declarations. They tend to vote the same way, or at least not against one another, in the UN General Assembly.[14] Nonetheless, the three governments have also not cooperated extensively within the United Nations, the G20, or other larger multinational institutions.

In recent years, the underlying nature of Russia-Indian ties has changed in ways similar to the Russia-China relationship. Both Beijing and New Delhi have become less reliant on economic ties with Moscow since the Cold War as they have opened their borders to Western trade and investment. The Russian government faces strong third-party competition even in its defense and civilian nuclear collaboration with India though not from China. During the Cold War, Moscow was New Delhi's dominant partner in these profitable high-technology sectors, but Western governments and companies have recently undertaken vigorous campaigns to expand their presence in both areas. In addition, the Indian government is striving to increase the share of indigenous production. In the past, Russia routinely sold certain cutting-edge weapons to India before offering them to China, but as India has developed closer defense industrial ties with the United States, Moscow has ceased its preferential treatment of India. Like China, India is decreasing its previously heavy dependence on Russia for advanced weapons systems. For instance, India has pulled out of developing the Russian-Indian Fifth Generation Fighter Aircraft (FGFA) after more than a decade of joint R&D due to technical problems related to its engines, avionics, sensors, and stealth capabilities, as well as disagreements over the project's cost and work shares. Though New Delhi aspires to follow Beijing's path to enhanced domestic defense industrial production, India can, unlike the PRC, import Western weaponry. The reciprocal military modernization programs of China and India both reflect, and contribute to, conventional, nuclear, and missile proliferation in neighboring countries. The PRC has surpassed India in the fifth-generation stealth fighter jet business, building on its own stealth jets. Beijing now depends on foreign imports only for select cutting-edge advanced technologies, such as high-performance warplane engines. The decreasing Russian-Indian defense relationship will, however, reduce one source of Sino-Russian tension, as Beijing dislikes Russian military assistance to countries like India that could engage in armed conflicts against China.

Moscow's changing priorities have been evident in how Russian-Chinese collaboration regarding Pakistan has increased, further decreasing Indian enthusiasm for joining a Sino-Russian bloc. For decades, relations between Moscow and Islamabad were severely strained. Russian analysts described Pakistan as a state sponsor of terrorism and worried how the country's extremist groups might seize control of Pakistan and its nuclear weapons.[15] Russia and China diverged sharply on the Kashmir issue. Moscow backed New Delhi's position that Kashmir was a bilateral issue between India and Pakistan and should be resolved through direct talks between them, while Beijing supported Islamabad's call for multilateral diplomacy to address the dispute. Over the past decade, however, Moscow and Islamabad have reconciled, with diplomatic and military exchanges increasing. For example, in November 2014, Sergey Shoigu became the first Russian defense minister to visit Pakistan since 1969. During his sojourn, the two governments signed an unprecedented bilateral defense cooperation agreement that provided a framework for more specific collaboration, such as holding joint military exercises. Russian and Pakistani officials have also engaged in a broad dialogue on Afghanistan, arms sales, terrorism, and regional security issues. Furthermore, Russia has begun its first direct weapons transfers to Pakistan and permitted China to coproduce with Pakistan JF-17 fighter planes powered by Russian-made RD-93 engines.[16] Moscow had previously eschewed such sales to avoid antagonizing India. Beijing has taken advantage of the Russia-Pakistani reconciliation to collaborate with both countries on Afghanistan, including by holding high-level diplomatic meetings that have included Iran, India, and the Afghan government. Still, the deepening defense relations between Russia and Pakistan may turn Moscow into an arms sales competitor with China in the Pakistani market.

IMPLICATIONS AND RECOMMENDATIONS

During the Cold War, Washington and New Delhi often found themselves on opposite sides of great-power issues. Whereas the United States wanted partners against Soviet communism, Indian leaders strove for nonalignment between the East and the West. In the 1970s, the United States pursued better relations with China to balance Moscow's expansionism, leading to Washington backing Beijing's ally Pakistan during the 1971 war with India, a decision that strained U.S.-Indian relations for years. The conflict drove India and Pakistan to seek nuclear weapons, which, due to U.S. nonproliferation policies, impeded U.S. security cooperation with both parties.[17] Fearing a nuclear war in South Asia as well as incentives for further nuclear weapons proliferation, U.S. officials imposed sanctions on both India and Pakistan for their nuclear weapons activities. New Delhi's Cold War tilt toward Moscow, despite India's commitment to nonalignment, also posed a perennial challenge for U.S.-India relations. During the 1980s, the Reagan administration gave Pakistan billions of dollars in economic and military aid to assist the armed resistance against the Soviet occupation of Afghanistan. To India's chagrin, the United States continued providing Pakistan substantial additional military and economic assistance after the Cold War.[18] Following the Cold War, however, Indian-U.S. ties have strengthened considerably. The two countries have established stronger military, economic, and political ties based on mutual interests in promoting democracy, countering Islamic terrorism, preventing weapons of mass destruction (WMD) proliferation, and addressing China's ascent. During his September 2018 visit to New Delhi, Secretary of Defense James Mattis said that the U.S. goal was "together to enhance and expand India's role as a primary major defense partner to elevate our relationship to a level commensurate with our closest allies and partners."[19] The Trump administration's 2017 National Security Strategy, like those released by the Obama and Bush administrations, delineated that the administration "welcome[s] India's emergence as a leading global power and stronger strategic and defense partner" and offered Washington's support in the "geopolitical competition between free and repressive visions of world order taking place in the Indo-Pacific region." The 2018 National Defense Strategy says the United States "look[s] to India to assume greater responsibility as a stakeholder in the international system, commensurate with its growing economic, military, and soft power." Reflecting the Pentagon's increased attention to the Indian Ocean region, on May 30, 2018, the U.S. Pacific Command was renamed as the Indo-Pacific Command (INDOPACOM). During his two-day trip to India in late February 2020, Trump joined with Narendra Modi in pledging to work together to make 5G technology more secure. Though they did not finalize negotiations on a bilateral trade deal, Indian Oil signed agreements with Exxon Mobil to increase liquefied natural gas (LNG) imports from the United States.[20]

Through increased defense ties with New Delhi, Washington hopes to strengthen India against China while limiting Russian-Indian military cooperation. Compared with their minimal military interaction during the Cold War, India and the United States now engage in a robust series of arms sales, joint exercises, and other interactions. The growth in defense-industrial ties has been impressive, beginning with the lifting of some U.S. defense-related sanctions in 2001, the 2004 Next Steps in Strategic Partnership, the Defense Technology and Trade Initiative (DTTI) launched in 2012, and the 10-year framework agreement on bilateral defense cooperation that was adopted in 2005 and renewed in 2015. The DTTI is designed to facilitate India's obtaining more advanced U.S. military technologies and support joint R&D projects by decreasing bureaucratic and legal impediments to bilateral defense industrial cooperation. Since India is not a formal U.S. military ally, the Obama administration created a new category of "Major Defense Partner of the United States," which is categorically equivalent to that of a non-North Atlantic Treaty Organization (NATO) ally without using such sensitive language, in order to facilitate arms sales and bilateral defense collaboration. In August 2018, the Trump administration promoted India to the U.S. Department of Commerce's Tier 1 Strategic Trade Authorization level, which allows Indians to purchase many hi-tech "dual-use" U.S. products without applying for specific licenses or using a streamlined process. For example, India has received U.S. authorization to purchase two dozen MH-60 Romeo anti-submarine helicopters from Sikorsky-Lockheed Martin. New Delhi was also one of the first foreign buyers of the P-8 Poseidon maritime surveillance aircraft, purchasing a dozen of the planes for more than $3 billion, and became the first non-NATO member to receive permission to buy U.S.-manufactured armed drones.[21] Furthermore, Indian and U.S. officials have signed several major defense cooperation agreements that build a foundation for enabling broader and deeper security ties. The first major bilateral military accord, adopted in 2016, was the

Logistics Exchange Memorandum of Agreement (LEMOA), which allows the Indian and U.S. armed forces to access each other's facilities and supplies. In September 2018, the two governments finalized the bilateral Communications Compatibility and Security Agreement (COMCASA), which had been under discussion for more than a decade. The COMCASA permits the two armed forces to exchange secure data and enables the United States to install state-of-the-art encrypted communications technologies on the U.S.-provided weapons systems India has already purchased, such as C-17 Globemaster, C-130J Super Hercules, and P-8I Poseidon aircraft.[22] Not only will this allow for more secure messaging with U.S. forces than the commercial systems they already possess but Indian forces will also be able to access more U.S. regional defense data networks in real time and thereby enhance local situational awareness.[23] In October 2020, the two governments signed the Basic Exchange and Cooperation Agreement (BECA) on geospatial cooperation, the last of the foundational defense agreements. The BECA permits the exchange of several types of real-time imagery, maps, and other data useful for navigation, targeting, and other military operations. The agreement also allows India to acquire more advanced avionics and navigational equipment from the United States. Sovereignty concerns made New Delhi reluctant to sign these admittedly intrusive agreements. However, India's interest in employing more cutting-edge U.S.-origin weaponry, sharing intelligence with the Pentagon on mutual threats, and achieving greater interoperability with Western countries as well as between the Indian Armed Forces' own services apparently overrode these objections.[24] The United States has also become the main foreign military exercise partner of the Indian Armed Forces. In the past decade, the two militaries have participated in dozens of bilateral exercises and multinational drills, while senior defense officials from both countries hold frequent consultations. Indian-U.S. exchanges have included regular meetings between civilian and military national security leaders, formal military exercises, defense dialogues, and additional interactions. In 2019, the U.S. and Indian armed services held Tiger Triumph. This first tri-service drill demonstrated how their exercise program has expanded beyond single-service army, air force, and navy engagements. Their maritime Malabar drills have included Australian and Japanese warships as well as the Indian and U.S. fleets. These exercises have improved military interoperability, maritime domain awareness, and mutual operational understanding. India and the United States have also stationed liaison officers at each other's major military commands, including the deployment of a U.S. liaison officer in the Indian navy's Information Fusion Centre for the Indian Ocean Region and the deployment of an Indian officer to the U.S. Naval Forces Central Command.

Furthermore, the two governments have enhanced cooperation against South Asian terrorism threats, including al-Qaeda, the Islamic State group, and Pakistani-backed extremists. The Trump administration fully "de-hyphenated" the India-Pakistan relationship, treating India as a great power in its own right. The newly created hotlines between senior Indian and U.S. officials could help them manage major regional crises, including those involving Pakistan. In their frequent regular meetings, Indian and U.S. representatives have exchanged information about the financing, recruitment, and cross-border movements of Pakistani-based terrorist groups such as and Hizb-ul-Mujahideen, Jaish-e-Mohammed (JeM), and Lashkar-e-Tayyiba (LeT). The Trump administration cut or suspended millions of dollars in anti-terrorism aid to Pakistan due to complaints about Islamabad's half-hearted measures against terrorist proxies that use its territory for international operations primarily in India and Afghanistan. India and the United States collaborate on other regional security issues, such as Afghanistan. At the inaugural September 2018 meeting of the U.S. and Indian defense and foreign ministers, this "2 + 2" group reiterated support for "an Afghan-led, Afghan-owned, and Afghan Government-controlled reconciliation process."[25]

Despite these strengthened ties, New Delhi and Washington still diverge on important issues. Indian-U.S. economic differences have increased in recent years. Dissatisfied with the large bilateral trade deficit in India's favor, the Trump administration imposed tariffs on imported Indian aluminum and steel. Indians still object to what they see as excessive limits on their access to some U.S. defense technology, despite the Industrial Security Annex augmentation to the DTTI signed in December 2019, which further protects the classified data associated with the U.S. defense technology transferred to India. The deterioration of Russian-U.S. ties has made U.S. officials more concerned about potential Russian access to U.S. defense technologies provided to India. Current friction regarding Indian-U.S. relations has centered around India's impending purchase of the S-400 missile system. Among other concerns, U.S. experts worry that operating these sophisticated Russian air defense systems near the F-35, which will be the mainstay of the U.S. and many Western air forces for decades, could compromise the security of the plane's stealth and other advanced technologies.[26] Though the U.S. Countering America's Adversaries through Sanctions Act penalizes countries that conduct a "significant transaction" with Russia's defense sector, Russian analysts have argued that Western sanctions have not adversely affected their arms trade with India.[27] Indeed, despite Washington's pressing India not to buy the S-400s, and threatening India with sanctions under the act, New Delhi went ahead with the purchase.

Conversely, Indian-U.S. differences regarding Iran may decrease. Indian analysts still see Pakistan and China rather than Iran as the primary source of nuclear threats in Eurasia. They welcomed the 2015 nuclear deal with Tehran, which removed many U.S. sanctions on Indian-Iranian commercial ties. Indian officials and analysts were displeased by the 2018 U.S. decision to withdraw from the Joint Comprehensive Plan of Action (JCPOA) and reapply nuclear sanctions on Iran, which forced Indians to curtail their purchases of Iranian oil. If Iran and the United States reach a new nuclear deal, then these sanctions may be removed. Above all, shared Indian-U.S. concerns regarding China, which have grown during the past decade, have been a key driver of recent U.S.-Indian security cooperation. Washington and New Delhi have overlapping, if not identical, security concerns relating to Beijing's growing military power. The United States and India's democratic model of governance also contrasts with China's one-party political system. Under Modi, the Indian government has become more comfortable confronting Beijing on various issues. Though neither India nor the United States has expounded an explicit strategy for containing the PRC, their national security communities recognize that a stronger U.S.-Indian partnership would better position them both to manage the challenges posed by Beijing. According to media reports, the Pentagon supplied the Indian Armed Forces with military intelligence on the PLA forces facing off against Indian troops in Doklam, helping to overcome Indian hesitations about COMCASA.[28] Future areas of likely deeper cooperation include public health, 5G technologies, securing shared supply chains from undue reliance on China, outer and cyberspace, and expanding multilateral partnerships with Australia, Japan, and other democracies.

Chapter 4   **Eurasia**

The Sino-Russian interaction in Eurasia has generally been harmonious. Collaboration has been greatest in Central Asia but lags in the South Caucasus, East Central Europe, and the Balkans. In all these regions, the role of the People's Republic of China (PRC) has been primarily economic, while Russia has had a greater military presence. PRC policy makers have seemed content with Moscow's having the lead security role in these countries since Russia has not leveraged this asset to try to impede Chinese economic activities in Eurasia. Though this balance of Russian and Chinese interests has persisted for several decades, future developments could disrupt this alignment.

RUSSIAN GOALS AND POLICIES

Russian diplomacy seeks to induce the United States and its partners to accept Moscow's primacy in the former Soviet space. Moscow has historically seen the regions of Eurasia as central to its security and prosperity. Russian diplomats believe that the North Atlantic Treaty Organization's (NATO) primacy negates the core principle of indivisible and equal security by placing nonmembers like Russia at a disadvantage. They also object to the alliance's use of military force without the approval of the UN Security Council, which circumvents Moscow's veto power. They also insist that important European security agreements be legally binding rather than mere reciprocal declarations of intent. Under former Russian president Dmitry Medvedev, Moscow pressed NATO countries to adopt a new European Security Treaty that would embody these principles and dilute the dominant role of Western security institutions. NATO governments objected that Europe's existing institutional architecture already established the principles Moscow sought to embody in the treaty and that Russia could exercise sufficient influence on European security deliberations through the NATO-Russia Council, the Organization for the Security and Co-operation in Europe (OSCE), and other extant institutions. Although the Russian government deemphasized the proposed treaty after Medvedev retired from the presidency, Moscow had recently revived and expanded these demands in its new draft European security treaties Moscow submitted to Washington and NATO in December 2021. These make evident that the Russian leadership aspires to restore the sphere of influence Moscow enjoyed during the Cold War. The new treaties called for the removal of all foreign NATO forces deployed in countries that joined the alliance since 1997, a ban on additional countries joining NATO, and a cessation of all NATO military activities in Eastern Europe, Ukraine, the South Caucasus, and Central Asia. During the past decade, Russian military activities in Georgia, Ukraine, and other countries have radically altered the security equation in the Black Sea region, transforming the area into an acutely competitive arena between Russia and NATO. Russia continues to occupy Georgian and Ukrainian territory and contest these countries' sovereignty, territorial integrity, and ties with NATO and the European Union (EU).

Russia has taken steps to increase its regional multinational structures to complement its bilateral relations in Eurasia with Moscow-controlled multilateral institutions. Russia's main military structure in Eurasia is the Collective Security Treaty Organization (CSTO), a Moscow-controlled defense alliance that consciously tries to imitate NATO. Armenia, Belarus, Kazakhstan, Kyrgyzstan, and Tajikistan are members but not China. The CSTO allies hold regular meetings, exercises, and other activities. Russia also subsidizes arms sales to the other members' militaries and Moscow's dominant position allows Russia to control when the CSTO is employed. In the cases of the crises in Belarus, Kyrgyzstan, or Nagorno-Karabakh, Moscow chose not to use the CSTO, but after widespread violence erupted in Kazakhstan in January 2022, Russian troops led the "peacekeeping force" that entered Kazakhstan to restore order. Moscow manipulates periodic war scares in the former Soviet republics to keep these countries out of NATO, secure concessions from them and Western governments, and probe for divisions between the United States and its allies.

Large Russian companies, often partly owned or controlled by the Russian government, have retained a large presence in some Eurasian countries, especially Central Asia. These firms employ many local workers, invest in critical national economic sectors, and manage important trade flows with the Russian Federation and other Eurasian states. For example, some Russian energy corporations help extract oil and gas from Azerbaijani and Central Asian hydrocarbon deposits and transport these outputs to China and other states. Moscow also exerts leverage in Central Asian states whose populations send large numbers of migrant workers to Russia. For example, a significant share of Tajikistan's national income derives from the millions of Tajik laborers in

Russia who remit parts of their salaries to their families in Tajikistan. Russian policies can expand or reduce the size of this foreign labor pool and their remittance flows. Yet, Russia's potentially most valuable instrument, the Eurasian Economic Union (EEU), was crippled at birth. Putin personally proposed forming the Union in 2011 in order to create a tightly integrated bloc of former Soviet republics under Moscow's leadership that would rival the EU, the United States, and the Asia Pacific Economic Community. Its formal goal was to enhance its members' economic prosperity and political influence by promoting the free flow of capital, goods, labor, and services and coordinating their agricultural, energy, industrial, and transportation sectors. Putin's language also suggested a degree of political and potential security integration that many saw as recreating elements of the former Soviet Union, whose population and territory were substantially greater than that of the Russian Federation, but the other members resisted pursuing this course when the Treaty on the Eurasian Economic Union was signed in May 2014 and after it entered into force in January 2015. The leaders of the other former Soviet republics have jealously guarded their sovereignty and sought to constrain Moscow's influence over their policies, including by developing ties with alternative powers such as China. In addition to these impediments to deeper integration among EEU members, the breadth of the Union has remained less than Moscow has hoped. Most important, a popular revolution deposed the pro-Moscow government in Ukraine that was seeking to join the EEU, depriving the bloc of Ukraine's 50 million people, substantial territorial connections with other Eurasian countries, and other resources. In addition, Azerbaijan and Georgia along with Turkmenistan and Uzbekistan have stayed out of the Union, denting its potential. One reason Moscow may have attacked Ukraine again in 2022 was to reverse this setback. As a result, its members consist solely of Armenia, Belarus, Kazakhstan, Kyrgyzstan, Tajikistan, and Russia. Furthermore, Putin's efforts to integrate the EEU closely with Beijing's BRI, Association of Southeast Asian Nations (ASEAN), and other non-Western economic blocs have proven largely unsuccessful. Due to its limited size and powers, the EEU's powers and influence have lagged far behind the former Soviet Union, depreciating its value to Moscow as a foreign policy tool and thwarting Putin's goal of leading a multinational bloc of tightly bound former Soviet republics. Though Moscow has made some gains recently by exploiting crises in several of these states, including Belarus and Kazakhstan, Russia's economic and technological power lags behind that of China in most of Asia and that of the EU in almost all countries in Europe.

CHINESE GOALS AND POLICIES

Since the Cold War, China has considerably expanded its economic and diplomatic presence in most of Eurasia. Through loans, investments, energy pipelines, and transportation networks, the PRC has become a leading trade and investment partner with many countries in Central Asia, the South Caucasus, and Eastern Europe, especially in the infrastructure and natural resource sectors. Many Eurasian leaders view China as an attractive source of investment, loans, trade, tourists, and technology, as well as a potential balancer and source of leverage with Russia and Western countries. Just as Russia's economic difficulties have provided China with opportunities to expand its economic role in the former Soviet republics, so the 2009 Eurozone crisis helped the PRC overcome EU resistance to PRC investment since European governments desperately needed more capital. Chinese foreign direct investment (FDI) rose substantially until 2016.[1] China's loans and investment have concentrated in the large countries of Western Europe, but the shares going to East Central Europe have increased in recent years. China's economic power has grown most in Central Asia, whose governments earn substantial revenue from the massive PRC purchases of their natural resources and would like China to finance large infrastructure projects that they cannot afford to build unilaterally. To remove barriers to PRC trade and investment by assuaging popular misgivings about the growing Chinese role in national economies, PRC diplomacy has emphasized mutual benefits through "win-win" cooperation with Chinese businesses. PRC representatives have strived to align Beijing's flagship BRI (previously known as the One Belt, One Road initiative) with other east-west silk road integration programs, such as those of Kazakhstan, Turkey, and Russia. Chinese firms often enjoy a critical commercial advantage over their Western, Russia, or Indian competitors due to Beijing's ability to force PRC entities into package deals. For example, the government can make proposed PRC investments more attractive by offering Chinese financing and various side payments, including bribes to local officials. The BRI has also benefited from its minimal requirements compared with the EEU or EU, which require partners to institute major changes in their economic laws and practices. Yet, China's economic magnetism, especially in Europe, has weakened in recent years due to setbacks affecting its BRI integration projects, partners' unfulfilled employment and revenue expectations, Beijing's assertive foreign policies, and its increasingly repressive domestic policies. Although the PRC and local partners frequently announce enormous commercial deals in memoranda of understanding, concrete projects in many Eurasian countries, including Russia, have been surprisingly few in number and limited in scope. In 2020, Chinese FDI in Europe fell to a 13-year low.[2]

Beijing's foreign security stakes have not grown as much as its international economic presence. Except in Central Asia, where the PRC has regularly conducted counterterrorism and border security drills with neighboring countries as well as provided some weapons and training, China's security role in most Eurasian countries remains small. PRC policy makers perceive the most serious security threats to Eurasia as the "three evil forces" of regional terrorism, religious extremism, and ethnic separatism. Being unconventional military threats, Beijing deals with them through counterterrorism, informational, diplomatic, and economic instruments. In almost all cases, the PRC works through the national governments, empowering and coercing them into suppressing local terrorists, religious extremists, and advocates of separatism within the PRC. That said, Beijing has several red lines, including insisting that Eurasian governments recognize Beijing's sovereignty over Taiwan, Hong Kong, and Xinjiang. Since Xinjiang lies in western China adjacent to several Eurasian countries, PRC policy makers are also concerned that the large diaspora of Uighurs, a Muslim Turkic people, in Central Asia will fight for greater autonomy and rights for Uighurs in China. Beijing has employed various coercive measures to control Uighurs and other minority ethnic groups in China. Concurrently, PRC diplomacy has pressed Eurasian governments to prevent Uighurs from organizing against Beijing's policies in Xinjiang.

Great power dynamics have substantially impacted China's status in Europe. In the early 2010s, the PRC benefited from the deterioration of Russia's relations with many European countries since Beijing was seen as a more palatable partner than Moscow. As U.S. tensions with the PRC rose during the late 2010s, however, Washington increasingly pressured European countries to curtail their ties with Beijing. The Trump administration particularly discouraged European states from developing close economic and security ties with either China or Russia. The Biden administration has continued this approach. As a result, institutional formats such as the EU-PRC "17 + 1" have not provided the benefits the participating states had hoped to see. Some EU members, such as the government of Hungary, have persisted in expanding economic relations with Beijing, while many European leaders want China to cooperate on managing global climate change, limiting nuclear proliferation, and other vital transnational issues. The PLA Navy and the EU Naval Force (EU NAVFOR) have collaborated on anti-piracy missions in the Gulf of Aden through Operation Atlanta.[3] EU countries also maintain scientific and academic exchange programs with Chinese universities. Yet, most European governments, seeking to strike a balance between benefiting economically through interactions with Chinese while limiting PRC leverage over EU vital interests, have been adopting a firmer line on Chinese investment in critical infrastructure such as ports and communication services. For example, under U.S. pressure, many European governments, including the United Kingdom, reversed earlier decisions to collaborate with China's Huawei corporation in building their 5G telecommunications networks. Pressure from Washington led Poland exclude Chinese involvement in the construction of its Central Communication Port and limited Huawei's access to Poland's 5G infrastructure market.[4] Additionally, the European Commission has been pressing Beijing to accept certain conditions aimed at guaranteeing reciprocity in research access and is asserting its right to block China from sensitive joint research projects, such as quantum technology, out of concern for intellectual property theft.[5] They also have been increasingly vocal in denouncing PRC repression in Hong Kong and Xinjiang. Some European countries have been sending warships to conduct freedom of navigation operations in Pacific waters claimed by Beijing. The Chinese government has responded with denunciatory rhetoric and, in some cases, economic sanctions. For example, the PRC curtailed economic ties with Lithuania after Beijing opposed the establishment of a "Taiwanese Representative Office in Lithuania." The PRC demands that foreign governments use "Chinese Taipei," "Taiwan Province," or other names that do not imply that Taiwan is an independent country.

RUSSIAN-CHINESE INTERACTIONS

Russian and Chinese policies regarding many Eurasian countries and issues have generally remained harmonious. In the past three decades, the PRC has achieved significant trade and investment throughout Eurasia, with minimal Russian opposition even as China's trade with several former Soviet republics has exceeded that of Russia. Moscow has not overtly complained about Beijing's expanding economic presence in Eurasia because Russian leaders do not want to risk worsening relations with the PRC and perceive advantages in China's balancing the EU's economic power. Though Russian and PRC businesses sometimes compete for trade and investment opportunities, they often focus on different geographic and commercial sectors. Additionally, Russian and Chinese firms have sometimes joined the large multinational projects that seek to finance and operate major infrastructure projects, such as the consortium established to extract hydrocarbons from Kazakhstan's offshore undersea deposits in the Caspian Sea. They both can benefit also from projects that help develop Eurasian markets. If China finances construction of east-west transportation infrastructure, Russian firms can use them to expand its activities as well. Russian and Chinese policies have independently supported integrating Eurasia into their regional integration initiatives since Moscow's EEU and Beijing's BRI both traverse many Eurasian countries. Russian and PRC diplomats insist that their regional initiatives are complementary, though in practice they can at best be seen as nonconflicting countries can join both initiatives if they wish. In the Balkans and Black Sea regions, Russia has not obstructed China's growing economic presence, probably because the PRC commercial activities supplant or replace potential ties between these states and the EU, which is viewed in Moscow as a more hostile bloc. Russian and Chinese information campaigns have both tried to undermine the EU's reputation for competency by criticizing how the body has dealt with pan-European challenges such as the COVID-19 pandemic and illegal migration into the EU. The Balkans have proven most receptive to this anti-EU messaging due to their historical ties with Russia, relatively weaker economies than most Western countries, and popular alienation from the EU (several Balkan states have yet to gain EU membership).

In Central Asia, Sino-Russian cooperation has sometimes extended beyond noninterference to encompass deeper coordination. Russian and PRC policy makers have agreed on the need to prevent Eurasian countries from becoming regional hotbeds of religious extremism, ethnic separatism, and other transnational threats. Concern about terrorism is at the forefront of Moscow's and Beijing's security calculations. Both Russian and Chinese authorities are concerned by the thousands of Central Asian nationals who joined the anti-regime forces in Syria, where they learned new combat skills that they could apply against their own governments if they return to their homelands. They have also become alarmed by how events in Afghanistan could result in transnational terrorist movements like the Islamic State—also known as the Islamic State of Iraq and Syria (ISIS), the Islamic State of Iraq and the Levant (ISIL), or its Arabic language acronym Daesh—spreading into neighboring Central Asian, Russian, and Chinese border territories. When the Taliban ruled Afghanistan in the late 1990s, they supported Islamist terrorists in Russia's North Caucasus and Xinjiang. Moscow and Beijing at times sharply criticized the U.S.-led military campaign in Afghanistan, especially its inability to suppress narcotics trafficking, and clearly do not want to see a long-term military presence in their backyard. They also castigated U.S.-backed movements that threaten to undermine authoritarian Eurasian governments aligned with Moscow or Beijing. Russian information campaigns have specifically accused Washington of orchestrating the overthrow of Russian-friendly governments in Ukraine and Georgia as well as failed attempts to depose other Eurasian regimes. Even so, the Russian and Chinese national security establishments have also worried that the Western military withdrawal from Afghanistan could worsen instability in neighboring countries and undermine their regional integration projects. Russian and PRC policy makers have consulted frequently about the terrorist threats in Central Asia and have, sometimes jointly, taken initiatives to fortify these states against potential terrorist threats.

Moscow's and Beijing's dual leadership of the Shanghai Cooperation Organization (SCO), established in 2001, has helped buffer Sino-Russian differences as well as underscore each other's intent to cooperate in the region. Though the organization has only a small permanent staff and few organic structures besides a modest Regional Anti-Terrorist Structure in Tashkent, the SCO enjoys a broad mandate to promote economic cooperation, counterterrorism efforts, and societal ties among its members. Besides Russia and China, the SCO also includes the Republic of Kazakhstan, the Republic of India, the Kyrgyz Republic, the Republic of Tajikistan, the Islamic Republic of Pakistan, and the Republic of Uzbekistan as full members. Though the organization lacks substantial authority or structures, its existence has provided Russia and China with a flexible multilateral framework to manage their sometimes-diverging policies in Central Asia. At times, Moscow and Beijing have utilized the SCO's unanimity rule to block one another from promoting some initiatives. For example, Moscow used the organization's unanimity rule to block PRC proposals to create a SCO-wide free trade zone, energy hub, or well-resourced development organs. Even so, the SCO's existence allows Russia and China to pursue essentially unilateral initiatives under the SCO's multinational gloss. Beijing has been particularly skilled at describing its economic deals with individual Eurasian countries as part of its SCO and BRI partnership programs. In practice, it is hard to see how these projects would have changed had the SCO or BRI never existed. Conversely, Russian and Chinese defense cooperation in Central Asia has been circumscribed. Russia has a considerably larger military presence than China that includes military bases, subsidized weapons sales, and more extensive multinational exercises, often undertaken within the Moscow-led CSTO. China is not a CSTO member and lacks a comparable foreign military alliance. Whereas the PLA deploys only a few times each year to Central Asia on exercises, the Russian armed forces have long-term facilities in several states. Throughout Eurasia, PRC officials have taken care not to overtly challenge Russia's security interests in these regions. In Central Asia, Beijing has welcomed Russian efforts to strengthen the national governments, including the January 2022 CSTO intervention in Kazakhstan, since political instability would threaten China's growing assets in these states while terrorist and extremist movements could threaten the PRC's internal security as well.

In European countries, Russian and PRC leaders both try to coopt sympathetic Western politicians and governments through information operations and economic inducements such as Russian energy deliveries or large Chinese investments. But their engagement with European countries occurs almost exclusively independently, with little if any over Sino-Russian coordination. Despite its Cold War history of confrontation with NATO, Russia has traditionally been more open to partnership activities with the alliance as an institution than China, which has distrusted the organization since the accidental NATO airstrike against the PRC Embassy in Belgrade during the Kosovo War, which many Chinese believe to have been intentional. Even the stunted PRC-NATO dialogue that developed during the 2000s to discuss Afghanistan and other regional issues has largely withered. China has yet to develop a major military presence in Europe. Despite conducting joint naval exercises in the Baltic Sea with the Russian navy in 2018, Beijing remains wary of being dragged into

European conflicts. Conversely, Russia has the largest military forces deployed in Europe. The Russian armed forces regularly conduct large military exercises in Europe and have stationed forces in Moldova, Georgia, and Ukraine despite the opposition from their governments. NATO governments constantly fear Russian military aggression against member or partner governments, such as Ukraine. The Black Sea has become an area of constant clashes as Russian and NATO naval and air forces operate in close proximity. Regarding the EU, Russia has sought to circumvent the EU as an institution and cultivate good relations with individual European leaders, whereas the Chinese government more comfortably deals with the EU as an organization as well as its individual member governments. Still, both Moscow and Beijing try to find friendly Western governments so that they can exploit the EU and NATO consensus requirements that permit a single member government to block sanctions, such as the imposition of sanctions on Russia or China. Although Russia and China do not visibly coordinate their policies toward Europe, from Moscow's perspective, the large PRC economic presence in Europe usefully weakens U.S. influence on the continent. Furthermore, China's large sales of industrial and consumer goods to Europe do not compete strongly with Russian sales to the EU, which focus on oil and gas.

The loose but harmonious Sino-Russian relationship regarding Europe has been evident in their policies toward the political crisis in Belarus that began when incumbent Alexander Lukashenko claimed an implausible 80% victory margin in the August 2020 presidential ballot despite widespread evidence of electoral fraud. The Russian and PRC governments recognized the declared election results soon after the ballot. Since then, Moscow and Beijing have both accepted Lukashenko's strategy of slowly dismantling the opposition by decapitating its leadership while they have been striving to prevent external (i.e., Western) interference. Yet, though Russia and China have adopted a similar public stance toward the crisis, their concrete cooperation on the issue has been minimal beyond their joint position at the UN Security Council that the Belarus election issue fell outside the Council's responsibility because the disputed ballot did not represent a threat to international peace and security. Otherwise, the PRC has not adopted a high-profile diplomatic initiative on the Belarus issue with Russia or anyone else. One reason for this paucity of Sino-Russian collaboration toward Belarus might be that Moscow's and Beijing's historical ties with that country have been very different. The Russian leadership's relations with Lukashenko had long been troubled. Lukashenko constantly carped at various Russian policies, demanded various Russian subsidies and subventions, and dragged his feet regarding Moscow-proposed regional bilateral and multilateral integration initiatives. The two countries are formally part of a common Union State as well as members of the Moscow-led CSTO, but Belarusian backsliding on its integration commitments has kept these ties rudimentary. Until the recent fraudulent election and mass government repression that followed, the United States and some European governments were searching for ways to exacerbate these Belarusian-Russian fissures to pull Minsk away from Moscow. Nonetheless, the Russian leadership tacitly backed Lukashenko's suppression of opposition protests, criticized Western governments for interfering in Belarus' internal affairs, and offered to deploy militarized police in the country on his behalf. The Russian government feared that the opposition, which was not originally anti-Russian, might nonetheless move closer to the West if it came to power. Moscow dreaded seeing another color revolution, as occurred in Ukraine and Georgia, in Belarus, which they view as machinations of the United States and its allies. The Kremlin understood that Lukashenko, while having tried to build ties with Western countries to gain leverage with Russia, had through his electoral fraud permanently alienated himself from the West as well as his own people, leaving him at the Kremlin's mercy. In contrast, China has avoided engaging in Belarusian domestic political affairs and focused on economic issues. The PRC's economic presence in Belarus has been growing for years, with Chinese entities financing highways, ports, railways, and other infrastructure to support the BRI connecting Asia and Europe. After the Ukraine revolution of 2014, the transfer of the Crimean Peninsula (where the PRC aimed to build a massive deep-water port) to Russia, and the subsequent large-scale fighting in that country, the more stable country of Belarus rapidly emerged as China's preferred "gateway to Europe." President Xi visited Belarus in 2015, the first Chinese leader to do so in over a decade. Conversely, Moscow's 2014 seizure of Ukrainian territory and support for separatists in eastern Ukraine intensified Belarusian interest in strengthening ties with the PRC to balance Russia's economic primacy in Belarus and hedge against the prospect of Russian intervention in their affairs.[6] Fueled by Lukashenko's frequent visits to China, PRC direct investment in Belarus grew by 200 times during the past decade.[7] Bilateral trade has also grown, propelling the PRC to the status of Belarus' third-highest trading partner, after Russia and Ukraine. The Russian government—perhaps confident of its primary position in Belarus, hopeful of benefiting economically from any China-Belarus transit through Russian territory (which also gives Moscow influence with Beijing), and following its overall foreign-policy priority of sustaining good relations with the PRC—has not openly objected to China's growing economic presence and other activities in Belarus. Yet, though Lukashenko remains in office, the mass protests in Belarus and the war in Ukraine will encourage the PRC's diversification of its Eastern European contacts even more to hedge against further instability. Unlike Russia, China wants Belarus and the PRC's other partners in East Central Europe to have good economic ties with the EU to facilitate the transit of China's trade to the large EU market through these countries. Furthermore,

Beijing will likely prepare for the possibility that Lukashenko's opposition will at some point come to power. The PRC has therefore adopted a low political profile, partly to avoid engendering opposition to China's growing economic presence.

IMPLICATIONS AND RECOMMENDATIONS

The U.S. decision to accept a major role in Central Asian security after the 9/11 attacks was an anomaly driven by the need to secure regional support for the U.S. counterterrorism objectives in Afghanistan. With the U.S. military withdrawal from that country, U.S. interests and influence in Central Asia have naturally declined. Due to their physical proximity and historical ties, the interests of both Russia and China in the region are larger and more sustainable. Central Asian countries welcome the U.S. presence as a balancing factor but are conscious that Russia and China have enduring interests due to their proximity, while the United States' role in Eurasia will remain more ephemeral. Moscow, in particular, has boosted its regional leadership among some former Soviet republics through its successful conflict mediation and military interventions in Belarus, Kazakhstan, and the Armenia-Azerbaijan conflict over Nagorno-Karabakh. Now that the Pentagon has withdrawn from Afghanistan, the U.S. military needs to rely on "over the horizon" drone strikes and other remotely based means of projecting power into the heart of Eurasia. The United States and its allies have never been able to offer Eurasian states an effective alternative to the massively resourced BRI. U.S. businesses still have a major presence in some commercial areas, such as Kazakhstan's hydrocarbon sector, where U.S. energy corporations have been active since the collapse of the Soviet Union, but the U.S. economic role is generally declining relative to those of Russia and China under the dual pressure of domestic nationalism and Sino-Russian economic penetration. The United States could amplify its impact by concentrating on a few niche areas—such as promoting female businesses and various rule-of-law initiatives—as well as better coordinating its regional initiatives with other Western partners such as the EU, Japan, and India. Nevertheless, the main challenge to the Sino-Russian alignment in Central Asia is that Moscow may not prove sufficiently powerful to maintain Eurasia's security with NATO's withdrawal from Afghanistan. Thus far, Beijing has assigned less strategic importance to the region than Moscow. PRC leaders also appreciate how Russia pursues many policies favorable to Chinese interests, such as suppressing regional instability and promoting Eurasian transit. In future years, however, China's growing economic interests in Eurasia, especially Central Asia, could lead Beijing to reconsider its policy of regional deference if Moscow seems incapable or unwilling of sustaining a favorable climate for the PRC's expanding commercial activities. The vacuum resulting from the decreasing Western military presence in Central Asia, combined with Russia's economic weakness and China's growing Central Asian equities (as well as PLA power-project capabilities), could drive Beijing (whose leadership has already crossed traditional red lines against PRC foreign activism) to elevate its security role in Central Asia regardless of Russian preferences.

In contrast, the United States retains major interests and influence in the Black Sea region. The U.S. military presence in the Black Sea has been growing. Since 2014, U.S. warships have regularly entered the Black Sea and expanded bilateral and multilateral military drills in the region. Yet, the U.S. deterrence mission in the Black Sea region faces a substantial capabilities challenge, given the complexities of mobility and logistics when operating in southeastern Europe in the face of Russia's local military superiority. The Montreux Convention Regarding the Regime of the Straits limits the time nonregional warships can deploy in the Black Sea, requiring their constant rotation. Major NATO powers such as France and Germany have not been very active in the region. Turkey faces constant Russian pressure to limit the presence of nonregional navies as well as restrict its security ties with NATO members and partners. Russian threats have also impeded the aspirations of Georgia and Ukraine to become full-scale NATO members since offering them full membership would require the unanimous support of all NATO governments, some of whom are unwilling to risk a possible armed conflict with Moscow over the issue. Recent U.S. diplomacy has instead focused on supporting those European governments willing to deepen economic and security ties with Russia's Eurasian neighbors independent of these organizations. Washington will need to continue this approach for the foreseeable future as well as, through diplomacy, encourage EU members to sustain their sanctions on Russia and China despite the costs. EU governments will continue to find it challenging to compartmentalize their economic cooperation with Russia and China from their deteriorating political-military relations with Moscow and Beijing.

5
Chapter

The Arctic

In the past, the Arctic has seen substantial international cooperation, but regional and global developments have been challenging collaborative norms. The region encompasses the seas and land north of the Arctic Circle. Eight countries possess territories there: Canada, Denmark (through possession of Greenland), Finland, Iceland, Norway, Russia, Sweden, and the United States. The Arctic's warming temperature and melting ice have been making the region's economic resources and sea-lanes more accessible. The prospect of accessing these Arctic riches has catalyzed international interest in the region, in a process that some compare to the great power scramble for Africa in the 19th century.[1] The melting of the polar ice caps can make it easier and more efficient for ships to carry goods and people through the area. Two major trans-Arctic shipping routes are potentially traversable: the Northwest Passage (NWP), which links Northeast Asia to northeastern North America via the Canadian Arctic Archipelago, and the Northern Sea Route (NSR), a system of sea-lanes above the Russian coast. The shorter distances of the trans-Arctic shipping routes compared with the longer maritime distances connecting Europe and Asia around Africa can reduce travel time, piracy threats, fuel consumption, and other shipping costs. Furthermore, the thinning ice sheets and melting ice caps are facilitating access to the Arctic's repository of fish, fossil fuels, and other natural resources. In addition to the massive deposits of oil and natural gas, the Arctic contains significant amounts of other metals and minerals. Many of these, including coal, copper, lead, tungsten, zinc, gold, silver, nickel, diamonds, manganese, chromium, and titanium, play critical roles in industrial production. Hitherto available only at a great financial cost, offshore extraction of oil and natural gas and the mining of seabed minerals would become easier with warmer temperatures and less icy waters. Yet, the Arctic melting could adversely impact many Russian, Chinese, and U.S. interests as well as those of other countries.[2]

The future of Arctic shipping and natural resource extraction is promising in the long term, but for the next few years, developing the Arctic will remain exceptionally challenging. The growth of fracking, renewable energy technologies, and liquified natural gas (LNG) have decreased interest in the region's still largely inaccessible hydrocarbon deposits. Forecasts of how soon the world can exploit the Arctic's riches have perennially been overly optimistic. The Arctic has long been discussed as a possible energy source, but the high costs and difficulty of operating in the region, and the existence of more easily accessible deposits elsewhere, made it an undesirable option. Even as the Arctic's physical geography becomes more favorable in some respects for commercial activities due to rising temperatures, many Arctic natural resources still require highly specialized equipment and complex logistical planning to acquire. Only a few Arctic shipping lanes have become marginally viable for limited summertime use. Polar ice is a serious threat to normal vessels and even more dangerous to ships and platforms that must maintain an exact position while drilling to avoid damaging equipment. The Arctic conditions necessitate expensive customized equipment and training of skilled laborers who can operate in the frigid temperatures, which affects the viscosity of oil and gas, raising the costs of storage and transportation. Climate change could improve access to Arctic waters in the coming decades, but meaningfully, Arctic shipping and resource extraction will require substantially more infrastructure investment. Many of the technologies required to fully develop the Arctic's resource and shipping potential remain to be developed. Until then, exploring, evaluating, and exploiting undersea resources will continue to prove difficult, expensive, and time consuming. The remoteness and severe climate of the region are major impediments to the construction of energy pipelines and transportation infrastructure. Tankers need icebreakers as well as modern navigation aids, precise hydrographic maps, port facilities, and search-and-rescue capabilities. In addition, environmentalists want to limit human activities that could jeopardize the Arctic's ecosystem. The rights and interests of the region's indigenous peoples will also need to be addressed. Preparing for and responding to a major oil spill in the frigid Arctic waters is a major challenge, requiring great expense and capacities that are not yet fully developed. Countries and firms need a more robust capacity to respond to potential environmental crises given the vulnerabilities of energy extraction efforts in the hostile climate.

The overlapping territorial claims of Arctic states also impede prospective exploitation of natural resources. Resolving the competing territorial claims and other resource management issues will require international agreement on guidelines regarding what resources may be developed, under what conditions, and by whom. The United Nations Convention on the Law of the

Sea (UNCLOS), adopted in 1982, offers each of the five littoral countries the opportunity to claim a 200-mile exclusive economic zone (EEZ) from their shoreline as well as exclusive rights to all the natural resources within the zone. Countries can also try to extend their EEZs beyond the standard 200 miles by convincing the UN Commission on the Limits of the Continental Shelf (CLCS) that the Arctic seafloor's underwater mountain ranges are geological extensions of their own continental shelves through rendering persuasive acoustic, visual, and other data. The UN Commission, which consists of expert geographers and hydrographers, evaluates these extension claims. All five Arctic circumpolar countries have launched exploratory missions, projects, or studies in order to advance their territorial claims in the Arctic, which sometimes overlap. For example, Russia, Canada, Norway, and Greenland all claim the Lomonosov Ridge, an underwater mountain range with vast fossil fuel deposits.[3] The five polar states have pledged to abide by the May 2008 Ilulissat Declaration, which affirms their commitment to resolve national territorial disputes in the Arctic on a peaceful basis, but the Arctic's economic opportunities have also enticed non-littoral states, namely, China, to seek greater assured access to the region. Since the United States is one of the few countries not to have ratified the UNCLOS, U.S. policy does not recognize EEZ extensions by other countries and stands on the traditional principle of freedom of the seas.

In addition to its scientific and economic value, the Arctic is a militarily important region. The United States and especially Russia have been sending ballistic missile–launching submarines under the Arctic for decades, since the ice helps conceal these nuclear deterrence patrols. These vessels are designed to be able to break through the Arctic ice to launch missiles, thus maximizing operational surprise and survivability through stealth. In addition, the flight paths of many Russian and U.S. strategic bombers and missiles pass through the Arctic Circle, as this is the most direct route between Russian and U.S. territories. The United States has joined with Canada to detect and defend against threats to North America from the Far North. As China's presence in the Arctic has grown, the Sino-Russian relationship has increasingly extended to encompass this region. Since Western sanctions have limited Russia's ability to effectively exploit the area's resource potential and develop NSR shipping lanes, Russian firms have turned to Chinese investments to fill the gap. However, the long-term endurance of Sino-Russian partnership in the Arctic is questionable given the two states' potentially diverging objectives.

RUSSIAN GOALS AND POLICIES

Russia possesses more territory, residents, and military forces in the Arctic region than any other country. Its northern coast comprises one-third of the entire length of Russia's national frontiers and extends from Norway on the Kola Peninsula eastward to the Bering Strait, encompassing the Barents, Kara, Laptev, East Siberian, and the Chukchi Seas. Several million Russians live above the Arctic Circle; the region generates almost one-fifth of the country's gross domestic product (GDP). The Russian military has several permanent bases in the region and sends additional forces there frequently on exercises. The Russian government's primary objectives in the Arctic are to maximize access to the region's natural resources, control emerging shipping lanes, secure Russia's northern borders from military threats, constrain the North Atlantic Treaty Organization's (NATO) military activities in the region, and leverage Moscow's Arctic activities for international influence and domestic prestige. The last objective has achieved an almost myth-like status in Russian political discourse, with Deputy Prime Minister Dmitri Rogozin having called the Arctic a "Russian Mecca."[4] Many Russians see the Arctic region as a core element of their national identity, and Russians take pride in their Arctic achievements. High-profile events, such as the 2007 stunt of having the Arktika research expedition plant a Russian flag on the seafloor at the North Pole, rally popular support behind the government's Arctic vision. Despite the perennial gap between Russian aspirations and Arctic realities, Moscow is unwavering in its long-term regional ambitions.

Following the Cold War, the newly established Russian government's interest and capabilities in the Arctic declined significantly from Soviet times. Drastic funding cuts and personnel reductions led the Russian military to curtail its Arctic presence. Meanwhile, since Russia lacked the capital and technology to develop the region's resources, Russian policy makers sought foreign partners and investment. More recently, the Putin years have seen a resurgence in interest and activity in the Arctic region. In 2014, Putin declared that the Arctic was "a concentration of practically all aspects of national security—military, political, economic, technological, environmental and that of resources."[5] Core Russian policy documents, such as its 2009 and 2020 Arctic strategies, affirm ambitious sovereignty claims and intentions to expand Russian resource and transportation development while calling for international scientific and economic collaboration to keep the Arctic a zone of peace.[6] Russian policies toward the Arctic also reflect this dual-track policy combining security and sovereignty competition with economic and scientific cooperation.

Moscow has ambitious territorial and resource claims regarding the Arctic, pursuing them through a combination of cooperative and coercive means, including both international legal instruments and an assertive stance. In 2010, Moscow signed a delimitation treaty with Norway, which resolved a 40-year dispute over boundaries in the Barents Sea. Yet, though Russia already has the largest internationally recognized EEZ in the Arctic region, Moscow has been eager to extend it. The Russian government makes claims to a number of underwater ridges, citing their connections with the Russian continental shelf, such as the Alpha Ridge, Mendeleev Ridge, and the Lomonosov Ridge, which runs directly under the North Pole.[7] The United States and other countries dispute some of Russia's territorial claims, including over the NSR and other Arctic sea-lanes. Even so, Moscow has been undertaking scientific research expeditions and other measures to substantiate its extensive claims. Though the CLCS has confirmed Russian claims in the Barents Sea and the Pacific Ocean, the Commission rejected Russia's 2001 submission, the first made by a national government, to claim the Lomonosov Ridge (which is also claimed by Canada and Denmark) due to insufficient supporting evidence. Russian scientists subsequently made substantial efforts to acquire such proof. In August 2015, Russia filed a claim with the United Nations for an additional 1.2 square kilometers of Arctic territory, where it hopes to encompass the Lomonosov, Mendeleyev, and Gakkel Ridges.[8]

Moscow aims to leverage its advantageous position in the Arctic Ocean to gain influence over other countries seeking commercial opportunities in the region. Russian firms have been building new maritime infrastructure to support expanded Arctic shipping, energy drilling, and other economic activities.[9] Developing the 5,000-km NSR, a system of sea-lanes that links the Barents and Kara Seas with the Bering Strait, represents an economic and strategic priority for Russia. Though a few large vessels have transited the route even without icebreakers, the environmental conditions severely constrain the movement of most ships through the NSR. Russians hope to make the NSR, hitherto used mostly by small craft in the summer traveling between Russia's northern ports, a viable conduit for international shipping. In this regard, the NSR would offer a commercial alternative to the Northwest Passage, which links Northeast Asia and northeastern North America via the Canadian Arctic, and the Suez Canal, which connects the Mediterranean Sea with the Red Sea in the Indian Ocean. The NSR has the potential to reduce travel time for goods transiting the Northern Hemisphere between Northeast Asia and northern Europe by approximately 10–15 days during the warmer months of the year. The government is building ports and rescue stations to support expanded shipping in the zone. President Putin has decreed that, while 20 million metric tons were carried across the Arctic in 2018, this figure should increase to 80 million by 2025.[10] In August 2019, Russia's Minister for the Development of the Far East and Arctic Alexander Kozlov said that the government and its partners "plan to synchronize the construction of icebreakers, cargo ships, the emergency rescue fleet, and port infrastructure" to attain this goal.[11] That year, the state nuclear corporation, assumed responsibility for developing the NSR, including the coastal infrastructure and Russia's fleet of polar icebreakers.[12] To provide electricity to remote Arctic locations, Russia has been developing floating nuclear power plants. Russian commercial ships have begun using the

NSR for maritime transportation and Arctic voyages between Russian ports. In 2018, the *Venta Maersk* became the first civilian container vessel to convey goods along the NSR from Vladivostok to St. Petersburg.[13] Russian companies are trying to develop the region's hydrocarbon resources—oil, gas, and high-quality coal. Moscow's regulatory demands in its Arctic waters are extensive and aim to generate revenue and leverage from companies and countries seeking to benefit from the faster route. Russian authorities must issue permits to foreign vessels to use the NSR with assistance from Russian icebreakers and Russian pilots. Russia has several dozen functioning icebreakers, including some with nuclear power, which can undertake lengthy trips without the need for remote refueling.

Russia has found it difficult to manage its two tracks of economic cooperation combined with security competition. Nonetheless, in increasing its civilian and commercial presence in the Arctic, Russia is also buttressing its territorial aspirations and military potential in the High North. Some of these "dual-use" capabilities that have both civilian and military purposes include search-and-rescue stations, Coast Guard vessels, and Russia's fleet of dozens of icebreakers of various capabilities and sizes. This civil-military fusion became evident in March 2015, when the Russian government appointed Rogozin, who also oversees the Russian defense industry, as head of a new federal commission for developing the Russian Arctic.[14] Russia is the only country that has been building nuclear-powered icebreakers in recent years; their extra power enables these ships to break through thicker ice. Following the Soviet Union's collapse, many of these icebreakers fell into disrepair, came under the control of private corporations, or were loaned to foreign countries, but the Russian government has since recovered control of many of these vessels and has devoted significant resources to building new ones for military and civilian use. Putin boasted that by 2035, Russia would have more than a dozen heavy-duty icebreakers, mostly nuclear-powered.[15]

Defensive and offensive considerations have produced a greater Russian military presence in the region. The Arctic provides a critical barrier against attacks from Russia's north and a bastion in which Russia's navy, including most of its strategic ballistic missile submarines, can patrol in relative safety under the protection of Russian land-based airpower and air defense missiles. The Eurasian landmass of Russia is effectively "walled in" by Siberia and the Pacific to the east, Asia and the Middle East to the south, and Europe to the west. The Arctic has for centuries served as the "fourth wall," restricting not only Russian but also foreign maritime activity near Russia. Russian doctrinal statements stress the military's role in protecting Russian interests in the Arctic. In peacetime, the mission of Russia's conventional forces is to sustain comprehensive maritime surveillance, protect northern sea-lanes, keep foreign submarines out of these waters, and support Russian sovereignty claims. In wartime, the Russian military must defend Russia's strategic submarines and northern coast from foreign attack. In addition to defensive considerations, the Arctic provides the Russian military a potential platform for projecting power into the North Atlantic, northern Europe, and the Pacific Ocean. The changes in the Arctic Ocean provide Moscow with economic and strategic advantages, opening more waters to Russian navigation and making it easier for Russian warships to circumvent NATO-controlled bottlenecks in the Baltic and Black Seas. But these changes also make Russia's northern ports more vulnerable to foreign attack, particularly those in the Kola Peninsula that house the majority of the country's ballistic missile submarine fleet—the Russian navy regularly test launches ballistic missiles from submarines sailing under the Arctic ice. Foreign warships will face fewer obstacles from floating ice when approaching the Russian coast. Russian concerns were evident in how Moscow has objected to Norway's growing defense cooperation with the United States, such as the decision to upgrade the Vardo radar station that monitors Russian naval activity, and Russian interference with allied Global Positioning System (GPS) communications during the 2019 NATO exercises in the Arctic.[16]

The Russian government, citing alleged NATO threats, has been upgrading its forces and facilities in the Arctic. In late 2014, Russia established the new Joint Strategic Command North for all Russian military forces in the region. Its main component is the navy's Northern Fleet, which has a variety of surface vessels, submarines, and naval aviation aircraft. The Command also includes additional air, ground, space, and other units.[17] The Northern Fleet's flagship is Russia's only Kirov class Project 11442 heavy guided missile cruiser, the *PyotrVelikiy* (Peter the Great). The fleet also has the Project 11435 *Admiral Kuznetsov* aircraft carrying cruiser, along with destroyers, corvettes, landing ships, strategic and attack submarines, carrier- and land-based aircraft, and helicopters. The Northern Fleet has been receiving some new ships and additional personnel in recent years. Russia has established several specialized Arctic fighting units and equipped other units with specialized military equipment designed to deal with the extreme weather conditions. Russia is also constructing a regional sensor network based on air and satellite coverage as well as maritime surveillance systems. On January 1, 2021, Russia elevated the status of its Arctic units into a New Northern Command, giving it the same status as its other four regional commands.

The Russian military has been building a multilayered forward line of defense in the northwestern regions of its Arctic territory by reactivating former Soviet-era military bases and constructing new ones. Moscow currently has several dozen military facilities in the region that includes major airbases and minor airstrips, search-and-rescue stations, air defense radar stations and missile batteries, and ports.[18] Russia's Alexandra Land Island, New Siberian Island, and Novaya Zemlya bases provide multilayered surveillance, early warning, and radar support for long-range interdiction and short-range coastal defense. The Tiksi North Air Base, on the Laptev Sea coast (Kola Peninsula), hosts the S-400 long-range air and missile defense system. The modernized Nagurskoye air base, located more than 1,300 kilometers north of Murmansk, has a hardened 3,500-m runway to allow for the deployment of most advanced modern bombers, fighters, and transport planes. Russia is laying deep-sea communication fiber-optic cables to connect many of these military facilities and considering serving some with floating nuclear power plants. Though many of these facilities serve a dual civilian-military purpose, supporting the coast guard and border patrol as well as the armed forces, Russia has been reinforcing its Arctic air-and-missile defense network by placing additional antiair, anti-surface, and anti-submarine missiles at some bases. Russia's deployment of missile defense systems on remote Arctic islands and the bolstering of its naval assets, including ice-capable corvettes armed with cruise missiles and enhanced anti-submarine warfare capabilities, aim to deny NATO forces access to the area, especially through control of the narrow sea passages in the region. The goal is to create a network of dispersed airfields, search-and-rescue stations, deepwater ports, air defense radar stations, missile batteries, and other facilities at strategic points throughout Russia's Arctic coast for multilayered air, sea, and ground defense. From the Pentagon's perspective, Russia's militarization could turn the Arctic into a A2/AD zone against NATO, building northward Russia's A2/AD wall, which already extends from Syria through the Black and Baltic Seas.

Not only has Russia been deploying additional military capabilities in the Arctic but its forces have also been more active in the region. The level of Russian submarine activity in the Arctic is the highest in decades, with many sightings throughout European and Scandinavian waters. The number of Russian strategic bomber flights flying near the Arctic territory of Norway, Canada, and the United States has also been increasing. More Russian ground forces are based, or rotate through, the Arctic region. During the past decade, the Russian military has conducted longer, larger, and more frequent exercises. These units rehearse air-assault drills, amphibious landings, dispersing and regrouping forces reinforcing remote outposts, and training for extreme weather conditions. At the tactical level, Russian exercises have practiced reconnaissance and surveillance, electronic warfare, and other combat procedures in harsh Arctic conditions. Defensive exercises focus on keeping foreign militaries away from Russia's northern frontier. Offensive drills have included rehearsing maneuvers to disrupt NATO activities in the North Atlantic Ocean, such as through the routes connecting Greenland, Iceland, and the United Kingdom (the GIUK gap).

CHINESE GOALS AND POLICIES

China has not commonly been seen as an Arctic country since the People's Republic of China (PRC) possesses no territory above the 60°N parallel, but China has strived to be seen as a legitimate Arctic stakeholder, influencer, and resource claimant. Beijing worries that other countries' sovereignty claims could constrain Chinese access to the Arctic. The PRC has therefore sought greater influence through expanded participation in Arctic governance mechanisms and increasing its economic and scientific presence in the region while striving to avoid provoking negative responses from other Arctic states. After years of lobbying, the PRC in 2007 became an ad hoc observer member of the Arctic Council. Comprising both Arctic countries and indigenous peoples, the Council is the most influential intergovernmental organization dedicated to Arctic issues. Though the Council acts by consensus and can only reach nonbinding decisions, membership bestows status as an important Arctic player. PRC officials initially argued that all countries, regardless of their geographic or historical connections with the Arctic territory, should have equal access to its resources since the region should be a "global commons" available to all. For example, People's Liberation Army (PLA) Rear Admiral Yin Zhuo maintained that the Arctic "belongs to all the people around the world, as no nation has sovereignty over it. . . . China must play an indispensable role in Arctic exploration as we have one-fifth of the world's population."[19] Chinese officials soon moderated their public position to avoid antagonizing Russia and the other Arctic states, specifically eschewing taking a position of the various sovereignty claims in the region. As in other regions, PRC discourse now characterizes its research, commercial, and infrastructure-building activities in the Arctic as aimed at mutually beneficially ("win-win") cooperation. Beijing's newly restrained stance helped the PRC become a permanent observer nation on the Council in 2013. China's upgraded position, though still lacking voting rights, has given the country more opportunities to present its interests to Arctic states and fortify its claims as a regional stakeholder.

Since 2012, PRC representatives have been describing China as a "Near Arctic State" and Major Arctic stakeholder.[20] Since then, PRC officials and scholars have regularly employed this term to highlight China's legitimate interests to shape Arctic norms and claim Arctic resources. A landmark January 2018 Arctic White Paper affirms that the PRC will adhere to the principles of "respect, cooperation, win-win result and sustainability" in its approach to the region. While affirming peaceful intent, the paper insists that China has a justified role as "an active participant, builder and contributor in Arctic affairs" because the "situation now goes beyond its original inter-Arctic States or regional nature, having a vital bearing on the interests of States outside the region and the interests of the international community as a whole." The text elaborates that "climate change, environment, scientific research, utilization of shipping routes, resource exploration and exploitation, security, and global governance . . . are vital to the existence and development of all countries and humanity, and directly affect the interests of non-Arctic States including China."[21] Beijing's emphasis on multilateralization and mutual gains echoes the narrative surrounding the Belt and Road Initiative (BRI), which the white paper extends to the Arctic as a "Polar Silk Road," envisaging the construction of airports, seaports, railroads, and undersea cables to help facilitate Chinese investment and trade. The PRC has capitalized on its elevated Arctic status to portray itself as a relevant stakeholder in global geopolitics and an active player in shaping international rules, consolidating its rising power status. Beijing has sought to strengthen its soft power and legitimacy by serving as the de facto spokesperson for major non-Arctic countries seeking a patron to promote their interests. The Arctic also offers China the chance to demonstrate adherence to the "peaceful rise" path by making cooperative efforts to maintain regional peace and stability.

The PRC has expanded its scientific and economic activities in the Arctic to bolster Beijing's claims to secure a "seat at the table" when the international community discusses Arctic issues. PRC researchers have assumed a more prominent role in Arctic-related research events and projects, establishing research ties with local partners in various fields, including climatology, geography, glaciology, oceanography, and geology, as well as offering resources and expertise to other nations launching such scientific research expeditions. In July 2004, the Polar Research Institute of China established the Arctic Yellow River Station on the Norwegian islands of Svalbard to monitor Arctic climate change and its effects on China's continental and oceanic environment. The PRC has also been building overseas satellite observation ground stations in several Nordic countries. In 2018, China inaugurated a weather research facility in Iceland and a joint research center in the Russian Arctic.[22] PRC experts also want to understand the possible effects of climate change in the Arctic region, such as the potential opening of new sea passages or natural resources, as well as the impact on China itself as well as the PRC's other global interests. As the 2018 White Paper explains, "The natural conditions of the Arctic and their changes have a direct impact on China's climate system and ecological environment, and, in turn, on its economic interests in agriculture, forestry, fishery, marine industry and other sectors."[23] Chinese scientific activism has helped Beijing shape the Arctic's rules, regulations, and governance. For instance, China has participated in adopting the Polar Code within the International Maritime Organization and is a part of the Agreement to Prevent Unregulated High Seas Fisheries in the Central Arctic Ocean. PRC representatives cite participation in these agreements and the collaborative scientific projects as manifestations of their "win-win" approach to Arctic issues.

As a large global consumer of natural resources and a country heavily dependent on maritime trade, China has a vested interest in the Arctic's economic potential. The region's energy and other natural wealth make it attractive for resource-hungry Chinese consumers. Furthermore, a significant portion of the Chinese economy hinges on international shipping, which could become substantially cheaper and faster by traversing Arctic sea-lanes. These interests converge in that the Arctic's own hydrocarbon riches, if they can be shipped to China, offer the PRC the prospect of energy security through import diversity. The PRC presently depends heavily on oil imports from the Middle East that pass through the Strait of Hormuz in the Persian Gulf, the northern part of the Indian Ocean, and the maritime chokepoint of the Strait of Malacca in Southeast Asia. This route is threatened by piracy attacks, naval interdiction, and political upheavals in the Middle East. Greater use of the Arctic would reduce these vulnerabilities as well as save time and fuel. Not only is China well placed to make use of maritime commerce through the Arctic but PRC corporations, with some of the world's largest shipyards, could also become leading manufacturers of the large vessels that would use such routes. The Chinese government has demonstrated a prodigious capacity to mobilize resources on behalf of its Arctic priorities by making substantial commercial investments in regional states. Through its strategy of bilateral "resource diplomacy," Beijing has offered various countries, especially smaller states, in or near the Arctic, lucrative trade and investment deals that China can leverage for influence.[24] For instance, Chinese economic engagement with Iceland has grown since the adoption of a binational Free Trade Agreement in 2013. PRC firms have also acquired shares in Canadian oil companies that could afford them access to Arctic drilling. China has also been helping develop port facilities in Europe that can support PRC ships that traverse the Arctic Ocean. Iceland's naturally deep harbors make it especially attractive for Chinese port infrastructure investment since these can facilitate reloading from large vessels to shallower ships for transshipment to southern ports in Europe and Asia. The PRC investments follow the familiar "anchor and cluster" strategy in which one major Chinese investment project soon leads to others. However, Western strategists are wary of PRC attempts to leverage its growing economic presence in the Arctic region for political influence.[25] For example, Icelandic authorities denied a land sale to a Chinese investor for security reasons, while Denmark has sought to monitor and limit PRC investment in Greenland, due to concerns that China is trying to acquire the island's rare-earth metals and bolster its independence movement.[26]

Although the PLA has been enlarging its presence in other regions, China has so far avoided a military role in the Arctic. Whereas Russian and U.S. policies overtly emphasize both scientific-economic cooperation and security competition, PRC public discourse eschews any discussion of a potential Chinese security role in the Arctic. Yet, there is also a Western concern that China's growing civilian activities in the Arctic could provide the foundation for a military presence. The reasoning is that, after having established a large commercial presence in the Arctic, the PRC will see the need to support its economic stakes through enhanced means of projecting military power in the Arctic, perhaps in cooperation with Russia.

RUSSIAN-CHINESE INTERACTIONS

Though Russia and China currently pursue different policy approaches in the Arctic, the region is an emerging area of Sino-Russian cooperation due to a fortuitous convergence of Russian assets and Chinese needs. Until a few years ago, Russian officials expressed clamorous concern about Beijing's growing Arctic ambitions. Moscow strove to limit the influence of all non-Arctic actors, including China, that could potentially challenge or undermine Russia's predominant status and strategic interests. For example, Russia was one of the leading proponents for limiting the participation rights of observers (which also include India, Japan, Singapore, and South Korea) in the Arctic Council.[27] Russian government representatives also strongly supported the 2008 Ilulissat Declaration's wording that asserted unique and extensive privileges for the five coastal states regarding territorial issues, resource development, and governance rights in the Arctic Ocean. In a 2013 interview with a Norwegian television company, Prime Minister Dmitry Medvedev emphasized that only Arctic states should define governance rules for the Arctic.[28] At the time, Russian authorities were resisting Beijing's application to become a full observer on the Arctic Council.[29] For Russians concerned with Beijing's rising international influence and power, keeping China out of the Arctic both limits the PRC's access to potential resources and helps secure Russia's economic and military power.

In the competition for the Arctic, Russia has many advantages: its physical geography (many estimated deposits lie along its northern shores), lengthy experience in the region, and extensive investment in polar equipment, including icebreakers. Nevertheless, Russia's Arctic infrastructure remains underdeveloped. Russia lacks the advanced technologies required to exploit the offshore oil and gas deposits in the Arctic waters, which present challenging geophysical conditions due to polar ice, severe storms, and other conditions. Additionally, many of the oil and gas deposits in the Russian Arctic remain unexploited because they necessitate new expensive overland or overseas transportation to connect them to international markets. Through joint ventures and other arrangements, Russian energy managers have sought foreign partners to bring additional capital, technologies, managerial skills, and other assets to the region. Before 2014, Russian companies favored working with U.S. and European energy firms since they generally possessed the most sophisticated technologies. Following the Cold War, U.S. and other Western companies created joint ventures with Russian firms to explore for and extract natural resources in Russian territory. In return for providing capital and cutting-edge technology, the Western firms received repatriated profits and access to oil, gas, and minerals in Russia's Arctic. Starting in 2014, however, U.S. and EU sanctions have prevented Western companies from investing in most Russian energy projects. For example, Eni, ExxonMobil, and Statoil had to abandon multibillion-dollar joint exploration and development projects for the Arctic with the Russian energy giant Rosneft. The sanctions have also limited possible Western use of the NSR for transpolar transit. As a result, Russian companies have turned to Chinese firms for alternative sources of capital and technologies. At the same time, China was launching major east-west projects to build transportation links with European markets; this PRC interest in transcontinental transportation networks naturally led to Chinese interest in using Russia's NSR as another, potentially faster and cheaper commercial conduit between China and Europe.

Since 2014, Russian politicians and analysts have typically cited many perceived near-term benefits in collaborating with China in the Arctic while downplaying the long-term risks.[30] As noted, PRC officials have facilitated this Russian policy change by moderating their rhetoric regarding the rights of non-Arctic states to the region's resources. Russian officials have allowed the China National Petroleum Corporation (CNPC) to join Rosneft and other companies to explore for hydrocarbon deposits in Russia's offshore Arctic territories and to purchase stakes in Russian Arctic ventures. Already in 2013, the CNPC acquired a minority stake in the large LNG project on the Yamal Peninsula of Novatek, Russia's largest private-sector investor in the Arctic. The project, which also includes France's Total, has been delivering LNG via the NSR to east China's Jiangsu province from Siberia since the summer of 2018.[31] In April 2019, the CNPC and China National Oil and Gas Exploration and Development Corporation reached another deal with Novatek to buy shares in the related Yamal LNG 2 project.[32] These investments support Xi's efforts to advance China's reliance on cleaner energy sources while enabling PRC companies to gain expertise about Arctic conditions. The two governments have also discussed possible PRC investment in developing Russia's deepwater Arctic port of Arkhangelsk and constructing a railway to link the port to other parts of Russia.[33] Chinese companies are investing in oil rigs off the coast of Murmansk, in conjunction with Russian companies Gazprom and Rosmorport.[34] Russian and Chinese scientists have initiated efforts to coordinate scientific explorations and share their research at symposiums and other exchanges.[35] In 2019, the two governments established a joint Arctic Research

Center. While environmentally focused, the center's work could also assist the NSR and other joint economic projects. Most important, the Russian and Chinese governments have agreed to develop the NSR cooperatively. Cosco, a large Chinese state shipping company, has been a leading foreign client of the NSR, making periodic test runs through the passage.[36]

If using the NSR proves commercially viable, coming years should see a progressive increase in the volume of PRC tonnage passing through the Russian Arctic, which will generate work for Russia's icebreaking fleet and transit fees for the Russian government. Russian regulations, as well as practical considerations, oblige Chinese vessels transiting the NSR to rely on Russian pilots, coastal infrastructure, search and rescue, and other services. Additional future Sino-Russian collaboration in the Arctic could include joint drilling, mineral extraction, and shipping projects that benefit from the likely improvement of relevant Chinese technologies. There might also be joint paramilitary search and rescue, counterpiracy, emergency response, situational awareness, or anti-smuggling drills. Though there is little evidence that China seeks a major military presence in the Arctic, Moscow and Beijing have expanded the geographic scope of their joint defense drills to the Mediterranean and the Baltic Seas, so a future exercise in the Arctic is possible. While comprehensive Sino-Russian collaboration has been limited to the development of Russia's designated Arctic shelf, Russian and Chinese coordination of Arctic exploration beyond Russian waters to include unclaimed land and resources is feasible. In this role, Beijing could overtly support Moscow's claims in the Arctic.

These interdependencies generally align the two countries' near-term Arctic interests and policies as well as boost their shared leverage. China is investing in the Arctic not to help Russia but to gain resources and shipping routes. By supporting Russia's Arctic activities, China benefits from access to Russia's hydrocarbon reserves and gains leverage in Moscow by becoming a financial backer of projects viewed as vital to Russia's national security and economy. Russia also has an opportunity to shift its international energy profile toward Asia and reduce Russia's dependence on European markets. The Chinese believe that joint projects could help mitigate Moscow's concerns about becoming a simple resource supplier to the PRC. The denouement of the global COVID-19 pandemic—with China's economy recovering much better than Russia or most other large countries—has made Russia even more dependent on Chinese investment and commerce in the Arctic. By granting Beijing access to the Russian Arctic, however, Moscow risks allowing China to become a more formidable economic and possibly security challenger. As in other areas of the world, China could pursue moderate policies toward the Arctic in the near term but, in the long term, develop a more assertive policy. To dilute China's relative influence, Russian officials have strived to develop other economic partnerships, extending to the Arctic region, with Japan, India, South Korea, and other Asian countries, though without much success. For now, Chinese entities have relied on Russia to safeguard the safety and security of the growing Chinese economic presence there. As in Central Asia, PRC policy makers perceive the Arctic as a lower priority region than their Russian counterparts. Unlike in Central Asia, which adjoins Chinese territory, the PLA does not have the option of supplanting Russian military power in the Arctic. In general, China has tried to downplay military issues due to its superior economic, diplomatic, and other nonmilitary power assets and concerns that militarization would impede China's access to the region.[37] In the future, however, the PRC might aim to enhance its search-and-rescue and other paramilitary assets in the region to support China's expanding commercial presence there as well as the safety of PRC nationals in the region. One reason China may be building its own polar icebreakers—the first named Xue Long, or "Snow Dragon"—is to reduce dependence on Russia's expensive and limited fleet of NSR escort icebreakers.[38] A growing Chinese military activity in the Arctic, even if primarily driven by economic objectives and the growth of China's military power in general, could eventually build the foundation for a PLA presence in the Arctic. For example, China could send submarines to patrol there.

Moscow's wariness of Beijing's future ambitions and growing power may preclude too deep a regional partnership, even if looser ties could weaken the prospects for some Russian projects in the Arctic. Sino-Russian disputes over Moscow's territorial and jurisdictional claims could arise given the divergence between Russian expansive sovereignty claims with China's wanting to keep the Arctic accessible to other states. PRC officials might again assume the position that the Arctic's resources should be available to all states and that, given China's large share of the world's population, the PRC has a substantial stake in the region, warranting correspondingly substantial influence. Moscow's concerns could intensify if Beijing tries to leverage Russia's growing dependence on PRC commerce to press Moscow for special privileges and concessions within its Arctic jurisdiction. Giving Beijing special privileges to utilize the Russian Arctic could alienate Moscow's other potential partners. Sino-Russian disagreements over Russia's environmental standards and hefty icebreaker and transit fees could also emerge. The Chinese want Russia to invest more in the NSR's commercial infrastructure, while Moscow prioritizes building additional military facilities. Notwithstanding their other effects, Western sanctions have accelerated Russia's expanding use of Chinese investment and technology for developing Russia's Arctic industries.[39] Likewise, U.S. tariffs on China have served to push China toward Russia since Beijing has retaliated by imposing tariffs on U.S. LNG imports, making Russian LNG more competitive.[40] If Western sanctions are relaxed, Russian companies might again seek to acquire Western investment or technology. Even if this does not occur, Russia might partner more with Indian, South American (such as Brazil), or other non-Western foreign partners. Likewise, PRC companies and officials are keenly aware that Russia is not the only Arctic player. If Arctic resources are more easily extractable from other states, or less politically costly than relying on Russia, China may intensify its pursuit of non-Russian resources. But if Sino-U.S. tensions are sustained, Beijing may see Moscow as its best available Arctic partner. Much depends on whether Sino-Russian collaboration in the Arctic can drive a general improvement in relations or whether the latter is a prerequisite of the former. PRC investment could require Russia to give up more control in the Arctic than Moscow might deem acceptable. Such cooperation might only occur in the context of a much stronger relationship between the two states—or the growing Chinese investment in the Russian Arctic could create precisely these shared interests.

IMPLICATIONS AND RECOMMENDATIONS

U.S. officials have become increasingly concerned about Russian and Chinese activities in the Arctic region. The Defense Department's 2020 report on the Chinese military noted, "The PRC's expanding Arctic engagement has created new opportunities for engagement between China and Russia."[41] The Obama administration, like its post–Cold War predecessors, had encouraged the PRC to become a responsible stakeholder in the Arctic, while the United States continued to cooperate with Russia on Arctic issues even after Moscow's illegal annexation of the Crimea. The Trump administration adopted a firmer line toward both countries. Notably, at the May 2019 Arctic Council meeting in Rovaniemi, Finland, Secretary of State Mike Pompeo described the Arctic as recently evolving into "an arena for power and for competition." Pompeo ridiculed the PRC claims to be a "Near-Arctic State," arguing that "only Arctic States and Non-Arctic States" are legitimate categories "and claiming otherwise entitles China to exactly nothing." Although Pompeo did not object to some PRC investment in the Arctic, he insisted that it needed to be transparent and constructive and avoid its "pattern of aggressive behavior elsewhere." Pompeo also expressed concerns about Russia's extensive territorial claims in the Arctic, intensified military presence in the region, and plans to join the NSR with Beijing's Maritime Silk Road. In response, Pompeo asserted that "under President Trump, [the U.S. government is] fortifying America's security and diplomatic presence in the area."[42]

The growing Sino-Russian alignment in the Arctic could challenge U.S. interests in the region and beyond. Beijing could back Moscow's territorial claims, which Washington opposes, and recognize Russian authority over the NSR, which the U.S. government considers an international shipping route. The expanded Russian and Chinese presence in the Arctic could impair U.S. freedom of maneuver as well as degrade U.S. access to Arctic shipping lanes and resource deposits. In January 2019, Air Force General Terrence O'Shaughnessy, commander of U.S. Northern Command, said the Arctic represented "the front line" of North America's defense.[43] The Pentagon's June 2019 Strategy report terms the Arctic a "potential vector for attack on the U.S. homeland" and warned of the potentially adverse consequences of Chinese military activities in the region for U.S. security.[44] Other U.S. priorities in the Arctic Strategy include maintaining comprehensive domain awareness, defending U.S. territory, limiting other states' sovereignty clashes, developing Arctic resources while protecting the environment, sustaining freedom of navigation and overflight, and enhancing transatlantic ties while limiting the Sino-Russian regional alignment against the West. The U.S. Navy's 2014 Arctic Roadmap rightly calls for ensuring fair access to these waters, preparing for search-and-rescue missions there, and maximizing use of the region's potential economic benefits. In May 2018, the Pentagon reestablished the Second Fleet and has increased navy patrols in the region to contest unrecognized maritime claims, while the U.S. ballistic early warning and missile defense facilities at Thule Air Base in Greenland, established in 1943, have recently been upgraded. Yet, in recent years, the United States has been the least active and assertive of the littoral countries and has lacked a clear, comprehensive, and consistent Arctic policy. U.S. administrations have not treated the Arctic as a U.S. national security priority on par with Europe, Asia, and the Middle East or pursued comprehensive or well-resourced policies toward the region. In February 2014, the United States issued its first Arctic plan in years, the Arctic Roadmap to 2030, but its three goals were vague: enhancing security, protecting the environment, and advancing international cooperation in the region. Neither the public summary of the January 2018 National Defense Strategy nor the February 2018 Nuclear Posture Review nor the December 2017 National Security Strategy addressed Arctic security issues in detail.

Though U.S. cooperation with Russia and China in the Arctic region will remain restricted pending a breakthrough in trilateral ties, the transnational nature of some nonmilitary issues—such as those related to climate, ecology, and the needs of indigenous peoples—warrants regular consultations on managing the consequences of climate change, environmental risks, and basic scientific research. Some Russians welcome a warming Arctic as making the region's resources and sea-lanes more accessible. However, other Russians recognize that Russia could suffer economic and human costs from excessive temperature rising, such as an increased spread of global diseases, larger fires in Russia's vast forests, and how the melting of permafrost threatens infrastructure in the Russian North. Furthermore, less Arctic ice removes an impediment to foreign as well as Russian activities in the region, creating more economic and security challenges for Moscow. PRC policy makers likewise understand that, though opening the Arctic to transpolar navigation, rising global sea levels will threaten China's ecosystems, agricultural production, and large coastal cities. The Biden administration could explore these shared trilateral interests in mitigating global climate change. Consideration should also be given to enhancing confidence-building measures among the regular armed forces as well as between Coast Guards and other paramilitary and law enforcement agencies operating in the region to avoid incidents and render mutual search and rescue support. At the same time, NATO should avoid direct engagement with China in order to discourage PLA military activities in the region. The United States and its partners should contest Beijing's claims to special Near-Arctic state status by pointing out that dozens of European and Asian countries are also located within 1,000 kilometers of the Arctic Circle. They should also warn Russia that continuing to militarize the Arctic will compel the West to increase its own military presence in the region, to the detriment of the region's overall security.

For purposes of both deterrence and defense, the Pentagon should increase its capabilities for Arctic missions. Given the lengthy defense acquisition cycle (building a modern icebreaker can take more than a decade and a billion dollars), the U.S. Navy and Coast Guard need to start building more icebreakers and additional vessels and planes suitable for Arctic missions. The United States currently has only one icebreaker capable of traversing through thick ice and only one permanent base above the Arctic Circle. Without new icebreakers, the United States will be forced to rely on foreign vessels for assistance. The United States and its allies can also expand use of uncrewed aerial and maritime vehicles since they can often handle the region's frigid temperatures better than humans, with fewer safety concerns. Their number should be sufficient to enable them to surge during crises, whether natural or deliberate, such as military contingencies. Still, the navy may need crewed warships for some missions, such as freedom of navigation operations that contest territorial claims. Furthermore, U.S. funding for non-platform enabling capabilities for mapping, communications, intelligence, surveillance, and reconnaissance must also be sustained. Many of these enhancements could support both civilian (e.g., commercial shipping and scientific research) and military activities in the Arctic.

The United States has a powerful advantage over Russia and the PRC, in the Arctic as elsewhere, due to the close U.S. defense partnerships with important regional players. Of the five countries with Arctic coastlines (Canada, Denmark, Norway, Russia, and the United States), Russia is the only one that is not a member of NATO. The Pentagon needs sustained access to bases and other facilities in allied countries to meet its Arctic commitments. To gain greater operational experience, the United States and its allies and partners should conduct more frequent and larger exercises in the region. They should rehearse search-and-rescue, coastal defense, amphibious operations, anti-submarine warfare, and logical supply and replenishment missions. The United States considers the Northwest Passage as an international route, while Canada claims that the passage is under Canadian jurisdiction, but the two countries should agree to set the dispute aside to address the greater long-term challenges to joint Canadian-U.S. interests in the Arctic. Though Canada has previously supported Beijing's increased role in the Arctic, its recent deterioration in relations with both Russia and China should offer greater opportunities for expanded Canadian-U.S. mutual defense initiatives regarding the Arctic, both bilaterally and within the NATO and North American Aerospace Defense Command (NORAD) frameworks. Europeans' strained relations with Russia and China should likewise present opportunities for Washington to enhance its partnership with the EU within the NATO framework on Arctic issues. Although NATO's 2010 Strategic Concept acknowledged new security challenges for the alliance, such as cyber and energy security, intra-alliance divisions have prevented NATO from fully addressing Arctic security issues. NATO has recently become more engaged in the region. The Trident Juncture 2018 military exercise was the largest alliance Arctic drill since the Cold War, incorporating 50,000 troops from even such non-NATO Nordic countries as Finland and Sweden. A U.S. carrier battlegroup, led by the USS *Harry S. Truman*, operated north of the Arctic Circle for the first time in almost three decades. Making further progress should become a significant item on the transatlantic agenda since all NATO members and partners would benefit from greater information sharing, situational awareness, and other Arctic-related security cooperation efforts. Denmark has been an excellent partner in countering Russian and Chinese influence in the Arctic, including by taking countermeasures against Chinese efforts to make large strategic investments in Greenland. In addition, the United States should work to strengthen the Arctic Council since NATO members have most of the permanent seats on it. Washington should also more directly engage with the non-Arctic states active in the Council, especially U.S. allies Japan and South Korea, and compete more successfully with China for their allegiances. This would require U.S. diplomats to elevate the Arctic issue in bilateral and multilateral engagements with these countries. For example, differences could emerge over U.S. opposition to European and Asian use of the NSR. The United States can trade directly with Europe and Asia from its North American coasts, but the NSR might be commercially advantageous for some maritime trade between Europe and Asia.

The United States can enhance its regional soft power by cultivating a reputation as a good environmental steward, demonstrating respect for the rights of the Arctic's indigenous peoples, and maximizing the development and sharing of scientific knowledge. The Trump administration's skepticism regarding climate change and perceived neglect of European environmental concerns risked alienated traditional transnational partners. The May 2019 U.S. refusal to sign an Arctic Council declaration highlighting climate concerns resulted in the Council, for the first time in its 23-year history, not issuing a joint declaration. PRC propaganda was quick to capitalize on the opportunity. Shanghai hosted an Arctic conference one month later that emphasized Beijing's lead in promoting Arctic cooperation.[45] More transatlantic cooperation with U.S. allies on this issue would yield low-cost dividends. The sanctions limiting Western companies from engaging in either technology transfer or capital lending to Russian hydrocarbon and transportation projects in the region limited economic development in the Russian Arctic. The United States and other NATO countries might also consider how environmental regulations and norms could impede large-scale Russian military activities in the region. The United States should cooperate to make Arctic allies, private companies, vulnerable populations, regional militaries, and other allied stakeholders more resilient against climate change impacts as well as help them develop a viable liability regime to deter and pay for environmental disasters. Senior U.S. military leaders have also recommended ratifying the UNCLOS to secure U.S. legal rights in maritime zones, which would give U.S. diplomats greater authority to criticize other countries' EEZ expansion and territorial claims. U.S. naval forces already adhere to the practices stipulated by UNCLOS as part of their standard operating procedure. In its messaging, U.S. officials should highlight to Russians the dangers of their assisting a major Chinese presence to emerge in the Arctic; once the PRC has built a strong Arctic foundation, it will never leave. Furthermore, if the PLA operates vessels there, this could make the Arctic a theater for Sino-American military competition, with the risk of Russian entanglement.

II
Part

Functional
Interaction

Chapter **6**   **Security Ties**

Russian and Chinese leaders have described the two countries' security ties as a critical dimension of their broader partnership. Their shared security objectives include averting bilateral conflicts, maintaining border security, advancing bilateral defense industrial collaboration, and influencing third parties such as the United States. From a historical perspective, their close defense ties stand as a relatively recent development. During the Cold War, the leaderships of Moscow and Beijing perceived each other as potential adversaries due to their territorial disputes, border skirmishes, ideological disagreements, and personal rivalries—though by the end of the 1980s, their tensions had been significantly reduced. During the 1990s, the Russian and PRC governments adopted several military confidence-building measures to constrain military activities and deployments that could impact the other country's security. In 2001, Moscow and Beijing signed a friendship and cooperation treaty based on the principles of mutual nonaggression, noninterference, strategic reassurance, equality, crisis consultations, mutual benefit, peaceful coexistence, anti-terrorism, international law, and respect for national sovereignty and territorial integrity. In June 2017, the People's Republic of China's (PRC) national defense minister Chang Wanquan observed, "In recent years, under the personal leadership of our national leaders, the level of mutual trust and interaction between the Chinese and Russian armed forces has steadily increased."[1] That same month, the two governments approved a roadmap for bilateral military cooperation for the 2017–2020 period. Their military and civilian defense leaders now regularly engage in bilateral and multilateral meetings as well as informal consultations in a variety of formats.

Russian and Chinese leaders view their defense partnership as a major policy success that they hope to sustain. Though both countries recognize the possibility of renewed Sino-Russian military tensions in the future, neither country's national security establishment views the other as a near-term military threat. Meanwhile, the 2018 U.S. National Defense Strategy identified both the Russian and the Chinese armed forces as primary threats to U.S. security, preventing the Pentagon from focusing its efforts against Russia or China alone. The Sino-Russian relationship is approaching a full-blown defense alliance, with the important exception that the two countries do not have a formal mutual defense pledge obligating each side to render military assistance to the other if the latter were attacked. The PRC's long aversion to formal alliances following the Sino-Soviet split of the late 1950s, as well as both countries' reluctance to commit in advance to fight on behalf of each other in conflicts with third parties, will hinder Moscow and Beijing from establishing a formal defense alliance. Nonetheless, through their arms sales, joint exercises, defense dialogues, and other bilateral and multilateral security cooperation, Russia and China have become a more formidable threat to U.S. security, especially in the Indo-Pacific region. For example, by exchanging weaponry and collaborating on defense research and development (R&D), Russia and China can better circumvent U.S. sanctions on their defense sectors. As long as Moscow nor Beijing cannot develop robust defense relationships with the United States, Russia and China have a powerful incentive to remain each other's most important military partners.

RUSSIAN GOALS AND POLICIES

Russia's national security community now perceive the PRC as Russia's most important defense partner. The Russian military cooperated with the North Atlantic Treaty Organization (NATO) during the two decades after the Cold War. A high point was when Russian troops served in a NATO peacekeeping operation in Bosnia under U.S. military command. Following Moscow's annexation of Crimea in March 2014, the United States and NATO ceased all combat collaboration with the Russian military. As a result, the Russian government has been eager to find other foreign military partners to underscore that Russia was not militarily isolated due to NATO's boycott and had other defense partnership options beyond the West. In this context, expanding security cooperation with China has made imminent sense. Due to China's enormous military power and other strengths, the People's Liberation Army (PLA) is a considerably more important partner than any other. Indeed, having security ties with China enhances Russia's own importance in Asia, giving Moscow greater leverage with India, Japan, Vietnam, and both Koreas. Furthermore, the growth of Chinese power promotes the development of a multipolar world in which power and influence of the United States are reduced. Another benefit of cultivating defense ties with China is that it allows Moscow to influence the future development of the PLA. For example, through joint Sino-Russian exercises, "the PLA's officers absorb the knowledge of Russian military traditions, strategies, and tactics."[2]

CHINESE GOALS AND POLICIES

China values its defense partnership with Russia given that the PRC's security ties with all its other important neighbors have turned adversarial. Additionally, the Chinese armed forces benefit from learning from the more experienced Russian armed forces. The PLA compensates for its limited foreign combat experience by learning from the actions and practices of more advanced militaries. Unlike the U.S. and Russian militaries, the PLA has not engaged in a major war since the 1950–1953 Korean conflict, excluding a brief intervention into northern Vietnam in 1979 as well as indecisive border skirmishes with India and the Soviet Union. Furthermore, though the PRC has been constructing a network of artificial islands in the South China Sea and aircraft carriers that provide mobile air cover, Beijing only recently opened its first foreign military base in Djibouti. Since the PLA has not fought in a major conflict in decades, the Chinese defense community has closely studied foreign militaries and their operations. Learning about modern combat conditions has also been an important motivation behind the PLA's participation in an expanding number and diversity of exercises with foreign partners. PRC analysts maintain that these drills advance mutual interoperability since they "allow both sides to better understand each other's way of combat and form better tacit understandings in future joint military operations and antiterrorist missions."[3] In the case of the drills with Russia, a PRC military representative observed, "Russia's battlefield experience in Syria, Crimea and Chechnya is very valuable to us, in particular on how they have adjusted their military strategy across time."[4]

The past few years have also highlighted for Beijing the value of having Russia as a diversionary antagonist. Though the Trump and Biden administrations wanted to make China the clear priority for U.S. defense efforts, Russian aggression against Ukraine, mercenary activities in Africa, and other threats to Western interests have prevented the U.S. national security community from putting the Russian-Western rivalry on hold, while the West deals with the rising China challenge. It is also advantageous for PRC diplomacy when Russia takes the lead in vetoing UN Security Council resolutions that China also opposes, signs joint Sino-Soviet declarations affirming principles favored by Beijing as well as Moscow, bears most of the burden in suppressing mutual security challenges in Central Asia, and does not itself present a near-term military threat along China's 4,200-km northern border with Russia.

RUSSIAN-CHINESE INTERACTIONS

Though Russia and China are not formal military allies, their defense ties have become more institutionalized and better integrated in recent years as Moscow and Beijing have built wide-ranging frameworks for security cooperation. Over the course of the 1990s, both states established confidence and security-building measures, mechanisms to avoid and manage military incidents, rapid communication networks, and regular consultations among their military and civilian defense leaders. For example, the annual sessions of the Russian-Chinese Intergovernmental Commission on Military-Technical Cooperation, an important Sino-Russian defense coordination body, cochaired by their respective defense ministers, discuss arms sales and other defense industrial cooperation. Senior Russian and Chinese military leaders also frequently participate in official visits, conferences, and summits involving both countries. For instance, high-level Russian defense officials regularly participate in the Xiangshan Forum, an annual high-profile conference hosted by the China Association for Military Science on Asia-Pacific Security, while the PRC defense minister regularly attends the annual Moscow International Security Conference hosted by the Russian Ministry of Defense. Moreover, Russian and Chinese defense officials meet frequently in other multinational formats, such as within the framework of the Shanghai Cooperation Organization (SCO) or the prominent multinational defense dialogues conducted regularly by the Munich Security Conference, and the International Institute for Strategic Studies. In May 2015, President Xi was the most prominent foreign guest at the Victory Day parade in Moscow, while Putin enjoyed similar status during Beijing's September 2015 celebrations commemorating the Japanese surrender ending World War II. Through these engagements, Moscow and Beijing have highlighted and, increasingly, exaggerated their wartime partnership and other previous eras of supposedly strong Sino-Russian defense ties. Routine contacts also occur among mid-level military officers, especially border units and functional specialists, such as Russian technicians training the PLA to use Russian arms. Since April 2015, senior civilian officials from the Russian and Chinese foreign and defense ministries have convened approximately one dozen consultations on Northeast Asia security to discuss Korean-related tensions and express joint opposition to U.S. military activities on the Peninsula.[5] Through professional military education exchanges, Russia and China can send military personnel to attend courses in each other's defense academies; thousands of Chinese officers have studied at Russian military institutions.[6] That the PLA has developed a cadre of Russian-speaking officers for engagement with the Russian armed forces testifies to the importance of Sino-Russian collaboration for the Chinese armed forces.[7] In June 2017, Russia and China signed a Roadmap on Military Cooperation for the 2017–2020 period, which has provided a framework for more concrete projects discussed at regular high-level Sino-Russian defense meetings.[8]

For almost three decades, Russia and China have conducted large-scale bilateral military exercises, which have included their land and naval components as well as joint aviation maneuvers and tabletop command post exercises. Defense Minister Shoigu has termed this cooperation "the most significant aspect" of their security partnership because the drills had improved the effectiveness and readiness of the two countries' forces "to respond to modern challenges and threats efficiently."[9] The purposes of these joint drills—which have seen a steady progression in complexity, diversity, and geographic expanse—have included improving operational proficiency by, for example, learning new tactics, techniques, and procedures for combined counterterrorist missions. They also send reassurance signals—displaying mutual trust and benign intentions to each other—as well as communicate warnings to other parties such as the United States.

The bilateral Sino-Russian exercises now involve an annual cycle of at least one ground component exercise (sometimes as part of the annual Russian strategic deals), a pair of naval component drills (called "Naval Interaction" by the Russians but termed "Joint Sea" drills by the Chinese) in two different regions of the world, and a joint strategic patrol in northeast Asia. Though the COVID-19 pandemic led Russia and China to cancel or reduce some drills in 2020, they resumed large-scale exercises in 2021. In August 2021, Russian ground and air forces were deployed at the PLA's Qingtongxia Combined Arms Tactical Training Base in northwest China. There they joined PLA Army and Air Force units affiliated primarily with the PLA's Western Theater Command in a two-stage drill, with an extensive planning and training phase followed by a day-long live-fire phase. This "Zapad/Interaction-2021" drill marked the first strategic-level Sino-Russian exercise on PRC territory. It replaced the previous practice of having PLA forces send contingents to participate in Russia's annual strategic exercise. Perhaps this was due to the location of these Zapad ("West") strategic drills, which occurred in September in European Russia and Belarus, uncomfortably close to Ukraine and NATO territory. The drills also marked the first time that Russian army units employed mostly Chinese gear, that the sides established a joint command and information system, and in which soldiers of both nationalities planned, trained, and drilled together in combined teams. The engagement also marked the first international exercise on PRC territory since the COVID-19 outbreak that began in the Chinese city of Wuhan at the end of 2019. Russia and China also jointly participate in exercises with additional countries, such as other SCO members in their Peace Mission exercise series. "Peace Mission 2021" occurred for two weeks in September in the Russian city of Orenburg. The PLA has also been a prominent participant in the Russian Ministry of Defense's annual International Army Games since 2014. Starting in 2017, China has cohosted some of the competitive events that occurred within the framework of the Games. In 2021, the PLA Army, Navy, and Air Force hosted three of the competitions in the northwestern area of Korta in Xinjiang. China further participated in a dozen events on Russian territory as well as competitions in Belarus, Iran, and Uzbekistan. The Russian and Chinese navies have additionally conducted several modest naval drills with Iran. Furthermore, Moscow and Beijing have exercised independently of each other with third partners, even when the other partner was a potential adversary of Moscow or Beijing. For example, Russia regularly conducts an extensive annual series of military drills with India, without any noticeable objection from the PRC government. Thus, there is no major cost to either country from sustaining these Sino-Russian drills—they have no opportunity to conduct major exercises with the most advanced Western militaries, while they can freely combine the Russian-Chinese drills with additional partners.

The Russian and Chinese governments also make frequent joint declarations on important global and regional security issues. In terms of content, these have regularly criticized various U.S. policies; pledged collaboration against separatism, terrorism, and religious extremism; and affirmed mutual nonaggression, noninterference, and respect for national sovereignty and territorial integrity. In their Joint Statement on Strategic Stability, issued during Putin's June 2016 visit to Beijing, the two governments warned against the threat to international stability from "some countries and military-political alliances" that "seek decisive advantage in military and relevant technology, so as to serve their own interests through use or threat to use of force in international affairs." They also expressed concern about the adverse strategic impact of "long distance (conventional) precision attack weapons" as well as "the unilateral deployment of anti-missile systems all over the world," which they claimed "has negatively affected global and regional strategic balance, stability and security." In this declaration, Russia and China called for "fair and balanced disarmament and arms control," new measures to keep terrorists from using biological and chemical weapons, respect for the UN Security Council and international law, noninterference in countries' internal affairs, refraining from enlarging military alliances, and for a wider conception of "strategic stability." The two governments released additional declarations during Putin's 2016 visit that offered their views on international law and cybersecurity.[10] The following year, they orchestrated a multilateral declaration at the June 9 SCO heads-of-state summit which warned, "The member states reaffirm that the unilateral and unrestricted build-up of missile defense systems by one state or a group of states, without taking into account the interests of other countries, is detrimental to international and regional security and stability. They find it unacceptable to ensure one's own security at the expense of others."[11] In a joint statement issued in June 2018, the two governments declared their intent to "enhance existing mechanisms of military cooperation, broaden practical military and military-technical collaboration, and jointly counter regional and global security challenges."[12] Speaking at the Moscow Security Conference in April 2019, PRC defense minister Wei Fenghe termed Beijing's defense ties with Russia as "the closest between large countries" manifested in reciprocal support regarding "the most important issues and strategic projects" and in "joint opposition to security threats amid instability and uncertainty prevailing in the world."[13] At the same conference, Russian defense minister Sergei Shoigu stated that due "to the efforts of Russian and Chinese leaders, our relations are reaching a new, unprecedented high level," to the general benefit of "ensuring peace and international security." Shoigu added that prominent Sino-Russian joint activities have included "joint operational and combat training activities, consultations between the general staffs," as well as collaboration between Russian and Chinese professional military educational institutions.[14] On numerous occasions, Russian and Chinese officials have jointly expressed concern about U.S. initiatives to strengthen ballistic missile defense capabilities, claiming that these strategic defense systems, in combination with the strong U.S. offensive nuclear capabilities, might give the United States nuclear superiority over Russia and China.

In the next few years, Sino-Russian defense collaboration will remain strong due to the momentum of past arms sales, the mutual benefits from the cooperation, and both parties' lack of major alternative security partners. For instance, the PRC has already signed contracts to procure billions of dollars' worth of Russian weapons in the coming years. Further, in June 2017, the two defense ministries adopted a framework agreement outlining bilateral military cooperation up to 2020. The PRC Defense Ministry stated that the new agreement showed "high level mutual trust and cooperation" and encouraged "both sides to face new threats and challenges in the security field and to jointly safeguard regional peace and stability."[15] A joint Sino-Russian statement, issued the following year, affirmed that the two countries would "build up cooperation in all areas, and further build up strategic contacts and coordination between their armed forces, improve the existing mechanisms of military cooperation, expand interaction in the field of practical military and military-technical cooperation and jointly resist challenges to global and regional security."[16] In June 2021, Russia and China renewed their 20-year Treaty of Good-Neighborliness and Friendly Cooperation, which provides for enhanced security collaboration. In a joint statement explaining their decision, the two governments boasted that their "new type" partnership was "based on equality, deep mutual trust, commitment to international law, support in defending each other's core interests, the principles of sovereignty and territorial integrity."[17] Their declaration pointedly argued, "While not being a military and political alliance, such as those formed during the Cold War, the Russian-Chinese relations exceed this form of interstate interaction" because "they are not opportunistic, are free of ideologization, involve comprehensive consideration of the partner's interests and non-interference in each other's internal affairs, they are self-sufficient and not directed against third countries."[18]

IMPLICATIONS AND RECOMMENDATIONS

Russian and Chinese officials regularly claim that the two countries' defense partnership promotes international security and peace. Though debatable, the Russian-PRC partnership has indeed provided each party a peaceful and secure "strategic rear" in the face of parallel confrontations with the United States, allowing Russia and China to concentrate attention on their distinct but compatible priorities. Beyond this passive reassurance, Sino-Russian defense collaboration has also enhanced Moscow's and Beijing's leverage with other countries, such as Japan, whose leaders have hoped to limit such security cooperation. Moscow's and Beijing's strained relations with Washington and its allies partly explain why Russian and Chinese leaders have viewed the Sino-Russian defense relationship as a major achievement to sustain. Russia has been unable to develop robust military relationships with Western countries, leaving Beijing as Moscow's most important defense partner outside the former Soviet Union. Meanwhile, though the PRC has pursued security ties with other countries, Russia remains the PLA's main foreign defense partner. Though their exercises have not attained the high level of interoperability that occurs, for example, between NATO members, this is not expected given their lack of necessity or expectation needing to fight together in a combined combat operation. Yet, they have practiced enough that some of their elite units seem sufficiently capable, if necessary, of jointly undertaking a counterterrorist campaign, a noncombatant evacuation operation, or rendering assistance in a humanitarian emergency. Observing the "Zapad/Interaction-2021" drill, in which Russian troops used PLA weapons and equipment, and which saw mixed Sino-Russian teams plan and operate together, Russian analyst Artyom Lukin argued that "it is getting clear that Russia-China military drills are not just symbolic shows of camaraderie, but are increasingly aimed at enhancing battlefield interoperability."[19] In the case of more demanding operational requirements, they would probably aim for deconfliction of their forces rather than a joint command. In the future, the Russian and PRC armed forces could continue pursuing a still wider range of combined defense exercises with more demanding tasks in additional regions of the earth, which would enhance the two countries' potential to conduct future joint military campaigns. They could also coordinate their defense cooperation with third countries hostile to the West, such as Iran or North Korea, to exert greater pressure on the United States. PRC national security decision makers have been investigating Russian tactics in Ukraine and Syria for lessons, which may have influenced Chinese tactics regarding PRC territorial disputes. Similar to Moscow's tactics in

Ukraine, Beijing has presented the world with a fait accompli in the East and South China Seas by declaring an air identification zone and by constructing artificial islands that are soon militarized. The 2018 U.S. National Defense Strategy has noted that both Moscow and Beijing "have increased efforts short of armed conflict by expanding coercion to new fronts, violating principles of sovereignty, exploiting ambiguity, and deliberately blurring the lines between civil and military goals," as well as "using other areas of competition short of open warfare to achieve their ends (e.g., information warfare, ambiguous or denied proxy operations, and subversion)."[20] Additionally, the expanding foreign military activities of Russia and China have increased the risk of inadvertent encounters between their forces and Western militaries. The prospects of war will rise if Moscow or Beijing overestimates the extent to which their alignment reduces the danger of confronting the United States and its allies.

Some constraints on Sino-Russian defense cooperation will persist. The recent, highly publicized arrests of Russian scientists and scholars working on military or dual-use technologies highlight Russian concerns about unauthorized technology transfers to other countries. Though Russian and Chinese political and military leaders have insisted that they do not perceive each other as threats, and Russian analysts still seem to genuinely believe that their country will retain decisive defense advantages over China for the indefinite future, some Russian policy makers undoubtedly harbor concerns about the long-term growth potential of China's military power. Additionally, this benign mutual non-threat perception could change. For example, worsening Sino-Indian tensions could antagonize Beijing if Chinese experts deem that Moscow prioritizes defense sales to New Delhi. Further, while PRC leaders have prudently avoided making public comments that imply concern about Russian military activities in Ukraine, Syria, and elsewhere, Chinese experts a few years ago privately expressed unease about how Russian weakness might create a security vacuum in Central Asia, which would threaten Beijing's regional interests. Russian military successes in Crimea and Syria subsequently quieted such comments.[21] But they could reemerge if the security environment in Central Asia deteriorated due to the Taliban victory in Afghanistan and other developments.

Russian and Chinese representatives have more openly acknowledged that their security cooperation is partly motivated by concerns about the United States. For example, PRC experts said that their Zapad/Interaction-2021 "exercise was forcing Washington to consider the worst case scenario of having to fight both China and Russia in the event of a regional conflict."[22] When PRC defense minister General Wei Fenghe went to Moscow in April 2018, he told the media that his trip aimed to emphasize to Washington and others the strength of Sino-Russian military ties.[23] Even before this acknowledgment, Russian and Chinese representatives undoubtedly appreciated that the two countries' high-profile defense contacts, military-technical cooperation, and joint exercises communicated deterrence signals to the United States and other countries. Many U.S. national security leaders and experts had, until recently, downplayed the potential threats generated by combined Sino-Russian security activities. During the last few years, the U.S. government has shown increasing concerns about Russian and Chinese military activities. Official U.S. national security documents and speeches now routinely warn of an era of renewed great power competition with both countries. Even so, U.S. analysts have still typically focused on the threats posed by each state separately rather than the challenges resulting from joint Sino-Russian defense initiatives. It is true that Russia and China have engaged in many disruptive military activities unilaterally as well as with security partners other than each other. For example, Russia and China each have been developing, deploying, and proliferating A2/AD capabilities (such as air defense systems, precision-guided weapons, mines, weapons of mass destruction, and innovative irregular warfighting tactics) that could impede U.S. operations and increase U.S. casualties in military conflicts. Yet, U.S. defense policy makers should more comprehensively assess the challenges to U.S. security interests presented by the growing Sino-Russian alignment as well. In particular, U.S. intelligence agencies should devote adequate resources to monitoring arms sales, military exchanges, and other interactions across Russia and China; many analysts seemed to have been caught off guard by some recent developments, such as the joint Russian-Chinese strategic aviation patrols near Japan and Korea or Putin's announcement that Russia would help the PLA construct its missile early warning network. Additionally, U.S. planners must prepare for contingencies involving both the Russian and the Chinese armed forces. Even if they do not operate as a combined force in a joint military operation, Moscow and Beijing could exploit conflicts between the other and Washington to advance their own security interests while the United States is preoccupied elsewhere. For example, if the United States were engaged in a conflict with Beijing over Taiwan, the Russian government might become more adventurous in the Baltics.[24] U.S. measures that effectively deter Russia and China concurrently could help avert such opportunistic aggression.

The diverging security environments in Europe and Asia have naturally shaped U.S. response options in each region. U.S. allies in Europe are more unified against Russian military threats than their Asian counterparts, whose views about how best to manage China vary considerably. Furthermore, the types of U.S. military force best suited to each region have differed. In Europe, the Pentagon has been deploying more ground forces near Russian land power, whereas in the Indo-Pacific region, the United States has relied more on independent and mobile U.S. air and naval forces to resist Chinese challenges. Even so, the United States has been pursuing innovative approaches toward European-Asian partnerships. A prominent recent initiative has been the launching in September 2021 of a trilateral Australia-United Kingdom-United States (AUKUS) defense industrial partnership to provide the Australian armed forces with nuclear-powered attack submarines, long-range precision-guided strike systems, quantum computing, artificial intelligence technologies, and other advanced military and dual-use capabilities designed to promote defense, deterrence, and strategic stability in harmony with U.S. regional goals. Yet, U.S. outreach will need to find methods to better integrate the more limited potential contributions of smaller Asian and European partners, especially those that are not formal U.S. allies. Many of these partners lack the resources to acquire complex military platforms and enabling capabilities available to the United States and its major regional allies. The United States should give these partners more opportunities to exchange views with U.S. national security leaders on U.S. defense and deterrence efforts to avoid the kind of surprised reactions we saw when they learned of the launching of AUKUS. Though AUKUS has increased partner interest in pursuing similar technology-sharing mechanisms with the United States, successfully launching similar technology-sharing arrangements requires assessing what credible military capabilities partners can bring, when they might arrive, and how they can be optimally supported. Even when partners cannot generate the same capabilities, they still might offer complementary contributions that sustain important areas of mutual military interoperability. For example, partners with more limited defense needs or capabilities could contribute to maintaining secure dual-use supply chains independent of Russia and China or help develop regional space, maritime, and cyber surveillance and defense networks.

7

Chapter   **Arms Sales**

Russia's vast military sales to China have constituted the most tangible aspect of the two countries' defense relationship. After Western governments imposed an arms embargo on China following the 1989 military crackdown at Tiananmen Square, Russia seized the opportunity and became the primary foreign weapons supplier of the People's Liberation Army (PLA). Since then, the People's Republic of China (PRC) has acquired more weapons from Russia than from all other countries combined. The transferred systems have included advanced warplanes, helicopters, air defense missiles, diesel submarines, high-performance engines, and electronic and aviation technologies. During the 1990s, Russian military exports to China constituted the most important dimension of the two countries' defense relationship as the PLA bought $1–2 billion worth of Russian weapons each year. Most recently, both armed forces may benefit from pooling some of their defense research and development (R&D) programs.

RUSSIAN GOALS AND POLICIES

When Western governments imposed an arms embargo on the PRC following the 1989 Tiananmen Square crackdown, Russia seized the opportunity to become the PLA's primary foreign weapons supplier. Major purchases have included complete weapons systems, some of which have been produced in China under license, such as Su-27 fighters, Mi-17 helicopters, Su-30 transport aircraft, Sovremenny class destroyers (with SS-N-22 SUNBURN missiles), Kilo class diesel-electric submarines (with Russian SS-N-27b SIZZLER missiles), several types of ship-to-ship missiles, and both S-300PMU (SA-10) and S-300PMU1/PMU2 (SA-20) surface-to-air defense systems. After Putin returned to the presidency in 2012 and Russian-West ties collapsed following Moscow's 2014 annexation of Crimea, Sino-Russian defense industrial collaboration reached new levels. For example, China has purchased more than 100 Russian combat helicopters to supplement its domestically produced models.[1] The PRC resumed buying complete Russian weapons systems rather than importing mostly components, licensed production, or spare parts. China has recently purchased some of Russia's most sophisticated weapons systems, such as the fourth-generation Su-35S Flanker-E advanced fighter jet and the S-400 Triumf (North Atlantic Treaty Organization's [NATO] designation: SA-21 Growler) surface-to-air defense system. The sales have been notable in that the PRC has become the first foreign purchaser of these advanced platforms, whereas India had typically enjoyed such a privilege in the past.

By generating more export revenue and larger production runs, these large Russian arms sales to China have supported Russia's military modernization program by providing substantial funds to the Russian military-industrial complex. In conjunction with energy exports, defense exports have represented the most important source of PRC-related trade revenue for Russia. Money earned from selling excess stocks of outdated weaponry has allowed Russian firms to extend production runs, upgrade platforms, and fund R&D projects for future weapons programs. The sales to China have also allowed Russian firms to advertise their defense technologies to other foreign buyers. The arms supplies may have also provided Beijing a greater incentive not to antagonize the Kremlin through intellectual property violations or other overt acts against Russian interests. By fueling the PLA's military buildup, moreover, Moscow has made Washington more concerned with China's rising military power and thereby diverted the Pentagon's attention from managing Moscow. The transactions also give Moscow a deeper understanding of the PLA's future development and activities and perhaps provide a means to influence their evolution. In addition, this high-tech defense industrial cooperation helps dilute the unwelcome perception that Russia is becoming a mere resource appendage to the PRC in a neocolonial relationship.

Moscow's willingness to sell advanced defense technologies to China despite the danger of reverse engineering reflects Russia's need for short-term revenue and non-energy exports, determination to maintain a major share in the PRC's defense market, and desire to maintain defense ties with China and the influence that such sales may give Russia with the PLA. The pressures of international isolation, Western sanctions, and depressed energy exports have induced Moscow to sell more advanced defense technologies to Beijing despite misgivings about facilitating PRC poaching of Russian intellectual property and thereby further strengthening China's military-industrial complex. The comprehensive Western sanctions, specifically on Russia's military-industrial complex, have made the revenue from sales to China more valuable for Russian defense companies. For example, some of these firms collectively earned several billion dollars from the S-400 and Su-35 transactions. Russia's determination to sustain a major share in China's defense market and to garner influence over the PLA might also have played a role in the restoration of massive Russian arms sales to the PRC, which Russian analysts may presume to be helpful for strengthening overall Sino-Russian relations as well as boosting Moscow's influence in China's national security community. Another reason that Moscow has encouraged Russian defense companies to supply even advanced maritime and air defense platforms to China is Russian confidence that the PLA would employ these systems only against other countries. Moscow has exercised caution in not selling weapons that could assist the PLA in a potential ground war with Russia. Instead of tanks, ballistic missiles, or strategic bombers, the transferred weapons have consisted of diesel-electric submarines and naval destroyers with advanced missiles designed to sink U.S. aircraft carriers. In turn, Beijing has refrained, at least in public, from interfering with Moscow's weapons sales to India, Vietnam, and other countries the PRC considers potentially hostile.

Russian analysts also seem to think that the PLA will continue to lag behind the Russian armed forces, which have more combat experience and possess more advanced equipment than their Chinese counterparts. Since the mixed performance in the 2008 Russian-Georgian War, the Russian armed forces have obtained new equipment and significantly improved their training, command structure, logistics, communications, and other enabling capabilities. The Russian military has made major investments in conventional and nuclear strike forces capable of establishing anti-access/area-denial (A2/AD) barriers against U.S. military forces that seek to operate near Russia's European and Asian borders. The Russian government has continued relatively high defense spending compared to the modest expenditures of the 1990s despite Russia's recent economic problems. The enhanced capabilities of the Russian military can be seen in all four of Russia's military districts, including in the Eastern Military District (MD) near China. Regardless, Russian decision makers have prudently avoided selling China the most advanced Russian weapons, waiting until even more advanced systems have entered, or are about to enter, service with the Russian armed forces. They have only made the leading-edge systems available to the PRC after more advanced systems (the fifth-generation S-500s and Su-57s) had been expected soon to enter service with the Russian armed forces. In response to PRC misappropriation, moreover, Russian arms dealers took steps to safeguard sensitive Russian technologies more effectively, such as requiring PRC importers to sign more rigorous intellectual property agreements. As a condition for the Su-35 sales, for instance, Russia has declined to allow PRC companies to manufacture the plane domestically and only provided turnkey models directly to the PLA Air Force (PLAAF).[2] Russian analysts have concluded that the transfer of even advanced weapons to the PLA would not present a near-term threat to Russia. They note that the Russian armed forces are more seasoned in combat experience and have anticipated that Russian defense equipment will remain ahead of PRC-manufactured military technologies for at least another generation of weapons modernization.

Some Russian analysts may also have reasoned that, if Russia waits too long to sell the high-tech weaponry China seeks, the PRC will eventually manage to manufacture these systems domestically through improvements in Chinese defense production, cyber theft of Russian intellectual property, or other means. Thus, they could have calculated that Russia might as well earn revenue through selling some units now rather than risk earning nothing by waiting too long. Another means by which Moscow has hoped to mitigate the risk entailed in the expanding Sino-Russian defense industrial collaboration with China is by pursuing more joint research, development, and marketing of new military technologies and systems, which could be accessed by both the Russian and PRC armed forces and sold to third countries. In the future, Russia could sell more advanced weapons to China and could further integrate the two countries' military-industrial complexes through more joint R&D and manufacturing, the wider sub-contracting and sourcing of weapons components to one another's defense industries, and wider reciprocal technological transfers.[3] Though Russian arms sales to China have constituted a decreasing share of overall Sino-Russian commerce since the value of their nondefense trade has grown, such military transactions have remained important given that Russia has represented the PRC's most important defense industrial partner. Additionally, their military sales, unlike other bilateral trade sectors, have involved high-technology exchanges with Russia earning a net surplus.

CHINESE GOALS AND POLICIES

Since 1989, China, needing modern defense technologies and lacking alternative suppliers, has been buying around $1–2 billion worth of Russian weapons each year. In addition to complete weapons sales, China has purchased Russian components and technologies as inputs into PRC domestic production and hired Russian technicians to train the PLA to employ these weapons. Since the PLA was initially equipped with primarily Soviet-origin military systems, the Chinese armed forces could readily absorb Russian defense technologies having the same legacy. Through purchasing Russian arms, the PLA has acquired many sophisticated defense technologies that the Chinese defense industry could not produce, thereby partly circumventing the West's post-1989 embargo. Meanwhile, since the PLA had already been based on Soviet-era military technology, the Chinese military likely found it, at least initially, easier to integrate the Russian defense imports than other foreign military technologies. Furthermore, buying expensive high-tech Russian weapons has helped China alleviate Russian complaints about the imbalanced nature of the two countries' bilateral trade relationship, in which the PRC has primarily purchased Russian energy and raw materials rather than high-value, high-technology items. Further, by affirming Russia's military advances, arms sales have assuaged Russian anxiety about China "passing" Russia as a global military power.

In the late 2000s, Chinese acquisitions of Russian arms slowed as the PRC became more selective in military purchases from Russia. Beijing failed to sign major new arms sale contracts with Moscow and procured only maintenance, specialized components, limited upgrades, and spare parts for already purchased systems. As a result, China had dropped to only the fourth-largest Russian arms importer by the mid-2010s.[4] Several factors during this period constrained Russian arms transfers to the PLA. China's improved ability to develop weapons had decreased PRC interest in purchasing low-quality Soviet-era weapons from Russia. The growing prowess of China's indigenous defense industry in the 1990s had resulted from the Chinese government's success in securing technology transfers from Russia in return for large weapons purchases; PRC access to former Soviet military technologies from Ukraine and other non-Russian suppliers; government appeals to the Chinese diaspora to contribute to the high-tech development of the motherland; and from Chinese skills in assimilating foreign defense technologies acquired through cyber theft and other nontraditional means. Given its improved indigenous defense production capabilities, the PRC demanded new and better weapons from Russia, which Moscow was unsurprisingly reluctant to offer in light of PRC success in incorporating Russian defense technologies into the Chinese military-industrial complex. Russian analysts cited past instances when PRC technicians copied Russian weapons platforms and, after making slight adjustments, sold the modified systems as knockoffs to third parties. The most notorious example that prompted accusations of intellectual property theft was the Chinese J-11B fighter jet, which showed a striking resemblance to the Russian Sukhoi Su-27. Russian policy makers understood the risks of such PRC reverse engineering of Russian defense technologies, which could diminish future PLA purchases of Russian weapons and eventually make Chinese firms more competitive against Russian sellers in international buyers.[5] Moscow therefore demanded that the PRC sign more rigorous intellectual property protection agreements and purchase sufficient weapons system to ensure that Russian sellers make a profit even if the PRC were to misappropriate the Russian technologies for its own substitute production. Unspoken Russian fears about aiding China's growing military power might also have contributed to the slowdown in Sino-Russian defense industrial collaboration.

Though initially reluctant since China's military-industrial sector had been improving so rapidly, the rising tensions with Washington in the past few years made the acquisition of Russia's cutting-edge weapons systems more urgent for Beijing. PRC leaders concluded that it was imprudent to wait several more years for equally advanced indigenously manufactured systems to enter service with the PLA. Furthermore, China no longer had access to advanced weapons technologies from other countries. Even Ukraine, the source of much of China's former Soviet defense technologies in the 1990s and 2000s, had curtailed such exports to the PRC due to U.S. pressure. Russia's latest defense technologies have been manufactured domestically, giving Moscow a monopoly decision on military export. PRC technicians had also proven unable to copy some advanced Russian defense technologies, such as Russia's top-line warplane engines. Despite decades of effort, the PRC defense sector has failed to manufacture a high-precision fighter engine capable of providing enormous power and maneuverability for complex aerial combat maneuvers. Consequently, since 2012, China has bought hundreds of advanced Russian engines to power the most sophisticated PRC fighter planes.[6] Meanwhile, the collapse of Russian-U.S. defense ties after 2014, which saw France and other NATO states cancel planned arms sales to Russia, likewise motivated Moscow to pursue more military technological cooperation with the PRC.

RUSSIAN-CHINESE INTERACTIONS

Though the value of this defense industrial cooperation has declined as a share of overall Sino-Russian economic cooperation in the past two decades, the Russian arms transfers to China have been mutually advantageous in many ways. Along with other defense collaboration between Russia and China, the sales have provided the foundation for a closer Sino-Russian security alignment against the United States and its allies. For instance, the weapons sales have increased Sino-Russian defense interoperability and facilitated more advanced joint exercises. Along with these imports, the PLA has also undertaken extensive modernization and reform initiatives. With its high spending, the PLA continues to replace Soviet-era weapon systems with modern equipment, including more advanced drones and attack helicopters for the army; larger blue-water combat vessels, including aircraft carriers, for the PLA Navy (PLAN); and more numerous and sophisticated planes for the PLAAF. Each PLA service has acquired improved Command, Control, Communications, Computers, Intelligence, Surveillance, and Reconnaissance (C4ISR) support. Comprehensive military reforms have included personnel cuts, organizational restructuring, and other measures to enhance effectiveness and optimize resources.[7] In late December 2015, the PRC established a People's Liberation Army Rocket Force (PLARF), a Strategic Support Force (SSF), a Joint Logistics

Support Force, and a separate PLA Army General Command headquarters. The Chinese Communist Party (CCP) has also tightened its control over the armed forces through various measures, such as reorganizing the Central Military Commission. The PLARF, which replaced the former Second Artillery Corps, centralizes all conventional and nuclear missile operations into one independent branch, playing a major role in implementing China's A2/AD, deterrence, and coercion strategies. This consolidation differs from the Soviet/Russian practice of only grouping long-range nuclear missiles into the Soviet/Russian Strategic Rocket Forces, or the U.S. approach of delegating shared operational control of nuclear platforms between the air force and the navy. Such measures of PRC military reforms have made the PLA more reliable, interoperable, and effective.

Furthermore, Russian and Chinese military planners have been pursuing asymmetrical approaches and systems to negate U.S. technological strengths as well as exploit U.S. defense vulnerabilities. These capabilities include cyber weapons, counterspace systems, and other instruments of deterrence, defense, and disruption. Russian and Chinese analysts perceive the U.S. reliance on information technology and space-based C4ISR systems, whose disruption could degrade defense capabilities, as potential vulnerabilities. By impeding these systems and constructing formidable A2/AD networks, Russia and China aim to deter, disrupt, and defeat the U.S. military. Both countries are also expanding their naval capacities. Russia plans to resume building larger capital ships and aircraft carriers and further develop maritime strike capabilities based on an array of antiship and antiair missiles. The latest Russian naval doctrine highlights the necessity of deterring and defending against foreign adversaries, protecting Russia's maritime resources and trade routes, controlling sea-lanes of communication, and pursuing naval engagement operations with friendly states like China.[8] The PLAN is modernizing and replacing older ships to deter and defeat U.S. military intervention, advance Beijing's claims to the South and East China Seas, secure commercial maritime lines of communication, and maintain an expansive maritime presence. The PLAAF is acquiring more advanced air superiority planes and longer-range strategic bombers. The PLA is also investing heavily in quantum communications, artificial intelligence, battle robots, and other next-generation military capabilities. Despite many similarities, differences persist between the Russian and Chinese armed services.

In an October 2019 presentation, Putin revealed that "we are now helping our Chinese partners create a missile attack warning system." He claimed that the new collaboration "will drastically increase China's defense capability," observing that only the Russian and U.S. armed forces have until now possessed early warning networks for detecting global missile launches.[9] Russian experts described the aid as primarily defensive, aiming to enhance PRC incentives to adopt early-launch policies and thereby decrease danger of inadvertent or deliberate nuclear war.[10] By improving the PRC's early warning capabilities, Russia is also enhancing China's ability to negate U.S. counterforce damage-limitation capabilities in a conflict. Another effect of Russia's helping China develop a more effective missile early-warning capacity is that it might facilitate the PLA's adopting a launch-on-warning posture in which some Chinese systems might begin to deliver their nuclear warheads to their targets upon detection of incoming foreign missiles. The head of the U.S. Strategic Command warned of the dangers of China's adopting such a posture "considering the immature nature of Chinese strategic forces and compressed timelines needed to assess and frame a response, increasing the potential for error and miscalculation."[11]

Russian arms sellers still worry that skillful PRC engineers might harvest the defense technologies sold to China and apply such knowledge to improve PRC-manufactured systems. Blatant cases of such renewed Chinese reverse engineering could lead Moscow to tighten export curbs on Russian defense technologies in an effort to counter such knockoff production. Russian suppliers have been confident that their most sophisticated weapons are so advanced that Chinese researchers would find it extremely difficult to reverse engineer such systems. This has indeed been proven in the case of the most advanced airplane engines. Nonetheless, the Pentagon has assessed that PRC technicians might manage to harvest important technologies from the PLA's newly acquired S-400s.[12] Not only would such Chinese misappropriation further reduce PRC demand for Russian-made systems but Chinese defense firms could also attempt to sell the PRC-made variants in third-party arms markets, especially those of developing countries that have predominantly relied on Soviet or Russian arms. For instance, in 2016, the Russian government had expected the Royal Thai Army to order Russian T-90 main battle tanks, but the Thai government opted for China's cheaper MBT-3000 tanks instead.[13] Whereas in the past the PRC sold only a limited type of weapons to only a few countries, the PRC's share of the global arms market has continually grown in recent years as the Chinese defense industry increasingly manufactures a wide range of sophisticated technologies that had previously been available only from Russian or Western sources. According to some estimates, having moved up the defense industrial value chain, China now sells more weapons by value than Russia. The continual modernization of the PLA will probably also result in the phase-out of large volumes of less advanced weapons; these arms could prove attractive to developing or economically strained countries that cannot afford Western or Russian weapons. In addition to charging lower prices compared to Western and Russian competitors for "good enough" weapons of only slightly lower quality, other advantages of PRC arms have included generous subsidies, loans, and tied aid packages for purchasing countries, as well as weak end-use monitoring requirements on governments that might employ the weapons for purposes unacceptable to Western suppliers. For example, the Chinese government offered a $500 million loan to the Philippines in 2017 to enable the country's armed forces to purchase PRC defense equipment.[14]

One silver lining to China's improving arms export industry for Moscow is that the Russian armed forces could acquire better defense and dual-use components from the PRC, such as information and electronics systems or naval platforms. These PRC imports could allow Moscow to circumvent Western sanctions, acquire technologies compatible with Russian weaponry and subsystems, and reduce PRC concerns about purchasing more Russian complete weapons systems by providing a kind of offset arrangement. The improving Chinese defense industrial sector also increases the potential value to both countries of realizing their plans to jointly research, develop, and market defense products. In theory, it could combine Russia's exceptional defense design bureaus and advanced military technologies with China's massive production and financial resources. The two countries have already made limited progress in this area. In May 2015, Russian Helicopters and the Aviation Industry Corporation of China signed a framework agreement on joint development of the Advanced Heavy Lift helicopter, which would incorporate major components from both companies and could be used for military as well as civilian missions. In August 2020, an official at Russia's Rostec Corporation, a leading arms manufacturer, said that Russia and China were jointly designing a next-generation non-nuclear-powered attack submarine.[15] Future coproduction projects might include transport aircraft, airborne refueling tankers, and a multiple barrel rocket system capable of launching reconnaissance drones.[16] In treating China more as a partner than a client, Moscow could keep Sino-Russian defense industrial cooperation robust even if the PRC ceases to purchase major Russian weapons systems.

Furthermore, given that Western sanctions have blocked Russia from acquiring many military-relevant technologies from European countries (including Ukraine), Moscow might take advantage of the PRC's improving capacity to manufacture advanced electronic circuits, naval vessels, robotic and autonomous systems like military drones, and other defense industries to acquire platforms and technologies that, due to the common Soviet origin, could be compatible with Russian-manufactured weaponry and subsystems. Such a reverse flow of arms sales would render Sino-Russian defense collaboration more balanced by offsetting large-scale PRC weapons imports from Russia. The increasing acquisition of defense technologies from China's growing military-industrial complex by Russia would also undermine the efficacy of U.S. sanctions against the Russian defense sector. Another challenge presented by China's growing defense industrial capabilities could be the difficulty in enforcing U.S.-Russian joint arms embargoes; even if Washington and Moscow agree to refrain from selling certain advanced weaponry to particular countries, the affected states could now appeal to the PRC to break such embargoes. Moreover, Russia's and China's growing military power, enhanced by Sino-Russian defense partnership, may have contributed to both countries' more assertive foreign policies in recent years. Russian and PRC policy makers might presume that the two countries' enhanced capabilities and security ties could weaken the credibility of Washington's defense guarantees to U.S. friends and allies.

IMPLICATIONS AND RECOMMENDATIONS

Until recently, Russian and Chinese representatives had routinely denied that the two countries' cooperation was directed against the United States or any other country. However, when General Wei Fenghe, China's new defense minister, visited Moscow in April 2018, he explicitly stated that his Russian trip aimed at alerting Washington and others to the growing closeness of Sino-Russian military ties.[17] Even before this acknowledgment, Russian and Chinese representatives undoubtedly appreciated that the two countries' high-profile defense industrial cooperation and military exercises communicated deterrence signals to the United States and other countries. The wide-ranging ties between Beijing and Moscow have challenged important U.S. national security interests and made both Russia and China more formidable rivals against the United States. As noted, Moscow has assisted Beijing in circumventing Western arms embargoes by transferring to the PLA some of Russia's most sophisticated air, naval, and missile technologies. Russia's augmentation of PLA capabilities has enhanced Beijing's capacity to coerce and threaten many countries, ranging from U.S. allies like Japan and Taiwan to important security partners such as India. In particular, the transferred Russian systems have enhanced China's power projection and A2/AD capabilities in multiple ways, eroding U.S. military advantages.

With new equipment and growing capabilities, Russia and China have improved their abilities to defend homelands, pursue counter-intervention operations against U.S. forward-deployed forces, project power in various regional security contingencies, and challenge long-standing U.S. conventional and nuclear military advantages. Both Russian and PRC defense establishments have undertaken comprehensive reforms to reduce the size, increase the readiness, improve the administrative efficiency, strengthen civilian control, tighten interservice coordination, and raise the combat effectiveness of their militaries. Their modernized command-and-control structures can better direct operations across military districts and services. Their most recent restructuring efforts have resembled the more comprehensive reforms the U.S. Defense Department undertook during the 1980s. Over the past decade, Russia and

China have also shown skills in using coercive sub-conventional instruments of power in gray-zone conflict areas to create "facts on the ground" in territorial disputes such as Moscow's seizure of Crimea and Beijing's island-building campaign in the South China Sea, in low-intensity aggression that remains below the level of coercion that would trigger a major military response.

In their arms sales to the PRC, Russia has deliberately aimed to enhance the PLA's ability to fight a war with the U.S. military and its East Asian allies. For instance, the weapons acquired from Russia have also strengthened the PLA's ability to conduct long-range precision strikes against U.S. forces and bases throughout the Indo-Pacific region, empowering PRC policy makers to challenge Pentagon practices that Beijing has long opposed, such as the U.S. Navy's Freedom of Navigation operations. These operations have drawn Russian protests whenever they occur in the Black Sea and PRC denunciations when they take place in the South China Sea. Thanks to Russian technology transfers, the PLAN has achieved a considerable boost in antiship and antiair missiles, long-range sensors, and other anti-submarine, anti-surface, air defense, and precision-strike capabilities.[18] Such enhancements have rendered China's fleet less dependent on land-based air defense systems and allowed it to operate at greater distances from shore. Equipped with improved radars and having a longer strike range, the S-400s Russia provided the PLA brought a significant upgrade to China's air defenses. Additionally, China's 2015 purchase of the Su-35s has complemented the S-400s by enabling the PLAAF to sustain a military presence at greater distances from the Chinese mainland, including throughout the East and South China Seas. The planes have also made it increasingly difficult for the U.S. military to achieve air superiority in conflicts near China. By boosting the PLAN's ability to conduct long-range precision strikes against U.S. warships, the transferred Russian weapons have challenged the preferred U.S. strategy of operating safely from ocean sanctuaries by impeding access to the waters and airspace in China's vicinity. Such military capabilities could also be used to prevent U.S. naval and air forces from entering the Korean Peninsula and to keep U.S. ground forces from approaching the Sino-Korean border in Korean unification scenarios. In essence, by strengthening the PLA, the Russian arms sales could have weakened U.S. deterrence against potential PLA aggression.

U.S. national security advisers will need to devote more resources to follow these Sino-Russian weapons transfers and defense industrial collaboration. Due to Western sanctions and other concerns, Russia and China have become less public about their military-technology collaboration. In recent cases, we have only learned of some Russian initiatives because Putin decided to announce them to foreign audiences. Furthermore, the United States must maintain defensive technological advantages over Russia and China in emerging military technologies, such as artificial intelligence, quantum computing, and robotics. The United States must also tend more to the long-term health of its foreign military partnerships, which present a substantial bulwark to Russian and Chinese military power. The 2018 U.S. National Defense Strategy notes that "[m]utually beneficial alliances and partnerships are crucial to our strategy, providing a durable, asymmetric strategic advantage that no competitor or rival can match."[19] Russia and China have both understood the importance of military alliances for the United States and have therefore attempted to weaken them. Beyond enhancing collective defense capabilities with key foreign partners, the United States should expand dialogues with them to limit the potential transfer of dual-use capabilities to Russia and China. Western defense sanctions should be designed to deny Moscow and Beijing military technologies that they cannot obtain from each other to avoid counterproductively strengthening the two countries' defense industrial ties by facilitating military transactions between them. Meanwhile, the United States and its allies need to more effectively discourage partners from purchasing Russian or Chinese weapons. For instance, the United States should undertake a critical assessment of the Countering America's Adversaries through Sanctions Act (CAATSA) enacted in mid-2017, which mandates sanctions on people, companies, and organizations that engage in "significant transactions" with Russia's defense and intelligence sectors. Although intended to dissuade states from buying Russian arms, the imposition of such sanctions in some cases, as with Turkey and India, has failed. The recent efforts to avert Turkish and Indian purchases of the S-400 have proven noticeably unsuccessful. In addition to imposing sanctions and signaling threats, Western governments should offer trade agreements, greater technology transfer, and other positive inducements to incentivize the targeted states to buy Western weapons. In some circumstances, the United States will need to make offsetting purchases or larger loans to match Russian and Chinese competition. The allies also should consider measures to address potential interoperability gaps due to the more rapid acquisition of the United States of strategic emerging technologies such as hypersonic delivery systems and long-range missile defense systems.

8

Chapter   **Arms Control**

Russia, China, and the United States are strengthening their nuclear forces and expanding their nuclear delivery systems. The renewed great power competition involving Russia, China, and the United States has substantially complicated negotiating and ratifying binding arms-control agreements among the world's most powerful countries. So have novel emerging technologies, mutual accusations of cheating, Russian and U.S. withdrawals from existing security agreements, disagreements over what weapons to limit and how to do so, and the proliferation of these capabilities to additional countries. Though the leaders of Russia, China, and the United States affirm that negotiated restraints on arms buildups can enhance stability, decrease risks, and reduce financial costs, the prospects for major arms control agreements during the next decade look bleak. Cooperation among Moscow, Beijing, and Washington on preventing the spread of nuclear arms and other weapons of mass destruction (WMD) to additional countries or nonstate actors persists, but this collaboration is also under threat due to the diverging goals and policies of the three great powers.

RUSSIAN GOALS AND POLICIES

The Russian government considers the maintenance of a powerful nuclear arsenal a national security priority. Russian planners measure the adequacy of their nuclear forces in potential scenarios involving the worst combinations of nuclear threats, such as having to fight a war against not only the United States and its allies but also China. Recent years have seen Moscow's political and military leaders elevate the prominence of their nuclear arsenal in rhetoric and actions. Specifically, they have repeatedly asserted their capacity and willingness to use nuclear weapons, conducted no-notice snap military exercises involving nuclear forces, increased strategic patrols with nuclear-capable bombers and submarines, and comprehensively upgraded Russia's strategic capabilities with additional nuclear delivery vehicles and enhanced supporting infrastructure. Russia currently has more than 4,000 nuclear warheads on its nuclear triad of long-range land-based intercontinental ballistic missiles (ICBMs), ballistic missile–launching submarines, and long-range heavy bombers. The country is developing and deploying new strategic missiles, such as the RS-24 Yars (NATO designation SS-27 Mod 2) ICBM, the RS-28 Sarmat (NATO: SS-X-30) heavy-liquid fueled ICBM, and a mobile solid-fuel RS-26 Rubezh (NATO: SS-X-31) system. Russia is also upgrading its Tupolev Tu-160 (NATO: Blackjack) strategic bomber, which carries nuclear-armed gravity bombs or long-range nuclear air-launched cruise missiles (ALCMs). Russia has also pursued more exotic long-range delivery systems, such as nuclear-powered cruise missiles, air-launched ballistic missiles that can fly at hypersonic speeds, and other novel weaponry poorly addressed by existing missile control agreements and have proven accident-prone under development and could prove destabilizing if deployed.[1]

Russian-U.S. arms control initiatives have made minimal progress since Moscow and Washington adopted the New START accord. Signed in April 2010, the treaty forced reductions in the Russian and U.S. strategic nuclear forces capable of delivering nuclear strikes at distances over 5,500 kilometers to totals of 800 deployed and nondeployed ICBMs and submarine-launched ballistic missiles (SLBMs), in each arsenal, with 1,550 "accountable" warheads as defined by the treaty's counting rules.[2] The treaty provides for extensive mandatory inspections, data exchanges, and other verification measures. Though Moscow and Washington agreed in early 2021 to extend New START by five years, the Obama administration had seen New START as a foundation for achieving substantially deeper cuts in nuclear arsenals. The Russian government rejected U.S proposals toward this end. Instead, Moscow sought to focus negotiations on limiting U.S. missile defenses and space defense programs. Moscow also wanted additional countries to engage in strategic arms negotiations, transforming what has been a largely bilateral process into a multilateral framework. Following Moscow's 2014 annexation of Crimea and intervention in eastern Ukraine, the U.S. government, especially Congress, imposed more restrictions on nuclear security collaboration with Russia. In 2019, Washington withdrew from "The Treaty between the United States of America and the Union of Soviet Socialist Republics on the Elimination of Their Intermediate-Range and Shorter-Range Missiles" (aka the "Intermediate-Range Nuclear Forces Treaty," or INF Treaty). This treaty had banned Soviet (and later Russian) and U.S. ground-launched missiles having ranges between 500 and 5,500 kilometers. Moscow and Washington had accused each other of violating this treaty.

The Russian government has also claimed that NATO's nuclear-sharing mechanism (through which the United States stores a limited number of nuclear bombs on the territory of select European countries) violates the Nuclear Non-Proliferation Treaty (NPT), which prohibits the transferring of nuclear weapons to other countries. The NPT, which entered into force in 1970, balances the goals of averting the further spread of nuclear weapons, promoting the peaceful application of nuclear energy, and eventual nuclear disarmament. The NPT recognizes five states as "authorized" nuclear-weapons states (NWS)—Russia, China, France, the United Kingdom, and the United States—as they developed their nuclear weapons prior to 1967. While NWS are not permitted to assist other countries to obtain such weapons, India, Pakistan, and North Korea acquired their nuclear weapons illegally after the NPT came into effect. Russia's strategic location between Europe and Asia allows its armed forces to deploy all its several thousand nuclear bombs on Russian soil. However, some U.S. nuclear weapons are stored on territory of several North Atlantic Treaty Organization (NATO) countries. Russians feel marginalized by Europe's NATO-dominated security architecture and have been trying to reduce NATO's current preeminent role in European security by limiting alliance membership enlargement, nuclear-sharing arrangements, and military activities in those East Central European countries that had been part of Moscow's former Soviet-led bloc but have since joined NATO.

In October 2016, moreover, Moscow suspended implementation of the Plutonium Management and Disposition Agreement (PMDA) with the United States to convert weapons-grade plutonium into nuclear fuel. The deal was first negotiated in 2000 and obligated both countries to dispose of a minimum of 34 tons of weapons-grade plutonium by irradiating the plutonium to produce so-called mixed oxide (MOX) fuel, which can be used in nuclear power plants, or immobilizing the material by imposing various radiological, chemical, and physical barriers. These, however, proved to be expensive processes for both countries. The United States unilaterally changed its elimination method from destroying the MOX to an alternative method of diluting and burying the plutonium. Moscow opposed this path, arguing that the Pentagon could later retrieve the weapons-grade material for military purposes. The Russian-U.S. divergences over the PMDA also reflected the different priorities of the two governments. The United States has been more concerned about proliferation to nonstate actors, for which the dilute and bury method would be effective, while the Russian government has been more concerned about a state actor (the United States) weaponizing the material and thus has insisted on more irreversible elimination.

Russian-U.S. differences over missile defenses have been long-standing. On May 26, 1972, the United States and the Soviet Union signed the Treaty on the Limitation of Anti-Ballistic Missile Systems, commonly known as the

Anti-Ballistic Missile (ABM) Treaty, which limited each country to two ABM sites (reduced to one after a 1974 protocol). In late 2001, however, President George Bush formally notified Russia that the United States would withdraw from the treaty following a legally mandated six months' delay. Since the Cold War, U.S. officials have affirmed that U.S. ballistic missile defense (BMD) capabilities have focused on countering threats from emerging nuclear powers like North Korea rather than the much larger and more sophisticated nuclear arsenals of Russia and China, which U.S. officials argue can overwhelm any conceivable defenses. The 2019 Missile Defense Review again states that U.S. missile defenses aim to protect the U.S. homeland from Iranian and Democratic People's Republic of Korea (DPRK) missile threats rather than Russian or Chinese nuclear forces. To parry nuclear threats from Russia and China, the Review affirms that the United States will rely on mutual deterrence—that neither country would dare to attack the United States with nuclear weapons since they are vulnerable to U.S. nuclear retaliation, creating a balance of terror through mutual assured destruction. Even so, Russian officials have demanded that the United States sign a binding legal agreement that would restrict the numbers, locations, and capabilities of its missile interceptors. Russian officials have been denouncing U.S. BMD programs for decades, claiming that the Pentagon has been pursuing the capacity to negate Russia's nuclear forces under the pretext of building defenses against other countries. They recognize that the U.S. missile defenses in Alaska and California cannot negate their enormous missile arsenals; they profess to fear that the United States could achieve a revolutionary breakthrough that could render the U.S. homeland considerably less vulnerable to Russia's nuclear deterrent. The U.S. government refuses to sign a treaty limiting its missile defenses since it could impede the capacity of the United States to defend itself and U.S. allies and partners from other countries' missile threats. In the late 2000s, Russian and U.S. officials engaged in extensive discussions on various cooperative projects and transparency and confidence-building measures (TCBMs) that NATO officials hoped could overcome Russian concerns while still permitting the United States and its allies to establish defenses against potential Iranian missiles threats to Europe. At one point, Russian officials were offering NATO permission to use a Russian BMD radar base in Azerbaijan, while NATO leaders were proposing a joint Russian-NATO missile shield to cover the Northern Hemisphere, but these efforts at compromise could never overcome the political and technological differences among the parties.

CHINESE GOALS AND POLICIES

Instead of matching the larger Russian and U.S. nuclear arsenals, China has traditionally prioritized improving its nonnuclear forces such as its naval and cyber capabilities. A PRC priority has been to expand and improve its ballistic and cruise missiles, some of which can carry nuclear warheads. The PRC sees these missiles as critical for deterring Taiwan's independence, driving U.S. forces away from China's naval regions and air space, and intimidating other countries, such as Japan, India, and South Korea. Until recently, the PRC nuclear modernization program has focused on improving the quality, rather than the quantity, of its arsenal, but China's warhead and missile arsenals continue to grow. The PLA's qualitative priorities have included enhancing the survivability of the force by replacing older, liquid-fueled ballistic missiles with solid-fueled missiles that are easier to store, move, and launch. Unique among the established NWS, the PRC has built a massive tunnel system, extending thousands of miles long and hundreds of meters deep, where it stores warheads, missiles, and other components of its nuclear deterrent. Beijing's tunnel-building and other nuclear opaqueness regarding its capabilities and employment practices have led to a vigorous Western debate regarding Beijing's nuclear intentions.

For years, many foreign observers believed that the PRC only sought a "minimum deterrence" of several hundred warheads that the PLA considers sufficient to survive any U.S. attack and inflict a devastating retaliatory blow on the United States.[3] Yet, the Pentagon has recently revised upward its estimate of Chinese nuclear weapons arsenal in the next decade. Speaking at the July 2020 Nuclear Deterrence Forum, Navy Admiral Charles A. Richard stated that "China is on a trajectory to be a strategic peer to us by the end of the decade. So for the first time ever, the U.S. is going to face two peer-capable nuclear competitors."[4] The PLA has obtained an impressive portfolio of advanced missile systems in recent years, which can carry nuclear as well as conventional warheads. It now fields more ground-launched missiles in the 500–5,500-km range than any other country, some 2,000 ballistic and cruise missiles capable of delivering conventional or nuclear warheads against ground, ship, and air targets from Chinese land, sea, air, and sub-surface launching platforms. The PLA's most important missiles include the single-warhead Dong Feng (DF)-31AG ICBM and the DF-41 three-stage solid-propellant ICBM. The latter is able to move on roads, unlike earlier silo-based, liquid-fuel missiles, which are more vulnerable to preemptive attacks. The DF-17 INF-1,500-km-range hypersonic glide vehicle (HGV) is carried aloft on a booster rocket into the upper atmosphere, where it separates and descends in unpredictable maneuvers toward the earth, which could potentially circumvent standard missile defenses. Moreover, the PLA's new strategic submarines and bombers are giving the PRC a genuine nuclear delivery triad for the first time in its history. The PLA Navy has also focused on deploying more advanced strategic submarines that, even when patrolling near home waters, can launch ballistic missiles with a range as far as the United States. The navy seems to have finally developed an effective intercontinental-range SLBM in its single-warhead Ju Lang-2 (JL-2), launched from China's Jin-class (Type 094A nuclear submarines) SSBNs. The PLA is also aiming to acquire its first long-range strategic bomber for launching air-to-surface ballistic missiles (against land or naval targets), the H-6Ns. Additionally, China has developed the intermediate-range DF-21D ballistic missile specifically to attack U.S. aircraft carriers. In 2021, open-source researchers found evidence that the PLA was constructing hundreds of additional missile silos in western China, suggesting that the PRC aimed to substantially increase its nuclear arsenal in coming years.[5]

Unlike the United States and Russia, the PRC government has stubbornly resisted negotiating binding constraints on their missile capabilities, even though many PLA missiles are dual-capable and can deliver China's growing number of nuclear warheads. The PRC's conventional ballistic and cruise missiles underpin the PLA's challenge to U.S. military primacy in the Indo-Pacific region. Among other goals, the growing PLA missile capabilities aim to weaken the credibility of U.S. security guarantees to allies and partners. Not only do these capabilities augment the PLA's potential to attack U.S. and allied forces preemptively but they also strengthen China's counter-intervention capabilities designed to negate U.S. power projection against PRC forces or territory.[6] The missiles can strike U.S. forces and bases throughout the Indo-Pacific area, sowing doubts among U.S. allies about the U.S. ability to intervene on their behalf in a regional conflict. The PLA has brandished these missiles through ostentatious testing in tense times. China's growing missile and nuclear threats could complicate U.S. military planning, reduce strategic predictability, decrease crisis stability by amplifying PRC preemption incentives, and weaken restraints on missile and possibly nuclear proliferation in Asia and beyond.

Though the PRC has refused to negotiate treaties with the United States that would limit its nuclear or missile capabilities, Beijing and Washington have cooperated on some nonproliferation issues, such as countering nuclear smuggling, reducing the risk of proliferation from nuclear reactors, and decreasing the availability of weapons-grade nuclear materials. Experts from the two governments have collaborated to convert some reactors in Africa to use low enriched uranium (LEU) rather than highly enriched uranium (HEU); the latter is easier to make into the fissile material needed for nuclear warheads. China and the United States also collaborate against nuclear terrorism and hold annual dialogues on nuclear security regarding civilian nuclear energy and research (mutual suspicions prevent cooperation on securing their nuclear materials). In 2016, the two governments launched a Center of Excellence of Nuclear Security in Beijing to train Chinese and foreign (primarily other Asian) personnel in best security practices, promote technological demonstration projects, and enhance collaboration with the International Atomic

Energy Agency (IAEA). Cooperation regarding the control of nuclear exports is less developed. Like the United States, China has joined the Nuclear Supplier Group (NSG) and the Zangger Committee, but it has yet to enter such important export-control regimes as the Wassenaar Arrangement or the Missile Technology Control Regime (MTCR). The PRC government is currently blocking India's entry into the NSG, expressing concern about New Delhi's unwillingness to join the NPT. However, Chinese objections appear more rooted in its general policy of limiting rival India's international status rather than in Beijing's aiming to contribute toward international nonproliferation.

RUSSIAN-CHINESE INTERACTIONS

Russian and Chinese representatives have coordinated their arms control stances on several issues. For example, when Moscow published its new nuclear deterrent doctrine in 2020, PRC Foreign Ministry spokesperson Zhao Lijian said, "China respects and understands Russia's efforts to safeguard national security interests."[7] Meanwhile, both governments have consistently objected to U.S. nuclear policies. They have denounced sanctions on Russian and PRC nationals and entities charged with abetting nuclear proliferation. The 2016 "Foreign Policy Concept of the Russian Federation" states, "Russia does not recognize the U.S. policy of extraterritorial jurisdiction beyond the boundaries of international law and finds unacceptable attempts to exercise military, political, economic or any other pressure, while reserving the right to firmly respond to hostile actions, including the bolstering of national defense and taking retaliatory or asymmetrical measures."[8] Whereas U.S. arms controllers want to constrain all three countries' nuclear weapons, China and especially Russia prioritize limiting U.S. conventional force capabilities, especially those applying novel strategic technologies.

Another area of trilateral friction is that, unlike Russia and China, only the United States offers extended security guarantees to other countries. These are unilateral pledges to defend U.S. allies with nuclear weapons if necessary. U.S. officials argue that these guarantees discourage nuclear proliferation since, when the United States credibly offers to protect another country with U.S. nuclear weapons, the other state does not need its own nuclear forces. In recent years, Moscow's and Beijing's hostility toward these U.S. nuclear alliances has grown. As noted, Russian officials describe NATO's nuclear-sharing arrangements—in which the United States deploys tactical nuclear bombs in select NATO countries with the declared intent of allowing these nations to take command of them in a war or crisis—as violating the NPT.[9] Although Russia pledges to defend its Collective Security Treaty Organization allies, implicitly with nuclear weapons, the Russian armed forces do not station nuclear weapons outside the territory of the Russian Federation. The draft security treaties that Moscow presented to NATO and the United States in December would require that NATO end its nuclear sharing program, that the United States withdraw all its nuclear weapons from Europe, and that the allies eliminate the infrastructure that could allow the rapid return of these weapons to Europe in a crisis. PRC officials also fault U.S. policy and note that the PLA does not place Chinese nuclear weapons in other countries. Yet, the PRC, unlike the Russian government, does not offer to defend other states with China's nuclear arsenal (or any other forces since China, again unlike Russia, does not have formal military allies or offer other states military security guarantees).

Similarly, Russian and Chinese strategists have long shared a mutual distaste for U.S. BMD systems, which they fear could undermine the viability of their missile deterrents against the United States. No existing treaty explicitly limits how many BMD systems the United States can develop and deploy. Washington has repeatedly rejected Russian demands to sign a new binding legal document specifying what the United States can and cannot do in the missile defense domain. Russian and Chinese representatives argue that the U.S. missile defense efforts could become so effective as to call into question their ability to retaliate after a U.S. first strike, could expand U.S.-led nuclear alliances that threaten their security, and could disrupt global and regional stability by reducing constraints on U.S. foreign military interventions. Until recently, Russian and Chinese BMD-related concerns were oriented toward different U.S. missile defenses. Russian analysts have long complained about U.S. BMD systems in Europe, whereas PRC concerns had focused on U.S. programs in Asia. Yet, this past decade has seen a growing harmonization in Russian and Chinese opposition to all U.S. missile defenses, in any region of the world. Not only do both Russian and Chinese officials denounce U.S. missile defenses in Japan and South Korea as well as in North America but PRC representatives now also support Moscow's position that U.S. BMD systems in Europe threaten global security. They see U.S. missile defense initiatives in Europe and Asia as designed to strengthen U.S.-led alliances intended to contain Russia and China generally as well as undermine their regional missile fleets.

Russian and Chinese officials regularly claim that the United States and its allies do not need defenses against Iranian and North Korean missile threats and that Washington is merely using these threats as a pretext to build defenses against Russian and Chinese missiles to gain strategic advantage. They argue that the best way to dampen any Iranian and DPRK nuclear weapons ambitions is through dialogue, negotiations, and reassurance rather than military buildups and threats. They express concern about U.S. defense experts' interest in constructing a more advanced BMD architecture that would counter emerging cruise and hypersonic missile threats through more comprehensive space-based surveillance and developing means of intercepting ICBMs sooner after launch, especially in their boost phase before they can deploy decoys and other penetration aides. (The technological and financial barriers to pursuing these options have so far proven insurmountable.) In the past few years, Moscow and Beijing have undertaken unprecedented bilateral counter-BMD exercises, discussed the establishment of a joint BMD program, curtailed security ties with South Korea to pressure Seoul not to deploy U.S. missile defenses, and pursued, albeit separately, offensive strategic technologies to overcome any missile shield. These include multiple independently targetable reentry vehicles, cyber strike weapons, and hypersonic delivery systems that could circumvent existing missile defenses.

A new Sino-Russian concern has focused on how the end of the INF Treaty could allow for the deployment of additional U.S. missiles in Europe and Asia. Since China had never signed the treaty, it had escaped the INF Treaty ban, whereas NATO governments believe that the Russian government went ahead and developed its own INF-range missile in violation of the treaty. Since withdrawing from the accord, the United States has resumed researching and developing land-based INF-range missiles, including a ground-launched version of the Tomahawk cruise missile, a new longer-range ballistic missile, and a proposed precision-strike missile stationed on a mobile launching platform. All these missiles would be armed with nonnuclear warheads. Russian and Chinese leaders have alleged that the United States invented specious Russian violations of the treaty as a pretext to leave the treaty and restart its own missile development program.

Despite their harmonious stance on many arms control issues, there are major differences between Russian and Chinese policies in this domain. For instance, only Russian officials have taken the extreme stance of threatening other countries that host U.S. BMD systems, claiming that such deployments would make them a prospective target for Russian attack in a conflict. Unlike Moscow or Washington, Beijing has offered a comprehensive no-first-use pledge to all countries and has called on Russia, the United States, and other nuclear-weapons-possessing states to follow China's example. This pledge includes a no-nuclear-first-use doctrine and negative nuclear security assurances (i.e., pledging not to employ nuclear weapons against other countries unless they first used nuclear weapons against China), though such a declarative policy is unenforceable, reversible, and vulnerable to changes in the strategic environment. Unlike Russia but like the United States, the PRC has not ratified the Comprehensive Test Ban Treaty, though all three countries have stopped testing fissile detonations. The Russian and Chinese governments also differ on the "multilateralization" of existing treaties like INF and New START. While Moscow and Washington have negotiated such arms control and reduction treaties for decades, Beijing has refrained from joining any formal strategic arms reduction treaties, arguing that Russia and the United States have to

cut their nuclear forces substantially first before China would consider negotiating limits on the PLA's nuclear forces. In contrast, the Russian government
has advocated that future strategic arms control treaties encompass additional
countries besides Russia and the United States—which would include China
as well as Britain, France, and possibly other states. Until recently, some Russian analysts argued that Western analysts underestimated the potential size
of the PLA's nuclear arsenal. Russian strategists likely plan to employ nuclear
weapons if the PLA directly attacked Russian territory.

IMPLICATIONS AND RECOMMENDATIONS

The U.S. national security community is struggling with how to manage
the growing nuclear arsenals of Russia and China. On the one hand, the United
States is maintaining its own strong nuclear deterrent and developing the next
generation of U.S. nuclear forces. This modernization has encompassed a
new Ground Based Strategic Deterrent ICBM, new penetrating B-21 Raider
strategic bombers, and a new Columbia-class strategic missile-launching
submarine. The United States is also upgrading its Command, Control, Communications, Computers, Intelligence, Surveillance, and Reconnaissance
(C4ISR) systems. Concurrently, the United States is searching for ways to
employ advancements in nonnuclear military technologies to generate additional capabilities to deter Moscow and Beijing, who might have a higher stake
in winning wars along their borders than the United States. Russian and Chinese leaders might calculate that they could employ conventional aggression
combined with threats of nuclear retaliation to compel the United States to
back down in a regional war rather than escalate to try to reverse the defeat.
The challenge of extended deterrence—pledging to use U.S. nuclear weapons
to defend other countries even at the risk of being attacked by the aggressor's
nuclear forces—has driven U.S. policy makers to develop concepts for strong
nonnuclear deterrence as well as for multi-domain operations that would
buttress nuclear weapons with conventional and other tools of power. The
Defense Department is now refining the concept of "Integrated Deterrence"
as an overarching conceptual framework for better synthesizing nuclear and
nonnuclear capabilities through enhanced cooperation with non-Department
of Defense (DoD) interagency partners along with allies and partners. The
intent is for Integrated Deterrence to encompass both vertical (across the spec-
trum of conflict) and horizontal (transcending regional and global boundaries) capabilities in conflicts ranging from nuclear crises to major conventional
war to non-kinetic political-military hybrid ("gray-area") actions at lower
conflict levels. The framework combines three approaches toward deterrence:
punishment through assured retaliation, denial of the benefits of aggression,
and entanglement in a rules-based order.

On the other hand, the United States is considering how to modernize arms control to address these novel challenges. The trilateral relationship between Russia, China, and the United States presents a poor climate for international arms control. The adverse conditions include quantitative and qualitative nuclear buildups in all three countries, Russian and U.S. withdrawals from existing agreements combined with the PRC refraining from entering new ones, and intensified great power competition among the three. Existing arms control treaties are fraying as all three countries undertake major nuclear buildups. The Trump administration strived to include China in future arms-control negotiations and address novel strategic weapons as well as nonstrategic nuclear capabilities hitherto excluded from previous Russian-U.S. treaties. Moscow and Beijing resisted. As noted, PRC officials have urged the Russian Federation and the United States to make progress toward nuclear disarmament without committing to reduce the PLA's arsenal. They claim that the PLA's nuclear force is defensive in nature, does not threaten any country, and is substantially smaller than the arsenals of Russia and the United States, with only a minimal nuclear deterrent needed for assured retaliation. Until recently, the United States has not pressed China to join strategic arms treaties, but since 2017, U.S. government has advocated including the PRC in future arms control agreements. The U.S. determination to constrain China's strategic capabilities within an arms-control framework will almost certainly increase if the PRC remains a leading strategic competitor of the United States. U.S. national security documents, including the Nuclear Posture Review and Missile Defense Review, explicitly reference the need to counter the PLA's growing military power. The PRC has developed the economic and technical capacity to quickly increase its nuclear arsenal. China's expanding capabilities have already impeded Russian-U.S. arms control. The failure of the INF Treaty to limit the PLA's massive missile buildup partly explains the loss of Russian, and especially, U.S. interest in sustaining that accord. Most of the PLA's ballistic missiles consist of intermediate-range systems that would have been banned had China been included in the original INF Treaty.

Russian officials had been pressing to include China in strategic arms limitation talks well before the Trump administration adopted the same position. Yet, the Russian government—whether out of an aversion to antagonizing Beijing, an animus for Washington, or, most likely, a combination of both—reversed its previous stance and ceased calling for China's inclusion in future Russian-U.S. strategic nuclear reduction talks even as Beijing's growing military power has weakened U.S. support for arms control measures that limit the Russian armed forces but not those of the PLA. Some Russians accuse Washington, by pressing to include Beijing in arms control agreements, of aiming "to drive a wedge between Russia and China."[10] Yet,

Russians presumably would like to constrain China's nuclear buildup and make the PRC nuclear policies more transparent. Russian nongovernmental experts acknowledge that Moscow would gain little by pressing China to join Russian-U.S. nuclear arms treaties since Beijing would probably reject this pressure and grow irritated at Moscow for siding with Washington on the issue. As with other foreign policy areas, Moscow probably wants Washington to take the lead in pressuring Beijing to constrain its nuclear and missile capabilities, hoping to gain from any Chinese concessions without suffering any degradation in Sino-Russian strategic ties. Perhaps fears regarding the worsening ties with Russia and the United States and alarm at the major Russian and U.S. military buildups and other elevated risks, coupled with China's own growing military power and security, will induce the PRC leadership to reverse its standoffish policy toward strategic arms control. Meanwhile, experts in all three governments should analyze how to incorporate China in strategic arms control in anticipation of a possible end to Beijing's opposition. Developing effective means of verifying trilateral arms control agreements is very important given how mutual accusations of alleged violations led to the weakening of several Russian-U.S. treaties.

The picture is brighter regarding nuclear nonproliferation. Russia, China, and the United States have encouraged universal membership in the NPT, which anchors the global rules and norms against the spread of nuclear weapons. The three countries have presented a united front against the proposed Treaty on the Prohibition of Nuclear Weapons (aka the Nuclear Weapon Ban Treaty), which would oblige them to eliminate all their nuclear weapons immediately. Instead, they favor a "step-by-step" approach toward nuclear weapons reductions, leading to the eventual elimination of their arsenals. They also have cooperated to promote the peaceful use of nuclear power. They provide aid to other countries to make their nuclear energy programs more safe and secure by providing human capital and regulatory infrastructure training. They also collaborate to encourage new proliferation-resistant civil nuclear energy technologies and pursue other multinational technical and scientific cooperation regarding nuclear research and development. Russia, China, and the United States are leading members of many important multinational nonproliferation organizations, such as the IAEA, which encourages the peaceful and safe uses of nuclear technologies while safeguarding their illicit use for nuclear weapons' development programs. All three countries support major nonproliferation export control regimes. Yet, Moscow and Beijing have strongly criticized Washington's withdrawal from the Joint Comprehensive Plan of Action (JCPOA), adopted by Iran and the five permanent members of the UN Security Council and Germany (P5 + 1) in 2015. Although Russia, China, and the United States have imposed comprehensive sanctions on North Korea for violating its nonproliferation commitments, Moscow and Beijing have frequently constrained the severity of these measures adopted by the UN Security Council. Russia and China have instead promoted alternative solutions to the Korean crisis designed to limit U.S. military activities on the Korean Peninsula, such as suspending of U.S.-South Korean military exercises and the non-deployment of U.S. missile defenses in northeast Asia. As discussed in the Korea section of this manuscript, many Russian and Chinese policy makers consider regime change in Pyongyang a greater threat to their interests than the North Korean nuclear and missile programs. Furthermore, the Russian, Chinese, and U.S. governments differ in their policies toward some of the nuclear weapon-free zones (NWFZs) scattered throughout the globe. The treaties establishing a NWFZ typically contain one or more protocols that define special rights and obligations of nonregional states and are open for signature by the five NPT-recognized NWS. One of these protocols usually obligates these NWS to not test or station nuclear weapons within the zone. Another common protocol found in NWFZs requires the NWS to pledge not to attack (or threaten to attack) the parties bound to the treaty with nuclear weapons. Countries join NWFZs in large part to obtain so-called negative security assurances. The PRC is the only NPT-recognized NWS that has signed all existing NWFZ protocols, whereas Moscow and Washington have been more selective in supporting these zones due to various concerns. Perhaps the most contentious one concerns the proposed WMD Free Zone in the Middle East, which all three governments pledged to work toward as part of their NPT-related commitments. At the 2015 NPT Review Conference, however, Moscow and Beijing declined to support Washington in its dispute with Egypt over the conditions needed to induce Israel (a non-NPT member) to embrace the zone. Russia, China, and the United States have also collaborated to counter nuclear terrorism through securing nuclear materials, technologies, and related items. During the past decade, these governments have helped many countries reduce fissile material holdings, ratify international nuclear security conventions, tighten their export controls and border security against WMD trafficking, and strengthen their nuclear security regulations and cultures. Through their joint participation in the Nuclear Security Summits held from 2010 to 2016, they contributed to the elimination of thousands of kilograms of HEU and separated plutonium, reducing the quantity of fissile material potentially available to nonstate actors like terrorists and criminals. The Summits, a U.S.-initiative supported by the Chinese and, at first, the Russian governments helped ensure that the nuclear security issue received the attention of senior global leaders. Yet, recent years have seen diminished Russian-U.S. nuclear security collaboration due to Moscow's boycott of the 2018 Nuclear Security Summit, the suspension of bilateral threat reduction projects, and disagreements over which multilateral institutions should lead further nuclear security efforts in coming years.

Moscow, Beijing, and Washington differ on many important arms control issues. These include Russian and Chinese concerns about U.S. conventional superiority, the U.S. desire to reduce Russia's tactical nuclear weapons, and mutual unease pertaining to each other's emerging artificial intelligence, cyber, space, and other defense capabilities. To address these concerns, nuclear powers could commit to a "grand compromise" of sorts in which they accept that they can achieve their national security goals through strategic equivalence rather than equal force totals across all categories. An asymmetric arms control provision could utilize either unbalanced reductions (as the USSR did when accepting the INF Treaty in 1987) or ceilings under which all parties could flexibly choose which types of forces to deploy. The limits put forth in such a treaty would apply to a larger array of weapon types than in previous treaties, to include nonstrategic tactical nuclear weapons, nondeployed and reserve warheads, space-based weapons, long-range conventionally armed HGVs, and BMDs. Verification regimes could involve extensive on-site inspections in addition to other forms of multinational and national monitoring programs to include nuclear warheads as well as their means of delivery. A comprehensive approach of this kind would extend the previous bilateral Russian-U.S. process to a multilateral format that includes China and perhaps other nuclear states. A less ambitious but more attainable scenario for arms control would be to pursue enhanced strategic stability and decreased risk of kinetic conflict through a patchwork of limited agreements in areas of common interest that would not require ratification of formal treaties or legally binding accords. Rather, they would focus on achieving less formal executive agreements, informal parallel unilateral actions, and strengthening international norms of behavior regarding the use of nuclear weapons. These areas could include decreasing incentives for nuclear escalation through reducing risks of miscalculation, removing first strike vulnerabilities, and other measures to decrease the risk of conflict escalation between great powers. Additional initiatives to voluntarily increase capability transparency and mutual understanding absent formal treaties could include regular strategic stability dialogues aimed at developing concrete measures to address the potential of new weapons or nuclear doctrines to destabilize great power balancing, limiting the proliferation of nuclear and other strategic offensive arms, and identifying and avoiding dangerous operational practices (e.g., deploying nuclear-armed missiles near to foreign nuclear powers). A collapse of strategic arms control would also adversely affect future global nonproliferation regimes, as they would compound existing conflicts and tensions between NWS and nuclear powers as well as place increased pressure on existing NPT restraints. Nuclear force buildups, resumption of nuclear weapons testing, overt threats to employ nuclear weapons against other states (even as a means of deterrence), and greater salience of nuclear weapons posturing in military doctrines would encourage other states to pursue similar capabilities. Conversely, renewed trilateral arms control commitments could increase international support for the NPT regime and steer states away from quixotic proposals (e.g., an immediate nuclear weapons ban). Furthermore, trilateral cooperation on nuclear security remains imperative for addressing existing global gaps. Russia, China, and the United States are well positioned to provide insights and resources to other partners on enhancing the sustainability of national-level frameworks for nuclear security. At the operational level, the three countries should renew and strengthen past efforts to help other countries reduce fissile material holdings; share best practices; fortify border security; strengthen security cultures; tighten export controls and related regulations; enhance and universalize international treaties, conventions, and institutions; and implement key items from the action plans adopted at the spring 2016 governmental, industry, and nongovernmental summits.

9

Chapter   **The Cyber Domain**

Russia, China, and the United States represent the most important nation-state actors in cyberspace; their policies and interactions will substantially determine the domain's future evolution. Russian and People's Republic of China's (PRC) leaders view controlling cyberspace as critical for societal control, economic power, foreign influence, and great-power conflict. They perceive cyber connections and other forms of transnational ties not only as potential threats to their domestic order but also as a cost-effective means to project international influence. The Russian and Chinese governments have been investing in offensive cyber capabilities to collect intelligence, penetrate public and private networks, execute computer network attacks, and if necessary, inflict damage on other states' critical infrastructure. Moscow and Beijing perceive their cyber capabilities as critical asymmetrical tools, along with other non-kinetic instruments, for countering U.S. primacy in both the economic and the military domains. In a war, their armed forces are prepared to disrupt the Pentagon's command, control, and communications networks. In their peacetime declarations and policies, Russian and Chinese officials advocate strong national government control of cyberspace. Their laws and regulations have carved out national cyber spheres in what previously had been a globalized World Wide Web of hyperlinked documents. The two countries' cyber policies are converging in other ways. During this COVID-19 pandemic, Russia and China have mobilized their lavishly funded government information agencies, their extensive portfolio of broadcast and print media, their covert social media networks, their intelligence agencies, hired contractors, and "patriotic" volunteers enthusiastically spouting nationalist narratives on behalf of their strategic messaging. The PRC has taken a page from Russia's playbook by conducting its own disinformation campaigns against the United

States, particularly centered around the pandemic. In Russia, meanwhile, the authorities have been implementing Chinese-style comprehensive internal information control. Instead of relying exclusively on disinformation and intimidation, Russian censors now more often implement fine-grained tools to remove opposing viewpoints from the web. The traditional U.S. preference has been for a largely free internet with minimal government regulation, though more recently, growing global cyber threats have been driving even the United States to bolster the government's offensive and defensive cyber capabilities. Russian and Chinese cyber operations are a major component of their broader "hybrid war" or "gray area" toolkit, which can also involve using elite capture, economic leverage, cyberattacks, intelligence operations, paramilitary proxies, and military maneuvers short of war. As such, information operations—involving media manipulation, sophisticated propaganda, exploitation of ethnic and racial strife, and courting agents of influence in foreign countries—constitute an important element that Moscow and Beijing wield to assert their national interests without resorting to armed conflict. The Obama, Trump, and Biden administrations have devoted a plethora of resources to countering cyber and other hybrid threats from Russia and China, with mixed results, so further efforts will be needed to reduce U.S. vulnerabilities and strengthen cyber deterrence.

RUSSIAN GOALS AND POLICIES

The Russian government's goals in cyberspace include protecting strategically important information and infrastructure, utilizing cyberspace to collect intelligence, shaping international perceptions and information flows, disrupting domestic and foreign opponents, and integrating cyber capabilities and non-kinetic military operations in combat missions.[1] Russian official discourse depicts cyberspace as an incessant battlefield against harmful influence. At home, Russian authorities have adopted new restrictions on domestic internet freedoms. For example, one law punishes those who spread "fake news" or show disrespect toward the Russian state or society or state symbols.[2] Another piece of legislation enhances the government's powers to protect Russia's domestic cyber sphere—the so-called RuNet (i.e., the Russian Internet)—during global internet malfunctions or attacks by external actors.[3] Regarding foreign audiences, Moscow uses cyber-enabled information operations to advance a particular narrative and influence targeted groups. In 2020, the U.S. State Department's Global Engagement Center identified five pillars of Russia's disinformation ecosystem: official government communications, state-funded global messaging, cultivation of proxy sources, weaponizing of social media, and cyber-enabled disinformation. According to the Center, this complex, flexible, and sometimes contradictory toolkit offers Moscow three major advantages. First, the numerous variations of Kremlin's false narratives allow operatives to target different audiences. Second, the complexity and relative decentralization of Moscow's disinformation architecture allow Russian officials to deny criticism and responsibility even as their proxy sites continue to spread dangerous disinformation. Third, the ecosystem amplifies propaganda through a "media multiplier" effect.[4]

In the military domain, the Russian Defense Ministry created a Cyber Command with various offensive and defensive missions. The Russian armed forces have conducted sophisticated cyberattacks in support of kinetic actions, such as disrupting opponents' communications networks prior to and during military operations through electronic warfare (EW), computer network infiltration, psychological manipulation, and disinformation campaigns. Russian tactics have included stealing embarrassing and sensitive data, weaponizing it to discredit targeted individuals or institutions, and promoting social discord to exploit foreign cleavages. The 2018 Department of Defense Cyber Strategy concluded, "Russia has used cyber-enabled information operations to influence our population and challenge our democratic processes."[5] By posing as American activists, Russian military assets spread inflammatory information about movements such as Black Lives Matter and the anti-gun movement in order to expose the ideological cleavages between the American people. By fomenting conflict and mistrust, Russia has tried to prevent the U.S. government from mobilizing U.S. resources in a unified strategy against it. During the 2016 U.S. presidential elections, Russian-linked operators purportedly strategically leaked hacked data to third-party outlets like WikiLeaks at opportune moments to embarrass foes and damage their credibility. Furthermore, Russian hackers breached private social media platforms and leaked emails stolen from the Democratic National Committee to embarrass the Democratic Party. Though assessing counterfactual situations is difficult, Russian interventions may have affected the outcome of the 2016 U.S. presidential elections as well as ballot outcomes in several European countries.

Over the past decade, Russian cyber offensive capabilities have become more visible, as Moscow has wielded them for a variety of political and military goals. The April–May 2007 cyber assault against Estonia disrupted public and private information networks through a massive distributed denial-of-service (DDoS) attack in which the perpetrators used thousands of hijacked computers to bombard websites with useless information until they became overloaded. The attacks targeted the websites of banks, telecommunication companies, media outlets, and government agencies, eventually forcing the country to block all foreign internet traffic. One year later, Russia's August 2008 political-military campaign against Georgia included a massive, well-integrated, and apparently extensively preplanned and rehearsed campaign against Georgia's internet infrastructure that degraded the effectiveness of Georgia's national response to the Russian campaign. These cyberattacks disabled dozens of important websites, including those of political leaders, financial institutions, and major news outlets. One of the major goals of the cyber offensive was to disrupt Georgian government communications both within the country and with the outside world.[6] Another example has been evident in Moscow's war in Ukraine, which began in 2014, as Russian-affiliated units employed a medley of malware, DDoS attacks, and spear phishing campaigns (where innocuous-looking emails include links to malware) against Ukrainian politicians, government offices, armed forces, communications nodes, and social networking websites. In December 2015, Russian hackers orchestrated an assault on the Ukrainian power grid, using malware called "Black Energy," which deprived 230,000 residents of power for several hours on Christmas Eve. Variations of this malware have since been discovered in U.S. systems.[7] Immediately before the November 2018 Russian-Ukrainian naval clash, moreover, Russian hacker groups conducted cyber reconnaissance on Ukrainian naval operations.[8] British and U.S. authorities believe that Moscow may also have engaged in a massive global cyber operation to penetrate Western governments, businesses, computer routers, firewalls, and other networking equipment to pre-position malicious code for potential future conflict.[9] In March 2018, the U.S. Computer Emergency Readiness Team (US-CERT) released a report on how Russian hackers collected information on industrial control systems, such as those equipping U.S. energy networks.[10] A cyberattack that had occurred in June 2017 illustrates how some of these hacks can spiral out of control. The NotPetya virus, a deletion virus disguised as ransomware, targeted Ukraine's accounting systems but inadvertently spread to 64 other countries and affected international companies, logistical operators, government agencies, telecommunication providers, and various financial institutions.[11]

Russia's cyberattacks have primarily been carried out by civilians working for the Russian government, its partner organizations, or as freelance hackers who might also engage in independent cyber operations for other clients. Even the campaigns against Georgia in 2008 and Ukraine in 2014 were, for the most part, not carried out by the Russian armed forces directly but rather by Russian civilians working with the military or at least enjoying exemption from Russian government prosecution as long as their foreign operations advance its interests.[12] During the 2016 U.S. elections, the Russian Internet Research Agency orchestrated trolls and bots on various social media accounts to sow discord and spread misinformation.[13] Meanwhile, the hacker group known as "Fancy Bear" infiltrated the Democratic National Committee's servers and selectively released sensitive information. For Moscow, the use of civilian hackers provides many benefits such as potential cost savings and deniability—making attribution of their activities to the Russian government more difficult, they can obscure Moscow's hand and thereby diminishing the risk of international backlash.[14] In 2020, a Russian cyber-hacking group called the APT29, also known as the "The Dukes" or "Cozy Bear," tried to illicitly access Britain, Canadian, and U.S. vaccine research.[15] The U.S. government has also identified connections between Russian computer companies, such as Kaspersky Lab, and the Russian military.[16]

CHINESE GOALS AND POLICIES

PRC leaders have endorsed the right of sovereign states to control online content within their borders—that is, the internet is a reflection of physical space within the state's sovereign territory.[17] They insist that the internet should be closed to foreign interference, and each country should have complete control of its domestic cyberspace. The "Great Firewall of China" comprehensively limits the Chinese public's access to the internet, allowing the government to filter the messages received by the population as well as, more recently, to monitor citizens' internet browsing habits.[18] PRC authorities use digital harassment and manipulation for ideological control and peer pressure campaigns against expatriate minorities, Chinese students abroad, and civil activist organizations.[19] Within China, PRC authorities have increased monitoring of Uighurs and other potential dissidents using advanced surveillance technologies. In their coverage of international affairs, the PRC media want the Chinese public to see how much foreigners respect China, in general, and President Xi, in particular. Such shifts correspond to the overall trend of tightening government control over Chinese society during the Xi presidency as well as the evolving PLA thinking concerning cyber conflict under its Active Defense concept. This framework sees "offense at the tactical and operational levels is consistent with an overall defensive orientation at the strategic level."[20] China's internet censorship framework includes an offensive component, the so-called Great Cannon, which, as part of an Active Defense strategy, can fire numerous repeated requests at a targeted website until it crashes.[21] In 2015, the Great Cannon was used in a DDoS attack on a California-based company that hosted a project designed to circumvent China's internet censorship, forcing the site to intermittently shut down over a five-day period.[22]

President Xi has delivered several authoritative speeches on cyber security. In a 2015 address to the Second World Internet Conference in Wuzhen, Xi presented "Four Principles" and "Five Propositions" to guide China's cyber policies.[23] The Four Principles were promoting sovereignty, peace and security, open cooperation, and positive order in the cyber sphere. The Five Propositions were as follows:

- Accelerate construction of a global network infrastructure and stimulate interconnection and interactivity.

- Build shared platforms for online cultural interaction to expand exchange and mutual learning.
- Promote innovation and development in the online economy to encourage global prosperity.
- Guarantee cybersecurity to stimulate orderly development of the internet.
- Build the internet governance system to stimulate fairness and justice.

During cybersecurity week in late April 2017, Xi called for strengthening PRC capabilities and governance capacity in four major areas: (1) managing internet content online and creating "positive energy" online; (2) ensuring general cybersecurity, such as in protecting critical information infrastructure; (3) developing an indigenous and independent technology base for software and hardware infrastructure to secure the internet in China; and (4) increasing China's role in "building, governing, and operating the Internet globally."[24] At the international level, the Cyber Security Association of China has helped promote these principles and propositions beyond China.[25] In line with these guidelines, PRC authorities have expanded their cyber defenses and technology transfer practices. Chinese laws and regulations force foreign companies to meet national requirements for technology transfer and domestic surveillance. The Chinese Cybersecurity Law of June 2017 compels foreign IT firms to separate local cyber operations from global networks, hold more data in China, and permit PRC authorities access to their software codes, raising the risk of cyber theft of their intellectual property.[26] The government's commercial cyber policies have evolved from prioritizing basic information technology to becoming the world's leading cyber power, most recently in fifth-generation (5G) telecommunications technology. PRC national security managers have long seen data as a strategic resource to control. With modern information technologies, they can exploit data collected by Chinese applications throughout the world to strengthen their artificial intelligence databases and foreign influence operations.[27]

The U.S. Department of Defense's (DoD) 2018 Cyber Strategy stated that Beijing has been responsible for numerous acts of cyber espionage, responsible for "eroding U.S. military overmatch" and U.S. "economic vitality."[28] The U.S. National Security Agency found that, between 2010 and 2015, China conducted more than 600 cyber operations aimed at stealing corporate secrets, military intelligence, and data about U.S. infrastructure.[29] The White House reported that PRC cyber espionage against U.S. businesses and inventors cost trillions of dollars of intellectual property theft.[30] Security experts believe that the Chinese government orchestrated the sophisticated "Titan Rain" global cyber network, which downloaded information from hundreds of unclassified defense and civilian networks.[31] Another suspected case of high-profile

Chinese cyber espionage was a security breach on computer systems belonging to the U.S. Office of Personnel Management. The attack compromised the Social Security numbers, fingerprints, addresses, financial histories, and other personally identifiable information of more than 20 million U.S. citizens.[32] This breach included the personal data of 4.2 million former and current federal employees.[33] Chinese hackers have also reportedly stolen information about U.S. weapon systems and vaccine development. Furthermore, China's Thousand Talents program aggressively woos top foreign scientists to steal intellectual property for PRC academic and business entities. In July 2020, FBI director Christopher Wray declared that the Chinese government's use of espionage and cyberattacks against the United States has amounted "one of the largest transfers of wealth in human history."[34]

The People's Liberation Army's (PLA) Strategic Support Force (SSF) has various cyber missions, akin to the Russian and U.S. Cyber Commands. PRC military doctrine emphasizes the importance of information, data, and networking in "winning informationized local wars."[35] In December 2013, an updated version of the PLA's *The Science of Military Strategy* for the first time included an entire chapter devoted to cyber war. It outlined four mission areas: network reconnaissance, network defense, network attack, and network deterrence. This confirms the PLA's interest in offensive as well defensive operations.[36] The 2015 Chinese Ministry of National Defense paper titled "China's Military Strategy" is the first official military document that addressed cybersecurity. It defined cyberspace and declared that "China is confronted with grave security threats to its cyber infrastructure."[37] In 2019, "China's National Defense in the New Era" declared that issues of "cybersecurity poses a severe threat to China" and regarded safeguarding the PRC's cybersecurity as one of its national defense aims.[38] The PLA also employs civilian "patriotic hackers."[39] Some of these were responsible for a March 2017 DDoS against the South Korean Lotte Group, who provided land for the U.S. Terminal High Altitude Area Defense (THAAD) system that China opposed.[40] In an October 2018 speech, Vice President Mike Pence accused the Chinese Communist Party (CCP) leadership of "employing a whole-of-government approach, using political, economic, and military tools, as well as propaganda, to advance its influence and benefit its interests in the United States." After reviewing Beijing's assertive economic and security policies toward other countries, Pence maintained that the Chinese government was trying to undermine the Trump administration's tough tactics toward China by intervening "in the domestic policies and politics of the United States." For instance, he claimed that China was trying to exploit divisions between federal and local officials, threaten to withhold commercial opportunities to U.S. businesses and regions, and use open and covert means to turn the American public against China. "To that end," Pence asserted, "Beijing has mobilized covert actors, front groups, and propaganda outlets [such as Chinese TV and radio] to shift Americans' perception of Chinese policies" as well as "taking steps to exploit its economic leverage, and the allure of China's large domestic market, to advance its influence over American corporations."[41]

RUSSIAN-CHINESE INTERACTIONS

Authoritarian governments like Russia and China dispose of a portfolio of information instruments to support their cyber-enabled foreign influence campaigns. Political campaigns, corporate advertisers, and other actors utilize some of these tools, but national governments, such as Russia and China, have many more resources and assets to apply to their campaigns. This is particularly true with waging coordinated disinformation campaigns. Whereas "misinformation" represents false information spread *without* malign intent, disinformation constitutes false information disseminated *with* malign intent, typically aiming to induce a visceral emotional response. Governments also have substantial cyber resources for conducting "malinformation"—the "hack and leak" of politically important private information with malign intent, as illustrated by the Russian operations to discredit the Democratic National Committee and leading U.S. politicians in 2016. It is important to distinguish between "fake news" (false information) and "public relations" or "public diplomacy," which seeks to advance a point of view using *accurate* information, albeit sometimes selectively. The Russian and Chinese execute information operations to support both their internal and external policies. The goals of the latter can include promoting positive portrayals of the propagators' actions, discrediting alternative sources of information, mobilizing their foreign-based diaspora communities to support the motherland, and (a frequent Russian priority) exploiting social, economic, and cultural divisions in targeted states to make them less able to resist external influence. For example, a perennial Russian objective has been to exacerbate racial tensions in the United States by posting emotionally charged messaging on social media. Democracies are vulnerable to these authoritarian influence tactics since they are generally open societies whose members want to encourage free speech and authentic debate.

Public diplomacy is a long-standing and accepted practice of national governments. Foreign ministries, including official spokespeople as well as national diplomats, normally are the main government agency involved in such campaigns. Governments can also hire foreign public relations companies and registered lobbyists to support their public diplomacy. These entities can overtly promote foreign-backed views through purchasing advertising in traditional media and lobbying politicians to adopt certain positions. Another technique, perfected by mass extremist parties such as the communists and the Nazis, is to establish front organizations that conceal their control in order to solicit support from independent groups. For instance, the Soviet Union would strive to coopt foreign peace movements and left-wing (but noncommunist) parties under the leadership of Soviet-controlled front organizations. The Communist Party of China continues such a practice today through use of government-organized nongovernmental organizations (GONGOs), coordinated through the United Front Work Department and other party oversight mechanisms, to build ties with foreign groups that might resist a comprehensive partnership directly with the CCP. Russia employs its own GONGOs to drown out the messaging of legitimate NGOs. In 2019, a seminar on press freedom in Russia-occupied Crimea was heavily attended by Kremlin-backed GONGOs who introduced themselves as hailing from "Crimea in the Russian Federation." These groups used up valuable speaking time to minimize the messaging of other NGOs in attendance.[42] Similarly, the Berlin-based "grassroots" media company Redfish has also aroused suspicion since its journalists hail largely from Russian state-owned media.[43]

State-controlled media—consisting of broadcast television, various radio outlets, and major newspapers—represent the second major national information tool. Russian television networks like RT are known for disseminating conspiracy theories, rumor mongering, and stretching truths in an entertaining manner. When the COVID-19 pandemic emerged, Russia's Channel One news network devoted a regular time slot to airing various conspiracies in which non-Russian entities were responsible for causing or exploiting the pandemic. These media outlets have strong multilingual internet presences that extend beyond the Russian Federation and the Russian ethnic diaspora. By the same token, China's CGTN (formerly CCTV) and other public TV networks have a domestic function of communicating government policies to viewers and persuading them to support them as well as offering entertainment and other services. Chinese foreign media operations have grown substantially, thanks to major government investment in building international networks. For instance, CGTN now has English, Arabic, and other foreign language broadcasts available in many markets.

In addition to these generally established techniques of foreign influence, governments pursue disinformation campaigns using communication entities whose ties to governments are obscured and denied. These nontransparent tools can involve human-staffed "troll" groups that can praise or damn postings through comments and "likes" as well as machine-driven automated "bots" that blast targeted content on multiple social media accounts (Twitter, Facebook, Instagram, YouTube, etc.) in what Twitter describes as "crossposting and amplifying content in an inauthentic, coordinated manner for political ends."[44] The latter software-driven postings can be dispersed across a wide geographic area, becoming "bot armies" of multiple masquerading profiles with many social media accounts operated by a concealed human or machine controller. These networks consist of fake and hijacked "core" accounts that generate falsehoods as well as "amplifiers" that replicate and endorse the content of the "core" accounts. They can communicate similar messages designed to reinforce a point or dissimilar ones to engender doubt, debate, and division about a topic. In conjunction with comments, trolls and bots can post doctored YouTube images and fake videos. Since these social media outlets are not formally affiliated with a government and less visible than state-owned media like TV, governments can more easily employ them to promote falsehoods, sow confusion, and exacerbate conflicts by conveying fine-tuned messages to discretely targeted audiences. For example, the infamous troll farm of the Internet Research Agency magnified political divisions through disseminating hyper-partisan messaging during the 2016 U.S. elections. In many cases, concealing their identity and location by means of fake or stolen accounts and professing either conservative or progressive values, these inauthentic actors posted on both sides of different political questions dealing with elections, racial and gender issues, or other divisive topics.[45] The volume of this inauthentic messaging across the various social media platforms aims to drown out authentic narratives emanating from independent media and other legitimate sources. For instance, the Russian disinformation ecosphere has generated a range of possible explanations to cast doubt on Russian government responsibility for the Skripal assassination attempt in Salisbury or the shooting down of Malaysia's M17 civilian airliner over Ukraine.

Modern social media facilitates microtargeting and obscures attribution. For example, Facebook's "groups" typically exclude external monitoring and consist of like-minded thinkers. Disinformation campaigns that target these entities aim to amplify malign messages by injecting them first into nontransparent closed social media groups or fringe publications in the hopes that they will enter mainstream discourse through adoption by prominent local media and influential commentators. When narratives come from clearly identified foreign state-controlled media, they are not trusted, but when they are repeated by local independent media, they can be more credible. This practice of disguising the origin of an idea or message that would be less credible if the audience knew its true origin has been referred to as "astroturfing." In this approach, even genuinely independent media can inadvertently "launder" foreign propaganda by lending credence to its content while obscuring its foreign origins, thereby making disinformation more credible.

Russian and Chinese officials favor new global internet rules that emphasize treating cyber sovereignty similarly to territorial sovereignty and "internationalization of internet governance" to dilute U.S. influence and contest Western norms in the cyber domain.[46] They favor national control of internet resources within a state's physical borders and the primacy of local legislation and national control of the transnational cyber domain. Moscow and Beijing want to replace the current multi-stakeholder model of internet governance, based on liberal norms of substantial free speech, with greater state control of internet resources and policies based on strong norms of noninterference with sovereign networks.[47] In 2018, Russia proposed a resolution at the UN General Assembly that would create an open-ended working group (OEWG) to work parallel to the UN Group of Governmental Experts (GGE) on issues of cyber norms. This action would have essentially given Russia an alternative forum to reinterpret existing GGE precedent in Moscow's favor.[48] The PRC also strives to achieve leadership in setting global standards for digital technologies. Moscow and Beijing have led efforts to undermine the U.S. position as sole monitor of the Internet Corporation for Assigned Names and Numbers.[49] The effectiveness of social media in the Arab Spring in organizing protests and rebellions gravely alarmed Russian and Chinese security managers.[50] Russia and China have exported their Internet-control technologies to foreign partners in Asia, Africa, and the Middle East.

Official Sino-Russian cyber cooperation has also been growing. In May 2015, Russia and China signed the Intergovernmental Agreement on Cooperation in Ensuring International Information Security, a high-level framework accord through which Russian and Chinese government agencies, corporations, and other entities have negotiated narrower but often more detailed limited agreements. In the Intergovernmental Agreement, Moscow and Beijing pledge not to conduct cyberattacks against each other and to instead collaborate against cyber threats designed to "destabilize the internal political and socioeconomic atmosphere," "disturb public order" or "interfere with the internal affairs" of either state.[51] The accord stipulates that Russian and Chinese officials will meet twice a year to coordinate their cyber initiatives and propose new ones.[52] At the 2015 World Internet Conference, Russia's Kaspersky Lab agreed to work with the state-owned China Cyber Security Company against an unnamed actor that had mounted sophisticated attacks against both countries.[53] During Putin's 2016 visit to Beijing, he and Xi demanded that all states respect nations' cyber sovereignty, eschew interference in another country's cyberspace, and fairly share internet resources.[54] The first Russia-China Information and Communication Technologies Development and Security Forum, held in Moscow in April 2016, also called for cyber sovereignty and shared internet governance.[55] In October 2018, Kaspersky signed a Strategic Cooperation Agreement with the China Industrial Control Systems Cyber Emergency Response Team under the Ministry of Industry and Information Technology.[56] In 2019, Moscow and Beijing signed a cooperation treaty on managing "illegal online content."[57] The two countries have established regular coordination mechanisms between their senior information officials, such as the China-Russia Media Forum and the China-Russia Internet Media Forum.

The COVID-19 epidemic has seen novel forms of Sino-Russian collaborative information manipulation. Major health crises such as those comparable to the COVID-19 pandemic provide receptive environments for disinformation campaigns since few people are epistemological experts and many have deep fears regarding how the pandemic could harm their health or those they love. Moreover, the public discourse is already replete with unsubstantiated claims about quack remedies and fictitious causes. Fear, uncertainty, and doubt provide opening for misinformation and disinformation. The COVID-19 pandemic offers malign actors additional fault lines to exploit due to the varying impact the virus has had on different countries, age groups, and socioeconomic classes. The economic downturns in most Western economies allowed destructive messages to play on the anxieties permeating Western nations. Indeed, creating conspiracy theories about Western biological weapons has been a well-established Kremlin strategy. One of the most effective Soviet propaganda campaigns was the KGB's malign information operation claiming that the Pentagon created AIDS. These fake stories alienated African Americans and harmed U.S. relations with African countries. Similarly, in the last decade, pro-Kremlin media falsely asserted U.S. responsibility for the Ebola outbreak, while Russian trolls promoted anti-vaccine sentiments in the West even as Russian leaders stressed the value of vaccines within Russia. The novelty of the COVID-19 pandemic and the resulting uncertainty over its origin, impact, and mitigation have provided a fertile ground for new state-orchestrated disinformation campaigns. Furthermore, people in lockdowns as a rule spend more time in the online world, making them more vulnerable to cyber-enabled propaganda.

There have been enduring Sino-Russian differences in the cyber domain. While Russia and China both want to protect their regimes from undesirable ideas disseminated through the internet, Moscow and Beijing have different approaches to domestic cyber control. Beijing utilizes a more comprehensive form of censorship in which its "Great Firewall" makes many sites and much content inaccessible to Chinese users. The government also closely censors social media platforms, like WeChat, and regularly removes unapproved content. In Russia, the government has taken care to control, either directly or through pro-Kremlin proxies, the country's main broadcast, social, and print media. Even so, political opponents of the current government can still express their opinions somewhere on the internet, such as on YouTube videos. Besides limited censorship and the control of the most popular domestic media outlets, Russian authorities attempt to drown out widely circulating disagreeable narratives rather than ban them outright while employing microtargeting to win over specifically targeted groups, such as westerners attracted to authoritarian values. For instance, "trolls" linked to the government strive to discredit unwelcome messages by making amusing and contemptuous comments that obscure the message and discredit the messenger. Russian authorities face an uphill battle when it comes to following China's example and separating their own country from the rest of the internet. The PRC's enormous domestic cyber market and ability to create its own web platforms means give China several advantages that Russia lacks. In its foreign campaigns, Russian foreign cyberattacks tend to be more immediately politically and militarily driven than those of China. Moscow uses its offensive information capabilities for its disinformation campaigns, spreading fake news, seizing private data, and disseminating secrets when the disclosure is best timed, is most impactful, and provides the most political leverage. For instance, Russia's foreign information operations have sought to disrupt other countries' national elections to erode public confidence in democratic institutions. Additionally, Russian groups have allegedly leaked emails to embarrass foreign political leaders. There is also a closer connection in Russia than China between cyber operations and information operations. Russian disinformation and propaganda campaigns rely heavily on cyber enablers, ranging from troll armies on Twitter that zealously back up Kremlin positions to DDoS attacks against hostile broadcasts and social media. Russian cyber personnel have mastered the art of clandestine manipulation, plausible deniability, and reflexive control—feeding misleading information to foreign counterintelligence agencies to shape their decision making in ways that primarily benefit Russia. In contrast, Beijing's immediate cyber goals have until recently been focused on gaining economic advantages though often with the concurrent objective of enhancing China's military-industrial complex. Stolen foreign commercial secrets can be transferred to PRC firms; such cyber espionage advances the country's corporate, financial, military, diplomatic, and related economic goals. Whereas Russian agencies selectively release targeted purloined secrets to advance the government's political goals, in the PRC, stolen information is largely kept private and utilized covertly for commercial or strategic gains. Not having fought a major war in decades, the PLA has not yet had opportunities to test its new cyber capabilities to support a conventional military campaign, while Russia had already done so in Georgia, Ukraine, and Syria. Furthermore, while Russians reflexively search for cleavages within and between countries to exploit them through disinformation, the PRC uses false messages more selectively to discredit narratives they oppose and the groups expounding on them. Russia's market power has been more limited, especially since the imposition of Western sanctions has made many foreign firms unenthusiastic about investing in or trading with Russian companies. China's leaders have, on the other hand, leveraged the PRC's enormous significance to the world economy to outright discourage foreign countries and sports teams from adopting positions on sensitive issues like the Taiwan Strait, pro-democracy protests in Hong Kong, and Xinjiang separatist movements that Beijing considers hostile. Exploiting their control over Chinese consumers and companies, PRC authorities have redirected contracts, tourists, and other economic benefits from some partners to others. As a result, many foreign businesses practice a form of self-censorship to avoid jeopardizing commercial ties with China. As a consequence of their large user base, Chinese apps like Weibo surpass Russian apps in international popularity. The growing proliferation of Chinese social media apps throughout the world has the potential to provide opportunities for further PRC media influence in the future. For instance, one factor driving PRC interest in becoming the world leader in artificial intelligence is its potential to strengthen these monitoring technologies even further. China also leads all other countries in developing, exporting, and maintaining foreign information control and surveillance technologies, which are popular with other authoritarian governments, such as in Africa and Central Asia.

In the past, Chinese media messaging exhibited a more positive orientation than that of Russia. Whereas Moscow-linked media strived to belittle the failings of the Western democracies, PRC news stories focused on praising Chinese actions and describing them as advancing the general global good by presenting "win-win" solutions. During the COVID-19 pandemic, though, the Russian and Chinese media approaches have been converging, with growing synergies between their tactics. PRC officials, perhaps emulating Russia, employed widespread information manipulation to defend their policies regarding the virus. Chinese diplomats and embassies used Twitter to amplify conspiracy theories about the coronavirus's origin. For instance, Foreign Ministry spokesperson Zhao Lijian promoted a conspiracy theory on his Twitter account to the effect that the U.S. military could have brought the virus to the PRC. China also exploited Russia's propaganda apparatus to promote conspiracy theories. The two governments have been promoting converging messaging about the virus through official media outlets as well as unofficial social media accounts. From the start of the pandemic, Russian official statements have regularly defended Beijing's position that the Western democracies failed to take advantage of China's effective response to the virus and ineptly allowed COVID-19 to spread throughout the world. The two governments have rallied behind a common narrative, with Russian officials and media readily endorsing Beijing's main talking points that:

- the Chinese government performed an admirable job at containing the virus domestically;
- the rest of the world should be grateful to China for giving them time to prepare for the pandemic's onslaught;
- China is a beneficial and beneficent actor;

- just because the virus first appeared in China does not mean it did not originate somewhere else, such as the United States; and
- rather than cooperate with other countries, the United States is seeking to isolate and blame them, especially China, for its poor response to COVID-19.

In a joint videoconference at the end of July, the heads of the media departments in the Russian and Chinese foreign ministries defended their media operations against Western criticisms and admonished Western governments who "adopt double standards, interfere in others' internal affairs or level groundless accusations on other countries' political systems, development path and state governance based on ideology and political prejudice."[58] Meanwhile, PRC diplomats, including ambassadors and embassies in other countries, have retweeted and reciprocally referenced false stories, many of which originated in Russia's more established infosphere, that advance Beijing's preferred narratives. Pro-Kremlin media outlets like RT and Sputnik were among the top five most-retweeted non-PRC news outlets by China's state-funded media.[59] Though this coordination may not represent a joint Sino-Russian disinformation campaign, by amplifying each other's messages, they help validate and amplify them.

IMPLICATIONS AND RECOMMENDATIONS

Notwithstanding their overlapping messages, occasional reciprocal coordination, mutual restraint on criticizing the other, and regular sharing of media experiences, questions arise as to how effective the Sino-Russian information cooperation has become. One analysis argues that Russian audiences find Chinese-made media pieces, of which there are more than 100 each month, stilted and unconvincing as the PRC information managers do not have substantial Russian area expertise, lack an effective mechanism to assess audiences' receptivity to PRC propaganda, and limit Russian media access to the main PRC media outlets.[60] If Russia implements Chinese-style information control on its own internet, moreover, it will likely do so using PRC-made software and hardware. This could give Beijing a backdoor into Moscow's network, a situation that could lead to suspicion between the two countries. On the international plane, as more authoritarian leaders aligned with Moscow, such as Russia's Central Asian allies, enact their own Chinese-style comprehensive domestic internet controls, they will turn to PRC technology and aid for help, decreasing Moscow's influence in this domain.[61]

Despite these long-term divisive tendencies, for the indefinite future, the United States will need to not only bolster U.S. defenses by reducing vulnerabilities but also enhance cyber deterrence, especially by displaying the capabilities and will to respond to major cyber threats. U.S. experts warn that the offensive capabilities of U.S. cyber adversaries will only increase in coming years.[62] For example, advances in artificial intelligence technology could facilitate the development of even more effective and complex cyber weapons in the future, such as "deep fake" videos simulating prominent personalities. Furthermore, the use of machine learning could enable the more rapid design, launch, maintenance, and refinement of automated disinformation attacks compared with the currently labor-intensive process. The essential challenge is that offensive cyber operations are attractive to U.S. adversaries since they plausibly hope to stay under the threshold of armed conflict that could trigger major U.S. retaliation. Though Washington has used a "name and shame" campaign to expose Moscow's and Beijing's activities to the world, the United States has been unable to change either actor's behavior.[63] As long as Russian and Chinese officials perceive the costs of cyber operations as low, and the potential benefits as high, they are unlikely to abstain from them. Moscow and Beijing enjoy certain advantages in their cyber competition with Washington. U.S. covert cyber operations are more difficult to keep secret in comparison to the two countries, as Russia's Duma and China's National People's Congress do not hold public oversight hearings comparable to those of the U.S. Congress. The U.S. media regularly exposes U.S. cyber vulnerabilities and operations, such as the Stuxnet virus that crippled Iranian nuclear centrifuges in the early 2000s or the statements made by Edward Snowden about the U.S. National Security Agency's global surveillance program. In contrast, the Russian and Chinese governments can more easily control their respective internal and external narratives. Their state-controlled media regularly dismisses U.S. leaders' allegations of cyber misbehavior as hypocritical in light of U.S. press coverage of U.S. cyber operations against other countries. Another advantage that the Russian and Chinese governments have is their substantial leverage to induce nongovernmental actors to support their operations, including national companies, hired contractors, government-tolerated cyber criminals, and "patriotic hackers."[64] By contrast, the U.S. government's ability to persuade independent private firms, academics, and other NGOs to follow its direction on cyber issues is limited. There have been high-profile recent incidents in which Google and additional U.S. IT corporations have distanced themselves from U.S. defense projects and other government programs. In addition, U.S. decision makers are naturally cautious about engaging in offensive operations in the cyber domain, given the unpredictability of this novel form of warfare.[65] Their Russian and PRC counterparts seem less constrained, though their reliance on stolen versions of Western software or inferior indigenous alternatives can create more cybersecurity vulnerabilities for Russian and Chinese entities. The aggregated effect of even modest Russian and Chinese cyberattacks could prove costly to U.S. economic competitiveness and national security.

Many U.S. government agencies contribute to cybersecurity. The DoD has offensive as well as defensive cyber missions. On the civilian side, the US-CERT, under the Department of Homeland Security (DHS), functions primarily as a defensive body, responding collaboratively with other U.S. government agencies as well as private-sector actors to respond to cyber incidents.[66] In September 2018, the DoD and the White House released new cyber strategies that singled out Russia and China as cyber threats to the United States and its allies. The 2018 DoD Cyber Strategy and Cyber Posture Review states that "China and Russia are engaging in great power competition via persistent, aggressive cyberspace campaigns that pose strategic, long-term risks to the Nation, our allies, and partners."[67] The DoD strategy highlights Moscow's interference in the 2016 U.S. presidential election and Beijing's history of stealing intellectual property of military importance. The White House National Cyber Strategy accuses Russia, along with North Korea and Iran, of "undermin[ing] our economy and democracy" and "sow[ing] discord in our democratic processes" through their cyber activities.[68] In response, this strategy says that the United States will detect, disrupt, degrade, and deter behavior in cyberspace that damages U.S. national interests. Toward this end, both the White House and the DoD support multifaceted response programs to bolster domestic cyber defenses and promote an open, interoperable, reliable, and secure internet. Furthermore, the National Cyber Strategy, the first such strategy to be released by the White House in the past 15 years, insists that "we will also work to prevent authoritarian states that view the open Internet as a political threat from transforming the free and open Internet into an authoritarian web under their control, under the guise of security or countering terrorism." The National Cyber Strategy further reiterated the federal government's commitment to protect sensitive new technologies and trade secrets to prevent adversarial nations from gaining "an unfair advantage at the expense of American research and development." The text reaffirms the priorities of protecting intellectual property, updating the method of evaluating foreign investment and operations under U.S. jurisdiction. The White House will also centralize management, improve oversight, strengthen the cybersecurity practices of federal contractors, and impose stronger penalties for cybercrimes.[69] Explaining the strategy, National Security Adviser John Bolton stressed that the United States would become more proactive in the cyberspace domain, stating, "[W]e're going to do a lot of things offensively, and I think our adversaries need to know that."[70] On October 27, 2015, Congress enacted the Cybersecurity Information Sharing Act, which mandates enhanced public-private cooperation in cyber risk management on the part of major U.S. government agencies. The State Department assists private-sector actors, including those in Russia and China, to evade and subvert government internet controls. The new White House's National Cyber Strategy reaffirms that internet freedom is an exercise of basic human rights, reflected in the First Amendment of the U.S. Constitution. To influence global norms, the United States will "expose and counter the flood of online malign influence and information campaigns and non-state propaganda and disinformation."[71] The United States could help other countries guard against cyber threats and espionage.

The Defense Department has become more proactive in the cyber realm and has authorized the Pentagon to conduct counterattacks against hackers under specific circumstances. Whereas previously the focus was on parrying attacks once they were launched at the United States, more recently the emphasis has become deterring and possibly preempting threats.[72] A Pentagon strategy adopted in 2015 selectively permits preemptive action to "terminate (an) on going conflict on US terms or to disrupt an adversary's military systems to prevent the use of force against US interests."[73] In explaining the new approach, defense secretary Ashton Carter said that "the United States must be able to declare or display effective response capabilities to deter an adversary from initiating an attack; develop effective defensive capabilities to deny a potential attack from succeeding; and strengthen overall resilience of U.S. systems to withstand a potential attack if it penetrates the United States' defenses."[74] In 2018, the Pentagon released a new cyber strategy that insisted the United States will "assertively defend our interests," with the military "build[ing] a more lethal force . . . for both warfighting and countering malicious cyber actors." According to a corresponding fact sheet released with the strategy, the DoD defines the concept of "defend[ing] forward" as "confronting threats before they reach U.S. networks." The concept will apply even to malicious cyber activities which "[fall] below the level of armed conflict."[75] Similar to covert action, offensive cyber operations usually require an interagency review process and direct authorization from the U.S. president.[76] Whereas the 2015 strategy delegated defense of critical infrastructure to other federal agencies, the 2018 strategy states that the DoD will assume more responsibility, building "trusted relationships with private sector entities" to defend "critical defense infrastructure," which the document defines as all U.S. military and civilian "assets essential to project, support, and sustain military forces and operations worldwide." Congress has supported the new approach. Section 1642 of the 2018 John S. McCain National Defense Authorization Act grants the Pentagon authority "to take appropriate and proportional action in foreign cyberspace to disrupt, defeat, and deter" when "an active, systematic, and ongoing campaign of attacks [are launched] against the Government or people of the United States in cyberspace." In 2018, President Trump issued National Security Presidential Memorandum 13 (NSPM-13), which gives broad powers to the DoD when it comes to conducting cyber operations, including delegating the presidential approval process for such activities to the Defense Department.[77] Ahead of the 2018 midterm elections, the U.S. military temporarily disabled Russia's Internet Research Agency to demonstrate U.S. intent and capabilities.[78]

Additionally, the Defense Department and other U.S. government agencies are decreasing their reliance on Russian and Chinese companies whose components or services may facilitate cyber espionage and sabotage. Congress has been supporting this process by expanding the power and scope of the Committee on Foreign Investment in the United States (CFIUS) to vet Chinese high-technology investments. For instance, CFIUS and the Trump administration blocked Huawei from expanding its telecommunications arm into the United States on the grounds that the company gives data to the Chinese government. PRC state-supported companies have had to curtail plans to purchase or invest in U.S. companies dealing with the most sensitive information sectors. U.S. civilian agencies will continue law enforcement and counterintelligence actions to thwart foreign-driven cyber commercial espionage.[79] Furthermore, the Pentagon is enhancing its resilience capabilities against all types of external cyber threats. Then undersecretary of defense for policy James Miller explained in 2017 that "[t]o be able to credibly impose unacceptable costs in response to a cyber-attack by major powers, Russia and China, the U.S. needs its key strike systems—cyber, nuclear and non-nuclear strike— to be able to function even after the most advanced cyber-attack."[80] In addition, U.S. Cyber Command (USCYBERCOM) has been elevated to the same status as the other major U.S. strategic commands, while the new Cyber Mission Force consists of thousands of military personnel capable of conducting defensive, offensive, and support missions.[81] USCYBERCOM released a new strategy, titled "Achieve and Maintain Cyberspace Superiority: A Command Vision for U.S. Cyber Command."[82] The strategy acknowledges that cyberattacks whose magnitude falls under the traditional threshold of armed aggression can still have a negative impact on vital U.S. diplomatic, economic, and military interests as well as societal cohesion. The Defense Department also aims to strengthen ties with interagency, industry, and international partners as well as cultivate domestic cyber talent while ensuring that military personnel are more "cyber fluent." Though recognizing that the United States will confront formidable state and nonstate cyber competitors for the indefinite future—including strategic adversaries, rogue states, and terrorist and criminal networks—the Pentagon will take measures to ensure that "the Joint Force can achieve its missions in a contested cyberspace environment."[83]

The United States also has diplomatic options for dealing with Russian-Chinese cyber threats, such as supporting the international coalition to sustain universal liberal cyber norms. The 2018 National Strategy advocates pursuing an international Cyber Deterrence Initiative to encourage "intelligence sharing, buttressing of attribution claims, public statements of support for responsive actions taken, and joint imposition of consequences against malign actors" among the United States and its partners. In theory, some form of cyber arms control could reduce these problems. However, the record of past agreements is poor. At the June 2013 meeting of the G8 summit in the United Kingdom, Presidents Putin and Obama signed a cybersecurity agreement to share urgent information that could "reduce the risk of misperception, escalation and conflict" between the two countries. A direct secure hotline was created between the U.S. cybersecurity coordinator and the deputy secretary of the Russian Security Council. Both governments also agreed to create a program under which the US-CERT and its Russian counterpart would exchange "practical technical information on cybersecurity risks to critical systems."[84] Moscow's annexation of Crimea the following March upended plans to set up the special working group on cybersecurity.[85] The agreement that Putin and Trump reached at the July 2017 G20 Hamburg summit to collaborate on cybersecurity was likewise never implemented after congressional objections led the White House to repudiate it.[86] U.S. attempts to foster cooperation with China have not fared any better. After a federal grand jury indictment of five PLA officials in May 2014 for cyber espionage and stealing trade secrets from Westinghouse Electric Company, U.S. Steel Corporation, and others, the Chinese government rejected these charges and suspended the China-U.S. Cyber Working Group that was established the previous year.[87] Beijing and Washington were able to reach a cybersecurity agreement during President Xi Jinping's September 2015 visit to Washington. The accord committed both sides to refrain from abetting state-sanctioned cyber theft of intellectual property for commercial competitive advantage and to cooperate on cybercrime issues.[88] However, the agreement had no enforcement powers, and PRC hacking of U.S. companies and other cyber espionage persist.[89] UN secretary-general Antonio Guterres correctly observed, "[T]here is no regulatory scheme for that type of warfare, it is not clear how the Geneva Convention or international humanitarian law applies to it."[90] Even so, the U.S. government can help potential allies and partners to strengthen their cybersecurity capabilities and policies, in exchange for greater support toward the U.S. vision of a free internet. Western experts recommend expanding cooperation among the United States and its allies to jointly study current Sino-Russian disinformation cooperation, forecast future coordination (through red teaming and other means), and develop better means to counter their digital influence campaigns.[91]

10
Chapter

Economics and Energy

Recent years have seen increasing connectivity between Russia and the People's Republic of China (PRC) in multiple economic sectors. For example, since the Cold War, Russia and China have constructed the infrastructure needed for Russia to supply China with large volumes of oil and gas. The financial crisis of 2008, the post-2014 Western sanctions, the COVID-19 pandemic, and other recent developments have resulted in Russian leaders doubling down on their economic ties with the PRC. Putin consistently disclaims anxieties about China's economic rise. In a newspaper article published during his 2012 presidential election campaign, he said that Russia aimed to rise along with China by catching the wind in China's sails.[1] Nonetheless, Russian hopes for massive Chinese loans, investment, and other aid in modernizing Russia's economy have not been fully realized. Sino-Russian economic ties remain small compared with China's trade and investment in Europe and the United States. Substantial impediments have hobbled the growth of Sino-Russian economic and energy ties. Two-way trade has only recently recovered from sanctions and COVID-19. Furthermore, Sino-Russian economic relations have become increasingly imbalanced as Russia has become increasingly dependent on China. Among other consequences of this dependency, Moscow's bargaining position has substantially weakened, making it harder to resist Chinese demands to buy shares in Russia's upstream market or Arctic hydrocarbon projects.

RUSSIAN GOALS AND POLICIES

With increasing urgency because of its constrained economic connections with the West due to almost a decade of increasingly severe Western sanctions, Russia has sought increased economic and energy cooperation with non-Western partners. The sanctions have discouraged foreign direct investment (FDI) in the Russian economy, complicated efforts to purchase advanced technologies from the West, encouraged capital flight, furthered the depreciation of the ruble, restricted Russian access to loans from U.S. and European financial institutions, and likely slowed Russian economic growth. In response, the Russian authorities have boosted domestic production in some sectors, such as agriculture, to compensate for depressed economic exchanges with the West. The Russian government has also maintained its support for the Eurasian Economic Union (EEU), a Moscow-led project that aims to strengthen Russia's economic influence in the former Soviet republics by facilitating commerce between members while raising economic barriers for countries outside the organization. Armenia, Belarus, Kazakhstan, and Kyrgyzstan have joined the EEU and agreed to unify their customs processes and promote a common economic framework.

There is a natural synergy between Russia's vast hydrocarbon sector and China's growing demand for energy imports. Russia is a global energy powerhouse. The Russian Federation possesses the world's largest natural gas reserves, is one of the world's largest oil producers, and remains a leading global exporter of hydrocarbons. Though Russia's hydrocarbon revenue varies depending on the global prices for oil and gas, fossil fuels comprise more than half of the value of Russia's total exports and almost one-third of Russia's national gross domestic product (GDP). Oil and gas are also the main sources of the federal government's revenue. Until recently, Russia's foreign energy ties were focused on servicing European markets. Russia's strong position as a major energy player in Europe is ensured through long-term energy contracts and other mechanisms. The Russian government has also assisted its state-owned enterprises to acquire strategic energy production and transportation infrastructure throughout Europe. Nonetheless, economic and political factors such as stringent environmental regulations, the growing availability of some alternative energy sources including liquefied natural gas (LNG) and Caspian hydrocarbons, and renewed post-Crimea concerns about the European Union's (EU) dependency on Russian energy supplies constrain opportunities for further growth in European hydrocarbon demand. Russia's preeminence in Western markets is also being eroded by the shale revolution in the United States and LNG exports from other countries.

Russian hydrocarbon exporters have therefore sought out additional markets to hedge against a decline in European energy purchases and to diversify their network of hydrocarbon partners. The Russian government has conducted a multipronged strategy to augment Moscow's influence in foreign energy markets. For example, it has invested billions of dollars to expand its transnational pipeline system, permitting Russia to export oil and gas directly to a variety of countries. Since many of these deliveries occur bilaterally, Russia can practice price, supply, and other types of discrimination. Furthermore, the government has restricted foreign investment in its energy resources and other sensitive sectors. Russia also exports small amounts of LNG and is seeking to expand sales of nuclear power technologies and services as well as other non-energy products. Asia has become the prime target of Russian interest since demand for energy in Asia is projected to grow faster than the rest of the world.

CHINA'S GOALS AND POLICIES

Since its implementation of market reforms in 1978, China has undergone one of the fastest sustained economic expansions in modern history. This growth has propelled the PRC to become the world's second-largest economy, after the United States. If present trends continue, the PRC could have the largest national GDP by the middle of this century. China has already become a leading trade and investment partner of many countries of the world. PRC companies have become global leaders in many fields. President Xi Jinping wants to increase the competitiveness of PRC industries still further by boosting domestic innovation and reducing China's reliance on foreign technology. He also aims to reduce income and wealth disparities by promoting the theme of "common prosperity." In the future, the PRC may aim to supplant the United States and create a PRC-led international economic order. So far, the China-U.S. economic war has not derailed these plans, but having good economic relations with Russia and other non-Western countries is a useful hedge against this pressure.

Furthermore, Russia can provide China with substantial natural resources, especially hydrocarbon gas. China is currently Asia's largest consumer and importer of natural gas and oil. The PRC plans to increase use of nuclear and renewable power sources dramatically to reduce its reliance on foreign energy sources as well as its carbon emissions. Nevertheless, China will need to import some energy for the foreseeable future if the PRC sustains high growth rates. The end of the Soviet Union opened opportunities in Eurasia for PRC businesses by removing barriers to east-west connectivity. During most of the Cold War, the border between China and the various Soviet republics was sealed and heavily militarized. Since then, PRC companies and finance have built several pipelines and other conduits from Asia to Europe that traverse Eurasian territory. China's landmark BRI consists of a series of rail, road, and other connections throughout the world, including through Eurasia via the "Silk Road Economic Belt" and in the Asia-Pacific region via its "Maritime Silk Road" component. The initiative—previously known as One Belt, One Road, or OBOR—aims to reshape Eurasia into a major transit zone for Chinese trade and transport with Europe. The BRI has used several PRC companies to construct various infrastructure projects across the Eurasian continent, which have included roads, bridges, and fiber-optic cables, among other things.[2] To secure foreign participation, China offers enticements such as diverse bilateral and multilateral projects to provide opportunities for PRC and foreign businesses as well as bind foreign partners to the Chinese economy.

RUSSIAN-CHINESE INTERACTIONS

After many years of false hopes and frustrated deals, Moscow and Beijing have made significant progress in consummating their long-anticipated energy partnership. Russia's enormous energy supplies and China's ravenous power demands are clearly complementary.[3] The PRC's rapidly growing economy places strong demands on it to secure energy imports, while Russia's economy is largely based on the demand for the export of natural resources. Until recently, large Sino-Russian energy agreements proved elusive. Russian and PRC representatives began discussing energy pipelines to connect their territories in the 1990s and began formal negotiations in the 2000s. Even so, both countries required many years to overcome such barriers as inadequate transportation infrastructure, diverging pricing perceptions, the availability of alternative partners, and a rapidly transforming energy market. For example, Russian negotiators spent years pressing China to pay the same price as Europeans did for Russian gas, while PRC energy importers insisted on paying Russia substantially less to match the lower price Chinese companies enjoy for Central Asian imports and to account for China's domestic price controls. The two sides repeatedly announced grandiose oil and natural gas deals that failed to materialize until recently. Many of their announced agreements were simply framework accords, memoranda of understanding, or declarations of intent to cooperate on concrete projects at a later date, which are only now reaching fruition. The first oil pipeline between Russia and the PRC was completed only in 2010.

Since then, however, Sino-Russian energy ties have expanded more consistently. In recent years, Russia has vied with Saudi Arabia as the PRC's main foreign supplier of oil. Natural gas transfers have also been increasing. As part of a 30-year energy agreement, the massive Power of Siberia natural gas pipeline, initially running from Chayanda field in Russia to Heilongjiang province in China, commenced operation as the first natural gas pipeline between the two countries in 2020. The volume of gas provided through this pipeline alone is scheduled to increase to 38 billion cubic meters in a few years.[4] In 2020, China imported roughly 8.1 million tons of natural gas from Russia, comprising some 8% of its total gas imports of 101.6 million tons that year.[5] The PRC commitment to reducing its carbon footprint in future years may eventually lead to reduced imports of Russian oil and gas, but the current focus on transitioning PRC energy use from coal to natural gas will have the opposite effect of increasing the Sino-Russian hydrocarbon trade. The two sides are discussing building another large gas pipeline, Power of Siberia 2, to meet this demand. Another factor that has accelerated progress is that China has been willing to provide loans or prepayments to Russian energy companies, giving them funds to build pipelines and modernize their production at low financial risk. For example, in 2009, China's offer to provide Russian state energy companies Rosneft and Transneft $25 billion to construct the Eastern Siberia-Pacific Ocean pipeline secured the launching of this long-discussed east-west oil pipeline. Furthermore, in light of China's decision to cease importing coal from Australia, Russia plans to nearly double the amount of metallurgical coal it exports to China.[6]

The Arctic has represented a growing area of Sino-Russian economic cooperation. After the United States and Europe imposed sanctions on Russian Arctic sector in 2014, Russia turned to China for financial support for several of these projects. The Russian government accordingly relaxed opposition to PRC investment in Russian energy production and other sensitive sectors of the Russian economy. PRC consumers have shown great interest in importing the growing volume of LNG being produced in the Russian Arctic. In February 2021, Russia's Novatek and China's Shenergy signed an agreement for Novatek to ship several million tons of LNG from the Arctic LNG-2 project in the Yamal Peninsula to terminals in Shanghai over the next 15 years.[7] Not only are several PRC companies helping develop natural resources in the Russian Arctic but Chinese corporations also look to become the main users of the Northern Sea Route that is being developed above Russia's northern frontier.

The Sino-Russian energy relationship has centered on oil, gas, and coal, but cooperation on nuclear, wind, and hydro power also occurs. Though the Sino-Russian nuclear energy partnership began in the 1950s, the last two decades have seen considerable growth due to Chinese interest in partnering with Russian companies with advanced nuclear technical capabilities. In May 2021, the PRC began constructing four advanced reactors powered by Russia's third-generation nuclear technology.[8] PRC representatives have framed the nuclear cooperation to be of great strategic significance in promoting Sino-Russian coordinated governance of the global energy industry. At a groundbreaking ceremony, attended by the presidents of both countries, President Xi called for Sino-Russian cooperation in establishing strong global safety principles, deepening Sino-Russian scientific and technological innovation, and advancing "the coordinated development of the global energy governance system."[9] Cooperation between Russia and China in other renewable energy sectors is more limited. In 2016, the newly established BRICS Development Bank— created as an alternative source of funding besides the World Bank and other Western-controlled international financial institutions for Brazil, Russia,

India, China, and South Africa (BRICS)—issued half-a-billion dollars' worth of "green bonds" to support renewable energy projects. The loans included considerable Chinese support for developing Russian solar and wind power.[10] The Sino-Russian renewable energy partnership may strengthen in the future if the Russian government becomes more committed to solar or other non-nuclear renewable energy sources, since China is a leading global supplier of such technologies. Outside the energy sector, Sino-Russian mutual trade and investment has been more limited. Russian and Chinese rail companies have pursued several joint projects. The Russian government has been pushing to prioritize hi-tech cooperation in industries such as biotechnology, nanotechnology, and aircraft manufacturing. With the strong backing of their two governments, Russian and PRC companies have signed deals to jointly develop and coproduce a wide-body passenger plane and a heavy-lift helicopter. Both governments are aiming to decrease their aviation industries' reliance on Western companies like Airbus and Boeing.

Both governments want to rely less on the U.S. dollar and Western financial institutions and more on use of their own national currencies in bilateral exchanges. To decrease their mutual dependency on the West, Russia and China have constructed financial structures within the Beijing-led Asian Infrastructure Investment Bank, the BRICS-sponsored New Development Bank, and the Shanghai Cooperation Organization to offer their businesses alternatives to using Western-led financial institutions. In 2014, the Russian and Chinese governments signed a three-year currency swap deal, since extended, to enable each country to use the other's currency without having to purchase it on the foreign exchange market.[11] Major Russian and Chinese banks have since constructed arrangements to bypass the U.S. dollar and pay each other in their domestic currencies. In March 2017, the Russian Central Bank, which has substantially increased its share of yuan in its foreign exchange reserves over the past decade, launched its first foreign office in China.[12] The two countries have also established a joint investment fund to finance mutually beneficial projects. Furthermore, the Russian state development bank Vnesheconombank (VEB) launched a new partnership with the China Development Bank to reduce its exposure to Western sanctions.[13] Russian and Chinese government agencies and companies frequently announce large trade and investment deals, new economic cooperation mechanisms, and additional initiatives to replace the U.S. dollar and weaken the other pillars of U.S. economic primacy. For instance, Gazprom Neft, the oil arm of Russian gas giant Gazprom, announced that it has started using the yuan for aviation fuel settlements, supporting the shift away from the dollar.[14] In 2019, during President XI's trip to Russia, the two leaders agreed to replace the U.S. dollar with national currencies for international settlements between them and develop alternative payment mechanisms to the U.S.-dominated SWIFT network for such trans-actions. Russia has reduced its dollar assets while increasing its Yuan holdings. In the first quarter of 2020, the dollar's share of trade between Russia and China fell below 50% for the first time.[15] Sino-Russian financial cooperation is also occurring in emerging economic sectors such as e-commerce and the novel tools of the digital economy. China is developing a digital yuan that Russia and other countries could use for international transactions.

In recent years, Russian and PRC leaders, including Putin and Xi, have pledged to harmonize their broader Eurasian economic integration initiatives, principally through linking the EEU and the BRI. For example, in his speech at the Far Eastern Economic Forum in September 2021, Xi highlighted the need for Russia and China to continue close economic cooperation and to deepen EEU-BRI collaboration.[16] Deeper Sino-Russian regional integration could increase bilateral trade and investment in critical areas, such as transportation infrastructure; strengthen security cooperation to preserve stability in transit countries; and expand people-to-people exchanges through tourism and other mechanisms. Interestingly, when Moscow launched the EEU in 2014, many observers saw the initiative as a counterweight to China as well as the EU and the United States, thinking Russia could use the EEU to erect barriers between its members and competing countries and regional blocs. The Russian government reversed its stance, however, after the Ukraine revolution, and Moscow's Crimea annexation led to the loss of Russian influence in much of Ukraine and triggered extensive Western sanctions. Russian policy makers came to accept Beijing's growing presence in Eurasia as both inevitable and potentially beneficial for Russia's economic objectives. The planned logistical and trans-portation infrastructure improvements connecting China and Europe would bring Russians more transit revenue and potentially more investment as well as facilitate Russians' own east-west commerce. Furthermore, Russian experts hoped that embedding the EEU within the BRI would promote Sino-Russian trust and ties. Conversely, they anticipated that the BRI would provide Moscow with leverage over Beijing due to China's reliance on transiting goods through the Russian landmass or neighboring territories under Moscow's security protection. By this reckoning, Chinese economic actors would make concessions to sustain Russian support for these east-west conduits. With Russia's support, Beijing secures a more reliable land route through Eurasia to Europe with lower political and security risks. Additionally, Russian officials may hope that, if China treated the EEU as a legitimate international actor, this would enhance the latter institution's status and enhance Moscow's prospects of joining other Asian multinational economic structures, such as the Regional Comprehensive Economic Partnership and the Comprehensive and Progressive Agreement for Trans-Pacific Partnership.

IMPLICATIONS AND RECOMMENDATIONS

Overall, the PRC has become the Russian Federation's most important trading partner due to China's high demand for oil, natural gas, and other raw materials. The PRC's exponential growth rates, along with Russia's stagnating economic ties with other countries, have also concentrated Russia's foreign economic ties on China. About one-fifth of Russia's imports presently originate from China, whereas some one-tenth of Russia's exports go to the PRC.[17] In 2020, the COVID-19 pandemic cancelled or delayed many Sino-Russian economic interactions since the PRC authorities, having adopted a zero tolerance toward the disease, largely closed China's borders to foreign nationals to prevent imported cases of COVID-19. As a result, Sino-Russian trade stagnated after several years of rapid growth. In 2021, though, Russian-Chinese trade rebounded. China's bilateral trade volume with Russia exceeded $120 billion for the first 11 months of 2021.[18] Cooperation has also been growing in new sectors such as e-commerce, mining, entertainment, construction, finance, and agriculture, with Russia benefiting from China's redirecting some food purchases away from the United States. The Russian and Chinese economies are essentially complementary, making it difficult for the United States or other players to impede their growing economic and energy ties. Russia has large quantities of natural resources, high-quality military equipment, and a pivotal location between Asia and Europe. Meanwhile, China can offer an enormous market, low-cost consumer goods, extensive manufacturing capability, and substantial investment capital. Beijing can encourage private PRC companies to invest in large projects with Russia through a combination of generous subsidies and loans with some negative pressure. To facilitate deals, the PRC has provided large loans and prepayments that provide Russian corporations with cash at decreased financial risk. Many of Russia's newest hydrocarbon fields are situated in eastern Russia closer to the PRC than the fields in European Russia. This location means that Russian oil and gas can enter Chinese territory directly without passing through international waters or third-party territories, as is the case with many other Chinese energy inflows. In some of their largest energy projects, Russia and China crafted a "win-win" model for developing their partnership: Russian firms received large Chinese advanced payments that allowed them to finance new hydrocarbon projects and transport the resulting oil and gas via pipelines to the PRC. Additionally, PRC companies have crafted favorable deals with Putin's associates to gain influence with the Russian elite.[19] Besides commercial considerations and other direct connections, their shared discontent with the U.S.-based liberal economic order also drives Russian-Chinese cooperation, within both bilateral and multinational frameworks. Putin has argued that governance of the world's major economic institutions should reflect the decline of the share of global GDP accounted for by the Western G7 bloc in favor of non-Western countries.[20]

Yet, in the Sino-Russian economic realm, there is often a chasm between declarations and developments. Mutual trade, investment, and other ties between Russia and China remain modest compared with the PRC's trade and investment links with Europe and the United States. Though Russia's trade with China has grown substantially, Russian expectations of receiving massive PRC investment and loans have not been fulfilled. While Beijing has become a more prominent trading partner for Moscow, Russia is by no means a leading trading partner of the PRC, which sends only some 1% of its exports to Russia. In 2021, 18% of Russia's foreign trade engaged China, whereas Russia accounted for a mere 2% of China's international commerce.[21] The overall volume of trade with Russia is significantly lower than that of China and other major economies, and Russia is not in China's top 10 major trading partners. A few years ago, Russian and Chinese leaders set the goal of raising their bilateral trade to $200 billion by 2020; the actual total that year was only half of that. Trade in 2020 between the PRC and Russia was only slightly over $100 billion. In contrast, China's trade volume with the United States that year exceeded $586 billion notwithstanding severe trade tensions.[22] Despite Russian aspirations for greater Chinese investment and technology, PRC investors have been as reluctant as other non-Russian entrepreneurs to make big bets on the Russian market. The Chinese government has formally refused to accept the legitimacy of the Western sanctions that have been adopted since 2014, but PRC investment in Russia decreased in the following years from already low levels. U.S. policy makers deliberately designed the sanctions to constrain Russian ties with China and other countries by raising the risk of doing business with Russian entities. The sanctions and the subsequent restrictions on travel after 2019 due to the COVID-19 pandemic have led PRC businesses to curtail its investment in many sectors in Russia, including manufacturing, transportation, and energy, with agriculture being the main exception. In 2019, PRC FDI accounted for merely $140 million of Russia's total $25.3 in inflows.[23] The largest PRC lenders to Russia have been the state-run banks that often make decisions on political rather than commercial considerations, are less exposed to the Western financial systems, and are more easily manipulated by the PRC authorities.[24] Similarly, with PRC government support and encouragement, some large state enterprises can hazard dealing with sanctioned Russian entities and sectors, but smaller Chinese businesses are more hesitant to take on the extra risk. Though Sino-Russian trade is balanced in terms of value, it is imbalanced in terms of quality. Russian exports to the PRC consist overwhelmingly of raw materials, especially natural resources like oil, coal, metals, and timber, along with fertilizer and agricultural goods, rather than high-tech and other high-value products, except for some advanced weapons and Russian nuclear power plants. Hydrocarbons account for almost two-thirds of Russian exports to the PRC. Meanwhile, Russians buy mostly Chinese electronics, machinery, base metals, textiles and apparel, and means of transport. More than two-thirds of Russia's imported technology products come from China.[25] Russian policy makers are eager to decrease their reliance on volatile raw material exports by reviving the Chinese purchase of high-value industrial goods and services. In public, PRC policy makers commit to do this. In practice, China continues to obtain most of its advanced technology from Western and other Asian countries. Though China is still importing nuclear reactors from Russia and other countries, the PRC has ambitions to become an exporter of nuclear reactors and services, positioning itself as a likely future competitor to Russia. The overreliance on oil and gas exports gives Russia an economic profile regarding China resembling that of a colony: selling natural resources in exchange for services and manufactured goods.

The Russian Far East has not been as strong a trade and investment magnet for China as Moscow has hoped. Russian authorities want to revive the Far East's fortunes, partially with the help of greater trade and investment from China. The vast region shares a 4,000-km border with China and is awash with natural resources such as natural gas, coal, gold, diamonds, timber, and seafood. But the region has experienced a continuous population exodus due to economic stagnation. PRC firms have invested in some border development projects encompassing the region. For example, the Russian Direct Investment Fund, VEB, and the China-Eurasia Economic Fund announced the creation of a finance mechanism to facilitate PRC exports to Russia and guide the flow of Chinese investment into projects into eastern Russia.[26] In 2018, Moscow and Beijing signed a six-year cooperation agreement for the Russian Far East, which included joint agricultural, tourism, and transportation investment projects. PRC capital accounts for almost three-fourths of all foreign investment projects in the Russian Far East.[27] Yet, the absolute volume of PRC investment remains relatively small. The Far East's small population size makes it challenging for factories that service local markets. Those Russians who remain are less fearful of Chinese immigration than they were in the 1990s, but anger over the environmental damage from China's Far Eastern investments persists. Another factor dampening PRC investors' enthusiasm is the existence of better opportunities in other locations, especially within China. Other conditions hindering investment in the Far East region include the region's poor transportation infrastructure and challenging climate conditions, all of which would add significant costs to any project.

Sino-Russian commerce experiences many hindrances, including language barriers, logistical problems, certification procedures, regulatory complexities, and cultural differences. Other unique factors are also at work. PRC banks have backed off from some projects to increase the volume of two-way trade settled in national currencies due to the volatility of the ruble, fears of devaluing the Chinese government's enormous dollar-denominated reserves, and to potential exposure to Western sanctions on Russia's financial sector.[28] So far, China's cash has not been as abundant as Moscow had hoped, and Beijing's preferences sometimes diverge from those of Moscow. Chinese purchases have made Russia an exporter of agricultural goods for the first time since the Soviet period, but China still imports more food products from other countries. The PRC also buys more LNG from the United States than from Russia. High-profile Sino-Russian projects, such as the planned high-speed railway between Moscow and Kazan, remain unrealized. Chinese investment in the Russian Arctic—aside from some high-profile flagship projects—has been minimal. Russian enthusiasm for BRI has waned as earlier hopes for substantially new Chinese investment in Russia or joint BRI-EEU projects have remained elusive. Conversely, Russian investment in China is dwarfed by the hundreds of billions of dollars of Western investment in the PRC.

Since China has considerably greater economic power than Russia, Beijing has less incentive to accept compromises for economic coordination, such as acting as a joint voting bloc in international financial institutions like the International Monetary Fund (IMF) or World Bank. Beijing has the weight to secure its own will in some of these structures—and even in opposing circumstances, securing Russian assistance is insufficient to shift the balance in China's favor. Progress on joining their Eurasian economic integration plans has remained limited due to the complexities of aligning these bodies and other challenges. While there has been agreement on some issues, and Russian and Chinese experts are developing more concrete implementation concepts, other critical issues such as reconciling diverging laws and regulations, establishing a system for protection of mutual investments, and forming investment dispute mechanisms remain unresolved.[29] The diverging nature of the two initiatives—the BRI is wider whereas the EEU is deeper—also complicates attempts to integrate them. The EEU has essentially become a limited customs union, whereas the BRI is a far more ambiguous program supported by significantly more financial and political capital. Though deeper, the EEU requires members to pursue similar policies and regulations, whereas the BRI, though more comprehensive, does not overly oblige participants to adopt stringent new laws or practices.

The Obama administration opposed the EEU, with Secretary of State Hillary Clinton characterizing Putin's initiate as an effort to restore the Soviet empire, but had adopted a generally neutral stance toward China's regional economic integration initiatives. These seemed to emphasize building infrastructure, removing barriers to trade, and addressing other challenges also faced by the United States and other economic actors in the region. Rather than outright objection, the Obama administration focused on promoting greater transparency in Chinese lending practices and other policies, adherence to internationally recognized lending standards, and ensuring that the United States and other nonregional states could remain active economic partners with countries within the region. In contrast, the Trump administration opposed both the BRI and the EEU as threats to U.S economic security and regional interests. The 2017 National Security Strategy maintained that "China and Russia target their investments in the developing world to expand influence and gain competitive advantages against" U.S. interests. The strategy warns that the kinds of state-directed investments favored by Moscow and Beijing often leave developing countries worse off. Instead, the United States "will promote a development model that partners with countries that want progress, consistent with their culture, based on free market principles, fair and reciprocal trade, private sector activity, and rule of law."[30] Yet, the United States has not yet launched a major competing initiative. Given budget constraints and the economic prioritization of other regions, the U.S. government might benefit most by supporting private-sector efforts as well as public-private collaboration where U.S. companies enjoy special skills and other competitive advantages. These projects might encompass expanding the use of U.S. commercial law and practices as well as improving managerial entrepreneurship and other human capital through targeted initiatives where local buy-in is strong. Congress should increase funding of the International Development Finance Corporation, which is subsuming the Overseas Private Investment Corporation, to support U.S. private investment abroad with more extensive loan and insurance guarantees.[31] Pooling resources with European and Asian democracies can also provide a more effective alternative for countering Russian and Chinese development programs. At home, strengthening the Committee on Foreign Investment helps shield critical U.S. emerging technologies and insulates industrial supply chains from Russian and Chinese meddling. The United States should encourage other countries to adopt similar oversight mechanisms.

11
Chapter

Outer Space

Outer space has become another arena of great power rivalry for Russia, China, and the United States. All three countries, which have the most advanced civilian and military space programs, believe maintaining a robust presence in space is critical for advancing their status, sovereignty, prosperity, and security. Historically, the United States and the Soviet Union (now Russia) had pioneered space technology and development. Unlike the first space race between Moscow and Washington during the Cold War, which was primarily defined by a quest for prestige and security, current space programs also strive for economic gains. The growth of the private-sector commercial space industry has also transformed what had previously been a domain dominated by states. Commercial firms now have space capabilities that previously had been available only to national governments. Another novelty is that more countries are asserting themselves in zero gravity. In particular, China has been investing enormous resources in developing its civilian and military space programs. These trends have resulted in space becoming more congested with an increasing number of satellites and other human-made objects.

Russia, China, and the United States have dedicated space defense projects as well as leading civilian space programs. All three countries possess several powerful space-launched vehicles (SLVs), operate more satellites than other states, and have access to spaceports throughout the world. Their ability to track and characterize objects in orbit—known as Space Situational Awareness (SSA)—through terrestrial and space-based sensors also exceeds that of other countries. Their space technologies are inherently "dual use" in that they can support military as well as civilian missions. Modern militaries use satellites, many commercial, for reconnaissance, navigation, communications, imagery, targeting, weather forecasting, and intelligence gathering. Common national security space missions include supporting combat communications, verifying arms control agreements, analyzing foreign defense developments, providing early warning of foreign missile launches, and monitoring long-term environmental conditions. But capabilities such as on-orbit servicing and end-of-life disposal can be used to disable or destroy other countries' satellites. At the same time, the international legal framework consists of a few narrowly tailored treaties and several discussion fora, such as the UN General Assembly and the Conference on Disarmament, that have made little progress negotiating even nonbinding norms and standards. The European Union admirably labored for a decade in a failed effort to secure agreement on a nonbinding Code of Conduct for Outer Space Activities without overcoming the opposition from Russia, China, and other countries.

Though Moscow and Washington have been space partners for decades, Russia has been increasing its cooperation in this domain with China, which has become an unacceptable space partner for the United States. In the words of an Indian scholar, "Today in the space domain there are two competing blocs. One consists of the US and its allies, and the other is Russia and China. They oppose almost each other's every idea in regards to space security."[1] Due to a 2011 law (the Wolf Amendment) passed by the U.S. Congress to prevent unauthorized technological transfer, the National Aeronautics and Space Administration (NASA), the primary U.S. government body for civil space exploration, has subsequently been prohibited from cooperating with China regarding most space issues. Though Russian-U.S. space cooperation has continued, strains over other issues have limited its extent. Most important, when Moscow annexed Crimea in 2014, the United States imposed sanctions against Russia, causing Moscow to pull away from many collaborative projects with Washington and look more favorably toward new partners, especially China. As Russia's agreement with the U.S.-led International Space Station (ISS) comes to an end in the next few years, Moscow may seize the opportunity to expand ties still further with China's space program. Such Sino-Russian collaboration could potentially leverage Russia's decades of experience in space with the People's Republic of China's (PRC) enormous financial resources and ambitions, forging a formidable anti-Western space partnership.

RUSSIAN GOALS AND POLICIES

Soviet and Russian space achievements evoke widespread feelings of national pride among Russians as a symbol of their country's global standing. The Soviet Union and the Russian Federation have had a long history of pioneering space exploration, having launched the world's first satellite (Sputnik, in 1957) and astronaut (Soviet cosmonaut Yuri Gagarin, in 1961). From 1986 to 2001, the USSR and later Russia also supported its own space station, the Mir.

In 1992, Moscow established the Russian Federal Space Agency, later renamed as the Roscosmos State Corporation for Space Activities, as the country's leading government space body, with the task of building on and surpassing Soviet achievements. Partnerships with the space programs of other countries (such as Kazakhstan, India, and Cuba) have been important elements in Soviet and Russian diplomacy and scientific-technological cooperation.

Despite various achievements and sustained strengths in advanced rocketry, satellite construction, and crewed spaceflight, Roscosmos has struggled to launch major space missions. Its last lunar lander reached the moon in 1976. Since 2014, falling prices for hydrocarbons, Western sanctions, and a recession have forced the Russian government to cut spending on its civilian space program. The United States and increasingly China spend many times more on space exploration than Russia. As a result, many Russian projects have been delayed or scrapped. Russia only recently overcame years of delays and corruption to open the new Vostochny Cosmodrome, which is to become Russia's main launch site, in the Amur Region in the Russian Far East near China. Russia has been using the Baikonur Cosmodrome in Kazakhstan for all crewed and most civilian satellite launches much longer than anticipated. (The Plesetsk launch site in northwest Russia also launches national security payloads.) Plans for a new Angara-A5 superheavy space launch vehicle and new crewed spacecraft (the Orel, intended for missions in Earth orbit and beyond) have been delayed for decades.

Nonetheless, the Russian government has continued to devote substantial funding to military space programs while still trying to revitalize its civilian and commercial space sectors. Russian military doctrine has come to view air and space as interlinked "into a specific field of armed conflict: an air-space theater of military operations."[2] Like the United States, the Russian Federation has reorganized and merged its military space forces with other branches and services over the years. In 2015, the government established the Russian Aerospace Forces by incorporating the preexisting Air Force with the Aerospace Defense Forces. This step reestablished space as an important realm for Russian military security while also encouraging integration of space into other Russian defense domains. The government has also made a sustained effort to rebuild its missile early warning capabilities, which atrophied in the 1990s, as well as its Arctic monitoring satellites. To maximize their dwell time, these satellites follow highly elliptical (aka *Molniya*) orbits pioneered by the Soviet Union designed to keep the satellites above certain parts of Earth, in this case the northern latitudes of the Arctic, for most of their orbits. More recently, Russia has been constructing additional surveillance, tracking, and communications support centers.

In November 2020, Russia shot down one of its own satellites, confirming the effectiveness of its PL19/Nudol anti-satellite (ASAT) weapon, which previously had only been tested against simulated targets. This weapon ascends directly from Earth's surface on a ballistic missile, which releases an exo-atmospheric kill vehicle that destroys its target by force of impact. Highlighting Russia's capacity to down U.S. space assets, Defense Minister Shoigu boasted that the "cutting-edge system" Moscow employed hit its target "with precision worthy of a goldsmith."[3] Russia has also conducted extensive research and development of uncrewed "co-orbital" spacecraft that maneuver near other space objects in order to study, shadow, disrupt, grab, hack, or smash them. With a persistent presence in space, these co-orbital ASATs could destroy other spacecraft with scant notice. Furthermore, Russia's "nesting doll" satellites have demonstrated an ability to expel smaller objects that could damage a target through kinetic collision at 700 kilometers per hour. The Soviet Union and Russia have also researched various directed energy weapons like lasers to track, disrupt, or, if strong enough, destroy objects in space.[4]

CHINA'S GOALS AND POLICIES

The Chinese government has a long-term plan to make the PRC a dominant player in outer space. A 2016 government white paper stated that achieving a presence in space is essential for advancing the Chinese economy and society.[5] Though China established its civilian space agency only three decades ago, the Chinese government has made extraordinary progress improving its civilian and national security space capabilities. The PRC has mastered many of the technologies and skills needed for space missions, including advanced rocketry, satellite construction, and crewed spaceflight. The PRC now has more than 400 satellites, second only to the United States, and their number is increasing more rapidly than that of any other country. For the past decade, China's average annual rate of government satellite launches has regularly exceeded that of the United States. The technical capabilities of China's satellites have continually improved. The PRC is also developing a new generation of Long March carrier rockets to send heavier payloads deeper into space as well as reusable rockets and spaceplanes. The government has been heavily promoting and developing its commercial space capabilities on international markets as part of a long-term plan to make China a dominant player in space and other technology sectors. China has concluded more than 100 space cooperation agreements and executed other forms of space cooperation with dozens of foreign countries and international organizations. Despite following the paths played earlier by Russia and the United States, the PRC has been unique in tightly integrating its commercial and defense space programs through its civil-military fusion policy.

In recent years, the PRC has conducted especially ambiguous long-range space exploration missions. In December 2013, China became only the third country to land a robotic probe on the moon's surface, after the United States and the Soviet Union in the 1970s. In January 2019, China's Chang'e-4 lunar mission deployed the Yutu-2 rover vehicle to explore the moon's far side, the first spacecraft to land on that surface, which is not visible from the Earth. In July 2020, the Chinese National Space Administration (CNSA) launched its first independent mission to Mars (a previous attempt proved unsuccessful when the Russian booster failed). This Tianwen-1 ("Heavenly Questions") package consisted of an orbiter, lander, and autonomous rover—the first time a country had packaged all three elements into a single Mars mission. The successful landing of the Tianwen-1 probe on Mars in May 2021 made China only the third country to realize such an achievement, after the Soviet Union and the United States. The PRC's crewed space capabilities have also been rapidly improving. In June 2013, China became the third country to independently send astronauts into space with its Shenzhou X mission. Since then, PRC astronauts (aka "taikonauts") have visited space more frequently and for longer intervals. The PRC demonstrated a mastery of automated and manual docking techniques by placing a pair of temporary space laboratories into orbit and successfully anchoring them to the Shenzhou spacecraft. In April 2021, China launched the core module for its planned long-term space station, the Tiangong. Since June 2021, rotating PRC crews have been configuring the module for future long-term occupancy.

RUSSIAN-CHINESE INTERACTIONS

The Soviet Union and later the Russian Federation helped the PRC to develop its space program by launching several Chinese space probes and training some of the first PRC astronauts. China's early space technologies, such as its SLVs, were based on Soviet designs. Nonetheless, for some two decades starting in the mid-1990s, the Russian government was cautious about cooperating with China's space program for fear of creating a formidable space competitor as well as antagonizing the United States, then Moscow's most important space partner. As in other areas, Russian policy makers have become more open to cooperating with China in the space domain due to limited national capacity, China's growing space capabilities, and the absence of alternative partners. In June 2016, the two governments signed an intellectual property protection agreement to support growing Sino-Russian collaboration regarding space exploration, rocket engines, and SLVs. Russia and the PRC have also linked their satellite-based terrestrial navigation systems, GLONASS and BeiDou, through data-sharing and other agreements. They have collaborated in the civil space research field, encompassing Earth monitoring, space debris research, and lunar exploration. Additionally, Russian and Chinese scientific bodies and companies have purchased important space technologies from each other. For example, the PRC has bought Russian spacesuits and RD-180 rocket engines, while Russia's space program has purchased Chinese microelectronics. In October 2019, President Putin announced that the Russian government was assisting the PRC to build an early warning system against U.S. missile launches. In March 2021, Roscosmos and CNSA signed a memorandum of mutual understanding on designing and eventually building a joint International Lunar Research Station. They plan to construct the structure, either entirely on the lunar surface or partly through a station that orbits the moon, through a series of phases through 2036. Then the station would host a series of robotic and crewed missions, including in deep space. Therefore, they are looking for lunar sites with ice and other resources in order to supply missions from the moon rather than the earth. Russian and Chinese representatives insist that they are open to collaborations with additional international partners.

In coming years, Russia and China may research, develop, and exchange military and dual-use space technologies. Of note, the Chinese media has called for greater Sino-Russian cooperation in the national security space domain.[6] For example, Russia and China could jointly develop SLVs and satellite constellations. They could also extend their joint military exercise program into outer space. Sino-Russian diplomatic collaboration regarding space security has been evident in various international bodies. For years, the two governments have been submitting draft treaties to the United Nations and other bodies designed to limit U.S. military activities in space. The United States and other countries have consistently rejected these drafts, the most recent being the "Treaty on the Prevention of the Placement of Weapons in Outer Space, the Threat or Use of Force against Outer Space Objects (PPWT)." Among other concerns, the text fails to limit ground-based weapons that target space objects, such as those employed in the PRC ASAT test in 2007 and the Russian test in 2021.

Conversely, China and the United States have cooperated only intermittently regarding outer space. A 1979 agreement on Understanding on Cooperation in Space Technology enabled the PRC to purchase U.S. satellite communication systems that were placed in orbit by NASA. The United States also built a ground station on Chinese territory to provide satellite images for the U.S. Geological Survey's Landsat remote sensing satellites. Cooperation grew more substantial in the 1990s, when the United States turned to China for affordable launching of U.S.-manufactured commercial satellites. Besides its lower costs, U.S. companies saw the PRC launch services as helping overcome the consequences of the 1986 Challenger explosion, which led to a two-year grounding of the U.S. Space Shuttle fleet and a permanent prohibition on commercial launches using the Shuttle. When some of these Chinese launches failed, U.S. companies provided technical assistance that likely improved the performance of PRC missiles as well as commercial rocket carriers. A congressional commission, besides censoring this assistance, found that China exploited academic exchanges to steal sensitive technologies that the PRC could use to improve its nuclear delivery systems. As a result of these concerns about inappropriate technology transfers as well as a lack of reciprocity and transparency, Congress has severely restricted Sino-U.S. scientific and technological space cooperation. NASA and the CNSA presently collaborate only on select space issues such as safety and diplomatic matters. They also have engaged in fresh confrontations over debris issues and the unguided rocket returns the Chinese space program have been generating during its recent missions.

Notwithstanding their Cold War rivalry, Moscow and Washington have experienced a lengthy history of space cooperation, exemplified by multiple joint missions. In the 1970s, the joint Apollo-Soyuz mission mated an Apollo command module with a Russia Soyuz spacecraft; the two spacecraft docked in July 1975, paving the way to a joint space station. Roscosmos focused its limited budget in the 1990s on international cooperation in space, specifically towards the new ISS.[7] The Russian Soyuz became the most reliable means of sending cargo and astronauts, American as well as Russian, to the ISS. The end of the Space Shuttle program in 2011 left NASA without a SLV for sending astronauts or large payloads into space. The Russian Soyuz rocket became the substitute means for U.S. astronauts to reach the ISS. Furthermore, the Atlas V rocket, operated by United Launch Alliance as an SLV for NASA and commercial payloads, used an imported Russian RD-180 engine to power its first stage. RD-180s are not refurbished after each use, but rather a new one is required, so the United States required a consistent supply of these engines. As a result, Russia earned substantial revenue by conveying U.S. astronauts to the ISS, selling rocket engines to the United States, and launching satellites for private companies and other countries. However, though this interdependence looked like a mutually advantageous bargain a decade ago, it became increasingly problematic for Washington as Russian-U.S. relations frayed and as the Russian authorities kept increasing fees for transporting NASA astronauts to the ISS. The practice of pursuing inconsistent acquisition policies, low production rates, and long development cycles for space launch systems weakened the U.S. space industrial base as well as U.S. space-related science and technology. The limited U.S. SLV capacity gave both Russia and China more opportunities to launch foreign satellites and build international relationships with partner countries. Though scientists and space companies in Russia and the United States wanted to continue cooperation on new scientific projects, they could not counterbalance the deteriorating governmental ties between Russia and the United States. In April 2014, the United States suspended most cooperative space projects with Russia, excluding only those required to manage the ISS, and tightened limits on the transfer of space technology to Russia. In response, Deputy Prime Minister Dmitry Rogozin, who oversaw the Russian space program, wrote on Twitter that the United States would need "to bring their astronauts to the International Space Station using a trampoline."[8] Russia also limited support for the U.S. Global Positioning System and threatened to end supplying Russian rocket engines to the U.S. space program. Russia's attack on Ukraine in February 2022 has erected another substantial barrier to an enduring Russian-U.S. space partnership.

IMPLICATIONS AND RECOMMENDATIONS

The U.S. government condemned Russia's November 2021 attack. U.S. secretary of state Antony Blinken denounced Russia's "recklessly conducted" ASAT test because it created a long-lived debris field that will "threaten satellites and other space objects that are vital to all nations' security, economic, and scientific interests for decades to come."[9] According to the U.S. National Defense Space Strategy that was published on June 17, 2020, space has become a distinct warfighting domain and new strategic environment that requires additional U.S. space-based capabilities as well as a novel approach toward space conflicts.[10] The Russian and Chinese militaries pursue counterspace capabilities to exploit the Pentagon's dependence on satellites. If they could even temporarily disrupt U.S. satellites, they could more easily seize disputed territories or take other aggressive actions against U.S. allies, partners, and interests. Their terrestrial and space-based ASAT capabilities include:

- direct-ascent kinetic kill vehicles launched from Earth that could destroy exo-atmospheric targets through force of impact;
- "co-orbital" systems on existing satellites that maneuver toward other space objects to observe, shadow, hack, disrupt, grab, or smash them;
- directed energy weapons such as laser, particle, or microwave beams with advanced aiming and control systems for disrupting, and possibly destroying, space objects; and
- ground-based and space-based electronic warfare (EW) systems for disrupting satellite sensors, communications, or navigation positioning systems by spoofing their signals, interfering with their transmissions, or overloading their radio frequencies.

Rather than "hard-kill" U.S. satellites with destructive means, Russia and China may preferably employ "soft-kill" methods, such as jamming and disabling satellites through cyber and EW attacks, to obscure attribution given plausible technical failures or accidental interference.

The leaders of U.S. Space Command (USSPACECOM) see the PRC as the most serious long-term threat to U.S. space interests.[11] A deeper space partnership between China and Russia, especially on national security space issues, could present still greater security risks. Several reasons make further Sino-Russian space collaboration likely. First, Moscow and Beijing are complementary partners. Since the collapse of the Soviet Union, Russia's space program, albeit possessing valuable experience, has suffered shortfalls in funding, qualified personnel, and other resource inadequacies. On the other hand, Beijing's burgeoning space program has ample resources but lacks Russia's decades of previous missions. Moscow and Beijing might plausibly try, in some areas, to combine China's resources with Russia's experience on joint projects. Additionally, constraints on their working with Western space partners, as well as their common aversion toward the United States, might drive them together.

Russia and China have analyzed U.S. dependencies in space and have developed doctrine and capabilities designed to deny U.S. access to and operations within the space domain. Their military doctrines indicate that they understand the importance of space to modern warfare and consider counterspace capabilities as means of reducing U.S. military effectiveness for winning future war. As discussed, Russia and China have developed a diverse portfolio of ASAT weapons. These range from direct-ascent systems that, launched from Earth, can collide with a target, as well as place satellites in the orbit that can then maneuver to disable or destroy targets in their proximity through ramming, detonating, or other means. Both countries also are developing ground-based lasers, electronic jammers, and cyber weapons to render adversary satellites blind, deaf, and impotent. Threats from North Korea and Iran in the space domain are also currently growing. Other challenges include lack of international agreements on unsafe, irresponsible, or threatening behavior in space and the critical reliance of U.S. military and civilian on space systems. As experts note, "The United States is considered to be particularly vulnerable to attacks in space due to the extent to which the nation is dependent on space. A potential adversary could asymmetrically disadvantage the United States through attacks against space systems."[12]

The United States has taken preparations to deal with the new challenges in space from Russia, China, and others. In the 2020 National Defense Authorization Act, Congress created a new U.S. Space Force to help counter these threats. In December 2019, the Space Force became the sixth branch of the U.S. armed forces. In June 2020, the Space Force established three mission-specific field commands: the Space Operations Command for conducting operations, the Space Systems Command for acquiring and developing capabilities, and the Space Training and Readiness Command. Though its architects and leaders stress that space has become a warfighting domain—joining the land, air, sea, and cyber domains—the Force focused on supporting terrestrial military missions, in peace and wartime, rather than waging battles in the cosmos. The Force is tasked with organizing, training, and equipping forces for the 11 Combatant Commands, which include the newly created USSPACECOM, which has assumed most of the space missions of the previous Air Force Space Command. In other words, the Space Force trains and equips military personnel to fight in space under the direction of USSPACECOM, which supports, and is supported by, the other U.S. Combatant Commands. It resembles a coast guard rather than a blue-water navy in that the focus of USSPACECOM and the Space Force is not to fight wars in space but to support operations on Earth, particularly by assuring U.S. access to space for terrestrial operations.

The National Defense Space Strategy directs the Pentagon to pursue four lines of effort to enhance U.S. military security in space: (1) build a comprehensive military advantage in space; (2) integrate military space power into national, joint, and combined operations; (3) shape the strategic environment; and (4) cooperate with allies, partners, industry, and other U.S. agencies. The Trump administration reestablished the National Space Council as a cabinet-level body within the Executive Office of the President, chaired by the vice president and supported by a prominent Users' Advisory Group, to coordinate overall U.S. government policies for civil, commercial, military, and international space policies. Its members helped draft both the 2018 National Space Strategy, which stressed the need for a "whole-of-government" approach in the space domain, and the Space Policy Directive (SPD) 1. The subsequent Deep Space Exploration and Development strategy for commercialization of most nonmilitary Low-Earth Orbit (LEO) activities addressed establishing a permanent presence on the moon, sending humans to Mars, extending scientific research deeper into space, and revitalizing U.S. space education and the U.S. space workforce. Its appendices list U.S. government agencies that pursue space missions and summarize proposed space programs. NASA's new Space Development Agency, established in 2019, aims to accelerate the research, development, and acquisition of innovative national security space capabilities.

The U.S. government has also successfully partnered with skilled U.S. space entrepreneurs to develop more viable means of LEO transport, for both astronauts and cargo supplies to space stations. Innovative public-private partnership arrangements have helped rebuild the U.S. SLV fleet. Under its Commercial Crew Program, NASA contracts to companies like SpaceX to convey astronauts into LEO using the companies own recoverable SLVs. The goal of commercializing all LEO missions achieved a major success in 2020, when a SpaceX Falcon 9 rocket and its Crew Dragon spacecraft conveyed a pair of NASA astronauts to the ISS. Such flights have since become routine. Meanwhile, NASA is developing its own Space Launch System (SLS) to convey crew beyond Earth's orbit. Under the Artemis program, the SLS is scheduled to convey astronauts, to include female crew members and people of color, to the moon in the next few years and later to Mars and other celestial bodies. Both NASA and the U.S. military may position more satellites in the so-called cislunar region between Earth and the moon, where the two bodies' gravitation pulls are negated. The Biden administration is reviewing the timetable for further missions as well as the extent to which the United States will cooperate with Russia and China on space projects. Citing the challenge from China's rapidly improving program and the scientific benefits, the administration announced in December 2021 that the United States would try to continue the existing ISS partnership, with Russia as the main partner, through 2030, by which time NASA hopes that private U.S. companies will build a replacement.[13] Russia's 2022 invasion of Ukraine has made this partnership substantially less likely.

The administration is also assessing what space arms control initiatives to pursue with Moscow and Beijing, such as agreements not to engage in destructive ASAT tests at a time when the number of satellites and spacecraft vulnerable to test debris is rapidly growing. In April 2022, the United States unilaterally pledged to eschew destructive ASAT tests and called on other countries to adopt a similar moratorium. A related issue is discussing how satellites of one country should behave when in proximity to other states' space objects. These arms control dialogues could occur through bilateral or trilateral discussions or in multinational structures, such as the United Nations. To deal with the Russian and Chinese space threat, the United States is expanding its surveillance of their space activities, hardening satellites against potential attacks, and preparing for the possible abrupt destruction or degradation of U.S. space-based networks. The United States should also continue cultivating new space partners. Many countries are now developing space launch and exploration capabilities. Building relationships with these new space powers will help the United States manage Russia's and China's growing capabilities in this domain.

Conclusion

Implications and Recommendations

Analysts have traditionally underestimated the potential for an enduring and comprehensive Russia-China alignment against the United States. Until recently, U.S. national security planners have shown little public concern about Sino-Russian economic, energy, diplomatic, or even security cooperation. Experts may have presumed that the Russian-Chinese security partnership was inherently limited due to the well-known differences between the countries, downplayed the military potential of both countries' armed forces given U.S. military strengths and the superior U.S. global network of allies and partners, or feared that expressing open unease about their collaboration would encourage it—or at least make Moscow and Beijing believe that they had gained leverage over the West from cooperating. However, prudence warrants more consideration of the negative effects of an enduring alignment of these two powerful countries on U.S. interests and how the United States can best manage them. This review of the case studies, encompassing both geographic regions and critical functional issues that are important both for the Sino-Russian relationship and the United States, provides comprehensive insights into these questions. Drawing on the cases, this concluding chapter considers the possible evolution of the Russia-China relationship, assesses past U.S. policies toward the Sino-Russian alignment, and offers additional recommendations for managing this great power triangle in coming years.

The cases confirm that, for many geographic and functional areas, the Sino-Russian relationship is stronger than at any previous point in recent history. Moscow and Beijing now engage in an unprecedented range of joint security, economic, and diplomatic initiatives. The two countries have resolved their territorial dispute, China has become Russia's most important economic partner, they routinely back each other in the United Nations and other multilateral fora, and they have become each other's most significant security partners. Their respective national leaders, Vladimir Putin and Xi Jinping, have accrued enormous power over their countries' foreign policies and will likely maintain control over their respective nations for years, given how they both have effectively secured removal of term limits on their rule. Moreover, the two men appear to collaborate, outwardly jovially, with each other more often and extensively than their predecessors. Not only do Russian and Chinese diplomats agree on which U.S. policies, principles, and institutions they oppose but they also increasingly promote alternate visions and projects to replace them. Their policy differences have narrowed in opposition to U.S. military alliances, missile defenses, and arms control. Toward nearby regions, both regimes trumpet nationalism and anti-Americanism to rally domestic support for their policies, while their political systems have been becoming increasingly authoritarian. At the regional level, Moscow and Beijing have sought a de facto condominium in Central Asia, launched a joint peace plan for the Korean Peninsula, and pledged to harmonize their respective Eurasian economic integration projects. At the global level, the two governments have promoted shared global norms for cyber and outer space, international economics, and other domains that would privilege their national interests at the expense of other states. They also accommodate each other's priorities and compartmentalize binational tensions in order to minimize the potential damage or disagreements to the relationship. Sino-Russian cooperation varies substantially by time, region, and functional area. While Moscow and Beijing act relatively closely in some areas, their policies remain largely uncoordinated regarding other questions. In many geographic and functional areas, the two governments still pursue parallel rather than coordinated policies. Their approaches are most harmonious regarding Central Asia and, increasingly, East Asia, and even the Arctic, while they are less aligned regarding Europe, South Asia, and the Middle East. In contrast, there is much less evidence of Sino-Russian collaboration regarding Latin America or Africa. In terms of functional areas, their ties are tightest regarding security issues, lag behind their hopes in the economic domain, and remain minimal in the social sphere, notwithstanding the two governments' best efforts to alter this situation. Moscow and Beijing each would like the other partner to alter some policies—and may privately welcome U.S. pressure toward that end.

Despite growing cooperation, the Sino-Russian defense partnership is still weaker than the military ties of the United States with its closest allies. Russia and China do not have a mutual defense alliance, lack permanent joint defense structures, and are not yet capable of conducting a large joint conventional military operation against a major adversary. Their economic relationship is glaringly unbalanced, with Russia considerably more dependent on China than vice versa. Many of their recent autarchic policies, compounded by the impact of the COVID-19 pandemic, have decreased their overall level of foreign, social, and economic connections, including with each other. Notwithstanding their efforts to expand Sino-Russian commercial relations or the Trump administration's decoupling policies, Western countries remain China's main economic partners. Fundamentally, the leaders of Moscow and Beijing strongly want to remain independent great powers. The contemporary Sino-Russian relationship could be described as an "alignment without alliance," in which both states can freely engage with third parties as long as they refrain from impeding the realization of each other's economic and military goals.[1] Keeping their distance even when siding with each other allows Russia and China to decrease mutual vulnerability. The durability of their strategic partnership is enhanced by this lack of constraints, exclusivity, or binding agreements. The COVID-19 pandemic provided an interesting, if inadvertent, stress test of their alignment. The massive slowdown in the Chinese economy at the beginning of the pandemic might have led Russian leaders to hedge against further setbacks and consider means to at least partly decouple their tightening economies. Instead, the subsequent slowdown in the Russian economy and its other main foreign economic partners, in conjunction with the People's Republic of China's (PRC) rapid economic recovery by the middle of the year, had the effect of inducing the Russian leadership to double down on its partnership with China.

FUTURE CHALLENGES AND OPPORTUNITIES

The next few years will most likely see a continuation of this pattern of decent, but not excellent, relations between Russia and China, in which they loosely cooperate on a few important issues but essentially ignore each other regarding most others. Though more than an axis of convenience, this situation does not represent a traditional security alliance, which typically includes legally binding mutual defense obligations. Nevertheless, alternate Sino-Russian futures are imaginable, and their probability could increase over time. In the face of a more direct U.S. military threat, Russia and China could form a genuine military alliance in which they pool their considerable economic and military resources and coordinate their defense policies to present the United States and its allies with a united front. This scenario would see the two countries commit to guarantee each other's defense and establish joint commands and other binational structures to enhance military collaboration in a conflict. A deeper economic partnership would entail Russia combining its skills in basic science and technology with China's enormous monetary, labor, and manufacturing resources. Conversely, several potential developments could worsen the Sino-Russian relationship and lead Moscow to join other countries in a strategy to balance Beijing's rising power. The PRC's massive military buildup could alarm the Russian national security establishment, as it has already in other countries.

Central Asia could serve as a bellwether for the overall Russian-Chinese relationship, reflecting the balance between cooperation and rivalry in Sino-Russian relations. Whereas Moscow strives to control the security policies of its Eurasian neighbors, Beijing's security goal has been to avert worst outcomes, such as regional terrorism or state failure. Should Beijing's confidence in Moscow's ability to maintain stability in Eurasia decline, Beijing might abandon its policy of deference to Moscow and assume a more prominent independent security role in Eurasia. The PRC's growing interest in Central Asian oil and gas could also lead Beijing to reconsider its policy of regional deference to Russia. The current harmony between Moscow and Beijing in Central Asia arises primarily because the PRC leadership considers the region of lower strategic priority than does the Kremlin. One could similarly imagine heightened Sino-Russian tensions over their adjacent border region. The demographic disparity that exists between the Russian Far East and northern China invariably raises the question of whether parts of underpopulated eastern Russia will, de facto if not de jure, fall under Chinese control.

Furthermore, the Sino-Russian partnership lacks popular foundation and is predominately a top-down project driven by the current governments in both countries, making it somewhat hollow and brittle.[2] Moscow and Beijing have coordinated themed years emphasizing tourism, language, and youth exchanges, with sports cooperation being the theme for 2022 and 2023, but societal ties between Russians and Chinese remain modest, with the COVID-19 pandemic abruptly curtailing tourism and other contacts. Throughout the pandemic, the PRC authorities have been treating Russian nationals the same as other foreign citizens in China, with no special treatment despite the claims of a "special relationship." New leaders in either country could bring a new perspective to the relationship. Status considerations may become a more serious impediment to their relationship in the future. Russian resentment could build if China continues to ascend as the sole near-peer rival of the United States, a position the Soviet Union had in the 20th century but has lost since then. Whatever deference and mutual respect they display in public, PRC analysts privately belittle Russia's long-term prospects of remaining China's great power peer, envisaging instead a G2 world of only two great powers, the PRC and the United States.[3] The growing Sino-Russian power gap will complicate their future relationship by amplifying Russian anxieties about falling further behind the PRC and becoming Beijing's subordinate partner. China's recent policy toward Russia has been atypically nonconfrontational, both in terms of the history of their bilateral relationship and compared with Beijing's policies toward its other neighbors. However, China might at some point exploit its increasingly superior power to pursue a more assertive policy toward Russia as well. Such a PRC overreach might prompt a Russian reassessment of its policy of appeasing and binding China.

More of the Same

The perpetuation of the current pattern of Sino-Russian relations, in which the two states cooperate in some areas but remain uncoordinated regarding others, is certainly plausible. Neither Moscow nor Beijing wants to antagonize the other at a time when relations with their other neighbors are so disturbed. Even more, both governments consider their strong relationship a major mutual asset. Russian leaders describe their alignment with Beijing as both comprehensive and enduring. In January 2021, Foreign Minister Sergey Lavrov observed, "Russian-Chinese cooperation . . . embraces . . . almost all spheres of human activity . . . ."[4] At his December 2017 news conference, Putin observed "that there is a nationwide consensus in Russia concerning the development of relations with China. Whatever the outcome of the [2018 Russian presidential] elections, Russia and China will remain strategic partners for the long-term historical perspective."[5] Many Russian leaders accept Beijing's growing power and influence as inevitable. They have decided that the best way to manage a rising China on Russia's doorstep is to bandwagon with the PRC by finding common ground, adopting supportive policies, and building bilateral ties. The goal of the Russian leadership is to solidify a close relationship sooner rather than later, as the two countries' diverging power paths indicate that Moscow's bargaining leverage with Beijing will likely decline in the future. Some Russian authors have developed a new conceptual framework to characterize the Russia-China relationship, referring to it as the "Greater Eurasian Partnership," a concept that connects growing Sino-Russian ties within the broader goals of revitalizing the Russian Far East's relationship with the rest of the country and strengthening Russia's presence and influence in Asia.[6]

Russian and Chinese leaders also have modest expectations of how much support they can expect from the other, limiting strains on their alignment. Both governments recognize that neither country is in a strong position to play a primary role in helping the other accomplish its core foreign-policy goals. Beijing's main objective is to dominate Asia, where Russia has little influence; meanwhile, Moscow has neither received nor asked for substantial support from China in managing its immediate challenges in Europe and the Middle East. Most of Russia's territory and natural resources lie in Asia, but its population, leadership, and diplomatic focus are directed toward Europe. These divergences lead them to temper their mutual expectations and accept their differences with equanimity. As long as Putin rules Russia, maintaining good ties with China will remain a priority. Putin's partisans describe Moscow's improved ties with Beijing as a major achievement of his presidency; challenging this assessment could be seen as questioning Putin's judgment and performance, an unwise career move. In effect, Moscow's "turn to Asia" strategy had become a "bet on China" policy, with Putin leading the charge. Until Putin leaves office, moreover, the Russian government's relations with the United States and many U.S. allies will remain poor. The pervasive hostility toward Putin among U.S. leaders, which is manifestly reciprocated, is unlikely to dissipate soon. Additionally, Russian defense experts doubt that Beijing will soon exploit its growing military strength to Moscow's disadvantage. Many Russian analysts have downplayed, if not underestimated, China's growing military capabilities. One reason that the Russian government has encouraged its defense companies to supply sophisticated air, navy, and air defense platforms to the PRC is Moscow's confidence that the People's Liberation Army (PLA) would only employ these systems, if at all, against other countries.

Relative to the U.S.-led world order, Russia and China are revisionist powers—they each would like to change key features to make it more beneficial to their distinct national interests. They presume hostile motives behind almost all U.S. government policies affecting their country. The Russian and PRC governments share discontent with the prevailing U.S.-led international system, which is based on classical liberal principles. They want to replace or radically change its U.S.-designed economic and security structures, which were established after World War II. For now, Russia has the ambition to challenge the U.S.-led global order but lacks the means, whereas China has the means but not the goal of establishing an entirely new international system. Moscow is more openly and immediately rejectionist than Beijing, employing more assertive means. The Kremlin desires a return to a multipolar world order in which Russia and China are also great powers, with independent spheres of influence, along with the United States. In contrast, PRC leaders profess a desire to reform, rather than upturn, the current international structures, though sometimes they suggest a more bipolar-plus arrangement, relegating Moscow to secondary status in a world defined primarily by China-U.S. competition. In his speech to the Munich Security Conference in February 2019, Yang Jiechi, the director of Chinese Communist Party's (CCP) Central Foreign Affairs Commission, said, "China has actively engaged in the reform of the global governance system [whose purpose] is not to overturn the current system or start something new, but to improve the existing framework to reflect new realities and increase the representation and voice of emerging markets and developing countries."[7] Thus, the PRC is no longer a "rule taker" but not yet a comprehensive "rule maker," though the number of areas in which Beijing has a major impact on global standards is increasing. In the long term, suspicions exist that PRC initiatives aim not only to improve China's economic power but also to attain economic dominance and, in turn, supplant the United States and present the world with an alternative economic order run from Beijing. Importantly, Russia and China generally dampen their fundamental differences regarding their preferred international order by not discussing the topic.

From a geographic perspective, Russia-China differences regarding regional issues remain modest and manageable. Despite expectations that Moscow and Beijing would become natural contestants for primacy in Central Asia, the region has thus far been a unifying force in the Sino-Russian relationship rather than an object of rivalry. Beijing has deferred to Moscow's dominant security and political roles in the region, while Russia has widely accepted the growth of PRC trade and investment in Central Asia to the extent that Chinese economic links have become comparable to those of Russia. The two countries seemingly resolved their centuries-long territorial dispute, mitigating a potentially divisive issue that could have presented a barrier to further coordination. Russia and China currently cooperate well on border security issues such as transborder crime, illegal migration, and frontier management. In the 1990s, this border area was a highly politicized issue in Russia, but during the following decade, under Putin's direction, Moscow reestablished central power over the region. Fears of Chinese immigrants flooding into Russian territory have also declined as the limited and transient nature of PRC migrants in the Russian Federation has become clearer. Chinese nationals typically worked in Russia for only a few years and then returned home. Long-term foreign immigrants in Russia still overwhelmingly come from Central Asia. If anything, Russian policy makers want to attract more PRC entrepreneurs and investment to the underdeveloped Russian Far East. Plans for joint Sino-Russian economic, energy, and agricultural projects in their border regions remain undeveloped, a source of mutual frustration though not tension. The slow but steady construction of new east-west energy pipelines and other transportation links will continually deepen economic ties. In the military domain, their joint exercise program has become routinized; analysts expect to see additional joint ground, naval, and air drills performed in the coming years. Given the lengthy number of military contracts already extant, Sino-Russian defense industrial cooperation will likely continue for some time, and future years will see the transfer of additional Russian weaponry to the PRC. Some Russian experts have viewed the PLA's rapidly advancing capabilities as a welcome means of helping balance U.S. global military power. In their interactions with their Russian colleagues, PRC officials show deference to Moscow's great power pretensions. Chinese representatives have been solicitous of Moscow's hurt pride, emphasizing their two nations' major power status, glorious history and culture, and enduring partnership.

A strength of their alignment is that Moscow and Beijing have regularly and adroitly managed their differences. For the most part, when Moscow and

Beijing diverge on issues, they do not pressure the other to yield in their disagreements. The two governments have been careful not to overcommit to
each other. Their relationship further benefits from the fact that Russian and
Chinese security priorities predominately focus on different geographic areas
and functional issues. Most Russian analysts identify countering terrorism
directed against Russian interests as well as decreasing U.S. influence in Eurasia and Europe as their main goals. In contrast, PRC policy makers primarily worry about separatist movements, Islamist terrorism in China, and U.S.
military activities in the Indo-Pacific region. Due to these differing priorities,
Russia and China do not presently have a major bilateral dispute where their
vital national interests conflict. Equally important, neither Moscow nor Beijing requires the other's help to achieve its most critical national goals, allowing them to accept with benign equanimity cases when the other fails to render
support, which lessens the potential for fissures. Since Russian officials prioritize European and Eurasian issues, while their Chinese counterparts focus
on Asian-Pacific questions, there are few issues where even a major bilateral
dispute could lead to a fatal break between them. They most often agree to
disagree. This practice makes their partnership less brittle, but the flexibility
does limit the depth of their collaboration on some issues. Given their national
political leaderships' shared desire to sustain good ties, even when Russian and
Chinese entities come into conflict regarding specific issues, such as when their
diplomats disagree over some regional question or their corporations compete
over contracts, these specific differences have not grown to damage the entire
Sino-Russian alignment. Although Russian and PRC policy makers would
like more support from the other in their disputes with third parties, they
are content to keep the other from openly siding against them. This dynamic
can be demonstrated by how Moscow and Beijing have managed their divergence over the question of enlarging the Shanghai Cooperation Organization's
(SCO) membership. In the past, Russia tried to raise India's status into the
SCO to dilute China's primacy, but for years, Beijing resisted elevating New
Delhi from an observer to full membership. Moscow and Beijing eventually
compromised by promoting Pakistan as well as India. Through this move, the
SCO acquired greater international status, but the balance of influence within
the organization did not change since the elevation of India was counterbal-
anced by that of Pakistan, China's ally. Additionally, their approach to managing disagreement can be seen in how Russia and China have not fully backed
the others' territorial claims. Moscow has not completely endorsed Beijing's
aspirations in the South or East China Seas and continues to provide arms
to Vietnam and India, China's regional rivals. Likewise, while Beijing has not
joined Western condemnation of Russian actions in Georgia and Ukraine, it
has not fully endorsed them. The presumed reason for this stance is Chinese
aversion to separatist movements, whether in the former Soviet republics or

in PRC-controlled Tibet, Taiwan, Xinjiang, and Hong Kong. While Chinese officials have opposed Western sanctions against Russia related to Ukraine, at least some PRC banks have refrained from conducting certain business with Russian financial institutions to avoid running afoul of these sanctions. Their mutual concerns of being dragged into a conflict by the other have led Beijing to distance itself from the Russian military activities in Ukraine; Moscow, in turn, has refrained from fully backing Chinese territorial claims in the East and South China Seas. In the future, Russia and China could continue to reach compromise solutions to their differences or contain any divergences within narrow bounds.

Tighter Ties

In October 2020, Putin remarked that the possibility of a full-blown Sino-Russian alliance cannot be precluded.[8] For Russia's current leadership, the United States represents an immediate threat to Russia's national security, whereas China signifies not only a long-term challenge but also an opportunity for promoting a multilateral world order, ideally in partnership with Moscow. Though the United States and Russia are not doomed to differ forever, Russian-U.S. cooperation has been at best episodic, transient, and shallow for at least the past decade; nothing on the horizon looks to alter this situation. Russian leaders seem to expect U.S. sanctions and hostility to last indefinitely given that the Biden administration has renounced trying to comprehensively reset relations with Moscow and Republican leaders in Congress have spearheaded efforts to impose more sanctions on Russia. Meanwhile, the recent abrupt downturn in Sino-U.S. relations may lead PRC leaders to hunker down for a long-term period of intense confrontation with the United States. Although Chinese leaders may want better relations with Washington, PRC analysts understand that American politicians, business leaders, and other influential U.S. actors have hardened their policies toward China on many issues in ways that will not be reversed soon. Indeed, an enduring improvement in U.S. relations in either Russia or China may not occur until more influential groups in both countries are interested in sustaining more functional bilateral ties. For years, there was no strong group in the United States that would lobby on behalf of better ties with Russia; now the same situation holds regarding China. During the past decade, the PRC has alienated some U.S. businesses with its predatory policies, farmers with its trade practices, and liberals with its human rights violations, while the Trump administration's extremely negative portrayal of PRC policies and motives has swung many Republicans as well as some Democrats against China. Opinion polls show general popular support among American respondents, Democrats as well as Republicans, for firmer U.S. stances on disputes with China.[9] If Russia's and

China's relations with other countries besides the United States also worsen, they will have additional incentives to improve their own relations.

Russia could become a considerably more important economic partner to China if other countries curtail commercial exchanges with the PRC due to concerns about China's unfair trade practices, mishandling of infectious diseases, or other factors. The extensive U.S. sanctions placed on both countries could strengthen their ties as they strive to reduce reliance on the U.S. dollar and demand major changes in international economic institutions to inhibit U.S. influence. In such circumstances, Moscow and Beijing could plausibly redouble their efforts to build an international economic system with a substantially decreased U.S. role. As the PRC is already the economically dominant partner in the Sino-Russian relationship, Russia needs China much more than China needs Russia. Since they cannot change this situation any time soon, Russian economic leaders may eventually accept that they would benefit from a deeper economic partnership with the PRC even if the Chinese might benefit more, focusing on Russia's absolute economic gains rather than China's superior relative gains. In the security domain, Russian and PRC policy makers could plausibly deepen their defense collaboration by further increasing the frequency, size, and ambitions of their military exercises. For instance, they could conduct even larger joint military operations, construct standing defense structures such as a joint missile launch warning center, or agree to permanently station liaison officers in each other's major military commands. Russia and China could also expand co-development of new dual-use and military systems, which they could use to equip their own armed forces as well as sell to other countries antagonistic to the United States. The Russian defense community may, for the first time, engage in substantial purchases from the PRC's military-industrial sector. Russian-Chinese collaboration in outer and cyber space could grow beyond their crafting of joint draft treaties that are designed to promote their norms in these domains to more concrete cooperative projects. Sino-Russian civilian and commercial space cooperation might extend to encompass collaboration on space security issues. The launch of the Chinese Tiangong Space Station will widen opportunities for Sino-Russian civil space cooperation, which may subsequently extend to military space issues. Additionally, Russia and China could expand their Arctic cooperation, which has focused on commercial issues, to include security and legal issues, with Beijing possibly offering to endorse Moscow's ambitious territorial claims there in return for Moscow supporting Beijing's sovereignty claims regarding the South or East China Sea. If Russia and China were to collaborate substantially more against the United States, Americans could face more serious challenges to their interests and values. For instance, Moscow and Beijing could simultaneously initiate military challenges in different regions of the world in order to stretch U.S. resources and capabilities.

Divisive Drivers

When Putin visited China on June 25, 2016, President Xi expressed his hope that the two countries might remain "friends forever."[10] Such an idyllic state does not exist in world politics. Indeed, several potential developments could significantly degrade Sino-Russian ties. For example, the PLA military buildup could eventually alarm Russia enough to change its Beijing-tilting defense policies and may press more vigorously to include the PRC in future rounds of nuclear arms control negotiations. Conversely, the Chinese government may cease tolerating Russian arms sales to nations, such as India and Vietnam, that could become PLA adversaries. Improvements in the Chinese military-industrial complex could further reduce the PLA's interest in Russian weapons. PRC arms dealers are becoming more formidable competitors of Russian weapons exporters—if not in all areas, then at least for some systems in certain markets that are seeking Soviet-type weapons and are willing to accept some degradation in performance for a lower price. Russia's fear about Chinese defense intellectual property theft could also rise sufficiently to impede further sales. Russian plans to create an European Union (EU)-like arrangement among the former Soviet republics could provoke Beijing's resistance since such a development could impede China's economic access to Central Asia. Russian diplomats may soon tire of Beijing's practice of hiding behind Moscow and relying on Russia to take the heat in blocking Western initiatives regarding Iran, Syria, and other global hotspots. PRC policy makers may consider the costs to China of alienating Russia tolerable given their own strategic independence and growing power. For instance, they can obtain energy from non-Russian sources, veto UN Security Council (UNSC) resolutions even without Moscow's support, and could soon have the means to manufacture domestically the major weapons systems they might otherwise obtain from Russia. Moscow and Beijing have both attempted to envelop the other in multilateral networks to constrain their policies—when projects involve other countries, their obligations are harder to break. At times, Russia has strived to strengthen the SCO, Eurasian Economic Union (EEU), and the Brazil-Russia-India-China-South Africa (BRICS) bloc to dilute and constrain China's power. Thus far, these structures have lacked the strength to play this balancing role. Beijing has been more successful in influencing Russian behavior through its offers of investment and other benefits within its Belt and Road Initiative (BRI) framework. PRC policy makers presume that Russia needs good relations with China due to Moscow's lack of alternative diplomatic options. Indeed, some PRC analysts highlight Russia's dependence on China to weaken other countries' interest in partnering with Russia and thereby reinforce that dependence. One major constraint on stronger Sino-Russian ties has been that both Russian and Chinese policy makers have parallel concerns of being dragged into a conflict by the other country. This traditional abandonment-entrapment dilemma would be exacerbated if either country's leadership behaves more aggressively than the other deems wise.

The governments in Moscow and Beijing also diverge in their general vision for a preferred world order. Russia is a revisionist power that wants to change the international system but lacks the capabilities to achieve this end. China is developing such capabilities, but until now, its revisionism has been selective, focused on remaking the Indo-Pacific regional order more to its liking but less assertive in other regions. Additionally, the current leaders in Russia often give the impression of wanting to go back to a Cold War order in which Moscow was, along with Washington, the most important global player. In the draft European security treaties published by Moscow in mid-December 2021, Russian diplomats called for measures that would roll back NATO advancements since the mid-1990s and restore a Moscow-led sphere of primacy in the former Soviet states. PRC policy makers seem to seek the same kind of sphere in Asia.

China's recent policy toward Russia has been atypically nonconfrontational, both in terms of the history of their bilateral relationship and compared with Beijing's policies toward its other neighbors. However, the PRC's increasing power might lead Beijing to "normalize" its Russian policies and pursue more assertive policies, as China has treated other countries. Exploiting its economic power, Beijing might eventually seek to leverage its stronger position to expand its influence in shared regions of interest at the expense of Moscow. In the Russian Far East, a combination of natural riches and sparse population imperils Moscow's long-term control. Beijing may soon reopen the question of the territories Imperial Russia seized from China in previous centuries. In the summer of 2020, some PRC commentators posted social media complaints when the Russian Embassy celebrated the 160th anniversary of the founding of Vladivostok, Russia's largest Pacific municipality.[11] The commentators recalled that Tsarist Russia had unjustly seized the region from a weak China in the mid-19th century.[12] Elsewhere, Beijing has not yet pressed Moscow to weaken its long-standing economic and security ties with India and Vietnam, confront Japan with a common front, or yield security primacy in Central Asia to Beijing. Given China's rapidly rising power relative to Russia, however, Beijing's willingness to share long-term regional primacy with Moscow in Asia is questionable. Until now, Beijing has been content with operating in the Arctic according to Russian rules, but the Kremlin cannot take this attitude for granted. Beijing might press Russia to allow PRC corporations a larger role in developing the Arctic. Moscow's sharp turn toward Beijing in recent years has already limited its freedom of action in Central Asia, where Russia has had to tolerate growing Chinese economic dominance. Beijing's BRI could reorient these and other former Soviet republics, which Moscow considers to be within its sphere of influence, toward the PRC. In turn,

China's increasing economic role in these countries has laid the foundation for a potential major PRC military role, which Moscow would find threatening. Russian arms sales and other ties with India, Vietnam, and other states that might engage in a conflict with the PLA could face stronger Chinese resistance. Such PRC overreach might result in Moscow's reassessing its strategy of appeasing and binding China.

Other regional factors could also contribute to a major downturn in their relations. Russian policy makers have been seeking a greater role in East Asia independent of their relationship with China—with Japan, South Korea, and certain Southeast Asian countries seen as providing possible opportunities to enhance Moscow's bargaining leverage with all regional players, helping situate Russia as a more important player in Asia, and hedging against any future problems in relations with Beijing. Moscow has had success maintaining ties with both India and China, two potential rivals, developing strong security and economic partnerships with both countries while avoiding siding with one against the other whenever possible. Russia has attempted but failed to reach out to other Asian players to pursue a more geographically diverse, less Sinocentric, Asia policy. Thus far, breaking out of Beijing's constraints has been difficult due to the limited inducements Moscow can offer other potential partners, including the two Korean states. But the future might bring better opportunities for a Russian change of course in Asia. In the military realm, Russian policy makers strive to make their partnership more valuable for China while also hedging against the long-term collapse of that partnership—often under the guise of strengthening defenses against the United States and its allies. Though Russian leaders do not see the PRC as an imminent military threat, they rightfully worry about their growing dependence on China.

Despite years of sustained efforts by both governments to promote humanitarian exchanges and the study of the other country's language, popular connections between Russians and Chinese remain minimal. The scant cultural and social ties between ordinary Russians and Chinese have remained a source of concern to both governments. They have therefore made a concerted effort to strengthen mutual ties. In addition to various student scholarships and state-sponsored foreign language programs, they have been promoting annual reciprocal theme years to showcase each other's cultural achievements. The reciprocal China-Russia National Years of 2006–2007 were followed by the China-Russia Years of Language 2009–2010 and of Tourism in 2012–2013. In 2014 and 2015, each country hosted a Youth Year of Friendship Exchanges. Nonetheless, their cultural ties remain heavily oriented toward other nations. Political and commercial elites in Russia and China generally prefer to send their children to schools in Europe and the United States rather than to each other's countries. Though excluded from their state-controlled media, culturally embedded negative stereotypes regarding the other nationality persist in popular discourse. The absence of a deep societal foundation binding the two nations makes it easier for future leaders to pursue other alignments outside the Sino-Russian nexus. Both the Russian and Chinese regimes are extremely personalistic; therefore, a change in the top leadership could result in radical changes in their foreign policies, including toward each other. The impact of individual leaders on their relations was evident earlier on how the personal animosity between Khrushchev and Mao helped drive the Soviet Union and the PRC apart. More recently, President Trump's atypically hard line regarding China substantially contributed to the recent deterioration in Sino-U.S. ties. Given this history, Russia's post-Putin government could plausibly move away from Beijing since, while Putin is so invested in his China policy that he cannot disengage, Putin's successor may not be so committed.

Relations between Moscow and Beijing have never been better. In sharp contrast, ties between Russia and the United States have never been worse since the end of the Cold War, while the third leg of the triangle, the Sino-American relationship, is still in flux. Beijing and Washington have had a mixed relationship in which they cooperate in some areas and disagree in others. Their disagreements have grown considerably in recent years, but an improved relationship in the future is certainly possible. Should U.S. power in the Pacific falter, Russia and China might also become natural rivals for the allegiance of other Asian states as they search for a new great power patron, either by aligning with or balancing against China's hegemonic potential in the Asia-Pacific region. For good reason, Russian policy makers fear that Beijing could exploit Moscow's lack of alternative partnerships to constrain Russian options regarding these regions. Already PRC pressure has been constraining Moscow's maneuvering room regarding Japan, India, and Vietnam. India has traditionally seen Moscow as a potential balancer against China and its regional ally Pakistan. Russian and Chinese fears of being entrapped into a conflict by the other with some third party could also intensify. Russian diplomats may also tire of allowing Beijing to hide behind Moscow to block Western initiatives in the UNSC regarding global hotspots. Renewed tensions over border regions could also arise. The demographic disparity that exists between the Russian Far East and northern China invariably raises the question of whether Chinese nationals will move northward to exploit the natural riches of underpopulated eastern Russia. Regarding commerce, Russian officials have repeatedly expressed concerns about their nation simply becoming excessively reliant on Chinese goods, services, and labor. A renewed Russian effort to create an exclusive economic union among the former Soviet republics could provoke stronger PRC resistance given the anticipated growth in China's economic interests to the former Soviet republics. Under these conditions, especially if Washington lacks the capacity to manage Beijing alone, Moscow could plausibly join other countries in a strategy to balance China's rising power.

A major worsening of relations would represent a regression to the historical mean for a relationship that has seen bloody wars, imperial conquests, and mutual denunciations. Some Russians regret the drastic change in fortunes between Moscow and Beijing in the post-Soviet period. Russian experts acknowledge that during the Cold War, "the Chinese leadership was unable to overcome the junior partner and apprentice complex in relation to the USSR."[13] It has only been during the past three decades, with the weakening of Russian political and economic power combined with China's surge toward global economic and military power, that the two countries have managed to strike a harmonious balance in their relationship. According to various metrics, while the PRC now has a much larger population and economy, Russia has a more powerful military, thanks to its larger nuclear force and greater combat experience. China has experienced an unprecedented economic rise in the past three decades, whereas its northern neighbor underwent a disastrous and humiliating degradation in the 1990s, which saw a major drop in living standards, military might, and international prestige. Since the early 2000s, coinciding with the Putin presidency, Russia has recovered, mainly thanks to the surge in export and prices of raw materials. Nonetheless, the Russian Federation is a markedly different country than the former USSR, having roughly half the population and gross domestic product (GDP) of the Soviet Union. The economies of Russia and China were roughly the same size in 1993; by 2020, China's economy had grown to almost 10 times the size of Russian economy. Hence, the PRC could plausibly surpass Russia according to other measures of status and power, thereby threatening to relegate Russia to permanent subordinate status. Based on current power trends, the economic, demographic, and military projections favor China. Furthermore, Russia faces years of strategic isolation, sanctions, and containment due to its actions in Ukraine and elsewhere. In contrast, the United States must manage a medley of Pacific security partners whose willingness to confront China in partnership with Washington is often limited. The PRC has built deep economic relationships with Asian countries that give its partners strong incentives to avoid confronting Beijing, especially since China tries to divide its potential opponents. The growing Sino-Russian power gap will complicate their future relationship by amplifying Russian anxieties about "China passing"—Russia's falling further behind the PRC and becoming Beijing's subordinate partner.

IMPLICATIONS AND RECOMMENDATIONS

Russian and Chinese officials deny that their collaboration is directed against any other country, but the wide-ranging ties between these revisionist powers present major challenges to the United States and other Western countries. By interacting in unanticipated ways through combined, coordinated, sequential, or opportunistic actions, their joint actions have challenged and will challenge important U.S. national security interests. Even if their opposition to democracy is motivated more by power than ideological considerations, including a prioritization of regime stability, their common stance threatens the vision of the world order supported by most Americans. The exchanges between the two countries have helped them circumvent U.S. sanctions against them. For example, by selling sophisticated air, naval, and missile technologies to China, Russia has substantially boosted the PLA's threat to many countries, including the United States, which now faces more formidable Chinese counter-intervention capabilities. The Sino-Russian defense interactions have also helped the PLA compensate for its lack of combat experience. In essence, the Sino-Russian defense partnership has weakened U.S. deterrence against potential Chinese aggression. Their defense cooperation looks to both deepen and widen in the future. PRC national security decision makers may have learned from Moscow's tactics in Ukraine to also present the world with fait accompli in contested regions like the South China Sea. The U.S. National Defense Strategy has noted that both Moscow and Beijing "have increased efforts short of armed conflict by expanding coercion to new fronts, violating principles of sovereignty, exploiting ambiguity, and deliberately blurring the lines between civil and military goals," as well as "using other areas of competition short of open warfare to achieve their ends (e.g., information warfare, ambiguous or denied proxy operations, and subversion)."[14]

The PRC government's de facto acceptance of Moscow's annexation of Crimea made it harder to dissuade subsequent Russian adventurism in eastern Ukraine, while the Russian arms transfers have helped fuel Beijing's territorial ambitions in the Pacific, which threaten key U.S. allies and interests. Moscow may be more openly and immediately rejectionist and employs more assertive means, whereas Chinese leaders have yet to call for a comprehensive replacement of the existing U.S.-created international economic and security institutions. Still, Russian and Chinese leaders have increasingly overlapped in their revisionist rhetoric and actions. As part of their strategies to challenge the United States without direct military conflict, Moscow and Beijing employ information operations and cyber tools, sub-conventional paramilitary force, proxy actions, weaponized corruption, sophisticated propaganda, exploitation of ethnic strife, economic threats, courting agents of influence in foreign countries, and other non-kinetic instruments. Besides directly strengthening the PLA's capabilities against Taiwan, Japan, and other U.S. partners, the large-scale Russian weapons transfers to China have indirectly bolstered Russia's own military power by generating royalties for the country's defense firms, which they can reinvest into additional military projects. The sales also compel the Pentagon to pay greater attention to Asian military contingencies rather than concentrating more on confronting Russian military power in Europe.

Both countries' growing foreign military activities may also increase the risk of accidents or inadvertent encounters with the U.S. and other militaries, given that confidence- and security-building measures are harder to negotiate on a trilateral, rather than bilateral, basis. Additionally, their hostile information policies reinforce one another's state-sponsored anti-American narratives, which they have promoted globally, including through joint statements and coordinated propaganda designed to shape international perceptions. Moscow and Beijing have launched information campaigns to weaken U.S. defensive alliances and constrain U.S. foreign military activities. For instance, their media misleads other states into thinking that hosting U.S. soldiers facilitates the spread of COVID-19 among their populations. In the UNSC, joint Russian-Chinese vetoes of U.S.-backed resolutions have impeded measures to enhance international peace and security. For instance, Moscow and Beijing have employed their UNSC vetoes to block sanctions against the Bashar al-Assad regime for chemical weapons attacks against the Syrian people. Russian arms sales to China circumvent Western arms embargos on the PLA, while Chinese loans, military purchases, and technological transfers weaken U.S. sectoral sanctions on Russia. Even when they render only passive support, such as restraining from criticizing each other's domestic and foreign policies, they effectively reassure each other and thereby embolden challenges to U.S.-backed norms and interests. For instance, their demilitarized joint border region provides both states a "strategic rear" that lies beyond the reach of the U.S. military and allows them to focus on other threats. Russian and Chinese leaders are more confident confronting the United States when they know the other backs them. For example, Moscow is under less pressure to cease threatening Ukraine or other U.S. partners and allies if Beijing declines to challenge these actions. Russian and Chinese leaders seemingly believe that what weakens the United States benefits them by default.

Moscow and Beijing present comparable challenges to the U.S.-led international system through their employing what are variously termed "asymmetric," "sub-conventional," "hybrid," "grey-zone," "non-linear," "ambiguous," "unrestricted," unconventional," and "next-generation warfare" tactics. The aggregate effect of these tools has presented a potent hybrid mix that the United States has found difficult to counter. Russian actions in Ukraine and Chinese moves in the Pacific have deliberately fallen below the threshold normally deemed suitable for collective defense countermeasures by the United States and its allies. The U.S. policy of nonrecognition of Russian and Chinese actions has not reversed Moscow's and Beijing's hybrid gains. For example, like Moscow in Crimea, Beijing has presented the world with a fait accompli by declaring an air identification zone and constructing more artificial islands in the South China Sea, which Beijing consolidated by subsequently enhancing its conventional military presence in areas first acquired by indirect means.

Through such "salami slicing" tactics, Beijing has also gradually expanded its control over other islands disputed with the Philippines. In the East China Sea, the PRC has been sending its coast guard and other paramilitary forces to the area as well as unarmed people to occupy contested islands. Though threatening, these kinds of activities do not constitute "an armed attack against Japan," rendering the old Japan-U.S. guidelines provide no definitive response on how the Japanese and U.S. militaries should respond. Traditionally, Japan has relied on its coast guard to counter these challenges, but China has made a major effort to strengthen its own maritime forces and combine them into a single structure independent of the PLA Navy, enhancing its paramilitary portfolio. Beijing's changing tactics may be based on PRC perceptions of Russia's success with hybrid warfare techniques though at the long-term cost of strategic isolation and containment. In several respects, China is better positioned to employ hybrid tactics successfully across a wider range of scenarios in neighboring regions than Russia. Despite these limited successes, Moscow faces the world's most powerful military alliance to its west, North Atlantic Treaty Organization (NATO), which is aligning its civilian counter-hybrid strategy more closely with the EU, the world's strongest regional economic and political union of independent countries. Meanwhile, in the Pacific, the PRC faces a multifaceted menagerie of more disunited opponents. While Russia has wielded powerful energy and economic assets in Eurasia, China has built deep economic relationships with Asian countries that give its partners strong incentives to avoid confronting Beijing, especially since China tries to divide its potential opponents. The Southeast Asian countries in the Association of Southeast Asian Nations (ASEAN) have never been able to maintain a sustained united front regarding Beijing.[15] Although Japan allies with the United States against China, South Korea and other U.S. military allies in Asia do not. Similarly, whereas in Europe many nominal neutral countries are very supportive of U.S. anti-Russian measures, in Asia even powerful states like India are wary of siding with the United States against China.

A complicating factor for U.S. policy makers is that Russia and China present different but complementary great power challenges to the United States. Both want a sphere of influence, but Moscow has been more aggressive in seeking its aims, using military power to seize foreign territory and sub-conventional means to subvert neighbors through hybrid tactics. Beijing is also flexing its muscles more than in the past though still less than Russia. The PRC is stronger economically and does not have to face a counterbalancing multilateral military alliance like NATO. Despite Russian efforts to diversify assets by enhancing its economic, diplomatic, and soft power, Moscow's main source of influence remains its military strength as well as its arms and energy exports. Of the three countries, the PRC and the United States enjoy a more robust power portfolio comprising economic and diplomatic as well as military assets. The high levels of economic and social interdependence between China and the United States mean that the PRC has many more means of retaliating for hostile U.S. economic measures than Russia. Since Chinese leaders believe that their relative power position will improve further in the future, they have adopted a generally risk-averse foreign-policy approach. In contrast, Russian leaders are less certain of their future trajectory, and therefore, they are more inclined to take risks, such as interfering in U.S. elections. Interestingly, Putin justified his decision to deploy Russian military units in Syria as a calculated risk.[16] The perceived diverging threats from Russia and China have directly affected the U.S. defense budget and global U.S. military posture. During the two decades after the Cold War, the United States substantially cut its military deployments in Europe due to a determination that the new Russian Federation, whose armed forces were in disarray after the collapse of the Warsaw Pact and integrated Soviet military-industrial complex, did not represent a near-term military threat. Following the U.S.-led military interventions in Afghanistan and Iraq, the Pentagon used Europe primarily as a staging point to project power into Central Asia and the Middle East. U.S. officials pressed European states to deemphasize territorial defense and instead focus on developing power-projection and counterinsurgency assets suitable for fighting insurgents in Afghanistan and responding to instability in Iraq and Libya. Meanwhile, during the past decade, U.S. military planners have begun to see China as a very serious military threat. A major component of the Obama administration's pivot to Asia was to rebalance U.S. military power from Europe to the Pacific region to reassure U.S. allies and partners while reinforcing deterrence threats to Beijing. The Russian military intervention in Georgia in 2008 did not appreciably change this approach.

In any case, it was only Moscow's coercion in Ukraine that led to a reversal of U.S. policy. In 2014, U.S. secretary of defense Ash Carter warned that the U.S. military was losing its competitive edge to Russia and China in key militarily relevant technologies and launched the Third Offset Initiative to sustain U.S. leadership in critical areas.[17] Following Moscow's aggression against Ukraine, the Obama administration perceived Russia as a more immediate threat to the United States than China. In January 2016, Army Chief of Staff General Mark Milley assessed Russia as the greatest threat to the United States due to its immense military capacity combined with its hostile intentions and aggressive actions, including overtly and covertly challenging Europe's existing borders in a manner not seen in decades. In contrast, Milley argued that China was less of an immediate challenge due to the fact that the PLA had not violated international boundaries and seemed to pursue a posture of strategic patience, given expectations that the military balance will continue to shift in China's favor.[18] The last defense budget submitted by the Obama administration increased allocations to countering "higher-end" threats from China but more so Russia. The budget supported the European Defense Initiative, a major increase in funding for U.S. forces in Europe, which provided for more U.S. rotational deployments to NATO countries, a quantitative and qualitative growth in U.S. military equipment based in Europe, and an improvement in the infrastructure required to reinforce U.S. military power in Europe in a potential Russia-NATO conflict. In contrast, the increased capabilities for countering China came mostly in terms of developing new military technologies rather than increasing U.S. forces in the Pacific.

During the 2016 U.S. presidential elections, some Russian and Chinese analysts favored Donald Trump's candidacy because they saw him as someone interested in bargaining and focused on advancing narrow, concrete U.S. national interests rather than promoting broad liberal democratic values. These analysts may have anticipated that Trump would follow realist presidents like Richard Nixon and George H. W. Bush in his foreign policy and eschew interference in other countries' internal affairs. Other observers expected that a potential Trump administration would reduce U.S. forces deployed abroad, deemphasize ties with allies, and perhaps pursue a grand bargain of accepting Moscow's and Beijing's primacy in Eurasia in exchange for concessions in other areas. Putin and other members of the Russian elite generally preferred Trump over former U.S. secretary of state Hillary R. Clinton, whom Russian leaders determined would be more hostile toward their interests. Some Russian policy makers welcomed the possibility that the United States might cooperate more with Moscow and less with Beijing since it could enhance Russia's leverage with China, the United States, and Europe. Sharing this sentiment, certain PRC media sources related that Russians, anticipating an improved bargaining position under Trump, began to backtrack in 2016 on earlier commitments to China.[19] Some PRC policy makers likely began to contemplate an unwelcome situation in which widening Sino-American tensions made Russia the pivotal partner in the strategic triangle. Nonetheless, some Chinese saw potential long-term benefits in a Trump presidency, hoping that President Trump would weaken U.S. military alliances and pursue international trade policies that were harmful to the United States.

In his early speeches as president, Trump argued for a de-escalation in tensions with Moscow and urged greater cooperation against common threats, such as international terrorism, and on non-security issues, such as energy and trade. Trump argued that his superior negotiating skills, strong leadership style, and his belief that Putin would respect him more than previous U.S. presidents would facilitate such collaboration. In many respects, Trump's worldview, as expressed during his election campaign, resembled that of the current Russian government. Trump blamed previous U.S. administrations for ruining relations with Moscow by failing to show or earn Russians' respect (such as by dismissing Russia as a failing and resentful former superpower) and for excessively interfering in issues of vital concern to Russians, such as their domestic politics and Moscow's relations with some of the other former Soviet republics. During his presidential election campaign, Trump had supported the Russian military's fight against the Islamic State in Syria. Looking for leverage, Trump suggested that he might reconsider U.S. policies regarding the nonrecognition of Moscow's March 2014 annexation of the Crimean Peninsula and the subsequent sanctions on Russia adopted by the United States (and its allies). Additionally, Trump characterized the Ukraine conflict as a primarily European concern, implying that Washington should let Europe incur the costs of any confrontation. In contrast to his positive tone regarding Russia, Trump employed some of his harshest language when referring to Chinese actions, denouncing its predatory trade practices, stealing of American jobs, currency manipulation, violation of intellectual property laws, and illegal export subsidies. Trump also suggested that he would more vigorously challenge Beijing's island-building and territorial claims in East Asia. Some of his advisers endorsed a large-scale naval rebuilding program and other defense initiatives aimed against China and want to organize a more explicit containment strategy against Beijing, involving traditional U.S. allies like Japan and Australia and new Pacific partners like India and Russia. Though Trump's attacks on China gained the most media attention, concern about Beijing's policies had been building within the United States for years, in both political parties. U.S. economic concerns center on PRC mistreatment of U.S. businesses, unfair trade practices, and alleged intellectual property theft. Washington's security concerns relate to Beijing's assertive territorial claims regarding neighboring territories and large military buildup. Other issues cover Beijing's policies toward Taiwan, Hong Kong, and Xinjiang as well as other authoritarian domestic policies. Concerns about PRC practices are likely to continue no matter which U.S. political party controls Congress or the presidency. Trump and his advisors initially argued that one reason to improve ties with Moscow was to wean Russia away from China. For instance, they hoped Russia would curtail its weapons deliveries to these two countries. They also worried that the U.S. sanctions on Russia deprived U.S. investors of business opportunities and drove Russia into China's arms. The Trump foreign policy team faulted the Obama administration for confronting Moscow and Beijing concurrently and therefore aligning their interests against the United States. Following his election, several of Trump's advisers indicated that they intended to work more actively to avert stronger Sino-Russian alignment by reducing tensions with Russia. Nevertheless, once in office, Trump made no visible effort to prioritize improving ties with Moscow, allowing the Defense, State, and Treasury Departments to pursue strong anti-Russian measures. A confluence of bureaucracy, politics, and pragmatism prevented Trump from pursuing better ties with Moscow. Trump's cabinet members had expressed more conventional views regarding Russia, while the domestic political situation in Washington severely limited Trump's ability to cooperate with the Russian government on almost all significant matters. Furthermore, strong congressional opposition precluded a comprehensive relaxation of U.S. sanctions on Russia. Most U.S. allies were also pressing the Trump administration not to soften its stance toward Moscow until Russia made concessions on Ukraine and other issues. Their opposition repeatedly blocked Trump's proposal that Russia rejoin the G7/G8. The U.S. forces assigned to NATO, the U.S. naval and air patrols near Russia, and U.S. military exercises with local partners have all increased during the Trump years. The administration's core national security documents, such as the National Security Strategy, were written by the bureaucracy and think tank experts, which described Russia and China as the two main "revisionist powers" seeking to usurp U.S. leadership and the international system that reflects U.S. values and impose their own different world order.

In the first months of the Trump administration, the Kremlin scaled back its confrontation with Washington since Russian leaders hoped that the new Trump administration might change some U.S. policies Moscow opposed. For example, they hoped that the Trump administration would remove some sanctions on Russia while not enforcing others or limiting their practical scope and not to pursue similar measures such as discouraging other Russian-U.S. business ties. Additionally, given Trump's previously anti-China rhetoric, Russian analysts were looking forward to positioning themselves as the swing state in an intensified Sino-American struggle for global primacy, seeing it as an opportunity to sustain Russia's status as a third pole in a global triangle. However, this hope faded after Trump stopped suggesting that the United States would not fulfill its security commitments to NATO members and his senior cabinet officials continued to severely criticize Russian policies. Russian leaders were also aware that Trump's pro-Russian policies faced major opposition in Congress, even among members of the Republican Party, and that many of his cabinet members were deeply skeptical about cooperating with Moscow, including Vice President Mike Pence. Russia's leadership soon realized that any improvement in bilateral relations under Trump would remain limited, contested, and transient. They complained about not knowing who was responsible for formulating Russian policy in the U.S. government due to the frequent turnover and vacancies among U.S. senior national security posts. They also faulted the Trump administration for pursuing traditional U.S. policies that make Moscow uneasy: regularly employing military force, disregarding international treaties, and refusing to accept international constraints on U.S. freedom of action. Given this calculation, Russian policy makers saw little benefit in making significant concessions to Washington regarding China or other issues. Even if Trump had overcome these obstacles to better relations with Russia, it is not clear if Moscow would have met him halfway since Russian leaders blamed previous U.S. policies for the poor state of their bilateral relations and expected Washington not just to abandon but also to "correct" these flawed policies in ways to make them more acceptable to Moscow. When Russian leaders initially thought that Trump sought to improve bilateral relations, their response was not to make concessions to facilitate this process. Instead, they claimed vindication on their position that the current tensions resulted from flawed U.S. policies. They further rejoiced that Trump's hoped-for pro-Russian policies would give Moscow new leverage in negotiations with China.

Recommendations

The United States has means to balance or weaken the Sino-Russian alignment. Despite their closer collaboration on many issues, Russian and Chinese perspectives and policies do not fully align. Nonetheless, since the Moscow-Beijing partnership is not binding, constraining, or exclusive, their low-cost, multipronged alignment may be resilient against potential U.S. countermeasures. Moreover, many U.S. strategies would have unpredictable effects on the Sino-Russian alignment, perhaps strengthening rather than weakening it. U.S. policy that was simply more assertive, for example, could have either impact. It is true that PRC analysts doubt Moscow's willingness to support Beijing in a possible confrontation with another Russian partner such as India or Vietnam. A Chinese perception that Moscow has failed to adequately support Beijing, such as when Khrushchev did not back Mao during a territorial dispute in the 1950s, could have an embittering effect. The Eisenhower administration deliberately heightened tensions with Maoist China to rupture the Sino-Soviet alliance by making it clear to PRC policy makers that Soviet leaders were unwilling to risk war with the United States on China's behalf.[20] Likewise, intensifying U.S. sanctions on Russia could deepen Moscow's irritation at Beijing if the Kremlin perceives that PRC support is inadequate. In recent years, Beijing has not recognized the self-declared separatist "governments" backed by Moscow in the occupied Georgian territories of Abkhazia and South Ossetia. Furthermore, though the Chinese government has denounced U.S. sanctions on Russia, PRC banks and corporations have de facto respected Western-imposed measures limiting commercial operations in Crimea to reduce their own exposure to U.S. countermeasures. Sanctions that weaken the Russian economy could also exacerbate Russian fears of falling further behind China as a global economic competitor. Still, a tougher U.S. approach toward either country risks driving Moscow and Beijing closer together. Alternatively, the United States could try to use positive incentives with one country to shape its policies in ways more favorable to U.S. interests. French president Emmanuel Macron has at times advocated this approach in order to give Russia an opportunity to avoid becoming "China's vassal."[21] Washington could alternatively try to divide Moscow and Beijing by seeking to improve ties with Russia or the PRC but not both, re-creating the kind of trilateral diplomacy that benefited the United States during the 1970s and the 1980s. For example, the United States could decrease some U.S. sanctions on Russia or China unilaterally to reduce one factor that may be deepening Sino-Russian ties.

Nevertheless, the U.S. leverage to break apart the entire multidimensional Sino-Russian alignment is limited. In the near term, there is probably no positive incentive that the United States could reasonably offer Moscow or Beijing that would lead them to comprehensively realign their policies toward Washington and away from the other. Both governments consider their historically atypical strong relationship a major mutual asset that they should strive to sustain. Furthermore, both governments would discount any U.S. inducements to defect given their suspicion of U.S. motives and doubts about the sustainability of any proffered concessions. They understand the volatile nature of American politics and deep congressional hostility to both authoritarian powers, which would impede presidential flexibility regarding, for example, sanctions relief. Even a complete U.S. disengagement from geographic regions that Moscow or Beijing consider as falling within their sphere of influence might not drive them apart. On the one hand, the reduced perception of a shared external threat could lead Russia and China to compete more directly for regional dominance. On the other, a U.S. withdrawal from regional hotspots could lead to greater cooperation between Moscow and Beijing to cooperate more in order to avert regional power vacuums that threaten their interests or to achieve joint gains with minimal mutual friction. From a long-term perspective, U.S. policies designed to improve relations with Russia—such as the possible repeal of some sanctions—could enable Moscow to better balance the rise of China's power in Europe, Eurasia, the Arctic, and the Middle East. Yet, if removing sanctions delays Moscow's continued economic and military decline relative to the PRC, this result would decrease possible Russian anxiety about falling behind China.

Additionally, the loose nature of the Russia-China alignment can make it harder and more dangerous to break. Historians believe that one reason why a local conflict between Austria-Hungary and Serbia escalated into World War I was due to the weak nature of the contemporary military alliances, which made the parties fear that their allies would defect unless they received clear evidence of support. German leaders felt that they had to offer Vienna a blank check in order to suppress Serbian terrorism, while both Russian and then French leaders concluded that they must commit to military action against Germany to avoid reneging on their security partnerships.[22] This reassurance-against-abandonment dynamic makes it harder for Russia or China to offer concessions to Washington for fear that such actions could undermine Sino-Russian ties. Moreover, an easy way to suppress their divisions is for Moscow and Beijing to focus against a common challenger—in this case, the United States. U.S. efforts at positive inducements could also be interpreted as a policy of appeasement and lead Moscow and Beijing to become even more confrontational toward the United States. In 2017, the prospect of U.S. sanction relief fueled Russian hopes for an end to U.S. opposition to their foreign policy and an increase in their leverage with China, but Moscow did not show a willingness to make concessions toward Washington—reflecting the Russian position that bilateral tensions all resulted from flawed U.S. policies. Even a comprehensive resolution of U.S. disputes with one of these countries might not prove sufficient to overcome the substantial benefits Russia and China gain from their mutual cooperation. Shared opposition to the United States is only one of many strategic, geopolitical, military, economic, or ideological variables that drive Moscow and Beijing together. U.S. policy makers should explicitly weigh the trade-off between the value of sanctions designed to weaken the Russian and Chinese economies against the impetus sanctions provide for driving Moscow and Beijing closer together. These measures can weaken Sino-Russian economic potential and military capacity as well as raise the risks for U.S. partners of dealing with Russia and China. On a broader level, overuse of sanctions can undermine their utility by allowing the targets to acclimate themselves and build resistance to them.

Even if the Sino-Russian alignment remains strong, the United States and its many powerful allies have the capacity to successfully manage their combined challenge. Due to their increasingly authoritarian political systems, Russia and China have inherent weaknesses—their elites' preoccupation with remaining in power, the distortion of information flow needed for effective decision making, and leadership succession problems that could abruptly change foreign policy orientations. U.S. policy makers should make a greater effort to identify and assess Russian and Chinese interests in their decision making, in order to understand potential trade-offs and complications as well as identify opportunities for potential joint gains. The United States should elevate the issue of the effect of Russian-Chinese collaboration in its dialogue with allies and partners. The recently released "NATO 2030" report appropriately recommends that a special unit of the alliance's Joint Intelligence and Security Division constantly evaluate and report the impact of Sino-Russian collaboration on allies' political, military, informational, and technological security.[23] Although the United States, NATO, and other U.S. allies devote copious resources to assessing Russian and Chinese developments, Western intelligence assets also must track their interactions more effectively. For example, Sino-Russian security cooperation has repeatedly exceeded the levels thought possible by many Western experts. One profitable example is how the U.S. government has collaborated in recent years with European entities as well as private-sector media companies to identify Russian-Chinese disinformation collaboration and, through mutual learning, develop better means to fortify Western information environments.[24]

Of course, not all Sino-Russian collaboration directly harms U.S. interests. The three countries do not need identical interests or views to cooperate directly. For example, the United States could benefit if Russia and China offered more support to the Afghan government. Both Russian and PRC analysts recognize that on balance, the NATO military efforts in Afghanistan have enhanced their security, denying the potential for terrorist cells to mass and launch operations against their countries. Conversely, they fear a premature U.S. military withdrawal from Afghanistan and have urged the United States to keep troops in the country until a peace agreement ends the fighting or until a stronger Afghan government can better promote security in Afghanistan and its neighborhood. However, a NATO military withdrawal would not necessarily obligate Russia or China to fill the security gap since both states could try to contain rather than resolve the Afghan security crisis. During the 1990s, Russian policy makers pursued such a containment strategy, seeking to fortify Central Asian border defenses and support various pro-Russian armed groups in the country. If peace ever takes hold in the region, meeting Russian and Chinese concerns probably requires accepting a neutral Afghanistan and excluding a permanent U.S. military presence in Central Asia. Russian-Chinese-U.S. cooperation within regional security institutions is also possible but remains difficult given the diverging interests of the institutions' members states. The Obama administration initially made a greater effort to engage the SCO as a possible regional partner regarding Afghanistan but soon lost interest due to uncertainty over the organization's intentions and effectiveness. Conversely, neither Moscow nor Beijing considers NATO a desirable security partner beyond Afghanistan. The different definitions of terrorism used by the governments will invariably complicate potential cooperation by leading to further charges of hypocrisy and double dealing. In their diplomatic exchanges and public messaging, U.S. policy makers can capitalize upon the mixed Russian and Chinese feelings about the NATO military drawdown in Afghanistan, emphasizing either its positive or its negative dimensions depending on the actors and circumstances involved. For example, highlighting progress in attaining stability might encourage further Chinese investment, while focusing on the continued threats posed by extremists might promote greater trilateral counterterrorism cooperation. Emphasizing a UN leading role in overseeing Afghan developments may help alleviate some Russian and Chinese concerns. By contrast, leaving Moscow and Beijing to assume a larger role in Afghanistan security could generate friction over each regional position. While this region has thus far not featured an open rivalry between Moscow and Beijing, due to their harmonious near-term interests, Central Asia's stability is becoming more crucial for Beijing's plans, both for east-west integration and for the security of its western borders against substate terrorist threats. PRC's doubts about Russia's will and capacity to maintain Eurasian stability have been less evident since Moscow moved against Ukraine in 2014 but could resurface. If PRC leaders believe it necessary to intervene militarily in Central Asia, Moscow would likely become uneasy about the implications of China supplanting Russian influence in Eurasia.

Russia, China, and the United States can further indirectly collaborate in complementary ways on overlapping or nonconflictual interests. For this to occur, however, policy makers in the three countries must think creatively about these opportunities. The three might, for example, cooperate better on Afghan projects within the framework of multilateral institutions and on economic issues rather than through bilateral security initiatives. Additionally, Russia, China, and the United States could find it easier to collaborate on Afghan-Pakistan issues rather than on Afghanistan alone since their shared security stakes are potentially greater regarding Pakistan, which has a much larger population than Afghanistan and nuclear weapons that could fall into the hands of the country's Islamist extremists. Similarly, Russia, China, and the United States can conduct complementary counter-narcotics efforts by independently training and equipping Afghanistan's counter-drug officers and by focusing their interdiction efforts on different sectors of Afghanistan's borders. Enhancing trilateral cooperation against terrorism, even if only in Eurasia, would prove useful. Other potentially profitable areas for trilateral functional collaboration could be nonproliferation, disaster management, mitigating global climate change, and promoting international public health, especially working together to avert another global pandemic. Washington needs to develop an effective strategy for managing its differences with Moscow and Beijing regarding North Korea in the short term, even as the United States pursues the long-term goal of persuading Russian and Chinese leaders of the benefits of incentivizing major reforms in Pyongyang's policies. Unrealized opportunities may also exist for cooperation on confronting climate change. PRC policy makers want to prevent flooding in China's coastal cities, while Russian leaders increasingly recognize their vulnerability to thawing permafrost, which is eroding the foundations of their northern and eastern infrastructure. More targeted policies concentrated on specific functional or geographic issues could have more predictable positive effects. For instance, since Russian officials will likely share U.S. concerns about China's growing military power and strategic opaqueness, arms control might become a wedge issue dividing Moscow from Beijing. By adopting additional sanctions on Russia designed to limit Sino-Russian defense cooperation, moreover, Washington could weaken this dimension of their partnership. Furthermore, skilled influence operations could exploit Russian anxieties about "China passing"— falling further behind the PRC due to the growing Sino-Russian power gap and becoming Beijing's subordinate partner. U.S. influence operations should stoke Russian suspicions that China wants to keep Russia in an unbalanced commercial relationship, a plausible argument given that PRC trade and investment has not substantially assisted Russia to diversify its economy away from exporting natural resources to China. They should also encourage Russian policy makers to adopt a longer time perspective in their decision making. PRC leaders seem to look decades ahead, while their Russian counterparts appear to think only in terms of a few years; as a result, they discount the challenge to Russia's long-term future status from China's rise. Russia and the PRC both face major demographic (and therefore socioeconomic) challenges, due to their aging workforce and low birth rates, but Russia's demographic difficulties are more severe. If Russians do not boost fertility and decrease mortality, the country could experience a substantial population loss in coming decades, which could undermine a foundation of great-power status.

Despite these complexities and complications, U.S. policy makers should prioritize measures that help the United States compete against Russia or China while neither driving Moscow and Beijing together nor inadvertently strengthening the nontargeted country. For example, an advantage of the U.S. energy sanctions imposed on Russia in 2014 was that they restricted the sale of U.S. technologies to Russia that were not readily available from Chinese sources. Other restrictions, however, have had less desirable effects. For instance, the recent U.S. strategy of constraining cooperation with Russian and Chinese students and scientists should be reviewed since they may unduly encourage Russian and Chinese nationals to study and work in each other's countries. The United States may want to relax some of these restrictions under appropriate safeguards. Academic exchanges can be mutually beneficial when they are conducted on the basis of transparency, reciprocity, and academic freedoms. Russian and Chinese funding of U.S. academic institutions must naturally be governed by strong safeguards to make sure such funding is not used to pursue foreign rather than U.S. interests. For example, funds received from foreign government institutions or state-controlled corporations like Huawei raise the risk that their funded projects will be used to divert scholars into working on projects that benefit the foreign government and could divert U.S. scholars and research to work on the economic development of Russia and China rather than the United States. Meanwhile, the United States should message the disadvantages to Russians and Chinese of studying or working in each other's countries, such as limited freedom of research and thought or decreased prospects of securing U.S. entry visas and scholarship opportunities.

The United States must balance preventing high-intensity competition with Russia and China that leads to war while avoiding being so preoccupied with risk avoidance that it encourages Russian and PRC nonmilitary assertiveness and hybrid coercion. U.S. policies have generally succeeded in deterring high-end aggression from Russia, China, and other states but failed to deter their sub-conventional challenges to U.S. interests. With some success, Moscow and Beijing have employed tailored "salami slicing tactics" that combine economic, political, legal, and diplomatic coercion short of war. Retaining overall U.S. and allied military superiority over Russia and China combined is critical. When deterrence fails, aggression, war, and international disorder can ensue as revisionist states press the dominant power's other extended deterrence commitments. Through miscalculation, low-level competition could escalate into a great-power conventional conflict. Conversely, successful deterrence strengthens factions in the targeted state that advocate foreign-policy restraint. History offers examples of how great-power deterrence can fail if revisionist powers believe that they can gain more from challenging the dominant power than by cooperating with it within the existing international system. Rising or dissatisfied powers must believe the credibility of the dominant power's pledges to protect its allies. Britain's inability to convince Germany before World War I that London would defend its allies led Berlin to underestimate the costs of aggression. Status quo powers must maintain military superiority over rising and dissatisfied powers and make credible commitments to defend their allies to persuade potential revisionists that accepting the existing system is better than challenging it. The United States should continue to strive to maintain its military technological advantages over both states in critical areas such as air power, naval superiority, networked information technologies, and missile defense. Of course, the types of military strength best suited to counter Russia and China differ by region and specific problem set. In Europe, the main threat is from Russia's land power, whereas in the Indo-Pacific theater, the Pentagon must focus on countering the PLA's growing air and naval forces.

Future U.S. administrations should also make a great effort to strengthen U.S. foreign defense and security alliances. Russia and China are trying to weaken the U.S. global network of security alliances and economic institutions because of its critical role in sustaining U.S. external power and the U.S.-backed international order. Washington now has a robust portfolio of alliances with various supporting institutions to help counter revisionist powers. This contrasts with Moscow and Beijing, which lack powerful military allies. The network of U.S. security partnerships, though entailing the stationing of soldiers abroad and substantial defense spending, provides the United States with an unparalleled strategic advantage over potential rivals such as Russia and China, including forward operating and staging bases, diplomatic and intelligence assistance, and international legitimacy for U.S. foreign military operations. For this reason, U.S. defense secretary Lloyd Austin has underscored the "power of partnership" in his speeches since alliances and partnerships represent a comparative U.S. strategic advantage in competition with Russia and China.[25] Moscow and Beijing employ various tactics to try to negate this U.S. advantage. For example, they exploit allies' fear of U.S. abandonment and the tandem allied anxiety of entrapment in U.S. conflicts on issues not central to their concern. Especially in Europe, Moscow tries to exploit divisions among U.S. allies and encourages anti-Americanism through various initiatives. In Asia and other continents, PRC propaganda plays upon countries' fears of economic and security abandonment by the United States (exemplified by trade wars and demands for excessive host-nation support) while suggesting to Americans that Japan, the Philippines, and other local actors are trying to entangle Washington into risky confrontations with Beijing for their own selfish interests. The United States should more directly counter Russian and Chinese propaganda, strengthen foreign institutions to remove vulnerabilities (such as political corruption) that could be exploited by malign foreign actors, temper critical comments regarding financial burden sharing by acknowledging allies' nonmonetary contributions to global security, and avoid actions—such as failing to enforce declared red lines or treating alliances as burdens rather than benefits—that raise allies' doubts about the U.S. commitment to defend them. Enhancing mutual consultations and assurances should also decrease partners' fear of entrapment. The United States and its allies also need to improve their nonmilitary tools to manage the increased great power competition. To address what Japanese commentators describe as these "gray area issues," the Japanese and U.S. militaries have adopted new guidelines for coordinated military action even without an armed attack against Japan. NATO and the EU should also further develop their capabilities for managing Russia and Chinese sub-conventional and political-military information hybrid threats short of war. More effectively countering Moscow's and Beijing's hybrid tactics also requires a U.S. counterstrategy that employs economic, diplomatic, legal, informational, coalitional, and other nonmilitary tools to parry Russian or Chinese sub-conventional assertiveness without escalating conflicts into armed exchanges. Additionally, trade agreements and related measures could improve defense industrial ties with key U.S. partners and discourage them from buying Russian or Chinese weapons or selling defense technologies to either country. Just as Western energy sanctions on Russia have focused on denying transfers that the PRC cannot substitute for, U.S. and other Western sanctions on Russia and China should target products and services that neither Beijing nor Moscow can supply to the other. Working with allies also enhances U.S. influence in international institutions. Russia and China aim to construct a rival world order based on illiberal domestic practices and mutually supported institutions linked to the United Nations and other multinational bodies. No matter how distasteful some of these bodies' actions, U.S. policies must engage with these institutions rather than ignore them. While standing alone, when necessary, in defense of American interests, U.S. diplomats should aim at public displays of consensus-building, especially among nontraditional U.S. partners. They should also highlight Russian and Chinese impediments to a better world, such as their joint vetoes in UN bodies of Western attempts to resolve regional conflicts.

Additionally, U.S. officials should encourage allies to strengthen their defense capabilities further to remove easy low-hanging fruit for Russian or Chinese aggression and make allies more resilient against low-cost probes and coercion. Conversely, the United States should avoid applying sanctions on allies and partners that result in a net loss of U.S. security. The Countering America's Adversaries through Sanctions Act (CAATSA), enacted in mid-2017, mandates sanctions on people, companies, and organizations that engage in a "significant transaction" with Russia's defense and intelligence sectors. Besides punishing Russia for its past "malign activities," the purpose of the CAATSA is to decrease the resources Moscow can employ against the United States and its allies and partners by discouraging countries from buying Russian weapons. The CAATSA has reinforced the credibility of the U.S. threat to sanction other countries presently contemplating buying weapons that fuel the Russian war machine. But it has not prevented China, Turkey, India, and other countries from buying advanced Russian weaponry even in the face of strenuous U.S. pressure—and in some cases, applications of the sanctions could push the targeted country into even deeper dependence on Russian weaponry. The U.S. Congress has thoughtfully debated a program to provide low-cost loans to NATO's former Soviet bloc members so that they can more easily replace their Russian weapons with U.S. weapons and equipment. This proposal could be expanded to cover non-NATO U.S. defense partners that also substitute the United States for Russian or Chinese arms.

U.S. and European sanctions can more directly aim to deny Moscow and Beijing technologies that they could obtain from the other—as with the U.S. and EU energy sanctions on Russia—to avoid strengthening their defense-industrial ties. Limiting the two powers' military resources would constrain their military modernization. Washington could expand its dialogue with other countries regarding major arms sales that could assist Russia and China so that countries understand the depth of U.S. concerns about such transfers and adopt better end-user and other export controls. Improved consultations and information exchanges would help avoid recent problems, such as when several EU governments sold sophisticated weapons to Russia before 2014 with little notice to their NATO allies, making the alliance look divided. Conversely, the United States and its allies can undercut the funds that Russia and China hope to earn through their planned joint research and development (R&D) efforts on the international arms market. Trade agreements and related measures could improve U.S. defense industrial partnerships with key allies and reduce the possibility of them attempting to buy Russian or PRC weapons. Increased U.S. purchases, or at least accessibility, for foreign weapons sellers would be a way for Washington to influence the global arms trade and security landscape. Given the size of the U.S. military budget, other states will naturally be inclined to sign mutually beneficial deals that allow both countries to sell more weapons to each other. The United States should continue its own arm sales reformation, unilaterally and with key partners, to match intensified competition from Russia, China, and other counties. Washington should also lobby the EU to continue its arms embargo on Beijing. Granted, it could be argued that relaxing the EU embargo on the PLA could help weaken China's ties with Russia by decreasing PRC's dependence on imported Russian defense equipment and technologies. Nevertheless, repealing the EU arms embargo could prompt Moscow to further relax its arms sales policies and permit Beijing to purchase its top-line weapons in order to retain Russia's share of China's defense market. Moreover, if Europeans offered to sell arms to the PRC, such sales could increase U.S. anxieties about Beijing's growing military capabilities, furthering perceptions that ungrateful Europeans were sacrificing joint transatlantic security interests in pursuit of commercial opportunities. A repeal could also communicate the wrong signal to Beijing—that Europe is unconcerned about China's human rights practices, its growing military potential, expansive territorial claims, or its self-claimed right to employ military force to recover Taiwan. The United States also fears that deepening ties between the EU and the PRC would risk weakening European support for U.S. efforts to deter PRC aggression. EU governments could become more unwilling to rebuke China on disputed issues in fear of Beijing's curtailing purchases of Western weapons. U.S. officials have seen this problem in the past when Russian-EU ties have been good. In return for maintaining the EU embargo on China, Washington can sustain a robust transatlantic dialogue regarding U.S. security policies in Asia that could affect European interests as well as improve transatlantic defense industrial partnerships that offer opportunities for European defense sales to the Pentagon. To counter joint Russian-Chinese military space initiatives, the United States should deepen cooperation with European and Japanese space programs to counter adverse Sino-Russian efforts to constrain U.S. defensive capabilities in international legal frameworks. The United States should also jointly monitor and mitigate threatening Russian and Chinese offensive counter-space capabilities.

In Asia, the United States should continue to strengthen ties with New Delhi since India acts as a natural regional counterweight to Beijing in Asia given its democratic government, large population, quickly growing economy, and advanced military capabilities. Keeping India outside any Russian-Chinese alignment is also important for complicating Sino-Russian relations. For example, having India as a full member of the SCO also makes it more difficult for Moscow and Beijing to employ the organization against U.S. interests. New Delhi's defense ties with Moscow can be limited through targeted U.S. competition, such as conducting more arms sales that displace possible Russian weapons transfers. Since there is a limit to the number of turnkey major U.S. weapons systems that New Delhi will purchase, both parties should also deepen binational defense industrial cooperation, especially regarding integrating their private military manufactures and defense R&D innovation efforts. India, meanwhile, should raise its defense foreign direct investment ceiling to international standards and relax some of its onerous offset requirements. India and the United States also should deepen their cyber and outer space cooperation. Given how Russia's support for the PRC's military and space power is threatening India as well as the United States, the two democracies could profitably pool their efforts to protect their terrestrial and space infrastructure from mutual threats, such as China's growing offensive cyber or counterspace capabilities. Furthermore, the United States should support the continued reinterpretations of the Japanese constitution to allow Tokyo to become more of a global net security provider. Despite Russian-U.S. differences, the United States should not oppose a Russia-Japan reconciliation to help balance PRC pressure against Tokyo and influence in Moscow. Until now, neither Moscow nor Beijing has backed the other's territorial claims against Japan. Long-standing territorial disputes between Russia and Japan over the Kuril Islands are unlikely to be resolved in the near future. U.S. officials should encourage their Japanese counterparts to keep diplomatic doors open to avoid inducing Moscow to side with Beijing on its territorial demands in the East and South China Seas. Russian-Japanese tensions complicate efforts to present North Korea with a united front, disrupt economic and energy cooperation in northeast Asia, and weaken a balancing factor that could help keep China's rise peaceful. In the specific case of northeast Asia, China and North Korea represent a greater threat to U.S. interests and regional stability than Russia. Reduced tensions with Moscow would enable Japan to concentrate more on managing Beijing's growing economic and military power, might induce Beijing to moderate its policies toward Tokyo, and could increase the likelihood that Russia would weaken its tight embrace on China and adopt a more geopolitically balanced approach. Trilateral security arrangements—especially the U.S.-Japan-South Korea, the U.S.-Japan-Australia, and the U.S.-Japan-India triangles—also help balance both Russia and China. The United States may need to more actively promote Republic of Korea (ROK)-Japan reconciliation. While Washington has so far taken important steps to further the military relationship between its two allies, including trilateral exercises and intelligence sharing, the United States should do more to promote economic and people-to-people reconciliation. Conversely, Washington is not well positioned to challenge Russian and Chinese influence in Central Asia. Neither

Afghanistan nor much of Central Asia offers great economic opportunities to the United States, and U.S. access to the region is impeded by the area's land-locked nature and civil violence. The regional governments want to continue multi-vector foreign policies based on flexible partnerships with multiple external countries, including the United States, but Washington's involvement in the region has been episodic and declining concomitant with the decreasing U.S. military presence in Afghanistan. Central Asians recognize that history, geography, and a Kremlin leadership determined to sustain a high profile in their region will keep Moscow engaged as a leading player in the region. Many Central Asian leaders welcome China's regional economic involvement as helping to develop their countries and preventing Russia from securing the kind of absolute domination over regional affairs that occurred during the Soviet period. Local elites welcome Beijing's noninterference in Central Asian states' internal matters, as the PRC neither restricts alternative trade opportunities (as does Russia) nor demands democratization (as does the United States) though with the notable exception of not criticizing Chinese policies regarding Xinjiang, Hong Kong, or Taiwan. Whereas Russian and Chinese presidents and prime ministers regularly visit the region or host bilateral and multilateral meetings with Central Asian leaders, no U.S. president has ever visited Central Asia. Nonetheless, the three countries can pursue complementary regional economic policies. For example, China is willing to fund long-term infrastructure projects in Central Asia that the Russian government cannot afford and private U.S. companies typically eschew as unprofitable. However, the electoral crises that Russia and its close partners experienced in 2020 have highlighted a fundamental vulnerability in the Kremlin's elite-focused influence strategy. Due to the renunciation of the Soviet-era Communist Party monopoly of power and the fundamentally Western orientation of many of these countries' citizens, their political leaders must hold periodic elections that they profess to be free and fair. Yet, these elections repeatedly arouse popular protests due to their fraudulent nature, undermining their claim to represent multiparty democracies. This strategic vulnerability provides opportunities for the liberal democracies to find local allies in the region. Additionally, the United States can promote free-market institutions and the rule of law in Central Asia and elsewhere. U.S. officials can also warn of the risks of relying excessively on Chinese loans or China's 5G surveillance technology, both of which could compromise the receiving nation's autonomy. The United States and its allies should also strive to induce Russia and China to make their aid more transparent (to reduce duplication), more conditional on better domestic governance and superior economic policies by the recipients, and more open to the United States and other economic partners.

Appendices

APPENDIX 1. RUSSIAN ARMS SALES TO CHINA

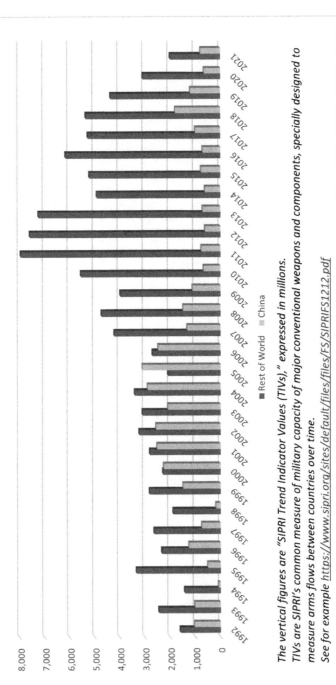

Russian Arms Exports to China

■ Rest of World ■ China

The vertical figures are "SIPRI Trend Indicator Values (TIVs)," expressed in millions.
TIVs are SIPRI's common measure of military capacity of major conventional weapons and components, specially designed to
measure arms flows between countries over time.
See for example https://www.sipri.org/sites/default/files/files/FS/SIPRIFS1212.pdf

Source: SIPRI Arms Transfers Database, accessed January 13, 2021

APPENDIX 2. CHINA'S SHARE OF RUSSIAN ARMS EXPORTS

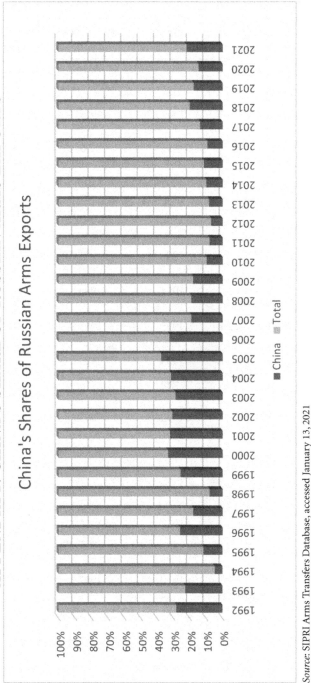

China's Shares of Russian Arms Exports

■ China ■ Total

Source: SIPRI Arms Transfers Database, accessed January 13, 2021

APPENDIX 3. MAJOR CONVENTIONAL WEAPONS TRANSFERS FROM RUSSIA TO CHINA

Weapon Designation	Designation	Year of Order/Deliveries		No. Produced/ Delivered
R-73/AA-11	SRAAM	1991	1992	300
Su-27S/ Flanker B	FGA aircraft	1991	1992	21
5V55U/ SA-10C	SAM	1992	1993–1997	150
76N6/Clam Shell	Air search radar	1992	1993	1
Il-76M	Transport aircraft	1992	1993	10
S-300PMU-1/ SA-20A	SAM	1992	1993–1997	4
ST-68/Tin Shield	Air search radar	1992	1993	1
Su-27S/ Flanker-B	FGA aircraft	1992	1992	2
53–65 533mm	AS torpedo	1993	1995–1999	75
Project-636E/ Kilo	Submarine	1993	1997–1999	2
Project-877E/ Kilo	Submarine	1993	1995	2
TEST-71	AS/ASW torpedo	1993	1995–1999	75
Mi-8MT/ Mi-17	Transport helicopter	1995	1996–1997	60
R-73/AA-11	SRAAM	1995	1996–2004	3000
Su-27S/ Flanker-B	FGA aircraft	1995	1996–1997	24
Ka-27PL	ASW helicopter	1996	1997	2
Su-27S/ Flanker-B	FGA aircraft	1996	1998–2007	105

Weapon Designation	Designation	Year of Order/Deliveries		No. Produced/ Delivered
Kh-31A1/ AS-17	Anti-ship missile/ARM	1997	2001–2015	700
Krasnopol-M	Guided shell	1997	1998–2002	1100
9M338/SA-15	SAM	1997	1999	400
Tor-M1/SA-15	Mobile SAM	1997	1999	15
9M119 Svir AT-11	Anti-tank missile	1998	2001–2015	1500
9M338/SA-15	SAM	1998	2000	500
9M38/SA-11	SAM	1998	1999–2000	150
Ka-27PL	ASW helicopter	1998	1999	5
Ka-32	Helicopter	1998	1999	3
MGK-335MS/ Bull Horn	ASW sonar	1998	2004	2
Mi-8MT/ Mi-17	Transport helicopter	1998	1999–2000	15
Moskit/ SS-N-22	Anti-ship missile	1998	2000	48
MR-90/Front Dome	Fire control radar	1998	2004	8
Project-956/ Sovremenny	Destroyer	1998	1999–2000	2
SA-N-12	Naval SAM	1998	2004	2
Tor-M1/SA-15	Mobile SAM	1998	2000	20
Kh-29/AS-14 Kedge	ASM	1999	2001–2002	100
Kh-59ME Ovod/AS-18	ASM	1999	2004–2006	150
Mineral/Band Stand	Sea search radar	1999	2004–2007	6
Su-27S/ Flanker-B	FGA aircraft	1999	2000–2002	28
Su-30MK	FGA aircraft	1999	2000–2001	38
AL-31	Turbofan engine	2000	2001–2005	54

(*Continued*)

(Continued)

Weapon Designation	Designation	Year of Order/Deliveries		No. Produced/ Delivered
Il-76M	Transport aircraft	2000	2002	1
RVV-AE/ AA-12 Adder	BVRAAM	2000	2002–2009	750
Fregat Top Plate	Air search radar	2001	2004–2007	4
48N6/SA-10	SAM	2001	2002	150
9M317/SA-17 Grizzly	SAM	2001	2004	150
Mi-8MT/ Mi-17	Transport helicopter	2001	2002–2003	35
S-300PMU-1/ SA-20A	SAM	2001	2003–2004	4
Su-30MK	FGA aircraft	2001	2002–2003	38
Zhuk	Combat ac radar	2001	2001–2005	100
AK-176 76mm	Naval gun	2004	2008–2018	30
3M-54 Klub/ SS-N-27	Anti-ship MI/ SSM	2002	2005–2009	150
48N6/SA-10	SAM	2002	2006–2007	150
53-65 533mm	AS torpedo	2002	2005–2006	150
9M311/SA-19	SAM	2002	2005–2006	200
9M38/SA-11	SAM	2002	2005–2006	150
Mi-8MT/ Mi-17	Transport helicopter	2002	2003–2004	25
Moskit/ SS-N-22	Anti-ship missile	2002	2005–2006	30
PMK-2	Naval mine/ torpedo	2002	2004–2007	100
Project-636E/ Kilo	Submarine	2002	2004–2006	8
Project-956/ Sovremenny	Destroyer	2002	2005–2006	2
S-300FM/ SA-N-20	Naval SAM	2002	2006–2007	2
TEST-71	AS/ASW torpedo	2002	2005–2006	150

Weapon Designation	Designation	Year of Order/Deliveries		No. Produced/ Delivered
Zmei/Sea Dragon	MP aircraft radar	2002	2003	1
Su-30MK	FGA aircraft	2003	2004	24
Mineral/Band Stand	Sea search radar	2004	2005–2018	30
48N6E2/ SA-10E	SAM	2004	2007–2008	297
AK-176 76mm	Naval gun	2004	2008–2015	20
Fregat/Top Plate	Air search radar	2004	2008–2015	21
Kh-59MK/ AS-18MK	Anti-ship missile	2004	2008–2015	200
MR-90/Front Dome	Fire control radar	2004	2008–2015	120
S-300PMU-2/ SA-20B	SAM	2004	2007–2008	8
AL-31	Turbofan engine	2005	2006–2009	100
Mi-8MT/ Mi-17	Transport helicopter	2005	2007–2012	54
48N6E2/ SA-10E	SAM	2006	2008–2009	750
Ka-27PL	ASW helicopter	2006	2009–2010	9
Ka-31	AEW helicopter	2006	2010–2011	9
Mi-8MT/ Mi-17	Transport helicopter	2006	2006–2007	24
S-300PMU-2/ SA-20B	SAM	2006	2008–2009	8
AK-176 76mm	Naval gun	2008	2007–2019	6
AL-31 for J-10 warplane	Turbofan engine	2009	2010–2012	122
D-30	Turbofan engine	2009	2009–2012	55
Mi-8MT/ Mi-17	Transport helicopter	2009	2010–2011	32

(Continued)

(Continued)

Weapon Designation	Designation	Year of Order/Deliveries		No. Produced/ Delivered
MR-123/Bass Tilt	Fire control radar	2009	2013–2014	2
AK-176 76mm	Naval gun	2010	2013–2015	59
AL-31 for J-10	Turbofan engine	2011	2012–2014	123
AL-31 for J-15	Turbofan engine	2011	2012–2015	125
D-30 for H-6K and Y-20	Turbofan engine	2011	2012–2015	184
AL-31 for J-20	Turbofan engine	2014	2017–2019	60
Il-76M	Transport aircraft	2011	2013	5
Mi-8MT/ Mi-17	Transport helicopter	2012	2012–2014	52
AL-41F	Turbofan engine	2015	2016–2018	10
Il-76M	Transport aircraft	2015	2015–2016	7
S-400/SA-21	SAM	2015	2018–2019	8
Su-35S	FGA aircraft	2015	2016–2018	24
RVV-AE/ AA-12 Adder	BVRAAM	2015	2017	192
48N6/SA-10	SAM	2015	2018–2019	300
AL-31 for J-10	Turbofan engine	2016	2016–2019	60

Source: SIPRI Arms Transfers Database, accessed January 13, 2021

APPENDIX 4. RUSSIAN-CHINESE TRADE
PROPORTIONS, 2018

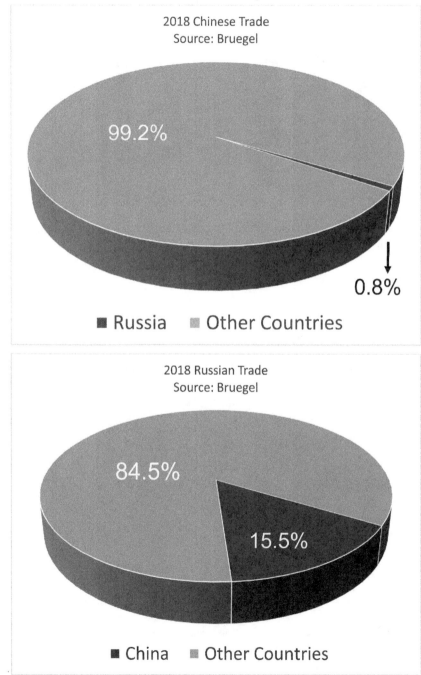

2018 Chinese Trade
Source: Bruegel

99.2%

0.8%

■ Russia   ■ Other Countries

2018 Russian Trade
Source: Bruegel

84.5%

15.5%

■ China   ■ Other Countries

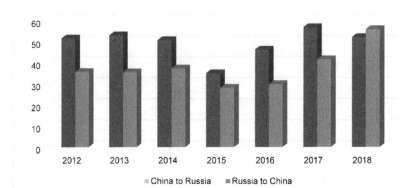

Sino-Russian Trade Desparity ($B)
2004–2018

Source: World Integrated Trade Solution Statistics

Source: https://wits.worldbank.org/CountryProfile/en/Country/RUS/Year/2018/TradeFlow/EXPIMP/
Partner/CHN/Product/all-groups

APPENDIX 5. SINO-RUSSIAN TRADE BALANCES

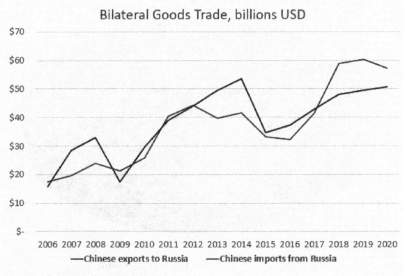

Source(s): UN COMTRADE

APPENDIX 6. MAJOR RUSSIAN-CHINESE JOINT INVESTMENT PROJECTS

Investment Project	Date of Investment	Investors	Location of Investment
Russian Forest Products Group (Russia's second-largest wood-processing company)	2013	Russia-China Investment Fund	Russia
DiDi (a transportation platform that provides transporting solutions to passengers via mobile app, from taxi, private car, chauffeur, and bus to test-drive services)	2014	Russia-China Investment Fund	China
Thalita Trading Ltd. (Thalita is the holding company of the Northern Capital Gateway, which manages Pulkovo Airport in St. Petersburg, Russia)	2017	Russian Direct Investment Fund (RDIF), Russia-China Investment Fund (RCIF), Mubadala Development Company (UAE), and Baring Vostok Private Equity Fund	Russia
Rostec City (a scientific and technological park on the former Tushino airfield in Moscow, Russia)	2017	Silk Road Fund, Russian Direct Investment Fund, Russia China Investment Fund, and Middle Eastern Funds	Russia

(Continued)

(Continued)

Investment Project	Date of Investment	Investors	Location of Investment
Zhaogang (a leading steel retailing e-commerce platform in China)	2017	Russia-China Investment Fund	China
Face++ (also known as Megvii—a facial recognition technology developer and servicing platform)	2017	Russia-China Investment Fund, Guo Feng Fund, Alibaba's Ant Financial, Foxconn Group, Sunshine Insurance Group, and S. K. Group	China
NIO (battery-based electrical passenger vehicle maker in China)	2017	Russia-China Investment Fund, Tencent, Baidu, GIC, TPG, Sequoia Capital, and Hillhouse Capital	China
Railway bridge over the Amur river on the Russia-China border to connect the Jewish Autonomous Region with the Chinese province of Heilongjiang	2018	Russia-China Investment Fund, OJSC Far East and Baikal Region Development Fund	Russia, China
Transneft (world's largest pipeline company that transports 83% of Russian oil)	2018	Russia-China Investment Fund, Russian Direct Investment Fund, and Middle Eastern Sovereign Wealth Fund	Russia

Investment Project	Date of Investment	Investors	Location of Investment
Sovcombank (a leading Russian private bank)	2018	Russia-China Investment Fund and Middle Eastern Fund	Russia
Intergeo (a metals and mining company)	2019	Russia-China Investment Fund and Middle Eastern Sovereign Wealth Fund	Russia
Alium (a pharmaceutical holding focused on commercial segment formed by the merger of two pharmaceutical companies Obolenskoe and Binnopharm)	2019	Russia-China Investment Fund, Middle Eastern Funds, Sistema, and VTB Bank	Russia
JSC Detsky Mir (Russia's largest retailer of children's goods)	2019	Russia-China Investment Fund	Russia

Source: Russia-China Investment Fund (RCIF), 2012–2019, http://rcif.com/en/portfolio-companies. htm; accessed January 31, 2021

Notes

INTRODUCTION

1. Andrea Kendall-Taylor and David Shullman, "China and Russia's Dangerous Convergence: How to Counter an Emerging Partnership," *Foreign Affairs*, May 3, 2021, https://www.foreignaffairs.com/articles/china/2021-05-03/china-and-russias-dangerous-convergence.

2. "Interim National Security Strategic Guidance," The White House, March 3, 2021, https://www.whitehouse.gov/briefing-room/statements-releases/2021/03/03/interim-national-security-strategic-guidance/.

3. Joseph Y. S. Cheng, "Convincing the World of China's Tradition to Pursue Universal Harmony," *Journal of Chinese Political Science* (2012), https://link.springer.com/article/10.1007/s11366-012-9191-5; David Kerr, "Central Asian and Russian Perspectives on China's Strategic Emergence," *International Affairs* (2010); and Robert H. Donaldson and Joseph L. Nogee, *The Foreign Policy of Russia: Changing Systems, Enduring Interests*, fourth edition (Armonk, NY: M. E. Sharpe, 2009).

4. Michael Mandelbaum, *The Case for Goliath: How America Acts as the World's Government in the Twenty-First Century* (New York, NY: PublicAffairs, 2005).

5. George Perkovich, "Are Nuclear Weapons Becoming More or Less Important to Deterrence in the Emerging International Security Environment?" Stratcom's 2012 Deterrence Symposium, 2012, http://www.carnegieendowment.org/2012/08/09/are-nuclear-weapons-becoming-more-or-less-important-to-deterrence-in-emerging-international-security-environment/dd88.

6. Andrew Osborn, "Russia Starts Biggest War Games since Soviet Fall near China," Reuters, September 11, 2018, https://www.reuters.com/article/us-russia-exercises-vostok/russia-starts-biggest-war-games-since-soviet-fall-near-china-idUSKCN1LR146.

7. Peter Toft, "John J. Mearsheimer: An Offensive Realist between Geopolitics and Power," *Journal of International Relations and Development* (2005), 381–408, https://link.springer.com/content/pdf/10.1057/palgrave.jird.1800065.pdf.

8. A. F. K. Organski, *World Politics* (New York: Alfred A. Knopf, 1968); Robert Gilpin, *War & Change in World Politics* (Cambridge, UK: Cambridge University Press, 1981); Robert Keohane, "Hegemony and After: Knowns and Unknowns in the Debate over Decline," *Foreign Affairs*, August 2012; and Matthew Kroenig, *The Return of Great Power Rivalry: Democracy versus Autocracy from the Ancient World to the U.S. and China* (New York: Oxford University Press, 2020). A good summary of this literature appears in Michael C. Webb and Stephen D. Krasner. "Hegemonic Stability Theory: An Empirical Assessment," *Review of International Studies* (1989).

9. John J. Mearsheimer, *The Great Delusion: Liberal Dreams and International Realities* (New Haven, CT: Yale University Press, 2018).

10. Nikolai Silayev and Anrey Sushentsov, "Russia's Allies and the Geopolitical Frontier in Eurasia," Valdai Discussion Club, April 2017, https://valdaiclub.com/a/valdai-papers/russia-allies-and-the-geopolitical-frontier/.

11. Padma Desai, "Russian Retrospectives on Reforms from Yeltsin to Putin," *Journal of Economic Perspectives* (2005), 87–106, http://faculty.nps.edu/relooney/00_New_13.pdf.

12. Scott Boston, Michael Johnson, Nathan Beauchamp-Mustafaga, and Yvonne K. Crane, "Assessing the Conventional Force Imbalance in Europe," The RAND Corporation, 2018, https://www.rand.org/pubs/research_reports/RR2402.html.

13. Cited in "Deng Xiaoping's '24-Character Strategy'," *Global Security*, 2022, https://www.globalsecurity.org/military/world/china/24-character.htm.

14. Yang Jiechi, "Working for a Community with a Shared Future for Mankind by Promoting International Cooperation and Multilateralism," Munich Security Conference, February 16, 2019, https://www.mfa.gov.cn/ce/cgcc/eng/xw/t1638902.htm.

15. Tom Waldwyn, "China's Naval Shipbuilding: Delivering on Its Ambition in a Big Way," The International Institute of Strategic Studies, May 1, 2018, https://www.iiss.org/blogs/military-balance/2018/05/china-naval-shipbuilding.

16. Sergio Miracola, "Beijing's Ultimate Goal: The Military-Civilian Fusion," Italian Institute for International Political Studies, August 2018, https://www.ispionline.it/en/pubblicazione/beijings-ultimate-goal-military-civilian-fusion-21110.

17. Graham Allison, *Destined for War: Can America and China Escape Thucydides's Trap?* (New York: Houghton Mifflin Harcourt, 2017).

18. Marc Bennetts, "Shunned by West, Putin Seeks Friend, Financier on China Visit," *Washington Times*, June 23, 2016, http://www.washingtontimes.com/news/2016/jun/23/putin-seeks-friend-financier-on-china-visit/.

19. DD Wu, "Xi-Putin Meet on SCO Summit Sidelines to Strengthen China-Russia Ties," *The Diplomat*, June 9, 2017, http://thediplomat.com/2017/06/xi-putin-meet-on-sco-summit-sidelines-to-strengthen-china-russia-ties/.

20. Timofei Bordachev, "Main Results of 2017: Energetic Russia and the Greater Eurasia Community," December 28, 2017, http://valdaiclub.com/a/highlights/main-results-of-2017-energetic-russia/.

21. "Foreign Minister Sergey Lavrov's Remarks and Answers to Questions during the Government Hour at the State Duma of the Federal Assembly of the Russian Federation," Embassy of the Russian Federation in the Kingdom of Thailand, January 25, 2017, https://thailand.mid.ru/en/key-issues/2088-foreign-minister-sergey-lavrov-s-remarks-and-answers-to-questions-during-

the-government-hour-at-the-state-duma-of-the-federal-assembly-of-the-russian-federation.

22. "Vladimir Putin's Annual News Conference," President of Russia website, December 14, 2017, http://en.kremlin.ru/events/president/transcripts/56378.

23. Vladimir Putin, final plenary session of the 16th meeting of the Valdai International Discussion Club, October 3, 2019, en.kremlin.ru/events/president/news/61719.

24. Brett Forrest, Ann M. Simmons, and Chao Deng, "China and Russia Military Cooperation Raises Prospect of New Challenge to American Power," *Wall Street Journal*, January 2, 2022, https://www.wsj.com/articles/china-russia-america-military-exercises-weapons-war-xi-putin-biden-11641146041.

25. "Statement by H.E. Mr. Vladimir Putin, President of the Russian Federation, at the 70th Session of the United Nations General Assembly in New York," Russian Federation Permanent Mission to the United Nations, September 28, 2015, https://russiaun.ru/en/news/vladimirputin70thsession.

26. "Foreign Policy Concept of the Russian Federation, Approved by the President of the Russian Federation V. Putin on November 30, 2016," Embassy of the Russian Federation to the United Kingdom of Great Britain and Northern Ireland, https://www.rusemb.org.uk/rp_insight/.

27. "Full Transcript: Interview with Chinese President Xi Jinping," *Wall Street Journal*, September 22, 2015, http://www.wsj.com/articles/full-transcript-interview-with-chinese-president-xi-jinping-1442894700.

28. Peter Ferdinand, "The Positions of Russia and China at the UN Security Council in the Light of Recent crises," Directorate-General for External Policies, Policy Department, European Council, 2013, http://www.europarl.europa.eu/RegData/etudes/note/join/2013/433800/EXPO-SEDE_NT(2013)433800_EN.pdf.

29. "Foreign Minister Sergey Lavrov's Remarks and Answers to Questions at a Roundtable Discussion with the Participants of the Gorchakov Public Diplomacy Fund in the Videoconference Format, Moscow, April 21, 2020," https://www.mid.ru/en/web/guest/meropriyatiya_s_uchastiem_ministra/-/asset_publisher/xK1BhB2bUjd3/content/id/4103828.

30. Shannon Tiezzi, "Does China Approve of Russia's Airstrikes Is Syria?" *The Diplomat*, October 8, 2015, http://thediplomat.com/2015/10/does-china-approve-of-russias-airstrikes-in-syria/.

31. Kenneth Anderson, "Text of Russia-China Joint Declaration on Promotion and Principles of International Law," *Lawfare*, July 7, 2016, https://www.lawfareblog.com/text-russia-china-joint-declaration-promotion-and-principles-international-law.

32. DD Wu, "Xi-Putin Meet on SCO Summit Sidelines to Strengthen China-Russia Ties," *The Diplomat*, June 9, 2017, http://thediplomat.com/2017/06/xi-putin-meet-on-sco-summit-sidelines-to-strengthen-china-russia-ties/.

33. DD Wu, "Xi-Putin Meet on SCO Summit Sidelines to Strengthen China-Russia Ties," *The Diplomat*, June 9, 2017, http://thediplomat.com/2017/06/xi-putin-meet-on-sco-summit-sidelines-to-strengthen-china-russia-ties/.

34. "China Committed to New Intl Relations Featuring Win-win Co-op," Xinhua, April 10, 2015, http://english.www.gov.cn/news/international_exchanges/2015/04/10/content_281475086322430.htm.

35. Vladimir Putin interview with *The Financial Times*, June 27, 2019, http://en.kremlin.ru/events/president/news/60836.

36. "Treaty of Good-Neighborliness and Friendly Ministry of Foreign Affairs of the People's Republic of China," PRC Ministry of Foreign Affairs, July 24, 2001, https://www.fmprc.gov.cn/mfa_eng/wjdt_665385/2649_665393/200107/t20010724_679026.html.

37. Andrew Browne, "The Danger of China's Victim Mentality," *Wall Street Journal*, June 14, 2016, http://www.wsj.com/articles/the-danger-of-chinas-victim-mentality-1465880577.

38. "Joint Statement between the People's Republic of China and the Russian Federation," PRC Ministry of Foreign Affairs, April 6, 2007, https://china.usc.edu/joint-statement-between-peoples-republic-china-and-russian-federation-april-6-2007.

39. "Vladimir Putin Meets with Members of the Valdai Discussion Club," transcript of the Plenary Session of the 13th Annual Meeting, Valdai Discussion Club, October 27, 2016, https://valdaiclub.com/events/posts/articles/vladimir-putin-took-part-in-the-valdai-discussion-club-s-plenary-session/.

40. "Chief of the General Staff of the Russian Armed Forces Spoke about Military Dangers and Threats to Russia in Modern Conditions," Ministry of Defense of the Russian Federation, April 16, 2015, http://eng.mil.ru/en/mcis/news/more.htm?id=12016242@egNews.

41. "Full Transcript: Interview with Chinese President Xi Jinping," *Wall Street Journal*, September 22, 2015, http://www.wsj.com/articles/full-transcript-interview-with-chinese-president-xi-jinping-1442894700.

42. "Russia Calls U.S. Accusations against China of Spreading COVID-19 Groundless," Xinhua, May 15, 2020, http://www.xinhuanet.com/english/2020-05/15/c_139057605.htm.

43. Richard Weitz, "The Sino-Russian Disinformation Axis during the COVID-19 Pandemic," *China Brief* 20, no. 14 (August 12, 2020), https://jamestown.org/program/the-sino-russian-disinformation-axis-during-the-covid-19-pandemic/.

44. "Diplomat Slams West's Biased 'Coronavirus Disinfo' Claims against Russia, China," TASS, May 14, 2020, https://tass.com/politics/1156487.

45. Paul Schwartz, "Russia-China Defense Cooperation: New Developments," *The Asan Forum*, 2017, http://www.theasanforum.org/russia-china-defense-cooperation-new-developments/.

CHAPTER 1

1. "Guidance on the North Korean Cyber Threat," U.S. Department of Homeland Security, April 15, 2020, https://www.us-cert.gov/ncas/alerts/aa20-106a.

2. Evans Revere, "North Korea's New Nuclear Gambit and the Fate of Denuclearization," Brookings Institution, March 26, 2021, https://www.brookings.edu/blog/order-from-chaos/2021/03/26/north-koreas-new-nuclear-gambit-and-the-fate-of-denuclearization/.

3. "Joint Statement by the Chinese and Russian Foreign Ministries on the Korean Peninsula's Problems," Russian Ministry of Foreign Affairs, July 14, 2017, http://

www.mid.ru/en/web/guest/maps/kr/-/asset_publisher/PR7UbfssNImL/content/id/2807662.

4. "Russia Condemns New U.S. Sanctions on North Korea," Reuters, March 7, 2018, https://www.reuters.com/article/us-northkorea-malaysia-kim-usa-russia/russia-condemns-new-u-s-sanctions-on-north-korea-idUSKCN1GJ175.

5. Uri Friedman, "Why China Isn't Doing More to Stop North Korea," *The Atlantic*, August 9, 2017, https://www.theatlantic.com/international/archive/2017/08/north-korea-the-china-options/535440/.

6. Lora Saalman, "Balancing Chinese Interests on North Korea and Iran," The Carnegie Endowment for International Peace, April 2013, http://carnegieendowment.org/files/china_interests.pdf.

7. "Foreign Ministry Spokesperson Wang Wenbin's Regular Press Conference on November 2, 2021," PRC Ministry of Foreign Affairs, https://www.fmprc.gov.cn/mfa_eng/xwfw_665399/s2510_665401/2511_665403/202111/t20211102_10440039.html.

8. Uri Friedman, "Why China Isn't Doing More to Stop North Korea," *The Atlantic*, August 9, 2017, https://www.theatlantic.com/international/archive/2017/08/north-korea-the-china-options/535440/.

9. Richard Roth, "UN Security Council Imposes New Sanctions on North Korea," CNN, August 6, 2017, http://www.cnn.com/2017/08/05/asia/north-korea-un-sanctions/index.html.

10. Alex Johnson, "China Proposes Deal to Ease Tensions Over North Korean Missiles," NBC News, March 7, 2017, https://www.nbcnews.com/news/north-korea/china-proposes-deal-ease-tensions-over-north-korean-missiles-n730436.

11. "Remarks by President Trump to the 72nd Session of the United Nations General Assembly," The White House, September 19, 2017, https://br.usembassy.gov/remarks-president-trump-72nd-session-united-nations-general-assembly/.

12. "Joint Statement by the Chinese and Russian Foreign Ministries on the Korean Peninsula's Problems," Russian Ministry of Foreign Affairs, July 14, 2017, http://www.mid.ru/en/web/guest/maps/kr/-/asset_publisher/PR7UbfssNImL/content/id/2807662.

13. "Russia, China Block U.S. Bid at UN to Halt Fuel Deliveries to North Korea," Radio Free Europe/Radio Liberty," July 20, 2018, https://www.rferl.org/a/russia-china-block-us-bid-un-security-council-halt-fuel-deliveries-north-korea/29377637.html.

14. Kelsey Davenport, "China, Russia Propose North Korea Sanctions Relief," *Arms Control Today*, December 2021, https://www.armscontrol.org/act/2021-12/news/china-russia-propose-north-korea-sanctions-relief.

15. "Foreign Ministry Spokesperson Wang Wenbin's Regular Press Conference on November 2, 2021," PRC Ministry of Foreign Affairs, https://www.fmprc.gov.cn/mfa_eng/xwfw_665399/s2510_665401/2511_665403/202111/t20211102_10440039.html

16. Fei Su, "China's Potential Role as Security Guarantor for North Korea," 38 North, October 24, 2018, https://www.38north.org/2018/10/fsu102418/#_ftnref14.

17. "Putin Says Korean Reunification Only Possible via Peaceful Means," Sputnik, November 12, 2013, http://sputniknews.com/politics/20131112/184670071/Putin-Says-Korean-Reunification-Only-Possible-via-Peaceful-Means.html.

18. "Pentagon Press Secretary John F. Kirby Holds a Press Briefing," U.S. Department of Defense, November 8, 2021, https://www.defense.gov/News/Transcripts/Transcript /Article/2837897/pentagon-press-secretary-john-f-kirby-holds-a-press-briefing/.

19. Dan De Luce and Elias Groll, "Trump White House Stays Quiet as Russia Flouts North Korea Sanctions," *Foreign Policy*, June 13, 2017, http://foreignpolicy.com/2017/06/13/ trump-white-house-stays-quiet-as-russia-flouts-north-korea-sanctions/.

20. "White House to Take 'Calibrated, Practical Approach' to North Korea," Axios, April 30, 2021, https://www.axios.com/biden-north-korea-diplomacy-denucleariza- tion-b38d20b5-d3a8-4eaf-a8f5-3eb6e8b38ec5.html.

21. Choe Sang-hun, "China Suspends All Coal Imports from North Korea," *New York Times*, February 18, 2017, https://www.nytimes.com/2017/02/18/world/asia /north-korea-china-coal-imports-suspended.html.

CHAPTER 2

1. "Joint Compendium of Documents on the History of Territorial Issue between Japan and Russia," Japanese Foreign Ministry, March 1, 2001, https://www.mofa.go.jp /region/europe/russia/territory/edition92/period2.html.

2. "77% of Russians Oppose Ceding Kuril Islands to Japan, Poll Says," *Moscow Times*, January 28, 2019, https://www.themoscowtimes.com/2019/01/28/77-percent- russians-oppose-ceding-kuril-islands-japan-poll-says-a64302.

3. "Japan's Prime Minister Plans a Steamy Tête-à-Tête with Russia's President," *Economist*, December 10, 2016, http://www.economist.com/news/asia/21711337- chances-breakthrough-two-countries-territorial-dispute-are-slim-japans-prime.

4. "Kuril Islands: What to Know about the Islands at the Centre of a Ter- ritorial Dispute between Russia and Japan," *South China Morning Post*, January 22, 2019, https://www.scmp.com/news/asia/diplomacy/article/2183225/kuril- islands-what-know-about-islands-centre-territorial-dispute.

5. Vladimir Isachenkov, "Russia Toughens Stance in Island Dispute with Japan," *The Diplomat*, January 14, 2019, https://thediplomat.com/2019/01/russia-toughens- stance-in-island-dispute-with-japan/; "Deep Gap Emerges between Japan, Rus- sia over Territorial Dispute," *Mainichi Japan*, January 15, 2019, https://mainichi.jp /english/articles/20190115/p2a/00m/0na/006000c; and "Russia Calls U.S.-Japan Secu- rity Alliance an Impediment to Peace Treaty Talks," *Japan Times*, March 2, 2019, https:// www.japantimes.co.jp/news/2019/03/02/national/politics-diplomacy/russia-calls-u-s -japan-security-alliance-impediment-peace-treaty-talks/#.XHsvRrhOnDc.

6. Ivan Timofeev, "Russia-Japan Dialogue: The Sanctions Factor," Valdai Discus- sion Club, January 21, 2019, http://valdaiclub.com/a/highlights/russia-japan-dialogue- the-sanctions-factor/; and Dmitry Streltsov, "Russia-Japan: Softening Negotiations with Unpredictable Prospects," Valdai Discussion Club, January 15, 2019, http://valda- iclub.com/a/highlights/russia-japan-softening-negotiations/.

7. Maria Shagina, "Japan and Russia Star-Crossed Economic Partners?" *Asia & the Pacific Policy Society*, April 2, 2019, https://www.policyforum.net /japan-and-russia-star-crossed-economic-partners/; and Chris Miller, "Japan's Fro- zen Far East Investment Giving Japan—Russia Ties Frostbite," East Asia Forum,

March 2, 2018, https://www.eastasiaforum.org/2018/03/02/japans-frozen-far-east-investment-giving-japan-russia-ties-frostbite/.

8. James Brown, "A New Cold War with Russia Forces Japan to Choose Sides," *The Diplomat*, April 23, 2018, https://thediplomat.com/2018/04/a-new-cold-war-with-russia-forces-japan-to-choose-sides/.

9. Francesco Sassi, "Japan in the Russian Arctic," *The Diplomat*, August 7, 2019, https://thediplomat.com/2019/08/japan-in-the-russian-arctic/.

10. Pan Mengqi and Cai Hong, "Tokyo's Defense Paper Lashed for Labeling Beijing a Threat," *China Daily*, August 29, 2018, http://usa.chinadaily.com.cn/a/201808/29/WS5b85b981a310add14f38844b.html.

11. Sarbhanu Nath, "Japan's Growing Strategic Footprint in South Asia," *The Diplomat*, January 11, 2019, https://thediplomat.com/2019/01/japans-growing-strategic-footprint-in-south-asia/; and Girard May, "China Faces a Stronger Japan," *The Diplomat*, May 31, 2019, https://thediplomat.com/2019/05/china-faces-a-stronger-japan/.

12. Mina Pollmann, "How Energy Security Shapes Foreign Policy," *The Diplomat*, March 16, 2016, http://thediplomat.com/2016/03/japan-how-energy-security-shapes-foreign-policy/.

13. "Center for Preventive Action, Tensions in the East China Sea," Council on Foreign Relations, May 4, 2022, https://www.cfr.org/global-conflict-tracker/conflict/tensions-east-china-sea.

14. Franz-Stefan Grady, "U.S. Air Force Flies 2 B-52H Bombers over East China Sea," *The Diplomat*, January 31, 2019, https://thediplomat.com/2019/01/us-air-force-flies-2-b-52h-bombers-over-east-china-sea/.

15. "Japan Wants Closer Relations with Russia. Good Luck with That," Stratfor Worldview, May 25, 2018, https://worldview.stratfor.com/article/japan-wants-closer-relations-russia-good-luck.

16. Anna Kireeva, "What Russia Thinks of Japan's Right to Collective Self-Defense," *Russia Direct*, July 15, 2014, https://russia-direct.org/analysis/what-russia-thinks-japans-right-collective-self-defense.

17. Magnus Lundström, "Why Are US Allies Japan and South Korea Drawing Closer to Russia?" *The Diplomat*, March 20, 2018, https://thediplomat.com/2018/03/why-are-us-allies-japan-and-south-korea-drawing-closer-to-russia.

18. Hiroshi Yamazoe, "Sino-Russian Cooperation from the Perspective of the U.S.-Japan Alliance," *Asia Policy* 13, no. 1 (January 2018), 32–38.

19. Joshua Walker and Hidetoshi Azuma, "Why Japan and Russia Are Working Together," *Foreign Affairs*, September 15, 2016, https://www.foreignaffairs.com/articles/japan/2016-09-15/abe-and-putin-make-peace.

20. Qi Wei, "Why Putin's Visit Matters to Japan?" Xinhua, May 13, 2009, http://news.xinhuanet.com/english/2009-05/13/content_11366710.htm.

21. Ankit Panda, "Japan Sanctions Russia over Ukraine," *The Diplomat*, July 29, 2014, http://thediplomat.com/2014/07/japan-sanctions-russia-over-ukraine/.

22. "Japan's New Sanctions against Russia 'Unfriendly, Short-Sighted'—Moscow," RIA Novosti, July 29, 2014, https://sputniknews.com/20140729/Japans-New-Sanctions-Against-Russia-Unfriendly-Short-Sighted—191427554.html?id=.

23. Stephen R. Nagy, "Pride and Prejudice with Chinese Characteristics," *Japan Times*, October 3, 2019, https://www.japantimes.co.jp/opinion/2019/10/03/commentary/world-commentary/pride-prejudice-chinese-characteristics/#.XZ0gcEZKiUk.

CHAPTER 3

1. "What Does Russia Import from India?" The Observatory of Economic Complexity, 2017, https://oec.world/en/visualize/tree_map/hs92/import/rus/ind/show/2017/.

2. Aleksei Zakharov, "Is This the Revival of Russia-India Economic Ties?" *The Diplomat*, September 20, 2018, https://thediplomat.com/2018/09/is-this-the-revival-of-russia-india-economic-ties/.

3. Shruti Godbole, "Future of the India-Russia Relationship Post Sochi Summit," Brookings Institution, July 2, 2018, https://www.brookings.edu/blog/up-front/2018/07/02/future-of-the-india-russia-relationship-post-sochi-summit/.

4. "India-Russia Bilateral Maritime Exercise Kicks Off," *Times of India*, December 15, 2016, http://timesofindia.indiatimes.com/city/visakhapatnam/India-Russia-bilateral-maritime-exercise-kicks-off/articleshow/55987598.cms.

5. Franz-Stefan Grady, "India, Russia to Upgrade Joint Military Exercise," *The Diplomat*, May 19, 2017, https://thediplomat.com/2017/05/india-russia-to-upgrade-joint-military-exercise/.

6. Shruti Godbole, "Future of the India-Russia Relationship Post Sochi Summit," Brookings Institution, July 2, 2018, https://www.brookings.edu/blog/up-front/2018/07/02/future-of-the-india-russia-relationship-post-sochi-summit/.

7. Aude Fleurant, Pieter D. Wezeman, Siemon T. Wezeman, and Nan Tian, "Trends in International Arms Transfers, 2016," Stockholm International Peace Research Institute, February 2017, https://www.sipri.org/sites/default/files/Trends-in-international-arms-transfers-2016.pdf.

8. Ayaz Gul, "Pakistan, Russia Sign Rare Military Cooperation Pact," Voice of America, August 8, 2018, https://www.voanews.com/a/pakistan-russia-sign-military-cooperation-pact/4519031.html.

9. "Why Developing the Chabahar Port in Iran Is Important for India: 10 Points," *Times of India*, February 16, 2018, https://timesofindia.indiatimes.com/india/why-developing-the-chabahar-port-in-iran-is-important-for-india-10-points/articleshow/62944859.cms.

10. Maninder Dabas, "Here Is All You Should Know about 'String Of Pearls', China's Policy to Encircle India," *Times of India*, June 23, 2017, https://www.indiatimes.com/news/india/here-is-all-you-should-know-about-string-of-pearls-china-s-policy-to-encircle-india-324315.html; and Steven Lee Myers, "With Ships and Missiles, China Is Ready to Challenge U.S. Navy in Pacific," *New York Times*, August 29, 2018, https://www.nytimes.com/2018/08/29/world/asia/china-navy-aircraft-carrier-pacific.html.

11. Ralph Jennings, "China Eyes Improved Indian Ties in Case of Sino-U.S. Trade War," *Forbes*, April 3, 2018, https://www.forbes.com/sites/ralphjennings/2018/04/03/china-moves-to-reconcile-with-india-amid-threat-of-sino-u-s-trade-war/.

12. Yang Xiaoping, "When India's Strategic Backyard Meets China's Strategic Periphery: The View From Beijing," *War on the Rocks*, April 20, 2018, https://

warontherocks.com/2018/04/when-indias-strategic-backyard-meets-chinas-strategic-periphery-the-view-from-beijing/.

13. James Heitzman and Robert L. Worden, eds., *India: A Country Study* (Washington: GPO for the Library of Congress, 1995).

14. "United Nations Digital Library," United Nations, accessed July 1, 2021, https://digitallibrary.un.org/search?cc=Voting+Data&ln=en&c=Voting+Data&fct__9=Vote&jrec=451.

15. Mark N. Katz, "Putin's Predicament: Russia and Afghanistan after 2014," *Asia Policy* 17 (January 2014), https://www.nbr.org/publication/putins-predicament-russia-and-afghanistan-after-2014/.

16. Joy Mitra, "Russia, China and Pakistan: An Emerging New Axis?" *The Diplomat*, August 18, 2015, http://thediplomat.com/2015/08/russia-china-and-pakistan-an-emerging-new-axis/.

17. Husain Haqqani, "India and the United States: Will a Strategic Partnership Emerge?" presentation at Hudson Institute, September 24, 2014, https://www.youtube.com/watch?v=cc2bAoABaH0.

18. Husain Haqqani, *Magnificent Delusions: Pakistan, the United States, and an Epic History of Misunderstanding* (New York: Public Affairs, 2013).

19. "Closing Remarks at the U.S.-India 2+2 Dialogue," U.S. Department of State, September 6, 2018, https://in.usembassy.gov/closing-remarks-at-the-u-s-india-22-dialogue/.

20. "Donald Trump in India: Key Deals Signed on Defense but Not on Trade," BBC News, February 25, 2020, https://www.bbc.com/news/world-asia-india-51625503.

21. Mike Stone, "Exclusive: U.S. Offers India Armed Version of Guardian Drone—Sources," Reuters, July 18, 2018, https://www.reuters.com/article/us-britain-airshow-india-drones-exclusiv/exclusive-u-s-offers-india-armed-version-of-guardian-drone-sources-idUSKBN1K820K.

22. Prateek Joshi, "The US-India 2+2 Dialogue: Implications and Challenges for the Indo-Pacific," PacNet, no. 64 (September 13, 2018), https://pacforum.org/publication/pacnet-64-the-us-india-22-dialogue-implications-and-challenges-for-the-indo pacific.

23. Dinakar Peri, "COMCASA Will Help India Track China's Indian Ocean Moves Better," *Hindu*, September 8, 2018, https://www.thehindu.com/news/national/comcasa-will-help-india-track-chinas-indian-ocean-moves-better/article24896647.ece.

24. Kallol Bhattacharjee, "India, U.S. Sign Landmark Military Communications, Security Agreement COMCASA," *Hindu*, September 6, 2018, https://www.thehindu.com/news/national/india-us-sign-landmark-comcasa-deal/article24881277.ece.

25. "Joint Statement on the Inaugural India-U.S. 2+2 Ministerial Dialogue," U.S. Department of State, Ministry of External Affairs, Government of India, September 6, 2018, https://mea.gov.in/bilateral-documents.htm?dtl/30358/Joint+Statement+on+the+Inaugural+IndiaUS+2432+Ministerial+Dialogue

26. Ashley J. Tellis, "How Can U.S.-India Relations Survive the S-400 Deal?" Carnegie Endowment for International Peace, August 29, 2018, https://carnegieendowment.org/2018/08/29/how-can-u.s.-india-relations-survive-s-400-deal-pub-77131.

27. "Expert Says US Sanctions Unlikely to Affect Russian Arms Deliveries to India," TASS, March 9, 2017, http://tass.com/defense/934600.

28. "US Provided India Intelligence Input on Chinese Troop Deployments during Doklam Stand-Off, Hints Report," *Swarajya*, September 5, 2018, https://swarajyamag .com/insta/this-is-how-us-helped-india-during-the-73-day-military-stand-off-with-china-in-doklam.

CHAPTER 4

1. "Value of Chinese Foreign Direct Investment to EU-27 and UK from 2012 to 2021, by ownership of investment," Statistica, April 2022, https://www.statista.com /statistics/1084385/china-foreign-direct-investment-to-eu-by-ownership-of-invest-ment/.

2. "Chinese FDI in Europe: 2020 Update," Merica, June 16, 2021, https://merics .org/en/report/chinese-fdi-europe-2020-update.

3. Zoe Stanley-Lockman, "A First: China, EU Launch New Combined Military Exercise," *The Diplomat*, October 18, 2018, https://thediplomat.com/2018/10/a -first-china-eu-launch-new-combined-military-exercise/.

4. Paweł Paszak, "Poland-China Relations in 2021: Current State and Prospects," Warsaw Institute, January 29, 2021, https://warsawinstitute.org/ poland-china-relations-2021-current-state-prospects/.

5. Cristina Gallardo, "Commission Seeks to Block China from Sensitive Joint Science Projects," *Politico,* March 30, 2021 https://www.politico.eu/article/ commission-plans-to-limit-research-tie-ups-with-china/.

6. Brian G. Carlson, "Why China Will Support Russia in Belarus," *The Diplomat*, August 31, 2020, https://thediplomat.com/2020/08/why-china-will-support-russia-in-belarus/.

7. Dimitri Simes, "China Scores Points over Russia with 'Mask Diplomacy' in Belarus," *Nikkei Asian Review*, May 2020, https://asia.nikkei.com/Spotlight/ Coronavirus/China-scores-points-over-Russia-with-mask-diplomacy-in-Belarus.

CHAPTER 5

1. Simon Tisdall, "Trump's Bid to Buy Greenland Shows That the 'Scramble for the Arctic' Is Truly upon Us," *Guardian*, August 24, 2019, https://www.theguardian. com/world/2019/aug/24/trump-greenland-gambit-sad-sign-arctic-up-for-grabs.

2. UN Environment Europe Office, "Temperature Rise Is 'Locked-In' for the Coming Decades in the Arctic," UN Environment Programme, March 13, 2019, https://www .unenvironment.org/news-and-stories/press-release/temperature-rise-locked-coming-decades-arctic.

3. Kristina Spohr, "The Race to Conquer the Arctic—the World's Final Frontier," *New Statesman*, March 21, 2018, https://www.newstatesman.com/2018/03 /race-conquer-arctic-world-s-final-frontier.

4. "Thawing Ice and Chilly Diplomacy in the Arctic," *New York Times,* April 28, 2015, http://www.nytimes.com/2015/04/28/opinion/thawing-ice-and-chilly-diplomacy-in-the-arctic.html.

5. Ekaterina Klimenko, "An End to Cooperation? Russia and the Arctic," Stockholm International Peace Research Institute, March 15, 2015, http://www.sipri.org/media/newsletter/essay/mar-15-russia-and-the-arctic.

6. "Russian Federation Policy for the Arctic to 2020," *Arctis*, March 30, 2016, http://www.arctis-search.com/Russian+Federation+Policy+for+the+Arctic+to+2020; and "Russian Federation Policy for the Arctic to 2020," Government of the Russian Federation, March 24, 2009, https://assets.aspeninstitute.org/content/uploads/files/content/upload/29%20Russian%20Arctic%20Strategy%20Until%202020%20BW.pdf.

7. David Auerswald and Terry L. Anderson, "China, Russia Move into the Arctic—and Put US at Risk," *The Hill*, May 14, 2019, https://thehill.com/opinion/national-security/443324-china-russia-move-into-the-arctic-and-put-us-at-risk.

8. "Minister: Russia Plans to Finalize by Autumn Studies to Confirm Its Arctic Shelf," TASS, August 13, 2019, https://tass.com/economy/1073258.

9. Reuters, "Russia Launches Nuclear Icebreaker as It Eyes Arctic Future," *Moscow Times*, May 25, 2019, https://www.themoscowtimes.com/2019/05/25/russia-launches-nuclear-icebreaker-as-it-eyes-Arctic-future-a65747.

10. Associated Press, "Russia's Vladimir Putin Outlines Arctic Expansion Program," *Los Angeles Times*, April 9, 2019, https://www.latimes.com/world/la-fg-russia-vladimir-putin-arctic-expansion-20190409-story.html; and Vladimir Isachenkov and Irina Titova, "Putin Presents Ambitious Arctic Expansion Program," *U.S. News and World Report*, April 9, 2019, https://www.usnews.com/news/business/articles/2019-04-09/putin-presents-ambitious-arctic-expansion-program.

11. "Minister: 80 Million Tonnes of Cargo to Be Transported along Northern Sea Route by 2024," TASS, August 29, 2019, https://tass.com/economy/1075621.

12. Atle Staalesen, "Rosatom Will Manage Russia's Northern Sea Route," *The Independent Barents Observer*, January 2, 2019, https://www.arctictoday.com/rosatom-will-manage-russias-northern-sea-route/.

13. Joanna Hosa, "Strategy on Ice: Has Russia Already Won the Scramble for the Arctic?" European Council on Foreign Relations, October 26, 2018, https://ecfr.eu/article/commentary_strategy_on_ice_has_russia_already_won_the_scramble_for_the_arct/.

14. "Russia Launches Arctic Commission with Military Overlord at Helm," *Moscow Times*, March 17, 2015, https://www.themoscowtimes.com/2015/03/17/russia-launches-arctic-commission-with-military-overlord-at-helm-a44842.

15. "Russia Launches Nuclear Icebreaker as It Eyes Arctic Future," Reuters, May 25, 2019, https://www.themoscowtimes.com/2019/05/25/russia-launches-nuclear-icebreaker-as-it-eyes-arctic-future-a65747.

16. Gerard O'Dwyer, "Nordic Countries See Russia Flex Its Missile Muscles," *Defense News*, August 5, 2019, https://www.defensenews.com/global/europe/2019/08/05/nordic-countries-see-russia-flex-its-missile-muscles; and Reuters, "Norway Says It Has Proof That Russia Messed with GPS Signals during NATO's Largest Military Exercise in Decades," *Business Insider*, March 19, 2019, https://www.businessinsider.com/norway-says-it-proved-russian-gps-interference-during-nato-exercises-2019-3?IR=T.

17. "Self-Sufficient Russian Military Force to Be Formed in Arctic by 2018—Defense Ministry," TASS, April 1, 2015, http://tass.ru/en/russia/786391.

18. Neil Shea, "Scenes from the New Cold War Unfolding at the Top of the World," *National Geographic*, May 8, 2019, https://www.nationalgeographic.com/environment/2018/10/new-cold-war-brews-as-arctic-ice-melts/.

19. Elizabeth C. Economy, "Beijing's Arctic Play: Just the Tip of the Iceberg," Council on Foreign Relations, April 4, 2014, https://www.cfr.org/blog/beijings-arctic-play-just-tip-iceberg.

20. China defines itself as a "near-arctic state," says SIPRI, "Stockholm International Peace Research Institute," May 10, 2012, https://www.sipri.org/media/press-release/2012/china-defines-itself-near-arctic-state-says-sipri.

21. State Council Information Office of the People's Republic of China, "China's Arctic Policy," Xinhua, January 26, 2018, https://www.uaf.edu/caps/resources/policy-documents/china-arctic-policy-2018.pdf. In Beijing's view, "States from outside the Arctic region do not have territorial sovereignty in the Arctic, but they do have rights in respect of scientific research, navigation, overflight, fishing, laying of submarine cables and pipelines in the high seas and other relevant sea areas in the Arctic Ocean, and rights to resource exploration and exploitation in the Area, pursuant to treaties such as UNCLOS and general international law."

22. Charles Digges, "Russian-China Relations Are Warming the Arctic," *The Maritime Executive*, May 25, 2019, https://www.maritime-executive.com/editorials/russian-china-relations-are-warming-the-arctic.

23. State Council Information Office of the People's Republic of China, "China's Arctic Policy."

24. Somini Sengupta and Steven Lee Myers, "Latest Arena for China's Growing Global Ambitions: The Arctic," *New York Times*, May 24, 2019, https://www.nytimes.com/2019/05/24/climate/china-arctic.html.

25. David Auerswald and Terry L. Anderson, "China, Russia Move into the Arctic—and Put US at Risk," *The Hill*, May 14, 2019, https://thehill.com/opinion/national-security/443324-china-russia-move-into-the-arctic-and-put-us-at-risk.

26. Humphrey Hawksley, "China's Arctic Plan Spreads a Chill," *Nikkei Asian Review*, February 16, 2018, https://asia.nikkei.com/Politics/International-relations/China-s-Arctic-plan-spreads-a-chill.

27. Nadezhda Filimonova and Svetlana Krivokhizh, "A Russian Perspective on China's Arctic Role," *The Diplomat*, September 27, 2014, http://thediplomat.com/2014/09/a-russian-perspective-on-chinas-arctic-role/.

28. Russian Government, "Prime Minister Dmitry Medvedev Gives an Interview to the Norwegian TV Company NRK," June 4, 2013, http://government.ru/en/news/2273/.

29. "Why China Wants to Expand Its Arctic Footprint," Stratfor, December 24, 2018, https://worldview.stratfor.com/article/why-china-wants-expand-its-arctic-footprint.

30. Sergey Sukhankin, "China's 'Polar Silk Road' versus Russia's Arctic Dilemmas," *Eurasia Daily Monitor*, November 7, 2018, https://jamestown.org/program/chinas-polar-silk-road-versus-russias-arctic-dilemmas/.

31. Donald Gasper, "China and Russia Want to Develop Arctic Energy Resources Together, and US Disapproval May Not Deter Them," *South China Morning Sea*, Septem-

ber 12, 2018, https://www.scmp.com/comment/insight-opinion/asia/article/2163719
/china-and-russia-want-develop-arctic-energy-resources.

32. Laura Zhou, "Could the Arctic Chill US-China Relations Still Further?" *South China Morning Post*, May 12, 2019, https://www.scmp.com/news/china/diplomacy /article/3009837/could-arctic-chill-us-china-relations-still-further.

33. Thomas Nilsen, "Railway, Port on Agenda for China's Vice Premier in Arkhangelsk," *Barents Observer*, March 27, 2017, https://thebarentsobserver.com/en /industry-and-energy/2017/03/railway-port-agenda-chinas-vice-premier-arkhangelsk.

34. Atle Staalesen, "The Chinese Oilmen Are Back in Murmansk," *Barents Observer*, June 27, 2018, https://thebarentsobserver.com/en/2018/06/chinese-oil men-are-back-murmansk; and Paul Goble, "China Pursuing Dominance of Northern Sea Route," *Eurasia Daily Monitor*, July 12, 2018, https://jamestown.org/program /china-pursuing-dominance-of-northern-sea-route/.

35. "Russian, Chinese Scientists Plan Joint Arctic, Antarctic Studies," TASS, March 25, 2019, http://tass.com/economy/1050272.

36. Laura Zhou, "Could the Arctic Chill US-China Relations Still Further?" *South China Morning Post*, May 12, 2019, https://www.scmp.com/news/china/diplomacy /article/3009837/could-arctic-chill-us-china-relations-still-further.

37. Marc Lanteigne, "Northern Crossroads: Sino-Russian Cooperation in the Arctic," National Bureau of Asian Research, March 27, 2018, https://www.nbr.org /publication/northern-crossroads-sino-russian-cooperation-in-the-arctic/.

38. Trym Aleksander Eiterjord, "China's Planned Nuclear Icebreaker," *The Diplomat*, July 17, 2018, https://thediplomat.com/2018/07/chinas-planned-nuclear-icebreaker/.

39. Nadezhda Filimonova and Svetlana Krivokhizh, "A Russian Perspective on China's Arctic Role," *The Diplomat*, September 27, 2014, http://thediplomat .com/2014/09/a-russian-perspective-on-chinas-arctic-role/.

40. Sherri Goodman and Marisol Maddox, "China's Growing Arctic Presence," *China-US Focus*, November 19, 2018, https://www.chinausfocus.com/finance-economy /chinas-growing-arctic-presence.

41. "Military and Security Developments Involving the People's Republic of China 2020," U.S. Department of Defense, https://media.defense.gov/2020 /Sep/01/2002488689/-1/-1/1/2020-DOD-CHINA-MILITARY-POWER-REPORT-FINAL.PDF.

42. Michael R. Pompeo, "Looking North: Sharpening America's Arctic Focus," Rovaniemi, Finland, U.S. Department of State, May 6, 2019, https://www.state.gov /looking-north-sharpening-americas-arctic-focus/.

43. Laura Zhou, "Could the Arctic Chill US-China Relations Still Further?" *South China Morning Post*, May 12, 2019, https://www.scmp.com/news/china/diplomacy /article/3009837/could-arctic-chill-us-china-relations-still-further.

44. "Report to Congress, Department of Defense Arctic Strategy," U.S. Department of Defense, June 2019, https://media.defense.gov/2019/Jun/06/2002141657/-1/-1/1/2019-DOD-ARCTIC-STRATEGY.PDF.

45. Charles Digges, "Russian-China Relations Are Warming the Arctic," *The Maritime Executive*, May 25, 2019, https://www.maritime-executive.com/editorials /russian-china-relations-are-warming-the-arctic.

CHAPTER 6

1. "Russia, China Deepen Military Cooperation with 'Mutually Beneficial' Road Map," Sputnik, June 6, 2017, https://sputniknews.com/world/201706071054403535 -china-russia-military-road-map/.

2. Alexander Korolev, "On the Verge of an Alliance: Contemporary China-Russia Military Cooperation," *Asian Security* 15, no. 3 (April 30, 2018), https://doi.org/10.108 0/14799855.2018.1463991.

3. Liu Xuanzun, "Russian Troops to Operate Modern PLA Equipment for 1st Time in Joint Exercise, 'Shows Mutual Trust,'" *Global Times*, August 4, 2021, https:// www.globaltimes.cn/page/202108/1230596.shtml.

4. Catherine Wong, "China-Russia Military Drill Makes Room for Combined Force against US," *South China Morning Post*, August 13, 2021, https://www.scmp. com/news/china/diplomacy/article/3145010/china-russia-military-drill-makes- room-combined-force-against.

5. "Military and Security Developments Involving the People's Republic of China 2018," U.S. Department of Defense, 2019, p. 113.

6. Vasily Kashin, "Russian-Chinese Security Cooperation and Military-to-Mil- itary Relations," Italian Institute for International Political Studies, December 21, 2018, https://www.ispionline.it/en/pubblicazione/russian-chinese-security-cooper ation-and-military-military-relations-21828; and Stephen Blank, "Military Aspects of the Russo-Chinese Alliance: A View from the United States," *The Asan Forum*, Feb- ruary 19, 2019, http://www.theasanforum.org/military-aspects-of-the-russo-chinese -alliance-a-view-from-the-united-states/.

7. William Ide, "Anti-Terror Drills Highlight China's Push into Central Asia," Voice of America, August 29, 2014, http://www.voanews.com/content/anti-terror- drills-higlight-china-push-into-central-asia/2432330.html.

8. DD Wu, "China and Russia Sign Military Cooperation Roadmap," *The Diplo- mat*, June 30, 2017, http://thediplomat.com/2017/06/china-and-russia-sign-military- cooperation-roadmap.

9. "Russia-China Military Cooperation Contributes to Global Stability—Defense Minister," TASS, September 2, 2015, https://www.rbth.com/news/2015/09/02/rusia- china-military-cooperation-contributes-to-global-stability-defense-minister_394051.

10. "China, Russia Sign Joint Statement on Strengthening Global Strategic Sta- bility," China.org.cn, June 27, 2016, http://www.china.org.cn/world/2016-06/27/con tent_38751766.htm.

11. "The Astana Declaration of the Heads of State of the Shanghai Cooperation Organisation," SCO Website, June 9, 2017, eng.sectsco.org/load/297146/.

12. "Joint Statement of the Russian Federation and the People's Republic of China," June 8, 2018, http://kremlin.ru/supplement/5312.

13. "China's Defence Minister Considers Relations with Russia as the Best among Large Countries," Russian Ministry of Defense, April 25, 2019, https://eng.mil.ru/en /news_page/country/more.htm?id=12227800@egNews.

14. "Russian-Chinese Relations—a Key Factor in Ensuring Global Security," Russian Ministry of Defense, April 25, 2019, http://eng.mil.ru/en/mcis/news/more .htm?id=12227799@egNews.

15. DD Wu, "China and Russia Sign Military Cooperation Roadmap," *The Diplomat*, June 30, 2017, http://thediplomat.com/2017/06/china-and-russia-sign-military-cooperation-roadmap/.

16. J. Berkshire Miller, "Large War Games Distract from the Complexity of China-Russia Ties," Al Jazeera, September 16, 2018, https://www.aljazeera.com/opinions/2018/9/16/large-war-games-distract-from-the-complexity-of-china-russia-ties.

17. "Joint Statement of the Russian Federation and the People's Republic of China on the Twentieth Anniversary of the Treaty of Good Neighbourliness and Friendly Cooperation between the Russian Federation and the People's Republic of China," June 28, 2021, http://static.kremlin.ru/media/events/files/en/Bo3RF3JzGDvMAPjH-BQAuSemVPWTEvb3c.pdf.

18. "Joint Statement of the Russian Federation and the People's Republic of China on the Twentieth Anniversary of the Treaty of Good Neighbourliness and Friendly Cooperation between the Russian Federation and the People's Republic of China," June 28, 2021, http://static.kremlin.ru/media/events/files/en/Bo3RF3JzGDvMAPjH BQAuSemVPWTEvb3c.pdf.

19. Catherine Wong, "China-Russia Military Drill Makes Room for Combined Force against US," *South China Morning Post*, August 13, 2021, https://www.scmp.com/news/china/diplomacy/article/3145010/china-russia-military-drill-makes-room-combined-force-against.

20. "Summary of the 2018 National Defense Strategy of the United States of America: Sharpening the American Military's Competitive Edge," U.S. Department of Defense, 2018, https://dod.defense.gov/Portals/1/Documents/pubs/2018-National-Defense-Strategy-Summary.pdf.

21. Author's interviews with Chinese security experts; 2012–2020.

22. Catherine Wong, "China-Russia Military Drill Makes Room for Combined Force against US," *South China Morning Post*, August 13, 2021, https://www.scmp.com/news/china/diplomacy/article/3145010/china-russia-military-drill-makes-room-combined-force-against.

23. "Chinese Defence Chief Says His Visit to Moscow Is a Signal to the US," *South China Morning Post*, April 4, 2018, https://www.scmp.com/news/china/diplomacy-defence/article/2140182/chinas-defence-chief-calls-his-moscow-trip-signal-us.

24. Hal Brands and Evan Braden Montgomery, "Opportunistic Aggression in the Twenty-first Century," *Survival* 62, no. 4 (2020), 157–182, https://halbrands.org/wp-content/uploads/2020/11/Opportunistic-Aggression-in-the-Twenty-first-Century.pdf.

CHAPTER 7

1. Peter Suciu, "Russia Is Quietly Selling New Helicopters to China," *The National Interest*, November 18, 2020, https://nationalinterest.org/blog/reboot/russia-quietly-selling-new-helicopters-china-172849.

2. "Adapt and Overcome: Chinese Pilots Learn Russian to Fly Su-35 Fighters," Sputnik, October 10, 2016, https://sputniknews.com/military/201610101046178395-china-fighter-aircraft-russian/.

3. Michael Kofman, "The Emperors League: Understanding Sino-Russian Defense Cooperation," *War on the Rocks*, August 6, 2020, https://warontherocks.com/2020/08/the-emperors-league-understanding-sino-russian-defense-cooperation/.

4. Aude Fleurant, Pieter D. Wezeman, Siemon T. Wezeman, and Nan Tian, "Trends in International Arms Transfers, 2016," Stockholm Peace Research Institute, February 2017, https://www.sipri.org/sites/default/files/Trends-in-international-arms-transfers-2016.pdf.

5. Maria Siow, "Could Russia Side with the US and India against China?" *South China Morning Post*, August 22, 2020, https://www.scmp.com/week-asia/politics/article/3098398/could-russia-side-us-and-india-against-china.

6. China Power Team, "How Dominant Is China in the Global Arms Trade?" Center for Strategic and International Studies, August 25, 2020, https://chinapower.csis.org/china-global-arms-trade/.

7. Adam Ni, "What Are China's Military Recruitment Priorities?" *The Diplomat*, August 10, 2018, https://thediplomat.com/2018/08/what-are-chinas-military-recruitment-priorities/.

8. Dmitry Gorenburg, "Russia's New and Unrealistic Naval Doctrine," *War on the Rocks*, July 26, 2017, https://warontherocks.com/2017/07/russias-new-and-unrealistic-naval-doctrine/.

9. Vladimir Putin, "Final Plenary Session of the 16th Meeting of the Valdai International Discussion Club," October 3, 2019, en.kremlin.ru/events/president/news/61719.

10. "China's New Missile Warning System to Reduce Probability of Big War, Say Russian Experts," TASS, October 4, 2019, https://tass.com/defense/1081529.

11. "Statement of Charles A. Richard, Command, United States Strategic Command before the Senate Committee on Armed Services," April 20, 2021, https://www.armed-services.senate.gov/imo/media/doc/Richard04.20.2021.pdf.

12. "Military and Security Developments Involving the People's Republic of China 2020," U.S. Department of Defense, https://media.defense.gov/2020/Sep/01/2002488689/-1/-1/1/2020-DOD-CHINA-MILITARY-POWER-REPORT-FINAL.PDF, p. 143.

13. Gleb Fedorov, "After 20 Years Russia Makes First Inroads into ASEAN," *Russia beyond the Headlines*, May 20, 2016, https://rbth.com/international/2016/05/20/after-20-years-russia-makes-first-inroads-into-asean_596093.

14. Patricia Lourdes Viray, "China Offers $500-M Arms Loan to Philippines," *PhilStar Global*, May 15, 2017, http://beta.philstar.com/headlines/2017/05/15/1700181/china-offers-500-m-arms-loan-philippines.

15. "Россия и Китай проектируютне атомную подводнуюлодку новогопоколения" ["Russia and China Are Designing a New Generation Non-Nuclear Submarine"], RIA Novosti, August 25, 2020, https://ria.ru/20200825/bezopasnost-1576269235.html.

16. "China Joins Russia to Develop Rocket-Launched Drone," DefenseWorld.net, March 31, 2018, http://www.defenseworld.net/news/22260/China_Joins_Russia_to_Develop_Rocket_Launched_Drone#.XI0yYShKhPY.

17. "Chinese Defence Chief Says His Visit to Moscow Is a Signal to the US," *South China Morning Post*, April 4, 2018, https://www.scmp.com/news/china/diplomacy-defence/article/2140182/chinas-defence-chief-calls-his-moscow-trip-signal-us.

18. Paul Schwartz, *Russia's Contribution to China's Surface Warfare Capabilities: Feeding the Dragon* (Washington, DC: Center for Strategic and International Studies, 2015).

19. "Summary of the 2018 National Defense Strategy of the United States of America," U.S. Department of Defense, January 2018, https://dod.defense.gov/Portals/1/Documents/pubs/2018-National-Defense-Strategy-Summary.pdf.

CHAPTER 8

1. Greg Walters, "All the 'Absurd' New Weapons Russia Is Building in the New Nuclear Arms Race," *Vice*, August 29, 2019, https://www.vice.com/en_ca/article/ne8nkw/all-the-absurd-new-weapons-russia-is-building-in-the-new-nuclear-arms-race.

2. "Treaty between the United States of America and the Russian Federation on Measures for the Further Reduction and Limitation of Strategic Offensive Arms (New START)," Nuclear Threat Initiative, June 29, 2017, http://www.nti.org/learn/treaties-and-regimes/treaty-between-the-united-states-of-america-and-the-russian-federation-on-measures-for-the-further-reduction-and-limitation-of-strategic-offensive-arms/.

3. Zachary Keck, "The Big China Nuclear Threat No One Is Talking About," *The National Interest*, June 2, 2017, http://nationalinterest.org/blog/the-buzz/the-big-china-nuclear-threat-no-one-talking-about-20983.

4. David Vergun, "China, Russia Nearing Status as U.S. Nuclear Peers, Stratcom Commander Says," DOD News, July 30, 2020, https://www.defense.gov/Explore/News/Article/Article/2294574/china-russia-nearing-status-as-us-nuclear-peers-stratcom-commander-says/.

5. "Military and Security Developments Involving the People's Republic of China 2021," U.S. Department of Defense, 2021, https://media.defense.gov/2021/Nov/03/2002885874/-1/-1/0/2021-CMPR-FINAL.PDF.

6. "Indo-Pacific Strategy Report: Preparedness, Partnerships, and Promoting a Networked Region," U.S. Department of Defense, June 2019, https://media.defense.gov/2019/Jul/01/2002152311/-1/-1/1/DEPARTMENT-OF-DEFENSE-INDO-PACIFIC-STRATEGY-REPORT-2019.PDF.

7. "Foreign Ministry Spokesperson Zhao Lijian's Regular Press Conference on June 3, 2020," PRC Ministry of Foreign Affairs, https://www.fmprc.gov.cn/ce/cgmb/eng/fyrth/t1785528.htm

8. "Federation V. Putin on November 30, 2016," Embassy of the Russian Federation to the United Kingdom of Great Britain and Northern Ireland, https://www.rusemb.org.uk/rp_insight/

9. "US Violates Non-Proliferation Treaty, Says Russian Foreign Minister," TASS, February 2, 2019, http://tass.com/politics/1042985.

10. "Deputy Foreign Minister Sergey Ryabkov's Briefing on Developments Involving the INF Treaty," Russian Foreign Ministry, November 26, 2018, http://www.mid.ru/ru/foreign_policy/news/-/asset_publisher/cKNonkJE02Bw/content/id/3420936.

CHAPTER 9

1. Michael Connell and Sarah Vogler, "Russia's Approach to Cyber Warfare," CNA Corporation, 2017, https://www.cna.org/cna_files/pdf/DOP-2016-U-014231-1Rev.pdf.

2. James Griffiths and Nathan Hodge, "New Law Lets Russia Jail People Who 'Disrespect' the Government Online," CNN, March 7, 2019, https://edition-m.cnn.com/2019/03/07/europe/russia-internet-law-intl/index.html.

3. "Russia Takes Steps to Survive Global Internet Shutdown with Its Own Web—MPs," RT, February 13, 2019, https://www.rt.com/russia/451292-russia-internet-cut-off/.

4. Global Engagement Center, "Pillars of Russia's Disinformation and Propaganda Ecosystem," U.S. Department of State, 2020, https://www.state.gov/wp-content/uploads/2020/08/Pillars-of-Russia%E2%80%99s-Disinformation-and-Propaganda-Ecosystem_08-04-20.pdf.

5. Eric Lichtblau and Eric Schmitt, "Hack of Democrats' Accounts Was Wider Than Believed, Officials Say," New York Times, August 10, 2016, http://www.nytimes.com/2016/08/11/us/politics/democratic-party-russia-hack-cyberattack.html.

6. David Hollis, "Cyberwar Case Study: Georgia 2008," Small Wars Journal, January 6, 2011, http://smallwarsjournal.com/jrnl/art/cyberwar-case-study-georgia-2008; and E. Lincoln Bonner III, "Cyber Power in 21st-Century Joint Warfare," National Defense University, 2014, https://ndupress.ndu.edu/Portals/68/Documents/jfq/jfq-74/jfq-74_102-109_Bonner.pdf.

7. Kim Zetter, "Inside the Cunning, Unprecedented Hack of Ukraine's Power Grid," Wired, March 3, 2016, http://www.wired.com/2016/03/inside-cunning-unprecedented-hack-ukraines-power-grid/.

8. Patrick Tucker, "Russia Launched Cyber Attacks against Ukraine Before Ship Seizures, Firm Says," Nextgov, December 8, 2018, https://www.nextgov.com/cybersecurity/2018/12/russia-launched-cyber-attacks-against-ukraine-ship-seizures-firm-says/153387/.

9. Jim Finkle and Doina Chiacu, "U.S., Britain Blame Russia for Cyber Global Attack," Reuters, April 16, 2018, https://www.reuters.com/article/us-usa-britain-cyber/us-britain-blame-russia-for-global-cyber-attack-idUSKBN1HN2CK.

10. U.S. Department of Homeland Security, "Russian Government Cyber Activity Targeting Energy and Other Critical Infrastructure Sectors," US-CERT, https://www.us-cert.gov/ncas/alerts/TA18-074A; and Kelsey Atherton, "It's Not Just Election: Russia Hacked the US Electric Grid," Vox, March 28, 2018, https://www.vox.com/world/2018/3/28/17170612/russia-hacking-us-power-grid-nuclear-plants.

11. Alina Pokyakova, "The Next Russian Attack Will Be Far Worse Than Bots and Trolls," Lawfare, March 20, 2018, https://lawfareblog.com/next-russian-attack-will-be-far-worse-bots-and-trolls.

12. "2015 in Review, and Predictions for 2016," Leksika, January 4, 2016, http://www.leksika.org/tacticalanalysis/2016/1/4/2015-in-review-and-predictions-for-2016.

13. Dave Lee, "The Tactics of a Russian Troll Farm," BBC, February 16, 2018, http://www.bbc.com/news/technology-43093390.

14. Michael Connell and Sarah Vogler, "Russia's Approach to Cyber Warfare," CAN Corporation, 2017, https://www.cna.org/cna_files/pdf/DOP-2016-U-014231-1Rev.pdf.

15. Zachary Cohen, Luke McGee, and Alex Marquardt, "UK, US and Canada Allege Cyberattacks on Covid-19 Research Centres," CNN, July 17, 2020, https://www.cnn.com/2020/07/16/politics/russia-cyberattack-covid-vaccine-research/index.html.

16. Franz-Stefan Gady, "Is Russia More Powerful Than China in Cyberspace?" *The Diplomat*, April 9, 2015, http://thediplomat.com/2015/04/is-russia-more-powerful-than-china-in-cyberspace/.

17. Jun Mai, "Xi Jinping Renews 'Cyber Sovereign' Call at China's Top Meeting of Internet Minds," *South China Morning Post*, December 3, 2017, http://www.scmp.com/news/china/policies-politics/article/2122683/xi-jinping-renews-cyber-sovereignty-call-chinas-top.

18. Jennifer Cheung, "China's 'Great Firewall' Just Got Taller," Truthout, July 22, 2015, http://www.truth-out.org/news/item/32001-china-s-great-firewall-just-got-taller.

19. Bethany Allen-Ebrahimian, "The Chinese Communist Party Is Setting Up Cells at Universities across America," *Foreign Policy*, April 18, 2018, http://foreignpolicy.com/2018/04/18/the-chinese-communist-party-is-setting-up-cells-at-universities-across-america-china-students-beijing-surveillance/.

20. Elsa Kania, "China: Active Defense in the Cyber Domain," *The Diplomat*, June 12, 2015, http://thediplomat.com/2015/06/china-active-defense-in-the-cyber-domain/.

21. Shaun Nichols, "China Weaponizes Its Great Firewall into the GREAT FIRE CANNON, Menaces Entire Globe," *The Register*, April 10, 2015, http://www.theregister.co.uk/2015/04/10/china_great_cannon/.

22. Dan Goodin, "Massive Denial-of-Service Attack on GitHub Tied to Chinese Government," *Ars Technica*, March 31, 2015, http://arstechnica.com/security/2015/03/31/massive-denial-of-service-attack-on-github-tied-to-chinese-government/.

23. Tian Shaohui, "International Strategy of Cooperation on Cyberspace Contents," Xinhua, March 1, 2017, http://www.xinhuanet.com//english/china/2017-03/01/c_136094371.htm; and Elsa Kania, Samm Sacks, Paul Triolo, and Graham Webster, "China's Strategic Thinking on Building Power in Cyberspace," *New America*, September 25, 2017, https://www.newamerica.org/cybersecurity-initiative/blog/chinas-strategic-thinking-building-power-cyberspace/.

24. Elsa Kania, Samm Sacks, Paul Triolo, and Graham Webster, "China's Strategic Thinking on Building Power in Cyberspace," *New America*, September 25, 2017, https://www.newamerica.org/cybersecurity-initiative/blog/chinas-strategic-thinking-building-power-cyberspace/.

25. Yuxi Wei, "China-Russia Cybersecurity Cooperation: Working towards Cyber-Sovereignty," The Henry M. Jackson School of International Studies, June 21, 2016, https://jsis.washington.edu/news/china-russia-cybersecurity-cooperation-working-towards-cyber-sovereignty/.

26. Jack Wagner, "China's Cybersecurity Law: What You Need to Know," *The Diplomat*, June 1, 2017, https://thediplomat.com/2017/06/chinas-cybersecurity-law-what-you-need-to-know/; and "China's New Cyber-Security Law Is Worryingly Vague," *Economist*, June 1, 2017, https://www.economist.com/news/business/21722873-its-rules-are-broad-ambiguous-and-bothersome-international-firms-chinas-new-cyber-security.

27. William Schneider, "China, 5G, and Dominance of the Global 'Infosphere,'" Hudson Institute, September 5, 2019, https://www.hudson.org/research/15290-china-5-g-and-dominance-of-the-global-infosphere.

28. "Summary: Cyber Strategy 2018," U.S. Department of Defense, https://media.defense.gov/2018/Sep/18/2002041658/-1/-1/1/CYBER_STRATEGY_SUMMARY_FINAL.PDF.

29. Rober Windrem, "Exclusive: Secret NSA Map Shows China Cyber Attacks on U.S. Targets," NBC News, July 30, 2015, https://www.nbcnews.com/news/us-news/exclusive-secret-nsa-map-shows-china-cyber-attacks-us-targets-n401211.

30. "National Cyber Strategy of the United States of America," Office of the White House, 2018, https://trumpwhitehouse.archives.gov/wp-content/uploads/2018/09/National-Cyber-Strategy.pdf.

31. Bradley Graham, "Hackers Attack via Chinese Sites," *Washington Post*, August 25, 2005, www.washingtonpost.com/wp-dyn/content/article/2005/08/24/AR2005082402318.html.

32. Julie Hirschfield Davis, "Hacking of Government Computers Exposed 21.5 Million People," *New York Times*, July 9, 2015, http://www.nytimes.com/2015/07/10/us/office-of-personnel-management-hackers-got-data-of-millions.html?_r=0.

33. U.S. Office of Personnel Management, "Cybersecurity Incidents," https://www.opm.gov/cybersecurity/cybersecurity-incidents/.

34. Amanda Macias, "FBI Chief Slams Chinese Cyberattacks on U.S., Calls It 'One of the Largest Transfers of Wealth in Human History," CNBC, updated July 8, 2020, https://www.cnbc.com/2020/07/07/fbi-chief-slams-chinese-cyberattacks-against-us-hudson-institute.html.

35. M. Taylor Fravel, "China's New Military Strategy: 'Winning Informationized Local Wars,'" *China Brief* 15, no. 13 (July 2, 2015), https://jamestown.org/program/chinas-new-military-strategy-winning-informationized-local-wars/.

36. Franz-Stefan Gady, "Why the PLA Revealed Its Secret Plans for Cyber War," *The Diplomat*, March 24, 2015, http://thediplomat.com/2015/03/why-the-pla-revealed-its-secret-plans-for-cyber-war/.

37. Lyu Jinghua, "What Are China's Cyber Capabilities and Intentions?" Carnegie Endowment for International Peace, April 1, 2019, https://carnegieendowment.org/2019/04/01/what-are-china-s-cyber-capabilities-and-intentions-pub-78734.

38. PRC Ministry of National Defense, *China's National Defense in the New Era* (Beijing: The State Council Information Office, 2019), http://www.xinhuanet.com/english/download/whitepaperonnationaldefenseinnewera.doc.

39. Larry M. Wortzel, "The Chinese People's Liberation Army and Information Warfare," U.S. Army War College, 2014, https://publications.armywarcollege.edu/pubs/2263.pdf.

40. Lorand Laskai, "When China's White-Hat Hackers Go Patriotic," Council on Foreign Relations, March 13, 2017, https://www.cfr.org/blog/when-chinas-white-hat-hackers-go-patriotic.

41. "Remarks by Vice President Pence on the Administration's Policy toward China," Hudson Institute, Washington, DC, October 4, 2018, https://trumpwhitehouse.archives.gov/briefings-statements/remarks-vice-president-pence-administrations-policy-toward-china/.

42. Ron Synovitz, "Attack of the GONGOs: Government-Organized NGOs Flood Warsaw Meeting," Radio Free Europe/Radio Liberty, September 30, 2019, https://www.rferl.org/a/attack-of-the-gongos-government-organized-ngos-flood-warsaw-meeting/30191944.html.

43. Charles Davis, "'Grassroots' Media Startup Redfish Is Supported by the Kremlin," *The Daily Beast*, June 19, 2018, https://www.thedailybeast.com/grassroots-media-startup-redfish-is-supported-by-the-kremlin.

44. "Disclosing Networks of State-Linked Information Operations We've Removed," Twitter, June 12, 2020, https://blog.twitter.com/en_us/topics/company/2020/information-operations-june-2020.html.

45. Nathaniel Gleicher, "Removing More Coordinated Inauthentic Behavior from Iran and Russia," Facebook, October 21, 2019, https://about.fb.com/news/2019/10/removing-more-coordinated-inauthentic-behavior-from-iran-and-russia/.

46. Lincoln Davidson, "Despite Cyber Agreements, Russia and China Are Not as Close as You Think," Council on Foreign Relations, June 30, 2016, https://www.cfr.org/blog/despite-cyber-agreements-russia-and-china-are-not-close-you-think; and Yuxi Wei, "China-Russia Cybersecurity Cooperation: Working towards Cyber Sovereignty," The Henry M. Jackson School of International Studies, June 21, 2016, https://jsis.washington.edu/news/china-russia-cybersecurity-cooperation-working-towards-cyber-sovereignty.

47. Jon R. Lindsay, "Exaggerating the Chinese Cyber Threat," Belfer Center for Science and International Affairs, May 2015, https://www.belfercenter.org/sites/default/files/files/publication/linsday-china-cyber-pb-final.pdf.

48. Guest Blogger, "The Sinicization of Russia's Cyber Sovereignty Model," Council on Foreign Relations, April 1, 2020, https://www.cfr.org/blog/sinicization-russias-cyber-sovereignty-model.

49. Eric Sterner, "China, Russia Resume Push for Content Restrictions in Cyberspace," *World Politics Review*, May 1, 2014, http://www.worldpoliticsreview.com/articles/13745/china-russia-resume-push-for-content-restrictions-in-cyberspace.

50. Sebastian J. Bae, "Cyber Warfare: Chinese and Russian Lessons for US Cyber Doctrine," *Georgetown Security Studies Review*, May 7, 2015, http://georgetownsecuritystudiesreview.org/2015/05/07/cyber-warfare-chinese-and-russian-lessons-for-us-cyber-doctrine/.

51. Olga Razumovskaya, "Russia and China Pledge Not to Hack Each Other," *Wall Street Journal*, May 8, 2015, http://blogs.wsj.com/digits/2015/05/08/russia-china-pledge-to-not-hack-each-other/.

52. Elaine Korzak, "The Next Level for Russia-China Cyberspace Cooperation?" Council on Foreign Relations, August 20, 2015, https://www.cfr.org/blog/next-level-russia-china-cyberspace-cooperation.

53. Jane Teufel Dreyer, "China and Russia: The Relationship Deepens," Foreign Policy Research Institute, January 7, 2016, https://www.fpri.org/article/2016/01/china-and-russia-partnership-deepens/; and "Russia's Kaspersky Labs Signs Deal with China Cyber Security Company as Beijing and Moscow Call for End to US Domination of Internet," *South China Morning Post*, December 17, 2015, http://www.scmp.com/news/china/policies-politics/article/1892257/russias-kaspersky-labs-signs-deal-china-cyber-security.

54. Lincoln Davidson, "Despite Cyber Agreements, Russia and China Are Not as Close as You Think," Council on Foreign Relations, June 30, 2016, https://www.cfr.org/blog/despite-cyber-agreements-russia-and-china-are-not-close-you-think.

55. Yuxi Wei, "China-Russia Cybersecurity Cooperation: Working towards Cyber-Sovereignty," The Henry M. Jackson School of International Studies, June 21, 2016, https://jsis.washington.edu/news/china-russia-cybersecurity-cooperation-working-towards-cyber-sovereignty/.

56. Russian International Affairs Council, "Russian—Chinese Dialogue: The 2019 Model," Moscow, 2019, p. 78, https://russiancouncil.ru/en/activity/publications/russian-chinese-dialogue-the-2019-model/.

57. Nadezhad Tsydenova and Tom Balmforth, "Russia and China to Sign Treaty on Combating Illegal Online Content," Reuters, October 8, 2019, https://www.reuters.com/article/us-russia-china-internet-idUSKBN1WN1E7.

58. Laura Zhou, "Beijing and Moscow Join Forces in 'Information War' as China-US Relations Rapidly Deteriorate," South China Morning Post, July 28, 2020, https://www.scmp.com/news/china/diplomacy/article/3094993/beijing-and-moscow-join-forces-information-war-china-us.

59. Jessica Brandt and Torrey Taussig, "The Kremlin's Disinformation Playbook Goes to Beijing," The Brookings Institution, May 19, 2020, https://www.brookings.edu/blog/order-from-chaos/2020/05/19/the-kremlins-disinformation-playbook-goes-to-beijing/amp/.

60. "It's So Hard to Find Good Help Chinese Broadcasters Are Making Inroads in Russia, but Beijing Has Stumbled due to a Shortage of Capable Propagandists," Meduza, July 28, 2020, https://meduza.io/en/feature/2020/07/28/it-s-so-hard-to-find-good-help.

61. Guest Blogger, "The Sinicization of Russia's Cyber Sovereignty Model," Council on Foreign Relations, April 1, 2020, https://www.cfr.org/blog/sinicization-russias-cyber-sovereignty-model.

62. Jared Serbu, "Foreign Cyber Weapons 'Far Exceed' US Ability to Defend Critical Infrastructure, Defense Panel Says," Federal News Network, March 7, 2017, https://federalnewsnetwork.com/dod-reporters-notebook-jared-serbu/2017/03/foreign-cyber-weapons-far-exceed-u-s-ability-defend-critical-infrastructure-defense-panel-says/.

63. Guest Blogger, "The Sinicization of Russia's Cyber Sovereignty Model," Council on Foreign Relations, April 1, 2020, https://www.cfr.org/blog/sinicization-russias-cyber-sovereignty-model.

64. Shane Harris, "China Reveals Its Cyberwar Secrets," The Daily Beast, March 18, 2015, http://www.thedailybeast.com/articles/2015/03/18/china-reveals-its-cyber-war-secrets.html.

65. Cory Bennet, "John Bolton, Cyber Warrior: Trump's Incoming Adviser Has Said the U.S. Should Launch a 'Retaliatory Cyber Campaign against Russia' and 'Use WikiLeaks for Target Practice,'" Politico, April 1, 2018, https://www.politico.com/story/2018/04/01/john-bolton-cyber-hawk-russia-451937.

66. "About Us," U.S. Department of Homeland Security, www.us-cert.gov/about-us.

67. "Summary: Cyber Strategy 2018," U.S. Department of Defense, https://media.defense.gov/2018/Sep/18/2002041658/-1/-1/1/CYBER_STRATEGY_SUMMARY_FINAL.PDF.

68. Arthur Herman, "A National Cybersecurity Strategy: Better Late Than Never," Forbes, September 24, 2018, https://www.forbes.com/sites/arthurherman/2018/09/24/a-national-cybersecurity-strategy-better-late-than-never/#71e01d7c2a2a.

69. "National Cyber Strategy of the United States of America," Office of the White House, 2018, https://trumpwhitehouse.archives.gov/wp-content/uploads/2018/09 /National-Cyber--Strategy.pdf.

70. Tommy Sears, "Trump Administration Unveils 'Offensive' and 'Deterrent' National Cyber Strategy," *Epoch Times*, September 26, 2018, https://www.theepoch-times.com/trump-administration-unveils-offensive-and-deterrent-national-cyber-strategy_2672308.html.

71. "National Cyber Strategy of the United States of America," Office of the White House, 2018, https://trumpwhitehouse.archives.gov/wp-content/uploads/2018/09 /National-Cyber-Strategy.pdf.

72. Robert Chesney, "The 2018 DOD Cyber Strategy: Understanding 'Defense Forward' in Light of the NDAA and PPD-20 Changes," *Lawfare*, September 25, 2018, https://www.lawfareblog.com/2018-dod-cyber-strategy-understanding-defense-for-ward-light-ndaa-and-ppd-20-changes.

73. David E. Sanger, "Pentagon Announces New Strategy for Cyberwarfare," *New York Times*, April 23, 2015, http://www.nytimes.com/2015/04/24/us/politics/penta-gon-announces-new-cyberwarfare-strategy.html.

74. David E. Sanger, "Pentagon Announces New Strategy for Cyberwarfare," *New York Times*, April 23, 2015, http://www.nytimes.com/2015/04/24/us/politics/penta-gon-announces-new-cyberwarfare-strategy.html.

75. Dave Weinstein, "The Pentagon's New Cyber Strategy: Defend Forward," *Lawfare*, September 21, 2018, https://www.lawfareblog.com/pentagons-new-cyber-strategy-defend-forward.

76. Chris Bing, "Lawmakers to Generals: Tell Us the Policies You Need to Launch Cyberattacks," *Cyberscoop*, March 13, 2018, https://www.cyberscoop.com /us-cyber-command-hacking-operations-government-funding/.

77. Sydney J. Freedberg, Jr., "Trump Eases Cyber Ops, but Safeguards Remain: Joint Staff," *Washington Post*, September 17, 2018, https://breakingdefense.com/2018/09 /trump-eases-cyber-ops-but-safeguards-remain-joint-staff/.

78. David E. Sanger, "Trump Claims Credit for 2018 Cyberattack on Russia," *New York Times*, July 11, 2020, https://www.nytimes.com/2020/07/11/us/politics/trump-russia-cyber-attack.html.

79. Michael Sulmeyer, "Cybersecurity in the 2017 National Security Strategy," *Lawfare*, December 19, 2017, https://www.lawfareblog.com/cybersecurity-2017-national-security-strategy.

80. Jared Serbu, "Foreign Cyber Weapons 'Far Exceed' US Ability to Defend Critical Infrastructure, Defense Panel Says," *Federal News Network*, March 7, 2017, https:// federalnewsnetwork.com/dod-reporters-notebook-jared-serbu/2017/03/foreign-cyber-weapons-far-exceed-u-s-ability-defend-critical-infrastructure-defense-panel-says/.

81. Cory Bennet, "John Bolton, Cyber Warrior: Trump's Incoming Adviser Has Said the U.S. Should Launch a 'Retaliatory Cyber Campaign against Russia' and 'Use WikiLeaks for Target Practice,'" *Politico*, April 1, 2018, https://www.politico.com /story/2018/04/01/john-bolton-cyber-hawk-russia-451937.

82. Richard J. Harknett, "United States Cyber Command's New Vision: What It Entails and Why It Matters?" *Lawfare*, March 23, 2018, https://www.lawfareblog.com/ united-states-cyber-commands-new-vision-what-it-entails-and-why-it-matters.

83. "Summary: Cyber Strategy 2018," U.S. Department of Defense, https://media.defense.gov/2018/Sep/18/2002041658/-1/-1/1/CYBER_STRATEGY_SUMMARY_FINAL.PDF

84. Fahmida Y. Rashid, "U.S. Russian to Share Cyber-Security Data to Defend Critical Systems, Avoid Cyber-War," *PC Magazine*, June 19, 2013, http://securitywatch.pcmag.com/security/312797-us-russia-to-share-cyber-security-data-to-defend-critical-systems-avoid-cyber-war.

85. Elena Chernenko, Vladislav Novyii, and Ivan Safronov, "Why Russia and China See Eye-to-Eye on Cyber Security," *World Crunch*, October 28, 2014, http://www.worldcrunch.com/world-affairs/why-russia-and-china-see-eye-to-eye-on-cyber-security/big-brother-george-orwell-internet-security-domestic-spying/c1s17328/#.VFFVlul0y20.

86. "Trump Backs Away from Working with Russia on Cybersecurity," *Guardian*, July 10, 2017, https://www.theguardian.com/us-news/2017/jul/10/close-to-the-stupidest-idea-critics-flail-trump-russia-cyber-security-plan.

87. Benjamin Kang Lim, "China Says It's Hard to Resume Cyber Security Talks with U.S.," Reuters, October 19, 2014, https://www.reuters.com/article/china-usa-cybersecurity-idINKCN0I80H020141019; and David Tweed, "Chinese Hackers Hit U.S. Firms Linked to South China Sea Dispute," *Bloomberg*, March 16, 2018, https://www.bloomberg.com/news/articles/2018-03-16/china-hackers-hit-u-s-firms-linked-to-sea-dispute-fireeye-says.

88. Adam Greer and Nathan Montierth, "How Are US-China Cyber Relations Progressing?" *The Diplomat*, November 1, 2017, https://thediplomat.com/2017/11/how-are-us-china-cyber-relations-progressing/.

89. Wenqing Zhao and David Stanton, "SinoTech: US Proposes Tariffs on $50B of Chinese Imports after Concluding China Violates Trade Rules," *Lawfare*, April 4, 2018, https://www.lawfareblog.com/sinotech-us-proposes-tariffs-50b-chinese-imports-after-concluding-china-violates-trade-rules.

90. Andrei Khalip, "U.N. Chief Urges Global Rules for Cyber Warfare," Reuters, February 19, 2018, https://www.reuters.com/article/us-un-guterres-cyber/u-n-chief-urges-global-rules-for-cyber-warfare-idUSKCN1G31Q4.

91. Daniel Kliman, Andrea Kendall-Taylor, Kristine Lee, Joshua Fitt, and Carisa Nietsche, "Dangerous Synergies: Countering Chinese and Russian Digital Influence Operations," Center for a New American Security, May 2020, https://www.cnas.org/publications/reports/dangerous-synergies.

CHAPTER 10

1. Vladimir Putin, "Russia and the Changing World," *Moscow News*, February 27, 2012, https://rusemb.org.uk/press/612.

2. Jonathan Hillman, "China and Russia: Economic Unequals," Center for Strategic and International Studies, July 15, 2020, https://www.csis.org/analysis/china-and-russia-economic-unequals.

3. Edward Chow, "Sino-Russian Energy Relations: A Match Made in Heaven?" Carnegie Moscow Center, January 29, 2021, https://carnegie.ru/commentary/83757.

4. "Power of Siberia: A Natural Gas Pipeline Brings Russia and China Closer," Congressional Research Service, April 21, 2020, https://crsreports.congress.gov /product/pdf/IF/IF11514.

5. "China-Russia East Route Natural Gas Pipeline Delivers 10 Billion Cubic Meters of Gas," *Global Times*, August 11, 2021, https://www.globaltimes.cn /page/202108/1231246.shtml.

6. Yohei Ishikawa and Shunsuke Tabeta, "Russia Deepens China Ties with Expanded Energy Exports," *Nikkei Asia*, January 6, 2021, https://asia.nikkei.com/Politics /International-relations/Russia-deepens-China-ties-with-expanded-energy-exports.

7. Francesco Sassi, "Energy Partnership Bolsters China—Russia Relations," East Asia Forum, April 8, 2021, https://www.industryweek.com/the-economy /article/21960574/russia-china-sign-unprecedented-270-billion-oil-deal.

8. Chu Daye and Yang Sheng, "Xi, Putin Witness Key Nuclear Energy Project Groundbreaking; Cooperation Has Strategic Significance," *Global Times*, May 19, 2021, https://www.globaltimes.cn/page/202105/1223955.shtml.

9. "Xi Jinping and Russian President Vladimir Putin Witness the Ground-breaking Ceremony of China-Russia Nuclear Energy Cooperation Project," Embajada de la República Popular China en la República de El Salvador, May 19, 2021, http:// sv.chineseembassy.org/exp/Hoy/t1877323.htm.

10. Alexey Lossan, "Russia and China Join Forces to Develop Green Energy," *G20 Executive Talk Series*, September 2016, https://digital.thecatcompanyinc.com /g20magazine/september-2016/green-energy/.

11. Dimitri Simes, "China and Russia Ditch Dollar in Move toward 'Financial Alliance,'" *Nikkei Asia*, August 6, 2020, https://asia.nikkei.com/Politics/International-relations/China-and-Russia-ditch-dollar-in-move-toward-financial-alliance.

12. "Bank of Russia Opens its First Representative Office Abroad," Bank of Russia, March 16, 2017, https://www.cbr.ru/eng/press/event/?id=970.

13. Ivana Kottasová, "Russia Gets Investment from China While Sanctions Keep U.S. Off Limits," CNN, July 7, 2017, http://money.cnn.com/2017/07/06/news/econ omy/russia-china-investment-deal-sanctions/index.html.

14. Amber Wang, "Russia's Gazprom Neft Signals Shift Away from US Dollar Payments in China," *South China Morning Post*, September 6, 2021, https:// www.scmp.com/news/china/diplomacy/article/3147743/russias-gazprom-neft-signals-shift-away-us-dollar-payments.

15. Dmitriy Frolovskiy, "Why China-Russia Economic Ties Will Emerge from the Coronavirus Pandemic Stronger Than Ever," *South China Morning Post*, August 25, 2020, https://www.scmp.com/comment/opinion/article/3098639/why-china-russia -economic-ties-will-emerge-coronavirus-pandemic.

16. Chris Devonshire-Ellis, "Xi Jinping Speech at the 2021 Far East Economic Forum," *China Briefing*, September 7, 2021, https://www.china-briefing.com/news /xi-jinping-speech-at-the-2021-far-east-economic-forum/.

17. Central Intelligence Agency, "Russia," *The World Factbook*, https://www.cia.gov /the-world-factbook/countries/russia/#economy.

18. Brett Forrest, Ann M. Simmons, and Chao Deng, "China and Russia Military Cooperation Raises Prospect of New Challenge to American Power," *Wall Street Journal*,

January 2, 2022, https://www.wsj.com/articles/china-russia-america-military-exercises-weapons-war-xi-putin-biden-11641146041; see also "China-Russia Bilateral Trade Up 20 Percent in January-April 2021," *China Briefing*, May 7, 2021, https://www.china-briefing.com/news/china-russia-bilateral-trade-up-20-percent-in-january-april-2021/.

19. Alexander Gabuev, "China's Pivot to Putin's Friends," *Foreign Policy*, June 25, 2016, http://carnegie.ru/publications/?fa=63916.

20. Lionel Barber and Henry Foy, "Financial Times Interview with Vladimir Putin," Russian presidential website, http://en.kremlin.ru/events/president/news/60836.

21. Karen M. Sutter and Michael D. Sutherland, "China's Economic and Trade Ties with Russia," CRS, May 24, 2022, https://crsreports.congress.gov/product/pdf/IF/IF12120.

22. Wang Cong, "China, Russia Need to Bolster Trade to Match Ever Close Bilateral Ties," *Global Times*, July 15, 2021, https://www.globaltimes.cn/page/202107/1228787.shtml.

23. Ankur Shah, "Russia Loosens Its Belt," *Foreign Policy*, July 16, 2020, https://foreignpolicy.com/2020/07/16/russia-china-belt-and-road-initiative/.

24. Alexander Gabuev, "Russia's 'China Dreams' Are Less of a Fantasy Than You Think," War on the Rocks, June 28, 2016, https://warontherocks.com/2016/06/russias-china-dreams-are-less-of-a-fantasy-than-you-think/.

25. Karen M. Sutter and Michael D. Sutherland, "China's Economic and Trade Ties with Russia," CRS, May 24, 2022, https://crsreports.congress.gov/product/pdf/IF/IF12120.

26. June Teufel Dreyer, "China and Russia: The Partnership Deepens," Foreign Policy Research Institute, January 7, 2016, http://www.fpri.org/article/2016/01/china-and-russia-partnership-deepens/.

27. Dimitri Simes and Tatiana Simes, "Moscow's Pivot to China Falls Short in the Russian Far East," *South China Morning Post*, August 29, 2021, https://www.scmp.com/week-asia/politics/article/3146505/moscows-pivot-china-falls-short-russian-far-east.

28. Johan van de Ven, "Fair-Weather Friends: The Impact of the Coronavirus on the Strategic Partnership Between Russia and China," *China Brief* 20, no. 4 (February 28, 2020), https://jamestown.org/program/fair-weather-friends-the-impact-of-the-coronavirus-on-the-strategic-partnership-between-russia-and-china/.

29. Gregory Shtraks, "Next Steps in the Merger of the Eurasian Economic Union and the Belt and Road Initiative," *China Brief* 18, no. 11 (June 19, 2018), https://jamestown.org/program/next-steps-in-the-merger-of-the-eurasian-economic-union-and-the-belt-and-road-initiative/.

30. "National Security Strategy of the United States of America," The White House, December 2017, https://trumpwhitehouse.archives.gov/wp-content/uploads/2017/12/NSS-Final-12-18-2017-0905.pdf.

31. Brandon Kirk Williams, "The New Arms Race: American Businesses vs. China's Government Money," *Washington Post*, December 10, 2018, https://www.washingtonpost.com/outlook/2018/12/10/new-arms-race-american-businesses-vs-chinas-government-money/.

CHAPTER 11

1. Ajey Lele, "Should India Join China and Russia's Lunar Research Station?" *The Space Review*, June 1, 2021, https://www.thespacereview.com/article/4185/1.

2. Alexey Arbatov, Vladimir Dvorkin, and Peter Topychkanov, "Entanglement as a New Security Threat: A Russian Perspective," Carnegie Moscow Center, November 8, 2017, http://carnegie.ru/2017/11/08/entanglement-as-new-security-threat-russian-perspective-pub-73163. According to the authors, "Russian military doctrine has come to view air and space as interlinked "into a specific field of armed conflict: an air-space theater of military operations."

3. "New Russian System Being Tested Hit Old Satellite with 'Goldsmith's Precision'—Shoigu," TASS, November 16, 2021, https://tass.com/science/1362219.

4. Todd Harrison, Kaitlyn Johnson, Thomas Roberts, Tyler Way, and Makena Young, "Space Threat Assessment 2020," Center for Strategic and International Studies, March 2020, https://www.csis.org/analysis/space-threat-assessment-2020.

5. "Full Text of White Paper on China's Space Activities in 2016," PRC State Council, December 28, 2016, http://english.gov.cn/archive/white_paper/2016/12/28/content_281475527159496.htm.

6. "China, Russia Must Resolutely Respond to Arrogant US Space Goal," *Global Times*, July 18, 2021, https://www.globaltimes.cn/page/202107/1228977.shtml.

7. "Mir Space Station," NASA, http://history.nasa.gov/SP-4225/mir/mir.htm.

8. "Trampoline to Space? Russian Official Tells NASA to Take a Flying Leap," NBC News, April 29, 2014, https://www.nbcnews.com/storyline/ukraine-crisis/trampoline-space-russian-official-tells-nasa-take-flying-leap-n92616.

9. Antony J. Blinken, "Russia Conducts Destructive Anti-Satellite Missile Test," U.S. Department of State, November 15, 2021, https://www.state.gov/russia-conducts-destructive-anti-satellite-missile-test/.

10. U.S. Department of Defense, "Defense Space Strategy Summary," June 2020, https://media.defense.gov/2020/Jun/17/2002317391/-1/-1/1/2020_DEFENSE_SPACE_STRATEGY_SUMMARY.PDF?source=GovDelivery.

11. Seth Robson, "'Our Pacing Threat Is the Chinese,' US Space Command Leader Says in Tokyo," *Stars and Stripes*, May 24, 2021, https://www.stripes.com/theaters/asia_pacific/2021-05-24/%E2%80%98Our-pacing-threat-is-the-Chinese%E2%80%99-US-Space-Command-leader-says-in-Tokyo-1572578.html.

12. Mariel John Borowitz, Lawrence Rubin, Brian Stewart, "National Security Implications of Emerging Satellite Technologies," *Orbis*, Fall 2020, p. 515.

13. Christian Davenport, "Amid Tension with Russia, Biden Administration Wants to Extend the Life of the International Space Station," *Washington Post*, December 31, 2021, https://www.washingtonpost.com/technology/2021/12/31/nasa-space-station-extension-russia/.

CONCLUSION

1. Yun Sun, "China-Russia Relations: Alignment without Alliance," *PacNet*, no. 67 October 7, 2015, https://www.stimson.org/2015/china-russia-relations-alignment-without-alliance/.

2. Harley Balzer, "Axis of Collusion: The Fragile Putin-Xi Partnership," Atlantic Council, December 2021, https://www.atlanticcouncil.org/in-depth-research-reports/report/axis-of-collusion-the-fragile-putin-xi-partnership/.

3. Alexander Gabuyev, "The Pandemic Could Tighten China's Grip on Eurasia," *Foreign Policy*, April 23, 2020, https://foreignpolicy.com/2020/04/23/coronavirus-pandemic-china-eurasia-russia-influence/.

4. "Russia-China Relations Built on Trust, Cooperation, Says Lavrov," Xinhua, January 19, 2021, www.xinhuanet.com/english/2021-01/19/c_139678255.htm.

5. "Vladimir Putin's Annual News Conference," President of Russia website, December 14, 2017, http://en.kremlin.ru/events/president/transcripts/56378.

6. Timofei Bordachev, "Main Results of 2017: Energetic Russia and the Greater Eurasia Community," Valdai Discussion Club, December 28, 2017, http://valdaiclub.com/a/highlights/main-results-of-2017-energetic-russia/.

7. "Full Text of Yang Jiechi's Keynote Speech at the 55th Munich Security Conference," Xinhua, February 17, 2019, http://xinhuanet.com/english/2019-02/17/c_137827311.htm.

8. Vladimir Isachenkov, "Putin: Russia-China Military Alliance Can't Be Ruled Out," Associated Press, October 22, 2020, https://apnews.com/article/beijing-moscow-foreign-policy-russia-vladimir-putin-1d4b112d2fe8cb66192c5225f4d614c4.

9. "Americans Most Likely to Name China, Russia, Iran as Greatest U.S. Enemy (Recent Trend)," in Jeffrey M. Jones, "Fewer in U.S. Regard China Favorably or as Leading Economy," Gallup, March 2, 2020, https://news.gallup.com/poll/287108/fewer-regard-china-favorably-leading-economy.aspx.

10. "'Friends Forever': Xi Talks Up China's Ties with Russia during Putin Trade Trip," *Guardian*, June 25, 2016, https://www.theguardian.com/world/2016/jun/26/friends-forever-xi-talks-up-chinas-ties-with-russia-during-putin-trade-trip.

11. "Now, Russia Faces China's Ire over Vladivostok Founding Day Celebrations," WIO News, July 3, 2020, https://www.wionews.com/world/now-russia-faces-chinas-ire-over-vladivostok-founding-day-celebrations-310368.

12. Maria Siow, "Could Russia Side with the US and India against China?" *South China Morning Post*, August 22, 2020, https://www.scmp.com/week-asia/politics/article/3098398/could-russia-side-us-and-india-against-china.

13. Timofei Bordachev, "Main Results of 2017: Energetic Russia and the Greater Eurasia Community," Valdai Discussion Club, December 28, 2017, http://valdaiclub.com/a/highlights/main-results-of-2017-energetic-russia/.

14. "Summary of the 2018 National Defense Strategy of the United States of America: Sharpening the American Military's Competitive Edge," U.S. Department of Defense, 2018, https://dod.defense.gov/Portals/1/Documents/pubs/2018-National-Defense-Strategy-Summary.pdf.

15. Jacob Koelsch, "Standing Up to Xi Jinping in the South China Sea," Baker Institute for Public Policy, June 17, 2020, http://blog.bakerinstitute.org/2020/06/17/standing-up-to-xi-jinping-in-the-south-china-sea/.

16. "Risks of Operations in Syria Carefully Calculated, Putin Says," Mehr, November 14, 2015, https://en.mehrnews.com/news/111919/Risks-of-operations-in-Syria-carefully-calculated-Putin-says.

17. Robert Haddick, "Preserving U.S. Military Might: How to Make the Third Off-set Strategy a Success," *The National Interest*, December 7, 2014, http://nationalinterest.org/feature/preserving-us-military-might-how-make-the-third-offset-11800; and Dave Majumdar, "America Reveals 'Great Power' Plans Against Russia and China," *The National Interest*, February 3, 2016, https://nationalinterest.org/blog/the-buzz/america-reveals-great-power-plan-against-russia-china-15103.

18. Sydney J. Freedberg, Jr., "The Pentagon's Four Horsemen: Milley Rates the Threats," *Breaking Defense*, January 21, 2016, http://breakingdefense.com/2016/01/the-pentagons-four-horsemen-milley-rates-the-threats/.

19. Yun Sun, "Sino-Russia Strategic Alignment and Potential Impact of a Trump Presidency," Norwegian Institute of International Affairs, no. 40 (2016), https://www.nupi.no/Publikasjoner/CRIStin-Pub/Sino-Russia-Strategic-Alignment-and-Potential-Impact-of-a-Trump-Presidency.

20. David Allan Mayers, *Cracking the Monolith: U.S. Policy against the Sino-Soviet Alliance, 1949–1955* (Baton Rouge: Louisiana State University Press, 1986).

21. Alexander Gabuyev, "The Pandemic Could Tighten China's Grip on Eurasia," *Foreign Policy*, April 23, 2020, https://foreignpolicy.com/2020/04/23/coronavirus-pandemic-china-eurasia-russia-influence/.

22. Barbara Tuchman, *Guns of August* (New York: Random House, 1962).

23. "NATO 2030: United for a New Era," NATO, November 25, 2020, https://www.nato.int/nato_static_fl2014/assets/pdf/2020/12/pdf/201201-Reflection-Group-Final-Report-Uni.pdf.

24. Margaret Taylor, "Combating Disinformation and Foreign Interference in Democracies: Lessons from Europe," Brookings Institute, July 31, 2019, https://www.brookings.edu/blog/techtank/2019/07/31/combating-disinformation-and-foreign-interference-in-democracies-lessons-from-europe/.

25. "Remarks by Secretary of Defense Lloyd J. Austin III on Middle East Security at the Manama Dialogue (As Delivered)," U.S. Department of Defense, November 20, 2021, https://www.defense.gov/News/Speeches/Speech/Article/2849921/remarks-by-secretary-of-defense-lloyd-j-austin-iii-on-middle-east-security-at-t/; see also Kathleen H Hicks and Lisa Sawyer Samp, eds., *Recalibrating U.S. Strategy toward Russia: A New Time for Choosing* (Washington, DC: Center for Strategic and International Studies; and Lanham, MD: Rowman and Littlefield, March 2017), p. viii, https://www.csis.org/analysis/recalibrating-us-strategy-toward-russia.

Index

About the Author

RICHARD WEITZ, PhD, is senior fellow and director of the Center for Political-Military Analysis at Hudson Institute, Washington, DC. His research includes regional security developments relating to Europe, Eurasia, and East Asia as well as U.S. foreign and defense policies. Weitz is also an expert at Wikistrat and a nonresident adjunct senior fellow at the Center for a New American Security. He is author of Praeger's *War and Governance: International Security in a Changing World Order*, *Global Security Watch—Russia*, and *Global Security Watch—China*.